The
1300s

HEADLINES IN HISTORY

Books in the Headlines in History series:

The 1000s

The 1100s

The 1200s

The 1300s

The 1400s

The 1500s

The 1600s

The 1700s

The 1800s

The 1900s

The 1300s

HEADLINES IN HISTORY

Stephen Currie, *Book Editor*

Bonnie Szumski, *Editorial Director*
Scott Barbour, *Managing Editor*

Greenhaven Press, Inc., San Diego, California

Every effort has been made to trace the owners of copyrighted material. The articles in this volume may have been edited for content, length, and/or reading level. The titles have been changed to enhance the editorial purpose.

Library of Congress Cataloging-in-Publication Data

The 1300s / Stephen Currie, book editor.
    p. cm. — (Headlines in history)
    Includes bibliographical references and index.
    ISBN 0-7377-0534-5 (lib bdg. : alk. paper)—
    ISBN 0-7377-0533-7 (pbk. : alk. paper)
    1. Civilization, Medieval—14th century. 2. Fourteenth century. 3. Indians—History. 4. Asia—History. I. Currie, Stephen, 1960– II. Headlines in history (San Diego, Calif.)

CB358 .A13 2001
909'.3—dc21

                                                          00-069509

Cover photos: (left) The Fortress at Dieppe defended against the English. One Hundred Years War, © Stock Montage; (right, top to bottom) Statue of warrior, © PhotoDisc; Aztec City, hand-colored engraving, © North Wind Picture Archives; Geoffrey Chaucer (c. 1342–1400) English poet. Author of *Canterbury Tales*, © Stock Montage
Pictures: Library of Congress, 16, 49, 102, 155; National Institute of Health, 177; North Wind Picture Archives, 223

Printed in the USA

CONTENTS

engagements was a sea battle fought off the town of Sluys.
The English won handily, but at some cost for the future.

to serve their lords, they worked the fields and paid taxes in exchange for the promise of protection in the event of war.

strongly moralistic, and they usually contained religious elements as well.

pears in the introduction to the Italian writer Giovanni Boccaccio's book the *Decameron*. Boccaccio describes the spread of the terrible plague—and the massive social disruption it caused.

century. In 1368, however, a rebellion led by Chu Yüan-chang successfully swept the Mongols from power and replaced them with native Chinese leaders instead.

2. Early Ming Wars and Successions

Taking back the throne from Mongol rulers was only half the battle. The early Ming years were marked by succession struggles and shifting alliances; a great deal of blood was shed before peace and unity returned to the empire.

3. Trade in Early Ming Times

Ming China saw a substantial growth in trade, both inside the country and with other nations. The trade helped bring wealth to China, but it sparked significant controversy as well.

FOREWORD

Chronological time lines of history are mysteriously fascinating. To learn that within a single century Christopher Columbus sailed to the New World, the Aztec, Maya, and Inca cultures were flourishing, Joan of Arc was burned to death, and the invention of the printing press was radically changing access to written materials allows a reader a different type of view of history: a bird's-eye view of the entire globe and its events. Such a global picture allows for cross-cultural comparisons as well as a valuable overview of chronological history that studying one particular area simply cannot provide.

Taking an expansive look at world history in each century, therefore, can be surprisingly informative. In Headlines in History, Greenhaven Press attempts to imitate this time-line approach using primary and secondary sources that span each century. Each volume gives readers the opportunity to view history as though they were reading the headlines of a global newspaper: Editors of each volume have attempted to glean and include the most important and influential events of the century, as well as quirky trends and cultural oddities. Headlines in History, then, attempts to give readers a glimpse of both the mundane and the earth-shattering. Articles on the French Revolution, for example, are juxtaposed with the then-current fashion concerns of the French nobility. This creates a higher interest level by allowing students a glimpse of people's everyday lives throughout history.

By using both primary and secondary sources, students also have the opportunity to view the historical events both as eyewitnesses have experienced them and as historians have interpreted them. Thus, students can place such historical events in a larger context as well as receive background information on important world events.

Headlines in History allows readers the unique opportunity to learn more about events that may only be mentioned in their history textbooks, or may be ignored entirely. The series presents students with a variety of interesting topics that span cultural, historical, and political arenas. Such a broad span of material will allow students to wander wherever their curiosity will take them.

INTRODUCTION

One of the more dramatic stories of the fourteenth century concerns King John of Bohemia. Though he ruled a small eastern European nation, John was the son of the king of Luxembourg, located many miles to the west, and he preferred to spend his time in France. In his eyes, therefore, he was truly a citizen of Europe. King John, moreover, defined himself not so much as a king but as a knight. He liked nothing better than fighting, and he roamed the continent joining battles whenever he could. The reason behind the conflict rarely interested him; for John, the point was simply to be a part of the action.

In between battles John participated in as many tournaments as he could manage. The tournaments of the time exhibited knightly fighting skills for all to see. They helped keep knights in fighting form, and they played an important role in determining a knight's importance. The knights who did well in tournaments were given the highest respect and were known for their fighting abilities. Some of these tournaments were known as jousts; they pitted two knights against one another, with the object to unseat one's opponent from his horse. Occasionally tournaments required the use of blunt lances that could knock the loser from his saddle without causing severe injury. However, many knights preferred to fight in the so-called à outrance style, which allowed sharp weapons and always left open the possibility of death.

Not all tournaments used one-on-one combat. Equally popular in fourteenth-century Europe were melée-style tournaments. These involved two teams of as many as thirty to forty knights apiece. The knights would assemble on a field and fight until one side had clearly won the upper hand. Again, if real weapons were used, many knights were seriously injured and others died.

By all accounts, John of Bohemia enjoyed both forms of tournaments. A strong and enthusiastic fighter, he was known as one of the finest knights anywhere in Europe. During one tournament, however, John was struck in the face and blinded. That might have put an end to his fighting, but John had other ideas. Rather than retire, he continued to join battles across Europe. He enlisted the help of other knights to lead him onto the battlefield and to tell him when the enemy was near. Lashing out furiously with his sword, John did his best to fight off the unseen foe.

As might be expected, fighting without the ability to see was both difficult and dangerous, and it eventually led to John's death. In 1346 John helped lead an army of five hundred knights to France to participate in the Hundred Years' War against England. There, the knights joined the forces of their ally, French king Philip VI. John enthusiastically helped France drive back the English, but he chafed at his limited role. Finally, at the Battle of Crécy, John begged to be taken into the center of the conflict; several of his knights agreed to do so. Putting John in the lead and lashing their horses together, they charged toward the scene of the heaviest fighting. The result was, perhaps, predictable. The following day all of the knights were found dead, John among them.

A Metaphor for the Century

The story of John of Bohemia is in many ways a microcosm of fourteenth-century life. John's preference for knighthood over kingship was common enough; this same preference was shared by a number of rulers of the period. As John's career indicates, moreover, warfare was of tremendous importance in Europe during the 1300s, and government was too often neglected. Valuing fighting over ruling had consequences, both for the rulers and for the people they ruled. The way John lived his life was well in tune with the ethos of the time.

Today, for example, we might describe John of Bohemia's rash actions as excessively macho. That would be an accurate description, for during the fourteenth century machismo was valued and applauded. In more strictly fourteenth-century terms, the concept of honor played an enormous role in society, both in Europe and beyond its borders. The whole social system of the upper classes was based almost entirely on the notion of protecting one's honor. Defeat in battle meant humiliation; even defeat in a tournament could mean a loss of respect.

But not participating was in all likelihood the worst of all. From any rational standpoint, a blind man such as John had no business charging into the heart of the battle at Crécy. The sensible alternative for him would have been to stay home, but for John that was not an option; and it is not an exaggeration to say that many knights of the time would have agreed with him. A knight who stayed home, even for as serious a matter as blindness, would lose face among his peers. He would be ignored; he would be demeaned; he would lose his hard-won position at the forefront of knighthood, and that was intolerable. Unfortunately, this overconcern with matters of honor did not just affect John of Bohemia. It affected dozens of other rulers, great and small, and in one way or another it led to the deaths of thousands upon thousands of lords, knights, and peasants.

John of Bohemia's career was also typical of the fourteenth century in that it ended so disastrously—and so apparently pointlessly. Few positive lessons can be drawn from his life, and there is little redemption in his death. John died not so much fighting for a cause, or even for loyalty to an ally, as he died to bolster his own self-image. His death

Fourteenth-Century Europe

scarcely spurred on his allies to greater efforts—the French over-whelmingly lost the battle—nor helped bring a quick end to the war, which instead would drag on for another sixty-nine years. Even his blindness had been avoidable, caused as it was in a tournament. Disaster and tragedy, preventable and purposeless—words such as these summed up not only John's life but also the century as a whole.

War and Destruction

The fourteenth century was indeed a difficult time. Wars raged for years, both in Europe and outside of it. From Japan to Mexico, from Turkey to France, thousands of men died while fighting, and many thousands more men, women, and children died while swept up in the destruction. As an indication of the level of violence prevalent during the period, Europe saw not one but two conflicts later called the Hundred Years' War. The more famous of these today was fought between France and England between 1337 and 1453. The other was fought between the Italian states of Genoa and Venice. This Hundred Years' War lasted even longer; beginning in 1256, it did not conclude until 1381.

The wars of the fourteenth century were bloody. At the 1346 Battle of Crécy, John of Bohemia was one of about four thousand French sol-

Many battles of the fourteenth century were waged more in sport rather than for a specific cause. Above, English and French soldiers fight near Brittany.

diers to lose his life. Ten years later the French lost at least as many men, probably more, in the Battle of Poitiers. During the Battle of Nicopolis at the end of the century, perhaps three thousand soldiers died on the losing Christian side. Though estimates of army strength and losses vary wildly, this figure probably amounted to at least a third of the total Christian force.

The destructiveness of these and other fourteenth-century wars was perhaps surprising in view of the available weaponry of the time. In the early part of the century, gunpowder became known in Europe—it had been invented in China a few centuries earlier—but its use in warfare was extremely limited. Consequently, people across the world still relied heavily on swords, lances, catapults, and bows to wreak havoc on their enemies. Yet the close nature of combat during the period allowed those relatively primitive weapons to make up in destruction what they lacked in firepower.

What made the wars particularly appalling and disastrous, however, was their apparent uselessness. More than at any other time during history, the wars of the fourteenth century seemed to have little to do with any well-articulated aim or goal. To be sure, a few of these battles were waged for somewhat high-minded causes. The struggle for Chinese independence from their Mongol overlords fits this category, as do several European uprisings against tyrannical rulers like the Italian Cola di Rienzo.

Most of the fourteenth century's wars, however, were fought solely for the thrill of the fight and for the honor and the glory of the participants. Knights fought in order to show off their prowess and, perhaps, to alleviate a sense of boredom. For public relations reasons, participants might try to invest their battles with a nobler purpose, but in the end personal bravery was what mattered most. Christian knights spoke of the Battle of Nicopolis as a religious struggle against Muslim supremacy in southeastern Europe. The overtones of holy war were completely lost when fighting broke out, though. The Christians went down to a bitter defeat because their leading knights persisted in making glorious and ill-fated charges while ignoring the details of military strategy that might have carried the day. Throughout the fourteenth century, even a great and costly victory rarely seemed to result in the deposing of an enemy king, the taking of substantial chunks of an opponent's realm, or the granting of more rights to the people.

Nobles and Peasants

But then, kings of the fourteenth century did not feel an especially strong connection to the people they ruled. Intermarriage between ruling families had helped create a situation in which kings like John of Bohemia could flourish. John was far from the only fourteenth-century ruler whose kingdom was miles from his birthplace, or who governed lands about which he knew little. Connected to other European rulers both by blood and by political alliances, kings routinely found themselves pulled into conflicts that did not concern their nations. Sometimes, too, they felt it necessary to come to the aid of an ally even when doing so was in direct opposition to the best interests of their people.

Other factors also affected relationships between kings and their subjects. Kings, knights, and other nobles ranked far above the masses. In the ethos of the period, the nobles were important and worthy of respect while the commoners had no particular value. There was little movement between the upper and lower classes: Few marriages linked families across class lines, peasants could not move out of their social station, and few nobles were in jeopardy of moving down. The social distance between the two groups removed kings and other members of the nobility from any real understanding of the day-to-day problems faced by their subjects.

Moreover, the social system called feudalism, which had been in force during much of the Middle Ages, was beginning to disappear. Feudalism was far from a perfect system, but it had offered peasants several definite advantages. Most obviously, feudal Europe had been a place of small, local government. Peasants lived on lands controlled by a single lord. They worked for the lord in exchange for the promise of protection in case of battle. The peasants and the lords thus had a legal relationship, with legal rights and responsibilities on both sides. It was in the nobility's interest to work with the peasants, to get to know them on some level, and to take into account their wishes and needs.

By the fourteenth century, however, Europe was moving toward a more centralized system. The power of the local lords was dwindling, shifting instead to more powerful—and more removed—kings and queens. Nobles no longer controlled "their" peasants as before, but by the same token peasants no longer had a local lord to rely on: instead, they were at the mercy of a faraway king who had no notion of their needs. The decline of feudalism, the rigid class structure, the intermarriages and alliances that further removed the king from his subjects—all of these factors meant that the common people's interests were increasingly ignored. The fourteenth-century peasants who served as foot soldiers, whose homes were destroyed, and who were heavily taxed to finance battles had no say in setting government policy.

This disconnection between the upper and lower classes had other damaging effects. The later part of the fourteenth century was rife with peasant revolts. A particularly violent one, the so-called Wat Tyler Rebellion, occurred in England in 1381. France suffered through a similar rebellion; so did parts of Italy and Germany, along with Flanders in the Low Countries. By the end of the fourteenth century most of the nations of Europe had undergone at least one such rebellion.

The exact causes of the revolts varied from place to place, but the basic themes did not. Peasants rebelled over low wages, relentless taxation, and lack of personal freedom. The ruling classes had lost touch with their populations. Life among the lower classes had become so bad that the peasants were willing to take enormous risks to complain. Though the battles did not typically result in major reforms, their frequency during the late fourteenth century demonstrates the separation many ordinary Europeans felt from their leaders—and the desperation they felt about their lives.

The Black Death

Not all of the calamities that befell fourteenth-century Europe were man-made. Famines struck from time to time, perhaps most notably in northern Europe during the early part of the 1300s. Some of the famines were sparked by the destructiveness of wars that laid waste to the countryside, but most were caused instead by the vagaries of weather. Storms and other unpreventable natural disasters also added to the list of the century's calamities.

The single greatest disaster of the time was neither weather-related nor the cause of wasteful human decisions. That disaster was the mid-century outbreak of bubonic plague in 1347. Spread by rats, fleas, and infected people themselves, the plague swept from India to Europe in a few short years, leaving a trail of death. Those who contracted the disease generally died from it within a week, sometimes in a matter of hours. Surviving a bout with the plague was rare; so was not contracting the disease in the first place. Though exact figures are impossible to come by, most scholars estimate that one out of every three people died in the affected areas of the globe. The outbreak was so disastrous that it is known today by a name all its own: the Black Death.

The Black Death was probably not the most destructive killer the human race has ever seen. Another outbreak of bubonic plague during Roman times killed more people, although over a much greater time span. Other diseases have spread even more quickly and had a farther reach. An epidemic of Spanish influenza, for example, killed at least 25 million people in just eighteen months after the end of World War I.

But the comparisons with other diseases would have held little interest for those battling the Black Death. Death was everywhere. Nothing seemed to stop the spread of the disease: not prayer, not the standard medical procedures of the day, not searches for scapegoats to blame. Whole families and villages were wiped out. Some towns and cities lost half their population. People buried their dead or, terrified of contagion, left them in the street to rot, and throughout they wondered if the plague marked the end of the world and the victory of Satan.

Indeed, few groups escaped the ravages of the plague. Those who lived in out-of-the-way villages had a better chance than city dwellers simply because they came into contact with fewer people during the course of a day. Still, all it took was the arrival of a single affected person, rat, or flea to introduce the bacteria—usually with disastrous consequences. Cloistered monks and nuns, isolated as they were from the outside world, likewise sometimes managed to escape infection. But with monks and nuns, it was all or nothing. The disease, once introduced into a monastery or a cloister, usually turned the tight quarters to its advantage. Leaping from person to person, the virus spread quickly through the entire community, often killing every last inhabitant of the house.

Nobles, the wealthy, and other educated classes probably stood the best chance of escaping. Even at the time, several observers noted that the rich seemed to avoid the disease better than did the poor. Only one reigning European monarch, a Spanish king, was killed by the disease, although several close relatives of other kings died as well. Roman Catholic bishops made up another group that was little affected by the pestilence. Current estimates indicate that perhaps only one out of every twenty bishops was killed—a far cry from the death rate in the general population.

The relative safety of kings, bishops, and the wealthy stemmed from their financial resources and their social rank. As a rule, they had not suffered from malnutrition and other health problems of poverty, which made them more able to resist the deadly virus. Perhaps more important, too, they had the means to arrange flight when the plague came close. Many of the rich in urban areas already owned country estates located far from the centers of infection.

Being able to stay away from the masses of infected people also played a role. Kings and bishops had staffs of servants and others who were charged with securing their employers' well-being, in some cases at the costs of the servants' own lives. Thus, visitors could be kept away until it was clear that they were not suffering from the disease. In some cases, men of noble rank were made virtual prisoners inside their houses. The strategy usually worked: They survived. Of course, the recognition that the rich had escaped much of the disaster suffered by the poor did not help calm tensions between the classes.

Effects of the Plague

The plague dominated life and thought during the time it raged—and during the remainder of the fourteenth century as well. Its effects were enormous. Villages were gone, and neighborhoods lay still. Nearly every survivor had lost a spouse, a parent, a child, or a neighbor to the scourge. The social and emotional fabric of the period was irretrievably damaged. There were not enough workers to farm the fields and not enough markets for the producers of goods. Governments lost what political hold they had on some areas.

But the effect on morale was most significant. The plague left psychic scars on its survivors. Some blamed themselves and believed that God was punishing them for sinful behavior. Others looked outward and blamed society's outcasts, often resorting to violence in their zeal to find a scapegoat. Medicine had failed dismally to provide a cure, to stop the spread of the plague, or even to shed any understanding into its causes. The church had done no better. Science and religion were ineffective. In the years after the plague, Europe was faced with a crisis of confidence unlike any in surrounding centuries. People wondered where—and whether—they could put their trust. What could still be believed? What could still give meaning and joy to life?

The plague did not end ever-present wars. The Black Death had only meant a temporary reprieve from the fighting that characterized the century. Wars stopped long enough for the pestilence to pass and then resumed with a vigor—even if with fewer available fighters. Even before the plague, the constant wars had led to a sense of tragedy and sorrow. To fourteenth-century Europeans, the world seemed an increasingly dismal place. The relative stability of the so-called High Middle Ages a century or two earlier had passed from the scene, and the outlook now struck most thinkers as a good deal less than rosy.

The difficulty of life had an impact on the culture of the times. In some areas of the world, such as China, culture thrived. Across most of the rest of the globe, however, cultural progress lagged or retreated. Only a few of the names of the century's artists, writers, and musicians are familiar to Americans today. Textbooks and historians tend to relegate the culture of the 1300s to a dusty corner of history. A series covering the history of European painting, for example, ends one volume with the works of twelfth- and thirteenth-century artists and begins the next with the start of the fifteenth-century Renaissance. The fourteenth century is completely neglected.

Similarly, studies of early European writers pass very quickly from the sagas of the 1100s to William Shakespeare, ignoring much of what came between. To be sure, Geoffrey Chaucer, Petrarch, and a few others are read today, but they are notable exceptions to the rule. Even the music of the period is known mostly to specialists. The Gregorian chant, which enjoyed a burst of popularity during the 1990s, is by and large an older art form, and best-known madrigals and other part-songs date largely from the Renaissance and other succeeding centuries. Although the fourteenth century was far from a cultural cipher, it is fair to say that the period is not noted for its contributions to the arts.

Shaped by Disaster

But the central story of the fourteenth century is not about culture, nor about the glories of the kingdoms that managed to expand into neighboring territories, nor about the plague itself. Instead, it is the story of the disasters that seemed to strike a frightened and weary populace in every conceivable way. Indeed, the litany seemed to have no end: plagues and famines and wars; the disconnection of nobles from the peasants they were supposed to serve; high prices, economic dislocation, greed. Every aspect of the century seemed to fit in with the general idea of decline. Writers of the period complained about a perceived rise in immoral behavior and a drop in civility. Anarchy and lawlessness were on the rise, observers mourned, while industriousness was falling and the social order was rapidly degenerating.

Politics, Government, and War in Fourteenth-Century Europe

The story of politics in fourteenth-century Europe is the rather sordid story of a series of struggles for power. In a quest for political control, kings and queens formed alliances with one another and then broke those alliances as suddenly as they had been formed in hopes of yet another political advantage. Revolutions broke out. Nobles opposed kings, kings opposed nobles, and the peasants faced off against everybody else. Political quarrels mixed into religious and cultural realms, too. Thus, violence erupted against Jews in Spain and France, against Muslims in the southeastern part of Europe, and even between factions of Roman Catholics.

To fourteenth-century Europeans, at times it must have seemed as though every nation was erupting in violence. Much of the worst fighting was between nations. England and France declared war on one another in 1337. By the time the fighting was over, the fourteenth century had been over for a full fifteen years; the original participants had long since been gone from the scene, yet the battles continued. England also waged war against Scotland, and France fought against Flanders. Various German states attacked one another and Austria, which in turn tried to take over Switzerland. Italy, Hungary, Bulgaria—the lists of wars seem endless.

Other political squabbles stayed more or less within a certain nation. Uprisings of the lower classes affected France, England, and the Low Countries. Arguments over royal legitimacy and proper succession of kingship turned into civil war in England, Bohemia, Germany, and much of Italy. These all began as primarily local issues, but as word of rebellion spread and beleaguered kings and princes called for help from their allies, most examples of civil strife turned out to be influential far beyond their original geographic area.

The situation was not helped by the forms of government most prevalent in fourteenth-century Europe. Kings, queens, and nobles ruled largely by force. With a few exceptions in a handful of scattered countries, individual citizens had no particular political rights. Often they had few legal rights that their leaders were bound to accept. A handful of leaders were relatively enlightened, but others oppressed their subjects. For many, the lure of war and the increased honor and respect a victory would bring overcame any sense of responsibility to the subjects who would ultimately have to fight and fund the adventure. Edward III of England, for example, bullied his country's Parliament into accepting confiscatory tax increases. Those increases hurt farmers and merchants, but they permitted Edward to wage the Hundred Years' War against France.

A strong and perhaps overly developed sense of honor reigned among the leaders of Europe. Petty insults—between monarchs and between claimants to the throne—were not forgotten; they were assumed instead to be the equivalent of high crimes. Suitably enraged, those who had been offended carried the quarrel to the battlefield. Small countries jockeying for position and power also added to the tendency toward war. The ethos of the day was expansion, and expansion at the expense of one's neighbors. Because the political and governmental systems of the time did not permit checks on the leaders, the bloodshed continued throughout the century.

The Battle of Bannockburn: The Scots Defeat the English

Thomas B. Costain

During the fourteenth century, Scotland was an independent nation—and one generally hostile to England. There had been battles and skirmishes between the Scots and the English throughout much of the thirteenth century, and matters carried over into the fourteenth as well. The bad blood culminated in 1314 at the Battle of Bannockburn on the border between Scotland and England. The Scots, led by their king, Robert the Bruce (commonly known to us today simply as Robert Bruce), routed the English despite a marked disadvantage in the size of the two armies.

This passage from Thomas B. Costain's book *The Three Edwards* sets the scene and explains how the Scottish army managed to succeed. However, as Costain makes clear, the victory did not bring about peace—and the fact that the pope was more or less on England's side did not help the Scottish cause, either. Costain is known as a novelist as well as a historian, and in this excerpt he adopts a novelistic approach, both in the writing style and in the exploration of motives and feelings of the participants in the battle.

Never before had such a well-equipped force of such size marched to the north to try conclusions with the Scots. The chronicles of

Excerpted from *The Three Edwards*, by Thomas B. Costain. Copyright © 1958 by Thomas B. Costain. Reprinted with permission from Doubleday, a division of Random House, Inc.

the day, which tend to exaggerate everything, fixed the English strength at one hundred thousand, but more recent calculations reduce this figure to something between twenty and forty thousand. Twenty-five thousand is probably close to the actual figure, and this would include the cavalry and the archers from Ireland and Wales. A larger force could not have operated on the narrow front beyond the Burn [creek] of Bannock, where Robert the Bruce waited with his army. This much may be set down as true, however: the army was splendidly equipped and caused a wave of awe and fear to spread through the Lowlands as it progressed northward. The train of carts following the army was twenty miles long!

The earliest reports estimated the Scottish army at thirty thousand, but this is absurdly high. Modern calculators have reduced the figure to something in the neighborhood of seven thousand, including a body of five hundred horse. The horse troops were light compared with the English cavalry, which consisted of knights armed to the teeth on huge Flemish chargers and numbered two thousand. One fact is clear: that the disparity was great, and that Scotland's only hope lay in the spirit of her sons and the skill of her king in selecting where he would stand and fight.

There was a moment when even the stout heart of the Scottish king almost failed him. It was early on the morning of Sunday, June 23, 1314. The Scot pipers and drums had roused the army early and mass had been celebrated. A light ration of bread and water was issued, for it was the vigil of St. John. Two of the Scottish leaders, the Black Douglas and Sir Robert Keith, who was the marshal of Scotland and had charge of the scanty cavalry, had ridden out before dawn to catch a first glimpse of the English. These two stout campaigners gazed with awe when the mist rose and the early sun shone on the burnished arms of the invaders. It was their lot to see first the approach of "proud Edward's power, chains and slavery." The cavalry was in the van; and two thousand mounted men with polished shields and helmets, with penons flying and trumpets sounding, can look as formidable as the army which someday will ride to Armageddon. Behind the horsemen came files of foot soldiers stretching back as far as the eye could see, marching steadily with swaying of shields.

The Black Douglas looked black indeed when he returned with Keith to tell what they had seen. Robert the Bruce was seated on a pony, because it was more sure-footed on such rough and marshy ground, and he was wearing a gold crown over his helmet, to identify him to his men. It would identify him also to the enemy and so can be classed as jactance, an open flouting of the foe, as though he said, I am Robert the Bruce, crowned at Scone, and if I fall the flag of Scotland will fall; and make what ye may of it, bold knights of the Sassenach [England]!

He listened to their story of the overwhelming might of Edward while he studied the thin ranks of his own men and their nondescript weapons. After sober reflection he advised them to say little, to let it be accepted that the English, while numerous, were disorganized, a plausible story after the rapid march of the invaders by the inland route through Lauderdale.

When a general has a defensive action on his hands he knows moments of serious doubt while watching the enemy advance. Has he overlooked any possibilities? Has he forgotten anything? Are his troop dispositions sound? The Bruce remained where he was for some time, gazing about him with anxious eyes. He studied the ground sloping away in front of him, up which the English must fight their way. It was narrow, with the junction of the Burn of Bannock at the Forth [River] on his left and the heavily wooded Gillies Hill and Coxet Hill on his right; much too narrow for the operations of a large army. The only stretch of open ground was the Carse, which lay between the river and the burn, and even this was studded with stunted trees and underbrush and the yellow of the sod was interspersed like shot silk with the green of the swampy mosses. In front of his permanent line, which faced the Carse, he had dug a row of pits and filled them with pointed stakes and iron rods known as calthrops. His position, in fact, was stronger than the one [Scottish patriot Sir William] Wallace had chosen at Falkirk [against England's Edward I in 1298]. But what of the archers who had won at Falkirk for the English? Douglas and Keith had said nothing of them, having seen only the chivalry [mounted men-at-arms] of the Sassenach in their steel harness and the foot soldiers with shields and spears. Had the English forgotten the lesson of Falkirk?

The Scottish army lay hidden back of the lines, but two corps were out in front, one covering St. Ninian's Church and village in the center, the other at the point where the burn turned sharply northward to empty into the Forth. Even the camp followers had been thought of; they had a place of concealment on Gillies Hill from which they could make their escape if the battle went ill; a thoughtful move, for an army in the exultation of victory will wipe out the fleeing camp followers as a playful gesture.

Had he left anything undone? He did not think so.

The Fight Begins

The English arrived at Bannockburn late in the afternoon following a twenty-mile tramp over heavy roads. They were tired and hungry, but Edward, basing his course on the precepts of his father, who always struck early and hard, decided to attack the two Scottish divisions which were in sight. A regiment of cavalry was sent forward to advance by the Carse Road. At first Scot commander Randolph did not see the approaching army, earning the reproof from his king, "a rose from your chaplet has fallen," but he started briskly to work then and routed the Englishmen.

The English vanguard [those in the front], commanded by the earls of Gloucester and Hereford, made an urgent advance in the hope of seizing the entry to the flat lands of the Carse, a strategic necessity. They found themselves opposed by a strong corps commanded by a knight on a gray pony and with a high crown fitted over his helmet.

"The king!" ran the word through the English ranks.

Perceiving that what they had thought was no more than a scouting party was in reality a formidable force led by the great Bruce himself, the English hesitated. Before they could retire, however, there happened one of the incidents which are told and retold in the annals of chivalry. One of the English knights, Sir Henry de Bohun, rode out into the open with his lance at rest and shouted a challenge to the Scottish king. Robert the Bruce lacked a lance but he seemed content with the battle-ax he was carrying, and so accepted the challenge by advancing from his own ranks. Bohun charged furiously, but almost at the point of contact the king's knee drew the pony to one side and the iron-clad challenger thundered past. Rising in his stirrups, Bruce had a second's time in which to deal a blow with his battle-ax. It landed squarely on the head of the charging knight and almost split his skull in two.

Returning to his party, the Scottish king was upbraided for having risked his life in this way. Bruce made no direct response but looked ruefully at the shaft of his ax.

"I have broken it," he said.

The shadows of night were falling by the time the English vanguard, very much chagrined by the defeat and death of their champion, had galloped back in a disorderly retreat.

The Upper Hand

At the break of dawn, in the far-distant region where the great spirits reside, [Scottish folk hero] St. Magnus must have been at work burnishing his spiritual armor; for, according to the word that later spread over all of Scotland, he had work to do that day.

The Scots had spent the night in prayer. The Abbot of Inchaffray had said mass and the foot soldiers were still on their knees when King Edward, arrayed in shining chain mail and jeweled tabard [tunic], and full of confidence in an easy victory, rode along his lines.

"They kneel," he remarked to those about him.

"Ay, Sir King," said Sir Reginald de Umfraville, who had been fighting Scots for ten grim years, "but to God. Not to us."

The English attack had been badly conceived. Because of the narrow front on which they must operate, the army had been divided into three main "battles," each of three lines. The first, made up of cavalry in the lead and foot soldiers behind, went across the Carse and up the sloping ground, behind the crest of which the Scots had been assembled in a dense adaptation of Wallace's *schiltrons* [a hollow circular formation]. The existence of the pits had not been suspected, and a toll of the horsemen was taken before the first of the attack came into contact with the hedge of Scottish spears. Their efforts to break through the clustering pike points was of no avail. In the meantime the second "battle" had followed up the hill. They could not get close enough to take a hand in the fighting and could do no more than halt and wait, conscious of the fact that the third "battle" had been ordered forward on their heels and would soon be on the hillside also. The attack, in fact, had been so clumsily contrived that the arrows of the English archers, massed on their right, were falling as thick on the attacking lines as among the Scots.

There was worse to follow. The lesson of Falkirk had been so faultily remembered that the archery division had not been provided with any form of protection. Robert Bruce, who was in personal command of the reserves behind the lines, saw at once the great opportunity which had thus been thrown his way. He ordered Keith to take his handful of cavalry around the left of the line and attack the English bowmen.

It was not an easy task, but Keith and his gallant five hundred accomplished it. They made their way around Milton Bog and came out against the flank of the archery corps. Great battles have often been won by a charge of cavalry in small numbers, delivered at exactly the right time and the right place. This was one, for in a matter of minutes Keith's horsemen, shouting a keening battle cry of *"On them!"* had thrown the bowmen into utter confusion and had slain large numbers.

Bruce, seeing victory in his grasp, led his reserves, who had been chafing for a share in the fighting, through the gaps between the *schiltrons* and fell on the fatigued first "battle" with claymore and pike. The first English line fell back on the second and forced a retreat into the laboring ranks of the third. It was utter confusion then on the slopes, which were already slippery with blood. Nothing much was left now of the bowmen who might have won the day for the English if the knights had been assigned to protect them up the slope to the point where they could riddle the Scottish ranks with steel-tipped death. Perhaps the gallant knights had refused to play pap-nurse to greasy varlets [that is, to give the archers protection]; this had been known to happen. Whatever the reason, the bowmen had no chance to display their worth on this tragic field.

The whole English line began to waver. Thousands of men who had not yet struck a blow fell into a panic and tried to break through the ranks of fresh troops coming to their aid.

The Final Thrust

And then the miracle happened which might be termed the Coup of the Camp Followers. The men and women of menial role who had been relegated to a place of safety back of Gillies Hill had been able to watch the course of the battle below them. It was clear to them now that the day was going very well indeed. Some unidentified and mute but not inglorious Wallace conceived a way to have a part in victory. The command was given and all of them—drivers, cooks, nurses, knaves—began to strip the leaves from branches. They used broken pike handles and broomsticks and even crutches and attached to them old clouts and the petticoats of the women and the tails of their plaid cloaks. Waving these improvised flags, they went charging through the underbrush, shouting at the tops of their voices.

To the panic-stricken English this could mean only one thing: that reinforcements had arrived for the Scots who were so eager to take a hand in the fighting that they had not chosen the slower course around the foot of the hill but had come charging over the crest. The faltering English line broke at this. Gilbert of Gloucester tried to rally the troops but was killed. . . . Twenty-seven other barons fell in the pandemonium.

Edward and his closest advisers had watched the confusion into which the army had fallen with bitter wonder and dismay. When the retreat from the hillside turned into a rout, Aymer de Valence, Earl of Pembroke, who knew a defeat when he saw one, having figured in many in his time, seized the reins of the king's horse. It was time for Edward to leave. Surrounded by the five hundred picked horsemen who served as the royal guard, they rode at a furious gallop around the left of the Scottish lines and cut north in the direction of Stirling Castle. One of the knights with the king was a Gascon named Giles de Argentine, who stayed with the beaten monarch until they shook off a fierce attack by Edward Bruce. "It is not my custom to fly," he said then. Wheeling about, he rode straight for the Scottish lines, crying, "An Argentine! An Argentine!" In a very few minutes he had begun a flight to wherever it is that brave soldiers are transported.

On other occasions Edward had not shown much courage in battle, but now, perhaps in desperation, he showed some of the Plantagenet mettle. They encountered more pursuers and an effort was made to drag him from his horse. He beat the enemy off. With a mace, which became a lethal weapon in his strong hands, he cut his way through to safety.

At Stirling Castle the royal party was refused admittance. It was pointed out that, inasmuch as the effort to relieve the fortress had failed, the castle must now capitulate. They did not want the king stepping into that kind of trap. Accordingly Edward and his morose followers rode sixty miles to Dunbar, where they made their escape by sea.

What part did St. Magnus play in the victory? All Scotland was thrilled with a story that late in the morning he appeared from the clouds above Aberdeen in a coat of shining mail and on a great white horse. He rode down the streets of the granite city, crying out in a mighty voice that Robert the Bruce had that day defeated Edward of England on the field of Bannockburn.

Aftermath

The pursuit of the English was conducted briskly but not to the exclusion of looting. The equipment of the beaten army had not only been ample but luxurious. An estimate places the loot taken from the field at two hundred thousand pounds, but this seems as exaggerated as the figures given of the size of the armies. It was considerable enough, however, to compensate the people of Scotland for the losses they had sustained in the twenty years of warfare. In addition to what had been left on the field there were many hundred knights captured, and the Scots saw that each of them paid a heavy ransom.

Scotland had been a poor country to begin with; and the continual burning of the countryside and the destruction of their herds and flocks had brought the people close to starvation. Bannockburn paid most of it back.

There were exchanges, of course. The Earl of Hereford had been taken prisoner on the field and the Scots demanded for him fifteen prisoners held by the English. These included the wife and daughter of Robert the Bruce and the venerable Bishop of Glasgow. . . .

The Scottish victory at Bannockburn did not bring peace. The Scots, having driven the last of the Sassenachs across the border, save for the city of Berwick, were willing and anxious to discuss terms. The English, humiliated and angered beyond measure, were not so disposed; they proceeded to take the military command out of the feeble hands of Edward and entrusted the army to Cousin Lancaster, who, as it soon developed, was no better. Realizing that the end to the long struggle was not yet in sight, Robert strove to make the English realize the cost of war by striking fiercely at the border counties. As a further measure he sent troops into Ireland in an effort to divert the attention of the foe. Edward Bruce was put in command, and it was announced that the King of Scotland intended to raise his resourceful and ever daring younger brother to the Irish throne. Roger de Mortimer, who has been mentioned as one of the young knights who won his spurs during the wholesale knighting of adolescent Englishmen by Edward I, was in command in Dublin at the time.

The resourcefulness and daring of Edward Bruce were not equal to the task. He established his rule over Ulster and remained there until 1318, when he sallied out to attack a large English force in a particularly foolhardy mood and was defeated and killed. In the meantime the mercenary Mortimer had also departed, leaving behind him personal debts contracted during his term of office amounting to one thousand pounds, "whereof he payde not one smulkin." A smulkin was a pleasantly characteristic Irish word for a brass farthing. This act of high-handed unconcern for everything but his own interests was the first in a career which would be marked by an insolence . . . and an avarice beyond all measure.

Bruce became doubly anxious for peace when he realized that a touch of leprosy which he had acquired in his wanderings was beginning to tighten its grip on his system and to rob him of power in his limbs. The *mickle ail*, it was called in Scotland, where it was widely prevalent. Every town had been obliged to provide some kind of leper hospital, which had its own churchyard, chapel, and ecclesiastics, even though the building itself might be no more than a frame shack on the edge of a wind-swept moor. It was highly ironic that the great fighting king, after struggling so long and enduring so much hardship, should thus be barred from the peace and comfort for which he had longed.

Realizing that his days were numbered, King Robert appealed to the Pope to bring about peace between the two countries. In 1320 he directed a message in the name of the barons of Scotland to Pope John XXII. It was a well-reasoned presentation and contained one clause which tells in a heartfelt way the plight of the northern kingdom.

> Admonish and entreat the king of the English, for whom that which he possesses ought to suffice, seeing that of old England used to be ample for seven kings or more, to leave in peace us Scots dwelling in this little Scotland, beyond which there is no human abode, and desiring nothing but our own.

It was unfortunate for Scotland that John XXII was Pope at this period. He was an appointee of Philip the Unfair and had been elevated to the papacy at Avignon through the efforts of that monarch; after, it may be added, a stalemate of two years. He proved to be a heavy-handed pontiff, as witness his course when a second pope was raised to the Vatican in Rome through German influence. This was a Minorite friar named Pietro Rainalducci de Corbara, who was given the title of Nicholas V. When the German influence declined, leaving Nicholas alone, he sought to make his peace with Avignon and was brought into the presence of John with a halter around his neck. A sentence of perpetual imprisonment was passed on him and he died in a prison cell in Avignon.

John disregarded the Scottish appeal. In fact, he went to the other extreme and in 1323 laid all Scotland under an interdict.

Women, Land, and Inheritance in England

Jennifer Ward

Elizabeth de Burgh was a fourteenth-century English noblewoman who had been widowed three times by the age of twenty-seven. She was wealthy in her own right, and she added the wealth of some of her husbands to what she already had. English law gave wives certain rights, especially where land was concerned. However, de Burgh was distressed to learn that those rights were limited. Her brother-in-law Hugh le Despenser used contacts in English government—apparently going as high as the king—to exchange certain of his lands with de Burgh's, over her objection. In this selection, she lists her complaints regarding her treatment. While some of what happened is based on politics (her husband Roger Damory had opposed the king), much also indicates the tenuous right of medieval women to hold land.

Editor's Note: The original of this letter is held by the British Library. The beginning of the letter and the end were written by a clerk in standard Latin legal language of the time; the clerk's contribution was simply to attest where, when, and under what circumstances Elizabeth de Burgh had prepared the document. The bulk of the excerpt was written in French and includes de Burgh's own words. It runs from "In the name of God, I Elizabeth de Burgh" and continues until "if fear of royal power with the peril that could follow did not stop me."

Excerpted from *Women of the English Nobility and Gentry, 1066–1500,* by Jennifer Ward. Copyright © 1995 by Jennifer Ward. Reprinted with permission from Manchester University Press.

In the name of God, amen. On 15 May, AD 1326, in the ninth indiction [a fifteen-year cycle of time] and the tenth year of the pontificate of the most holy father and lord John XXII, pope by divine providence, the noble woman Lady Elizabeth de Burgh, one of the sisters and heirs of Lord Gilbert de Clare, late earl of Gloucester, and formerly wife of the late Roger Damory knight, exhibited and recited word for word a parchment schedule written in French, of the tenor and contents written below, in her oratory [place of prayer] in the small chapel next to her chamber in Clare castle in Norwich diocese in the presence of the discreet men, Sir Thomas de Cheddeworth, rector of the church of Lutterworth, and Sir John Diccus of London, clerk of the diocese of London, her close advisers, specially summoned, and witnesses to those matters written below which were personally drawn up, and in the presence of my public notary. In the name of God, I Elizabeth de Burgh, one of the sisters and heirs of Sir Gilbert de Clare late earl of Gloucester, and formerly wife of Sir Roger Damory, wish that it be known by all people that, when certain disagreements occurred between our Lord, Edward king of England, son of King Edward, and several great men of his land in the fifteenth year of his reign [1321–22] on account of certain oppressions which caused them grievance, contrary to the law of the land, my lord Sir Roger was one of those great men and was harried and oppressed so that he died. While he was still alive I was captured in the castle of Usk, part of my inheritance, by power and command of the king, and taken to the abbey of Barking where after my lord's death I remained imprisoned more than half a year, and all my lands were taken into the king's hands. During that time, the king sent three letters of credit by [royal officials and courtiers] Master Richard de Clare, Sir John Lestourmy and Piers Mareschal in turn, the condition for the credits being that I should agree to exchange the land of Usk and all my inheritance in Wales with Sir Hugh le Despenser the younger in return for the land of Gower. In that the land of Gower was worth less than the land of Usk and my Welsh inheritance, the king promised fully to make up the difference at the true value with other lands more convenient to me, and to give me back all my inheritance of the earldom of Gloucester, my dower [lands belonging to her husband given to her upon his death], all my lands purchased jointly with my lord, all my castles, jewels, vessel [silver plates] and wardrobe. If I would not agree, I would never hold in peace the land of my inheritance, dower or joint purchase during the lifetime of our lord the king. I Elizabeth was distressed at these threats, and, seeing the great oppression done from day to day to the good people of the land, the danger to myself and my children who were imprisoned with me, and our disinheritance, agreed under protest to make the exchange, and this was done before Sir John de

Bousser, justice of our lord the king, Sir William de Clif, clerk of the chancery, and most of my household, and in return I was to receive suitable lands at their true value, and all my inheritance, dower and joint purchase, together with all my castles, jewels, vessel and wardrobe, as had been promised. After the exchange our lord the king delivered to me the rest of my inheritance and my dower, and retains the lands of joint purchase and all the other things promised except the manor of Holton in Oxfordshire. Then the king ordered me by letter to be with him at York at Christmas in the sixteenth year of his reign [1322], and put me in hope that at my coming I should have grace and the residue. On hearing this command I took the road to York.

Threats and Promises

On arrival the king kept me as it were under guard, ousting my council and household, until I sealed a quitclaim [legally promised to relinquish] against my will of the land of Usk and all my inheritance in Wales, and over and above this he ordered me to seal another writing, namely a letter obligatory binding me by my body and lands [requiring royal permission for her to remarry or sell the lands], contrary to the law of the land. Because of the argument I put up over sealing this writing, some of my councillors were taken and imprisoned for a long time, and I left the court to great ill will. When I had travelled five days on my way back to my castle of Clare, the king ordered me back, threatening that, if I did not return and seal the writing, all the land which I held of him would be taken away and I would never hold a foot of land of him. In order to avoid this great evil, I returned, and sealed that writing against my will, and the king has never carried out his promises. Soon after I was seised of [in possession of] Gower, Sir William de Braose through the abetting, help and maintenance of the aforesaid Sir Hugh brought a writ of novel disseisin [dispossession] against me naming the land of Gower, contrary to the law of the land which does not allow the king's writ concerning any free tenement to run in Wales. Sir Hugh, through his lordship and the royal power usurped by him, made the assize [judicial decision] go against me and made me lose that land in the presence of Sir John de Bousser and Sir William de Clif, the king's justices assigned to the case, although Sir Hugh was obliged to provide warranty to me and my heirs. After he had recovered that land, Sir William de Braose gave it to Sir Hugh le Despenser the elder who gave it to his son, Sir Hugh the younger, who still holds it. To injure me more, the king has taken back from me by his will and detains and distrains [seizes] all the wood of my inheritance in the chace [hunting park] of Tonbridge. I Elizabeth have sued on this at all the parliaments these three years by bill asking for the king's grace and redress of the above wrongs, and I could have no remedy, reply, nor have the bill endorsed, nor find a sheriff who was willing to make execution according to law of the writ of warranty that I have carried and prosecuted against Sir Hugh the younger for the land of Gower thus lost. Now Sir Hugh the younger, seeing the great scandal of the aforesaid wrongs, and in order to blind the people, and deceive and injure me more, offers me lands in recompense for Gower which are less than half the yearly value of Gower. In this I Elizabeth clearly see my disinheritance, the oppressions done by the king and the royal power which is in the hands of Sir Hugh the younger, the disgrace to myself to be thus disparaged or put in danger, the loss of my children, and all my lands and property, and, in view of all this and for fear of being reputed or surmised to be among those whom the king holds to be his enemies, I make the protest before you Notary and the witnesses who are here present that, if any lands should be delivered to me in recompense for Gower, I do not and will not accept them of my free will, nor will I receive them for any other reason than for fear of the king by the malice of Sir Hugh the younger who opposes me, and to avoid the above dangers, restore my goods and secure my right to the lands that are wrongly detained until the time that grace may be more open and the law of the land better maintained and common to all. I make the statement that I would wish to make this protest openly and publicly as civil law demands if fear of royal power with the peril that could follow did not stop me. I, John de Radenhale, clerk of the diocese of Hereford, public notary by apostolic authority, was present with the above witnesses while Lady Elizabeth recited each and every of the items mentioned above written in the French language, and thus made her declaration as stated above, and I saw, heard, wrote and recorded those things done, recited and carried out by the aforesaid Lady Elizabeth in this public form, and being asked I signed it with my accustomed mark, in the aforesaid year, indiction, pontificate, month, day and place.

Crime

May McKisack

During the fourteenth century, thieves and robbers roamed the countryside and the towns, and violence was prevalent throughout society. In this selection, historian May McKisack explains some of the reasons for the crime problem and discusses why the judicial systems seemed powerless to stop it. McKisack was a history professor from England. This excerpt is drawn from her extensive one-volume history *The Fourteenth Century.*

It did not make for good order in the land that, the clergy apart, almost the whole male population of fighting age should have been not only armed, but trained in the use of arms. Under Edward I's Statute of Winchester (modified in points of detail by the Statutes of Northampton, 1328, and Westminster IV, 1331), laymen between the ages of fifteen and sixty were bound to possess arms, ranging from the helmet, hauberk [chain mail], and sword of the knight down to the poor man's bow, arrows, and knife. The object of this legislation was, of course, the defence of the realm and the maintenance of the peace. Constables were in command of the forces of township and hundred which made up the *posse comitatus* [peacekeeping force of citizens] under the command of the sheriff; and on many occasions and in many places, most notably on the northern border, the *posse* did good service. But to arm the population entailed arming its numerous criminals and accustoming ordinary citizens to the expert handling of weapons, a tendency further encouraged by Edward III's exhortations concerning the practice of archery. Doubtless, the ordinary man needed no official encouragement to carry a knife in his belt when he went abroad; but it was a more serious matter that the able-bodied men of the village, trained to act as a military unit, could without difficulty organize themselves in defiance of the law. It may well have been the experience gained by the country folk in the *posse* which made it necessary for the Black Prince himself, with Lancaster and other lords, to take armed forces into Cheshire to suppress the rising of 1353; or which facilitated the rising of Oxfordshire villagers, . . . at the time of the Oxford riots on St. Scholastica's day, 1355; or, indeed, of the men of Kent and Essex in 1381 [during the so-called Wat Tyler Rebellion].

Mass movements on this scale were exceptional; but no student of the period can fail to be impressed by the general prevalence of criminal groups and gangs, the *compaignies, conspiratours, confederatours,* which were the subject of so many parliamentary complaints. The "draw-latch," "wastor," or "roberdesman" might work alone; but it was the roving bands of criminals, many of them highly organized, for whom the sparsely-populated, thickly-wooded countryside afforded such ample cover, who terrorized the ordinary citizen and defied the officers of the law. The activities of the Folvilles . . . show six brothers of a knightly family (one of them a priest) forming the nucleus of a criminal gang in Leicestershire in the early years of Edward III, a gang which after sixteen years of recorded crime was still untouched by the law. Besides countless less conspicuous crimes, the Folvilles were responsible for the murder of a baron of the exchequer (Roger Bellers) on the high road, near Leicester, and for the capture and holding to ransom of Sir Richard Willoughby, a justice of the king's bench. In one of his indictments, Eustace de Folville is referred to as *capitalis de societate* [leader of society]: and we know that his associates included a village parson, a clerk (described also as *miles*), and the constable of Rockingham castle, Sir Robert de Vere. Crime on this scale among the landed gentry can hardly have been general; but the exploits of the Folvilles do not appear to have been very different from those of Sir Robert Holland and Sir Adam Banaster in Lancashire, or of Sir Gilbert Middleton in Northumberland; and the extraordinary letter sent to a Yorkshire parson, by one describing himself as "Lionel, king of the rout of robbers," from his "Castle of the North Wind," is unlikely to have been the work of a common footpad. No doubt, as is often alleged, crime and disorder increased as a result of the Black Death and when disbanded soldiers began to return from the wars; criminals were said to be flocking into London after the cessation of the pestilence and the chroniclers refer to an increase of crime, particularly of crimes of sacrilege, in the sixties. But there is abundant evidence to show criminal gangs at work before the war began and those who joined the army included many professional criminals, enticed into service by the offer of a royal pardon for their past misdeeds. Murderers, robbers, and poachers are said to have been responsible for the victory of Halidon Hill (1333); and over 200 holders of royal pardons for crime are to be found among the shire levies [soldiers] serving in Scotland in 1334–5. Of the notorious Folvilles, one, Eustace, went overseas in the retinue of the earl of Northampton in 1337, another, Robert, was summoned, together with several of his associates in crime, to serve in Flanders in 1338. So late as 1390 the commons were still protesting against the issue of such pardons to men convicted of murder, treason, or rape.

Justice

Impartially administered justice was not to be looked for in such a world. Officials from the highest to the lowest were corruptible and the people knew it. Even the judges, with their high professional qualifications, salaries, fees, and pensions, were by no means above suspicion. In 1341 John Inge, a justice of the common pleas, pleaded guilty to the charge of having taken money on many occasions from accused persons and litigants while he was acting as justice of assize [court sessions] and jail delivery; Sir John Willoughby was accused "by clamour of the people" of selling the laws as if they had been oxen or cows. In 1350 Sir William Thorp, chief justice of the king's bench, was deprived [removed from his duties] and imprisoned for taking bribes. Fifteen years later Sir Henry Green, one of his successors in office, and Sir William Skipwith, chief baron of the exchequer, suffered a like fate on account of what are described as their *enormes infidelitates* [enormous crimes]. The commons, in 1339, alleged that trailbaston commissions [a type of court] did more harm to the innocent than to the guilty; in 1365 they were protesting against the appointment of commissioners of *oyer et terminer* [certain criminal courts] for life, with a grant of a third of the fines and amercements [other punishments involving money or goods]; an arrangement which encouraged the justices to hold superfluous sessions, to bribe jurors, and to procure false indictments. Attacks on judges during the rising of 1381 may have derived much of their impetus from hatred of the labour laws in particular; but it is hardly to be doubted that they also owed something to widespread popular suspicion of the integrity of even the most highly placed administrators of the law.

The corruptibility of the sheriffs was notorious. Though shorn of most of their judicial powers, they were still indispensable to the smooth running of the machinery of justice. The commission to the justices of the peace was always accompanied by the writ *de intendendo* to the sheriff whose duty it was to summon panels of jurors and, if the persons accused pleaded not guilty and put themselves on the country, to summon a trial jury, usually for a later session. Thus, it was open to the sheriffs to empanel jurors to suit one of the parties, to procure wrongful indictments, and to make false returns. In 1314 the commons of Suffolk petitioned against false indictments preferred by subordinate officials for their masters' advantage; outcries against the sheriffs' habit of compelling people to prefer indictments led, in 1330, to the removal of all the sheriffs and their subordinates throughout the country. In the case of *Ughtred* v. *Musgrave* (1366) the sheriff of Yorkshire, Thomas Musgrave, was accused of malicious arrest, false imprisonment, extortion of money, and an endeavour to entrap complainants into an attempt to abuse the forms of law by arranging for a collusive indictment by a packed jury. Musgrave was said to have seized Ughtred's servant, one Robert Woolman, put him in durance [confinement] and tortured him to within a little of death until he agreed to lay false accusations of felony and larceny against his master. The number of cases of corruption which found their way on to the assize rolls proves, however, that such offences did not always go unpunished. . . .

The government was by no means indifferent to the prevailing lawlessness and petitions on the subject seldom failed to elicit a favourable response. The four main methods of defeating the ends of justice—bribery; maintenance (the unlawful upholding of another's suit by word, writing, encouragement, or other act); embracery (the attempt to influence a jury by money, promises, threats, or persuasion); and champerty (maintaining a suit in consideration of receiving a part of the land, damages, or chattels recovered) were all forbidden by statute under Edward III and Richard II. But statutes were of little avail when a session of the commissioners of *oyer et terminer* could be broken up by a knight invading the hall with drawn sword and seizing one of the justices by the throat; when the earl of Devon himself could send a message to a justice of the peace telling him "that he was false and that he should answer with his body, that he (the earl) knew all the roads by which he must come and go and that he should not escape the hands of the said earl who was sure of him"; when a canon of Sempringham and the cellarer of a Cistercian house could be found among those who employed the Folvilles to destroy a rival's water mill; and when a country parson could be dragged from his bed at daybreak and carried away to Sherwood.

Trade and the Hanseatic League

Robert S. Lopez

During the fourteenth century commerce steadily rose throughout many parts of Europe. In northern Europe a group of German cities banded together in a group they called the Hanse, or the Hanseatic League. Founded in 1369, this league strengthened commercial relationships in northern Germany by bringing together a network of merchants, bankers, and shippers; it enabled trade goods to reach their destinations faster and more cheaply.

This excerpt, from *The Commercial Revolution of the Middle Ages, 950–1350* by Robert S. Lopez, describes the growth of the Hanseatic League. Lopez takes particular care to contrast the Hanseatic League with similar organizations that had sprung up in Italy during the fourteenth and earlier centuries. In his view, the Hanseatic League was never as powerful, as well organized, or as successful as its Mediterranean counterparts. Lopez also compares the Hanseatic League with the nations of Scandinavia, the great powers in the area since the days of the Vikings.

In Germany as in Italy, the agricultural revival and military recovery from the tenth century on enabled a number of towns to develop their local and long-distance trade, to challenge the authority of the emperor and his vassals, and eventually to build up a commercial and colonial empire. Trade was the main driving force, but economic penetration often was supported by the sword. Again, as in Italy, some of the towns that played a prominent role in the early period—Cologne, Mainz, and Ratisbon above all—were old Roman centers where a

Excerpted from *The Commercial Revolution of the Middle Ages, 950–1350* (Englewood Cliffs, NJ: Prentice-Hall, 1971) by Robert S. Lopez. Reprinted with permission from Ms. Claude Lopez.

trickle of trade had never ceased flowing, if only because a resident bishop or lay lord maintained a cluster of potential consumers within their walls. They were joined, however, by new urban nodes and episcopal sees sprouting in the wake of the German eastward expansion under the Carolingians [early medieval emperors] and their successors: Bremen, Hamburg, and Magdeburg, like Venice and Amalfi, were children of the Middle Ages. Even the internal structure of the urban society in the early period of expansion, so far as we can tell through a much scantier documentation than that of Italy, was not unlike that of many Italian towns. Closely knit groups of interrelated families (the "patricians," as modern historians rather improperly call them) all but monopolized public offices; they also were leaders in long-distance trade and owned much land, including valuable plots around the market place. Some of their ancestors may well have been petty noblemen who felt the attraction of trade.

Analogies, however, go no farther than this. The German urban development was slower than the Italian one and did not attain as much. Not before 1288 did Cologne finally break the power of her archbishop in the battle of Worringen, and to achieve that goal she needed the help of other feudal lords; still the archbishop and other vassals continued to rule over most of her district. Hemmed in and often harassed by the territorial princes in their vicinity, the German towns generally had to settle for something less than the rugged independence and all-pervasive commercialism of the Italian communes [small political units]. They invited imperial protection and, finding it inadequate, often huddled together in regional leagues. They let lingering feudal and agrarian interest weaken the main commercial and industrial bent of the urban community. As a partial compensation for the resulting mediocrity of their economic and political progress, they were spared some of the dramatic business crises and fierce conflicts that filled with tension the urban history of Italy. Moreover, the relations between merchants and princes did not have to be unfriendly; common interests in Germany produced remarkable instances of collaboration. As early as 1120 the duke of Zähringen joined twenty-four prominent merchants in founding [the city of] Freiburg-im-Breisgau, and the same pattern was followed in the foundation of Bern [in Switzerland]. Prolonged collaboration with princes was instrumental in Germany's greatest urban success, the formation of what was eventually to be called the Hanseatic League.

Hansa, it must be noted, was a term commonly used in northern Europe, chiefly but not exclusively to designate associations of merchants; its original meaning probably was "armed convoy," which appropriately describes the military underpinning of trade. Long before the thirteenth century several hansas appeared and disappeared at different points along or near the southern coast of the North Sea; but the

Hanseatic League "par excellence" was founded only in 1369, when Cologne and other Rhinish towns joined a preexisting, informal alliance of German seaports of the "northern Mediterranean" [North and Baltic Seas]. This alliance, however, was the crowning product of the relentless commercial and military expansion of Germanic people from the ninth century on. In the ninth and early tenth centuries, when the prowess and seamanship of the Vikings dominated the entire northern world, only the Frisians, a hardy folk of peasant-traders living between Rhine and Weser, dared to compete with the Scandinavians. With less primitive methods Westphalian merchants carried forward the challenge between Weser and Elbe in the late tenth and early eleventh centuries, but did not yet threaten the Scandinavian predominance in the Baltic. The tide began to turn in 1143, when Lübeck, originally a Slavonic settlement whose ruler had welcomed German settlers but had succumbed to the aggression of a German lord, was founded again as a wholly German town by Henry the Lion, the cousin and rival of [medieval emperor] Frederic Barbarossa.

Simple Commerce

Lübeck, placed on the eastern side of the narrow neck of land that separated the Baltic from Hamburg and the North Sea, was ideally located to serve as the master link between the two halves of the northern Mediterranean while the Scandinavians still had the Jutland straits firmly in their grip. . . . German merchants hopping from one river mouth or natural harbor to another used their naval and commercial proficiency to found a series of towns, all of which looked upon Lübeck as the kingpin of their trade and the ancestral home of their leading families. German knights sweeping through the inland plains used their superior armament and organization to crush the resistance of thinly settled Slavs and Balts, and made the wilderness alive with settlements of peasants brought in from as far as Westphalia and Flanders. Ever since the beginning the German advance into pagan or scarcely Christian countries had been wrapped in vaguely religious colors; it became officially a crusade in Latvia and Estonia, where the Teutonic Order of knights preceded or assisted the merchants with its remarkable combination of ruthless force and business talent. Lithuania alone resisted to the end. Poland and Russia, which had long been Christian and fairly well developed, held out against conquest but welcomed commercial penetration. A belated attempt by the Danes to stop German penetration failed. By 1274 Reval, originally a Danish outpost in Estonia which had been subsequently absorbed into the German sphere, could write to Lübeck: "Our two towns belong together like the arms of Christ crucified." Theirs was a silver cross, wrought of German conquering trade.

As a matter of fact, between the late eleventh and the late thirteenth centuries the Scandinavian military and economic power collapsed.

No doubt the merging of the Scandinavian elites with much larger native populations in Russia, Normandy, and southern Italy was an inevitable consequence of overexpansion; so was the fall of the Viking possessions in the British Isles. But the contraction of their power in their home waters of the northern Mediterranean calls for still another explanation, especially as their unruly tribes at the same period should have gained strength through consolidation into the three kingdoms of Denmark, Norway, and Sweden. Indeed the king of Norway brought under his control the remote, poverty-stricken Scandinavian communities in Greenland and Iceland; the king of Sweden annexed peripheral Finland; but the vigorous campaigns of several Danish kings could not for long prevent the Germans from evicting the Danes from their once extensive domains on the southern and eastern Baltic shores. Again, the Scandinavian "brotherhood" of merchants at Visby in the central Baltic island of Gotland was eclipsed by the community of "German visitors of Gotland," which was the first core of the future Hanseatic League. More than that, by a combination of diplomacy and warfare the German merchants gained special privileges at the great fairs of Skanör (in the Danish-dominated part of southern Sweden), in all ports of the Swedish kingdom, and in all those of Norway except the extreme north.

All told, the German pattern of penetration into the Scandinavian sphere of influence and home ports resembled that of the Italian merchants on Byzantine and Islamic shores. Like the Greeks and the Muslims, though in a much more primitive context, the Scandinavians were early starters who failed to keep up with economic and social progress. Sea trade with them was not so much the business of free townsmen as that of noblemen and peasants with a knack for navigation. Their ships, which had supplied models to all northern peoples, were now smaller than the German cog, a sturdy sailship fitted for the bulkiest cargoes. They lagged behind the Germans in replacing the traditional lateral rudders with a central rudder, more effective to steer ponderous ships. All of their commercial techniques were getting out of date.

Let us not infer that the "Easterlings" [German traders] . . . had caught up with Italian or Catalan techniques. It was enough for them to be more advanced than their competitors in the northern seas. Their versions of the partnership and *commenda* contracts [sophisticated types of loans and agreements common in Italy during the period], possibly derived from still simpler Scandinavian models, were cruder and hazier than their Mediterranean counterparts. Double-entry accounting and insurance were totally unknown. Credit organization was rudimentary, although commercial interest rates in Lübeck became as low as in Italy and the bankruptcy of [banker] Hermann Clendenst in 1335 shook the town as thoroughly as the contemporary bank failures in Florence. Literacy was fairly widespread, but not as much as among Italian or Belgian burghers. The cities of the Easterlings in the course of the thirteenth century became nearly as independent as the Italian communes, but their ruling classes were more closed, and the hinterland, as that of the Catalan ports, escaped their control. On the other hand, the Easterlings were less embroiled than the Italians in party strife, mutual competition, and fights for oversea empires. They generally avoided inter-city rivalry by accepting Lübeck's leadership, and reduced the quest for permanent colonies by shuttling rapidly across narrow stretches of sea and back to home ports. One establishment at the eastern end of their longest route—the "yard" at Novgorod [in present-day Russia], which they captured from the Scandinavians— and three at the outer prongs of the western end—the "steelyard" at London, the "kontor" at Bruges [in Belgium], and the autonomous quarter at Bergen [in Norway]—took care of most of their oversea needs. Even here their holdings were no larger than the earliest Italian enclaves: the establishments and privileges were permanent, but the population consisted chiefly of temporary callers, and sovereignty rested with the local rulers.

Most of the objects of German sea trade reflected a less developed economy than that of the classic Mediterranean. Oriental spices and refined wares, which for a short time around the tenth century had reached Scandinavia through the Russian rivers, now came to Germany from the west, as did other luxuries of French and Italian origin. The demand, however, was limited to the fairly small number of people who could appreciate and afford them. Far more important was the flow of raw materials from Russia, Poland, and the new and old German hinterland: rye, grain, timber, pitch, tar, honey, wax, and furs. More timber, pitch, and tar came from Scandinavia. Bohemia and Hungary sent some of their precious and non-precious metals; England, her wool and hides. The odor of salted herring, less sweet but more substantial than that of spices, dominated the scene. Without the salt of nearby Lüneburg, Lübeck might never have risen above mediocrity, but she soon had to supplement it with French and Portuguese salt. The herring trade had its main center at the Skanör fairs: the king of Denmark still collected tolls and his subjects unloaded the fish, but the Lübeck merchants were the most important buyers. . . . By 1368 their purchases came close to 34,000 barrels and rose steadily thereafter. In conclusion, the list of commodities included very few noble items, but it missed none of the basic necessities of life.

Victory at Sea

Desmond Seward

The Hundred Years' War began in 1337, when King Philip of France took a small principality from England and King Edward III of England responded by claiming the whole of France for himself. Edward instantly set most of his energies and most of his nation's funds toward fighting the French. He used up so much money during just the first three years of the war that he was forced to pawn his crown. He also borrowed heavily from bankers in Ghent, now part of Belgium; indeed, he had to leave his wife and children in Ghent as collateral until he could repay the money. In the meantime, the French fleet had massed and looked quite formidable.

Edward, however, decided that he would continue to fight the war. As historian and medieval specialist Desmond Seward explains in this excerpt from his book *The Hundred Years' War: The English in France, 1337–1453*, the policy led to a quick and glorious sea victory in 1340 off the coast of the Low Countries—but also sentenced Edward to dissension and loss of support at home.

When the King [Edward III] arrived back in England from Ghent in the spring of 1340, he summoned Parliament and told it that unless new taxes were raised he would have to return to the Low Countries and be imprisoned for debt. Parliament made plain that it was very unhappy about Edward's extravagance, but reluctantly granted him a "ninth" for two years—the ninth sheaf, fleece and lamb from every farm, and the ninth part of every townsman's goods. In return the King had to promise to abolish certain taxes and make a number of reforms in government. However he could now return to Ghent to redeem his wife and children and recommence operations against Philip. He collected reinforcements, assembling a fleet on the Suffolk coast for their transport. En route he intended to deal with the French armada at Sluys.

Contrary to what the [fourteenth-century] chronicler Geoffrey le Baker seems to have heard, the King had been planning this move for some time. The enemy invasion fleet was now dauntingly large; it included not only French but also Castilian and Genoese vessels, Castile being an ally of France while the Genoese were mercenaries under the veteran sea-captain Barbanera (or "*Barbenoire*" as the French called him). Edward had requisitioned all the ships he could find, literally pressganging [kidnapping] men to sail and to fight on them. Even so, his sailing masters, Robert Morley and the Fleming Jehan Crabbe, warned him that the odds were too high. The King accused them of trying to frighten him, "but I shall cross the sea and those who are afraid may stay at home." On 22 June 1340 he finally set sail from the little port of Orwell in Suffolk, he himself on board his great cog *Thomas*. En route he was joined by Lord Morley, Admiral of the Northern Fleet, with fifty vessels—together their combined force amounted to 147 ships.

Probably these vessels were nearly all cogs. The English government had commissioned a number of converted cogs, the "King's Ships," which for all their shortcomings were intended for war. The cog was basically a merchant ship, designed for carrying cargoes which ranged from wool to wine and from livestock to passengers. Shallow-draughted [able to maneuver in very little water] and small-sized—usually 30 to 40 tons, though sometimes as big as 200—it could use creeks and inlets inaccessible to bigger ships. Clinker-built, broad-beamed and with a rounded bow and poop, it was a boat for all weathers and for the North Sea. But while the cog made an excellent troop transport, it was hardly a warship—even though special fighting tops could be built on the fore and stern castles. Tactics were brutally simple—to move to windward of the enemy ship and then try to sink her by ramming or by running her aground.

With its single square sail and rudimentary rudder, a cog was slow to maneuvre. The King's Ships were particularly at risk when confronted by a purpose-built battle-craft, like the Mediterranean galley which was armed with a proper ram and a stone-throwing catapult, and whose oars gave it superior speed and maneuvrability. For the last forty years the French had maintained a royal dockyard, constructed by Genoese experts, which specialized in producing these galleys—the Clos des Galées at Rouen—and a battle on the open sea might have placed Edward at a considerable tactical disadvantage.

The English fleet anchored off the Zeeland coast, opposite Blankenberghe, on 23 June. Scouts were landed and sent out to reconnoitre. They returned to report how they had seen at Sluys "so great a number of ships that their masts seemed to be like a great wood." Edward stayed at sea and spent all day discussing what to do.

The French Admirals, Hue Quiéret and Nicolas Béhuchet, were

"right good and expert men of war" but no seamen—Béhuchet was a former tax collector—and there was a marked lack of liaison with their Castilian and Genoese colleagues. Barbanera begged the Admirals to put to sea, no doubt so that he could use his three galleys against the English cogs, but they insisted on staying in the estuary where they could fight a land battle, which was just what Edward wanted. The French massed their fleet in three squadrons, one behind the other, the ships lashed together with chains and barricaded by planks and by small boats weighted with stones. The first squadron had captured English cogs at one end of the line, each vessel mounting four cannon and defended by crossbowmen and crewed by Flemings and Picards. The second squadron was manned by men from Boulogne and Dieppe, the third by Normans. But the 20,000 men on board were largely pressganged and few of them had ever seen a battle. There were no more than 150 knights and 400 professional crossbowmen all told in the whole of this Grand Army of the Sea—the rest were frightened fisherfolk, bargees and longshoremen.

That night King Edward divided his own fleet into three squadrons, marshalling his ships in threes—two filled with archers flanking one of men-at-arms. He kept in reserve a fourth squadron, of ships defended entirely by archers. Then at 5 in the morning he tacked away from his anchorage into the wind and waited for the tide to turn. When his sailing-masters finally put their helms over and steered towards Sluys, they had the wind and the sun behind them and the tide running with them. Barbanera at once realized the danger. "My Lord," he told Béhuchet, "the King of England and his fleet are coming down on us. Stand out to sea with your ships, for if you remain here, shut in between these great dykes, the English, who have the wind, the tide and the sun with them, will hem you in and you will be unable to maneuvre." But this last desperate warning went unheeded, whereupon the Genoese galleys slipped anchor and escaped just in time.

At about 9 o'clock the English fleet sailed straight into the French ships who, still at their moorings, were "arrayed like a line of castles." According to an enthralled English chronicler, "an iron cloud of quarrels from crossbows and arrows from long-bows fell on the enemy, dealing death to thousands." Then the English ships crashed into the French and grappled together. The men-at-arms boarded with swords, axes and half-pikes, while the bowmen continued to shoot flight after flight and seamen threw heavy stones, iron bolts and quicklime from the mast-tops; there were even divers who tried to sink the enemy ships by boring holes in their hulls below water. The battle surged backwards and forwards from one vessel to another.

An early casualty was a fine English cog which was carrying "a great number of countesses, ladies, knights' wives and other

The naval battle at Sluys in the English Channel was the first important battle of the Hundred Years' War. It was a decisive English victory.

damosels, that were going to see the Queen at Ghent." Although strongly guarded by archers and men-at-arms, their ship was sunk— it is said—by cannon. The screams of the drowning ladies must have maddened the English.

[French chronicler Jean] Froissart, who had met men who were there, writes: "This battle was right fierce and terrible; for the battles on the sea are more dangerous and fiercer than the battles by land; for on the sea there is no reculing nor fleeing; there is no remedy but to fight and to abide fortune, and every man to shew his prowess." The King was in the thick of the mêlée and was wounded in the leg— his white leather boots were covered in blood. There was an especially murderous struggle to regain the great cog *Christopher* which was defended by Genoese crossbowmen, but at last it was "won by the Englishmen, and all that were within it were taken or slain." The English found considerable difficulty in capturing the Castilian ships because their sides were so tall. The battle "endured from the morning till it was noon, and the Englishmen endured much pain."

Eventually archers gave the advantage to Edward's men—they could shoot two or even three arrows for every one crossbow quarrel—and the first French squadron was overwhelmed. Many of the enemy jumped overboard, their wounded being thrown after them. The sea was so full of corpses that those who did not drown could not tell whether they were swimming in water or blood, though the knights must have gone straight to the bottom in their heavy armour. Hue Quiéret, after being badly wounded, surrendered—to be beheaded immediately. Béhuchet was also captured, to be strung up by English knights within a matter of minutes.

The sight of their Admiral's corpse swinging from the yardarm of the *Thomas* (the King's flagship) caused panic among the French second squadron, many of whose crews leapt overboard without resisting. The onset of dusk went unnoticed, so bright was the light of the burning ships. When darkness fell the King remained before Sluys, "and all that night abode in his ship . . . with great noise of trumpets and other instruments."

During the night thirty enemy vessels slipped anchor and fled, while the *Saint-Jacques* of Dieppe continued to fight on in the dark—when she was finally taken by the Earl of Huntingdon, 400 corpses were found on board. Those French ships who stayed were attacked from the rear by Flemish fishermen in barges. When morning came Edward sent Jehan Crabbe and a well-armed flotilla in pursuit, but he had no reason to be dismayed that a few enemy vessels escaped. The entire French fleet, with the exception of those who had fled during the night, had been captured or sent to the bottom, while thousands of its men had died—"there was not one that escaped but all were slain," Froissart boasts with pardonable exaggeration.

The Aftermath for England

Edward made a pilgrimage of thanksgiving to the shrine of Our Lady of Ardembourg. Later he commemorated the battle of Sluys on a new gold coin, the noble of six shillings and eight pence; he is shown on board a ship floating on the waves, crowned and bearing a sword and a shield which quarters the royal arms of France and England. These coins so impressed contemporaries that some people said they had been made by alchemists in the Tower of London. They gave rise to a jingle:

> Foure things our Noble showeth unto me,
> King, ship, and sword, and power of the sea.

But Sluys had not won Edward command of the Channel, let alone of the seas—only two years later the French sacked Plymouth for a second time. None the less, he had rid England of a very real threat of invasion.

With hindsight one can see that Sluys marked the passing of the initiative to the English—indeed, to the men of 1340 God had shown he was on their side.

However, King Edward still seemed no nearer to achieving the conquest of France. Towards the end of July, accompanied by seven earls and an army which included 9,000 archers, several thousand Flemish pikemen, and a multitude of mercenaries, he laid siege to Tournai. But though he may have had as many as 30,000 troops, he had no siege engines—mangonels [devices used to throw missiles] or battering-rams—and could do little apart from camping before the walls. And, as in 1339, his army included Dutch and German lords who had been hired under the indenture system; these quarrelled incessantly with each other, insisted on being paid on time, and left when they felt like it.

Meanwhile Philip who was "very angry at the defeat of his navy"—only his court jester had dared tell him the news—marched to relieve Tournai with an army even bigger than Edward's and mustering nearly 20,000 men-at-arms. The French King adopted his usual tactics, refusing to offer battle and keeping his troops in the surrounding hills from where they raided Edward's outposts and ambushed his supply lines. The English King grumbled to the young Prince of Wales, in a letter: "He dug trenches all round him and cut down big trees so that we might not get at him." Edward's army was already unpaid and mutinous, and soon supplies and fodder began to run out. Shorter of money than ever and totally unable to pay his angry mercenaries, the English King was forced to negotiate a truce, at Espléchin on 25 September. For once even Edward seems to have been discouraged; in October he had told the Pope's envoys that he was ready to surrender his claims to the French crown if Philip would give him the Duchy of Aquitaine (as it had been in Henry III's day) in full sovereignty. For he could expect no money from England; many of his subjects had refused to pay the promised ninth and in some places tax collectors had been met with armed resistance. Two months later, Edward fled secretly from the Low Countries to escape his clamorous creditors.

The King returned to England in a fury. As he saw it, years of work had been ruined by the failure of his government to find him enough money. The chief villain in his eyes was the Chancellor, John Stratford, Archbishop of Canterbury, whom he believed to have mishandled the taxes. Edward actually informed the Pope that Stratford had deliberately kept him short of money in the hope that he would be defeated and killed; incredibly, the King insinuated that the Archbishop had adulterous designs on the Queen and had tried to set her against him. Stratford saved himself by bolting to Canterbury where he took sanctuary, but many of his officials were arrested. However, after casting himself as a second Thomas à Becket [the famed twelfth-century archbishop of Canterbury], the wily prelate then managed to shift the dispute from the administrative to the constitutional field—he accused Edward of infringing Magna Carta, insisted on the right of ministers to be tried by Parliament, and maneuvred him into summoning one in April 1341. The Archbishop found massive support in the Parliament, and the King was wise enough to give way in return for supplies; soon he was reconciled with Stratford. Edward knew very well that he had to keep his subjects' support, above all that of the magnates, not only to continue with his French ambitions but to keep his throne.

Despite the subsidies granted in 1341, King Edward could not repay his loans. These included £180,000 which he had borrowed from the Florentines [Italian banking houses]. In 1343 the Peruzzi, who were owed £77,000 (quite apart from interest) went bankrupt; the Bardi followed them three years later. For a short time the small group of native English financiers . . . who controlled the wool trade tried to make a profit by lending money to the King, but in 1349 they in their turn crashed. However, by then Edward was at least able to rely on the *maletote* or export duty on wool. The Parliament, which included many wool producers, had at last grown reconciled to this hateful tax becoming an annual subsidy, partly because they had wrested from the King the right of controlling taxes. Indeed the growth of parliamentary power was one of the most important side effects of the Hundred Years' War for the English.

Anti-Semitism in Spain

Michel Mollat and Philippe Wolff

Anti-Semitic feeling among Christians was never far from the surface
in medieval Europe. Even European rulers who had an official policy
of "tolerance" usually restricted where Jews could live and what type
of work they could do. In other countries, and in tolerant countries at
certain times as well, anti-Semitism could grow violent. Among these
acts of violence was a series of pogroms, or organized massacres of
Jews, which took place in Spain during the last decade of the fourteenth
century.

This excerpt, from *The Popular Revolutions of the Late Middle Ages*
by French historians Michel Mollat and Philippe Wolff, describes some
of these pogroms. Mollat and Wolff's book focuses on uprisings during
the period, and so they evaluate the anti-Semitic violence very much in
these terms. They point out, for instance, that Spain's upper classes and
nobility tended to support and protect the Jews while the lower and middle classes were much more likely to take part in the violence; in this
way, the violence was at least in part a rebellion against Spain's rulers.
Mollat and Wolff also recognized, however, that most of the violence
stemmed from fear and hatred of Jews among Christian Spaniards of the
time. Unfortunately, the same scene would be played out again through
medieval Europe—and, as we know, well into our own time, too.

A ll over Europe the position of the Jews had steadily deteriorated
during the fourteenth century. In 1290 Edward I had expelled
them from England. In France since the time of Philippe le Bel ex-

Excerpted from *The Popular Revolutions of the Late Middle Ages,* by Michel Mollat and Philippe
Wolff, translated by A.L. Lytton-Sells. Copyright © 1973 by George Allen & Unwin, Ltd.
Reprinted with permission from Taylor & Francis Books, Ltd.

pulsions had followed periods during which the Jewish communities had been able to reestablish their business; which might be called the policy of the sponge. They were scarcely popular with the public, as was shown by the *Pastoureaux'* movement [an uprising of shepherds] in Languedoc (1320) and by the anti-Jewish episodes in the civic disturbances of 1382. Nowhere, however, did the Jewish question exhibit the same seriousness as in the Iberian peninsula.

The number of Jews living in fourteenth-century Spain has been very variously estimated: a million and a half in the kingdom of Castille alone according to some, about twenty thousand according to others. The best way of judging is to start from the presumed number of the Jews who were expelled in 1492, and it is agreed that between 100,000 and 150,000 left Castille at that time. Prior to this, massacre, emigration and conversions had reduced their numbers in proportions difficult to estimate. It is not unreasonable to suppose that towards 1370 they may have numbered about 200,000, that is, between 3 per cent and 5 per cent of the total population. The most important communities were living in Toledo, Seville, Jerez and in Murcia; but small *aljamas* (seventy-one in Castille proper) were scattered throughout the kingdom. They were even more widely dispersed in the kingdom of Aragon, which probably contained nearly 60,000 Jews, a relatively greater number, namely 6–7 per cent of the population. One is averse however to adopting the figure . . . proposed for Barcelona: 5,000 Jews, or 12–14 per cent of the population. If there were 1,500, this is a fair estimate, but at least we may suppose that this was the most numerous community in the kingdom.

Were these Jews as rich as has been said? Increasingly, since the thirteenth century, a prosperous minority of great financiers and administrators had become isolated from the mass of the (Jewish) community. A certain Yucaf Pichon was virtually director of the royal finances for Enrique II, King of Castille, between 1369 and 1375. The Jews monopolized the posts of tax-farmers or receivers, posts for which their means and experience commended them. Even the nobility had recourse to their services. One suspects that this contributed to making them unpopular. Doctors like Yucaf ibn Wakar, in the service of the King of Castille, who entrusted him with diplomatic missions; or the Rabbi Haym el Levi who in 1389 was physician to the Archbishop of Toledo; or . . . astrologers such as Hasdai Cresques, in the service of Yolanda of Aragon, rose to very high office. These rich Jews often became less devout, and the Rabbis loudly deplored the fact, but the great majority of Jews remained ardent believers, and these included usurers, but also small farmers, artisans and merchants. There were also poor Hebrews, for whom a hospital had been founded at Barcelona; but Christians in general did not make these distinctions. The Jews had won a strong social and economic position, they were rough in recovering the moneys owing to them, they refused to be assimilated and so represented a "cyst" in the State.

The conflict became particularly acute in the kingdom of Castille where passions had been inflamed by a dynastic dispute. Pedro I, whom his enemies called "the cruel," had openly leaned for support on the Jews. This encouraged immigration on the part of large numbers, people who had been made uncomfortable by the attitude of their various governments. His half-brother, Enrique de Trastamare, who led the insurrection against him, strongly reproached him with his pro-Jewish policy. This was only one of the grounds of contention. But Enrique was overtaken by his own propaganda. His troops destroyed several *aljamas*; the one at Toledo was partly sacked in 1355; and when the people of Valladolid rose against Pedro I in 1367, eight synagogues paid the price of this "emotion." When Enrique II was victorious in 1369, the Jews rallied round him, and he continued to use them, though less blatantly. One may suppose that the events of 1391 were the culmination of these conflicts.

Anti-Jewish feeling subsisted on instinct. It also adopted the old conception of the collective and hereditary responsibility of the Jews in the Passion of Christ, and for this reason showed itself most strongly in Holy Week. But definite claims, precise demands were formulated. What was demanded was, first, a moratorium, or even a reduction of the debts owing to the Jews. . . . Certain crafts, such as medicine and finance, were to be closed to them. Generally speaking, a Jew's profession should give him no power over Christians. He was also to be distinguished from Christians by special signs worn on his clothes, by confinement in a ghetto, and by being forbidden to assume a Christian name. In the law courts, a Christian's testimony should always prevail over a Jew's. Finally, any sign of increased activity, such as the building of new synagogues, or embellishment of old ones, was jealously watched and opposed. The *aljama* of Cordova was compelled to demolish a new religious building, and the principal synagogue in Valencia, which had been enlarged and adorned, was given by the Queen to her principal chaplain (1379). One can clearly distinguish the social and economic character of these grievances against the Jews.

They were still further exasperated by the propaganda of new converts, not then very numerous, but full of hatred for their former co-religionists; and also by fanatics among whom Ferran Martinez, archdeacon of Ecija, was outstanding. Some went as far as preaching in favour of a "definite solution" of the Jewish question. The *aljama* of Seville had several times to complain of the archdeacon of Ecija, and Juan I of Castille had to write to moderate his zeal. But the King died on 9 October 1390, leaving an heir who was a minor, and Enrique III's reign was marked from the outset by great agitation.

Pogrom

It was in these conditions that the pogrom started. To fix the chronology and measure the extent of this drive would be useful, though much further research in local archives will be needed. We may begin by recording what is known from—among other sources—the letter which Hasdai Cresques, the Queen of Aragon's astrologer, wrote to the community at Avignon. Violence started at Seville on 6 June 1391, directly encouraged by Ferrán Martinez. Two synagogues were converted into churches, murders and thefts followed. The contagion spread to nearly all the *aljamas* of the archdiocese. Cordova was soon the theatre of scenes as frightful, and the wave of violence moved on to Ubeda, Baeza, Jaén, Muradal, Ciudad Real, Huete and Cuenca. At Cuenca a subsequent trial was to prove that several members of the municipal council took part in the massacre. Toledo was affected on 18 June.

By way of Orihuela and Alicante the flame of hostility reached Valencia. We are fairly well informed about the pogrom at Valencia by an account which was written by order of the city magistrates themselves. Despite the precautions inspired by the disquieting news, forty to fifty young men appeared at the gateway to the *Juderia* [ghetto], uttering threats. Some of them even managed to invade the ghetto, the Jews having shut the gate too late. Responding to the shouts of the Christians who had remained outside, the crowd was joined by soldiers and vagabonds. The Infanta [daughter of the king], escorted by the Knights and sworn aldermen, asked the Jews to reopen the gates, in order to reassure the crowd as to the fate of the intruders; but in vain. While the Jews were refusing, the barrier round the ghetto was crossed and the massacre began. Some Jews fled to the churches and let themselves be baptized.

Repression began on 11 July, when the aldermen ordered those who were in possession of clothes, jewels and money stolen from the *Juderia* to bring and deposit them in front of a special commission. They arrested nearly 100 persons, of whom about eighty were men of the people, though ten were men "of high lineage." This detail and several others emphasize the view that elements of all ranks had taken part in the riot. When however on 8 November 1392 the King granted a general pardon, and made an exception for only twenty of the culprits who were to be named, these were all artisans. What strikes one, moreover, about these events is the religious enthusiasm amid which they took place. The aldermen, in their letter to the King, pointed to several miracles as having occurred, some of them officially certified by notaries, and they concluded that this could be explained only by divine intervention. Thus a repudiation of the excesses committed at the expense of royal property (the Jews being regarded as such) was combined, in spite of everything, with a belief in an overruling providence; both circumstances having led to so many conversions.

In the meantime the contagion had spread north to Catalonia. On 2 August the same atrocities were perpetrated at Palma de Mallorca; though there a new element crept in. After plundering the *aljama*, the mob attacked the property of certain Christians.

Of events in Barcelona we have the means of offering a more detailed picture. On receiving the news from Valencia, on 17 July, the council had decided to establish a force, armed and sworn in, which would prevent any possible assault on the *Call*, or Jewish quarter. Then, as all remained calm, anxiety died down. On 2 August the council seemed to be absorbed by problems of food supply; it was a question of sending two ships to Sicily, in particular two Castilian ships which happened to be in the harbour.

It was then that the four terrible days began. On Saturday 5 August, towards half past one in the afternoon, a small band, which had come from the port and included Castilian sailors, set fire to the gates of the *Call* and killed some hundred Jews. During the whole evening and night the mob shared in the pillage, while the surviving Jews took refuge in the royal Castillo Nuevo, near by. Sunday the 6th witnessed a lull in the tempest and an attempt at reaction. A number of the culprits were arrested and confined in the Provost's gaol [jail]. The royal officials, the councillors and many "honoured citizens" mounted guard round the *Call* and the Castillo Nuevo. These measures were continued on the Monday. The citizens assembled under arms, as commanded by the councillors, and a well-attended council unanimously condemned ten Castilians to be hanged. Guilhem de Sant-Climent, the royal Provost, was preparing to execute the sentence when towards half past one in the afternoon a far greater rising took place, amid cries of "Long live the King and the people!" The documents agree in making the lower class responsible. After a turmoil which left one man dead and several wounded, the rioters attacked the Provost's (*viguier*) gaol and freed the prisoners. For a short time sedition turned into a social conflict. The houses of several "honoured citizens" were threatened. Canon Mascaro, our best source of information, indicates a Knight, Pons de la Sala, as having under cover of two royal flags diverted the common people towards the royal castle and then laid siege to it. Meanwhile, the cathedral bells were sounding the alarm. In the evening the peasants belonging to the militia (the *sagramental*) flocked to the castle. During the night the archives of the *batle* (that is the bailiff) were burned. Finally, on Tuesday 8 August, the Jews, who had taken refuge in the new Castillo and were dying of thirst and hunger, surrendered; and a procession, setting out from the cathedral, came to receive them. Mascaro records the memory of a monk, standing on the castle mound and holding up a cross. Numerous baptisms were at once celebrated in the cathedral and in other churches. Recalcitrants were lodged in families and instructed in Christian dogma. Some more were converted, but many, especially women, refused and were killed; three hundred, according to a fairly reliable source.

Then came a long period which Mascaro describes as follows:

> They [the rioters] threatened to kill all the clerics, and forced them to pay taxes and to contribute in everything as if they were laymen. Next they menaced the silversmiths, merchants and rich men, without putting them to death, though they were not far from it. During this time when a council was held in the city all the common folk were admitted to the general council. Various embassies were sent to the King, containing men of the upper, middle and lower orders.

The register of the council for this period, which has been preserved, confirms the above. The city lived under pressure from the populace, and many artisans took part in the councils held in August and September. It was decided to inquire into the past administration of the city's finances, and a commission of auditors was appointed, containing one, two or several members of each craft, a few citizens and merchants, and two of the royal accountants—who were therefore in a very small minority. The object was to punish past abuses, but also to lighten fiscal burdens on the city. Meanwhile, the taxes were reduced, the duty on wine being lowered from an eighth [of the price] to a sixteenth. A letter of remission [relief from taxes] which was granted to a courier from the city throws light on the circumstances in which these decisions were taken. We see this man mounting a bench and crying out: "My Lords, may it please you to remove these impositions, for a great throng is outside, awaiting the good news!" An embassy (including two artisans) was sent to the King, praying him not to come, or in any case not with armed men. The council was busy trying to restore order, and to remove weapons (except swords and daggers). There being still some question of the Jews, it was decided to expel those who refused conversion and at the same time to separate the converts from the recalcitrant; but the last allusion to them dates from 21 August.

Reaction followed little by little. After 9 October the councils were composed as before the riots, the exceptional presence of artisans being no longer mentioned. On 30 November, the usual date, five new councillors were elected, and new members of the Council of the Hundred appointed. It was agreed that the former should swear to continue the examination of the accounts. On 13 December the commission of inquiry underwent a significant change. The artisans were to succeed each other monthly, in groups of ten; but, of these ten, only four would in fact sit at one time, facing four citizens or merchants.

Repression had by now begun. On 6 December the first royal troops entered the city. On the 13th the gibbets [gallows] were set up, and on the 14th eleven men were hanged in the principal squares of the city, the bodies remaining exposed for a week. On the 22nd ten more were hanged and two were quartered. Mascaro gives us the name of one of the latter, N'Armentera, a tailor, and he enumerates with a detail tinged with satisfaction the places where the fragments were to be exposed. One desire was clearly manifest: to inspire terror in the public. The King and Queen were able to make their solemn entry on 10 January 1392.

No less than eighty-two letters of remission, affecting ninety-two persons, have been preserved in the registers of the royal chancellery: these inform us of the sequel to the whole affair. The formula is practically repeated in each case. The crimes and faults of the beneficiary were remitted, even if he had taken part in the attack on the *Call*, in the attack on the Castillo Nuevo, in breaking into the Provost's gaol, in burning the Bailiff's archives, or in the massacre of the Jews—on condition, however, of satisfying the civil courts. The price for these pardons was usually fixed at a low figure, and these remissions evidently concern poor people, but the figure was sometimes higher. The same impression arises from a study of the beneficiaries' occupations. Seven were slaves, three were freed men; there were six sailors, two cobblers, two weavers, and a carpenter; but there were also three innkeepers, a notary and two silversmiths. A whole family—parents, two sons and three slaves—received a collective pardon. Some ten persons were strangers to Barcelona. A few collective remissions were granted to parishes near the city. In fact, there were many who managed to pass through the meshes of the net. Yet this insurrection cannot be regarded as a simply popular one.

Deposing King Richard

Adam of Usk

Adam of Usk was a priest and a lawyer who is remembered today for having written a chronicle of life in England at the end of the fourteenth century. The chronicle covers the years from 1377 to 1404, but the bulk of the book covers the period between 1397 and 1402. This excerpt from Adam's work tells of events from the year 1399.

This was a troublesome time for England. King Richard II was unpopular and becoming steadily more so. In particular, he had run afoul of several influential nobles of the house of Lancaster. The Lancasters were politically powerful—so much so that, fearing for his kingdom, Richard had exiled their leader, Henry Bolingbroke, the duke of Lancaster. The move was not successful. In 1399, disgusted with Richard's reign, the Lancastrians helped Henry back into the country, overthrew Richard, and installed Henry as king in his place.

The Lancastrians spread stories about Richard's parentage to make the deposition seem more legal. They questioned, for example, whether one of his ancestors had been a true heir to the throne. They also started rumors, such as the one mentioned in Adam's chronicle, that his biological father was not actually his legal father and that he was therefore not in the line of succession at all. Whatever the truth of the matter, Richard's career as king was over, and Henry ruled for the next fourteen years. During the next century, partly as a result of the events Adam describes here, wars would break out between the powerful Lancasters and another noble house, the Yorks.

Excerpted from *The Chronicle of Adam of Usk* (London: John Murray, 1876) by Adam of Usk, edited by Edward Maunde.

Editor's Note: Adam takes up the narrative here soon after Henry arrived back in England. One of Henry's first targets was the county of Chester. Chester had given support to Richard, and so Henry was anxious to subdue it. He did this by destroying the countryside as well as by using more standard military tactics, such as storming castles.

Richard had been in Ireland, but he hurried back to England when word reached him of Henry's return. He assembled an army to attack Henry but was hampered by the refusal of some of his allies to obey orders. Without the command of an army, Richard's reign was effectively at an end.

The same day, the duke of Lancaster with his host reached Chester. But first he reviewed his troops in a large field, in which was a fair crop of standing corn, some three miles from the city, on its eastern side, marshalling their ranks to the number of one hundred thousand fighting men. And it may be truly said that the hills shone again with their shields. And thus he entered the castle of Chester; and there he remained for twelve days, he and his men, using king Richard's wine which was found there in good store, laying waste fields, pillaging houses, and, in short, taking as their own everything they wanted for use or food, or which in any way could be turned to account.

On the third day of his arrival there he caused the head of Perkin de Lye, who was reckoned a great evil-doer, to be cut off and fixed on a stake beyond the eastern gate. This Perkin, who as chief warden of the royal forest of Delamere, and by power of that office, had oppressed and ground down the country people, was taken in a monk's garb; and because, as it was said, he had done many wrongs in such disguise, he deservedly was put out of the world in that dress. One thing I know, that I thought no man grieved for his death.

King Richard, hearing in Ireland of the landing of the duke, set out in the full glory of war and wealth, and made for the shores of Wales at Pembroke with a great host, and landed on the day of St. Mary Magdalene (22nd July), sending forward the lord [Thomas] Despencer to stir up his men of Glamorgan to his help; but they obeyed him not. Stunned by this news coming in from all sides, and acting on the advice of those who I think were traitors, and hoping to be relieved by the succour of the men of North Wales and Chester, he fled in panic at midnight with only a few followers to Caermarthen, on the road to Conway castle in North Wales. Whereupon the dukes, earls, barons, and all who were with him in his great host, according to the [biblical] text: " Smite the shepherd and the sheep shall be scattered," disbanded, and making their way through by-ways into England were robbed of everything by the country people. And I saw many of the chief men come in to the duke thus stripped, and many of them, whom he trusted not, he delivered into divers keepings.

On the eve of the Assumption of the blessed Virgin (14th August), my lord of Canterbury and the earl of Northumberland went away to the king at the castle of Conway to treat [discuss terms] with him on the duke's behalf; and the king, on condition of saving his dignity, promised to surrender to the duke at Flint castle. And so, delivering up to them his two crowns, valued at one hundred thousand marks, with other countless treasure, he straightway set forth to Flint. There the duke coming to him with twenty thousand chosen men—the rest of his army being left to guard his quarters, and the country and castle and city of Chester—sought the king within the castle (for he would not come forth), girding it round with his armed men on the one side and his archers on the other; whereby was fulfilled the prophecy: "The white king shall array his host in form of a shield." And he led him away prisoner to Chester castle, where he delivered him into safe keeping. Thus, too, he placed in custody certain lords, taken along with the king, to be kept till the parliament which was to begin on the morrow of Michaelmas-day.

While the duke was then at Chester, three of the twenty-four aldermen of the city of London, on behalf of the same city, together with other fifty citizens, came to the duke, and recommended their city to him, under their common seal, renouncing their fealty to king Richard. They told, too, how the citizens had gathered in arms to Westminster abbey to search for the king, hearing that he had in secret fled thither; and that, not finding him there, they had ordered to be kept in custody, till parliament [until parliament would next meet], Roger Walden, Nicholas Slake, and Ralph Selby, the king's special councillors, whom they did find. And so the duke, having gloriously, within fifty days, conquered both king and kingdom, marched to London; and there he placed the captive king in the Tower, under proper guard.

"Setting Aside King Richard"

Meanwhile the duke sent to Ireland for his eldest son Henry, and for Humphrey, son of the duke of Gloucester, who had been imprisoned in the castle of Trim by king Richard. And when they had been sent over to him, along with great treasure belonging to the king, the said Humphrey, having been poisoned in Ireland, as was said, by the lord Despencer, died, to the great grief of the land, on his arrival at the isle of Anglesey in Wales. But the duke's son came safe to his father, and brought with him in chains sir William Bagot, a knight of low degree, who had been raised by the king to high places.

It was of king Richard's nature to abase the noble and exalt the base, as of this same sir William and other low-born fellows he made great men, and of very many unlettered men he made bishops, who afterwards fell ruined by their irregular leap into power. Wherefore of this king Richard, as of Arthgallo, once king of Britain, it may well be said in this wise: Arthgallo debased the noble and raised up the low, he took from every man his wealth, and gathered countless treasure; wherefore the chiefs of the land, unable longer to bear such great wrongs, revolting against him, put him aside and set up his brother to be king. So in all things was it with king Richard; concerning whose birth much evil report was noised abroad, as of one sprung not from a father of royal race, but from a mother given to slippery ways of life; to say nothing of much that I have heard.

Next, the matter of setting aside king Richard, and of choosing Henry, duke of Lancaster, in his stead, and how it was to be done and for what reasons, was judicially committed to be debated on by certain doctors, bishops, and others, of whom I, who am now noting down these things, was one. And it was found by us that perjuries, sacrileges, unnatural crimes, oppression of his subjects, reduction of his people to slavery, cowardice and weakness of rule—with all of which crimes king Richard was known to be tainted—were cause enough for setting him aside . . . and although he was ready himself to yield up the crown, yet was it determined, for the aforesaid reasons; that he should be deposed by the authority of the clergy and people, for which purpose they were summoned.

On St. Matthew's day (21st September), just two years after the beheading of the earl of Arundel, I, the writer of this history, was in the Tower, wherein king Richard was a prisoner, and was present at his dinner, and marked his mood and bearing, having been taken thither for that very purpose by sir William Beauchamp. And there and then the king discoursed sorrowfully in these words: "My God! a wonderful land is this, and a fickle; which hath exiled, slain, destroyed, or ruined so many kings, rulers, and great men, and is ever filled and toileth with strife and variance and envy;" and then he recounted the histories and names of sufferers from the earliest habitation of the kingdom. Perceiving then the trouble of his mind, and how that none of his own men, nor such as were wont to serve him, but strangers who were but spies upon him, were appointed to his service, and musing on his ancient and wonted glory and on the fickle fortune of the world, I departed thence much moved at heart.

The Great Schism

Walter Ullmann

The word *schism* means "a split," and what happened in the Catholic Church in 1378 was most certainly a split. The issue at stake was who should become pope. Some of the College of Cardinals, who were to decide the matter after the death of Gregory XI, supported the archbishop of Bari, who was to become Pope Urban VI. Others held out for his rival, Robert of Geneva, who was to become Pope Clement VII. Both ultimately claimed victory and set themselves up in different cities, each calling himself the one and only true leader of the Catholic Church.

Another issue was related to the location of the seat of the Church. Popes had traditionally been Romans, and the papacy had been located in Rome. Increasingly, there had been French popes who had preferred to have their seats in France. Political leaders got into the act, too. A few kings and princes, such as those of France and Scotland, recognized Clement while rulers in England, Hungary, and other countries supported Urban. But the central issue was one of religion, and the cardinals did not fully resolve their differences until the Council of Constance in 1414—nearly forty years and several popes after the Great Schism took place.

This excerpt is from Urban's account of his election in a document called *Factum Urbani*, as reprinted in Walter Ullmann's *The Origins of the Great Schism*. Keep in mind that the document was intended as a justification for Urban's legitimacy as pope.

When it became known that [Pope] Gregory's death was imminent, the officials of the city, i.e., Guido de Primis, a French knight, the city counsellors and the district governors, together with all those who were entrusted with the management of public affairs

Excerpted from *The Origins of the Great Schism* (North Haven, CT: Archon Books, 1967) by Walter Ullmann.

and many other citizens of repute, approached the cardinals in the church of the Holy Ghost and expressed their regret for the illness of Pope Gregory XI and declared themselves ready to help the cardinals in this grave hour and to obey all their wishes. At the same time, in case of Gregory's death, the deputation asked the cardinals to elect a man who would be suitable for the government of the Church in those days. The cardinals replied that, without any undue influence being brought to bear upon them, they would elect one who was suitable for this post and whose choice was inspired by God. The cardinals requested the city authorities to do everything to take care of the maintenance of public order and discipline. This request was granted: guards and sentries were to be posted all over the city, in the Borgho and around the Conclave, thus protecting the cardinals against all violence and insults.

"On 27th March, 1378, Gregory died and the apostolic see was vacant. . . . On the following day, however, when all the cardinals were in the church of S. Maria Nova (in which the body of Gregory XI had been buried), the Senator and other officials approached them and humbly and civilly submitted the request that a worthy man of the Italian nation should be elected, adding that this would be in the interest of the universal Church and of the whole of Christendom. This request was repeated by them on subsequent days when they gave their reasons: that the Roman see, which was and is apostolic, had suffered greatly through the long absence of the pope; also that the state of the city of Rome itself was ruinous and near collapse; that churches, monasteries, cloisters, palaces and many other buildings were in a lamentable and deplorable state; that ecclesiastical goods and possessions in and around Rome were neglected, and that this bad example was now being followed in other parts of Italy, whereby enormous and almost irreparable damage was inflicted upon many churches, monasteries, etc. The only way to remedy this state of affairs was to elect a pope who was a Roman (*Romanus pontifex*) and, furthermore, for the cardinals themselves to reside at Rome and not, as hitherto, to despise the city. In the opinion of the officials, it was because of the French origin of the popes that they had treated Rome with so much contempt; they felt themselves foreigners in the city. . . .

"After listening to this address of the officials, the cardinals consulted each other and replied to them *constanter et intrepide* that they did not favour any particular nation and that, eliminating all undue influence, they intended to elect a pope to the advantage of the Church of God and the world, as God and their consciences bid them do. At the same time they requested the officials and senators to protect them, the palace, the conclave and the Borgho of St. Peter as well as the bridges leading to the Borgho. The officials immediately appointed as guards certain Roman district governors and four other Roman citizens of repute. The cardinals trusted these guards and made them take the oath . . . to the effect that they would protect the cardinals and their households.

"Nevertheless, the cardinals ordered the remainder of their personal goods and property belonging to the Church to be brought immediately into the castle of St. Angelo; moreover, the papal *camerlengo* (i.e., the head of the Treasury) was ordered to move into the castle with many strong soldiers and warlike nobles as well as with a good supply of foodstuffs. There he remained until the pope was elected. . . .

"One must bear in mind, however, that before the cardinals went into the conclave they had a meeting in which the person of the future pope was discussed. But no agreement was reached as to the personality of the candidate. For it became known that five of the cardinals, i.e., the Cardinals of Limoges, Aigrefeuille, Poitiers, de Vergne and Marmoutier, had nominated the Cardinal of Poitiers. Upon being told that this was an impossible choice, they proposed the Cardinal of Viviers who was their *vicinus* (neighbour) and one of their party (*de sequela eorum*). Five other cardinals, all of whom are called the Gallic or French proper, i.e., Glandève, Brittany, Geneva and St. Eustace, and the Spanish Cardinal Peter de Luna, were equally anxious to have one of themselves; they seemed to have been supported by Cardinal Orsini. The other three cardinals, the Italians, appeared desirous to have an Italian candidate. Nevertheless, the Limousins attempted *per varias inductionés* to persuade the French cardinals and also the Italians to elect a Limousin, i.e., the Cardinal of Poitiers. The French strongly declared that they would never consent to such an election: the Limousins must not think that they had rented the papacy because the last four popes had been of their nationality.

"Since these negotiations had broken down, the French cardinals approached their Italian colleagues and told them that they would prefer an Italian pope to a Limousin. The Limousins, on the other hand, declared that should they not have a sufficient number for their candidate, or at least for the Cardinal of Viviers, they would elect the Archbishop of Bari, hoping that the other cardinals also would agree with this choice, in view of the learning and experience of this candidate, who was well informed in all curial matters and known to all of them: he belonged to the household of the Cardinal of Pampeluna (himself a Limousin) and was his chaplain; moreover, since this cardinal had stayed behind at Avignon, Gregory XI had appointed the Archbishop of Bari as vice-chancellor for the Italian lands. Until Gregory's death he had carried out that office efficiently and faithfully. The cardinals considered him as a Frenchman who conformed to their way of life, because he had lived for a long time in Avignon and had always been in their company. He was by birth of the kingdom of Naples which was now ruled by Queen Joanna, a princess very devout and loyal to the Church. It was common knowledge in Rome that, even before the cardinals had entered the conclave, they had in mind the Archbishop of Bari as future pope.

Conclave and Election

"The cardinals, sixteen altogether, entered the conclave on 7th April, 1378. As they entered, a crowd of Romans standing around the palace shouted: 'We want a Roman.' These words were also heard repeatedly during the conclave. The conclave itself was firmly locked on all sides. Then the Cardinals of Aigrefeuille and Poitiers approached the Cardinal of St. Peter and asked him whether, if they should give their votes to the Archbishop of Bari, he would support them. The Cardinal of St. Peter . . . repeated his consent.

"On the morning of 8th April . . . they began the election proper in the chapel of the palace, where the Cardinal of Poitiers remarked to the party of the Cardinal of Milan: 'What do you think? Does not the Archbishop of Bari appear to you a good pope?' The cardinal's answer was in the affirmative. The Cardinal of Poitiers now consulted the Cardinal of Aigrefeuille and all the other Limousins, and they found that they had already the necessary majority. Whereupon the same cardinal spoke to all others present thus: 'My Lords, let us sit down, for I am certain we will very soon have a pope.' After these words Cardinal Orsini, seeing the unanimity of the cardinals, rose and made the following speech, in order to delay the election (or, as was thought, to hinder it altogether): 'My Lords, let us postpone this election, so that we can delude the Romans who want a Roman pope, and let us send for a Roman Friar Minor, put upon him the cope and mitre [symbols of bishops] and pretend that we have elected him pope; then we may retire to a safe place and elect another one.' The Limousins replied: 'Certainly not, my Lord Orsini, we shall not do as you say, because we do not want to deceive the Roman people nor to damn our souls: no, we intend to elect a real pope at this very moment, and we refuse to take notice of the clamourings and petitions of the people.'

"The Cardinal of Florence also had the intention of putting off the election in order to prevent the choice of the Archbishop of Bari, and he proposed that they should elect the Cardinal of St. Peter. The Cardinal of Limoges replied that the Cardinal of St. Peter was a good and saintly man, but firstly he was a Roman (and a Roman was asked for by the populace, therefore they could not have a Roman), and secondly, he was too infirm and decrepit, and, therefore, unsuitable for the office of supreme pontiff. Addressing the Cardinal of Florence, he said: 'You come from a city which is hostile to the Roman Church and, therefore, we shall not elect you. The same holds true of the Cardinal of Milan, and Cardinal Orsini is a Roman and too partial and too young, and therefore we shall not elect any of you Italians.'

"Immediately after these words, whilst the conclave was still firmly locked and complete silence reigned both within and without the palace, the Cardinal of Limoges gave his vote for the Archbishop of Bari. . . . The archbishop was freely elected by two-thirds of the cardinals, including even the Cardinal of Florence.

"After this election the cardinals discussed the advisability of making the result known to the public. They decided to postpone the announcement until after dinner, because the elect was not present in the palace; if the candidate were to appear, the fact of his election would become known and might have unpleasant consequences for him (since he was no Roman and the population would have very much liked a Roman as pope). . . . Soon after that, the rumour spread amongst the Roman crowd that the cardinals had already elected a pope, although no one knew his identity, or even his nationality. Therefore the crowd shouted and made it clear to the cardinals in the conclave that they wanted to hear the result of the election. Whereupon the Bishop of Marseilles, the *locum tenens* of [substitute for] the chamberlain, was sent out to the crowd, who told them in French: 'Allez à St. Pierre'; he meant to say that they should go to St. Peter's (i.e., where they would hear more). Some of the crowd, however, understood that the Cardinal of St. Peter was elected, went to his quarters in the city, entered it and carried away a good deal of his belongings, justifying their action by saying that this was an old custom when the Roman pontiff was elected. The rest of the Roman crowd stayed behind in the vicinity of the palace and exclaimed: 'We want a Roman, we have a Roman.' The cardinals sent for the Archbishop of Bari, the Patriarch of Constantinople and several more prelates and dignitaries of the Church, who were outside the city boundaries, and they were all requested to come to the palace to discuss important business concerning the Church. Most of the prelates arrived at the palace, where they dined, whilst the cardinals took their meal inside the conclave. . . .

"A Better One Has Been Elected"

"Believing him [the Cardinal of St. Peter] to be the rightful pope, [the crowd] paid homage to him. The cardinals, however, taking advantage of this, disappeared one by one from the palace under the cover of the general commotion and went to their quarters, some of them accompanied by Roman citizens of high standing. The Archbishop of Bari, nevertheless, remained in the palace. The Cardinal of St. Peter said to the multitude: 'I am not the pope, nor do I want to be an antipope. A better one has been elected, the Archbishop of Bari.' . . .

"On the following day, 9th April, the election was made known to the officials and governors of the city of Rome. They were pleased with the election and immediately entered the palace to pay homage to the newly-elected pope. But he did not allow this and said that he would not like to be addressed other than as Archbishop of Bari. On the same evening the . . . five cardinals who had remained in their quarters, came to the palace and to the elected pope and congratulated him upon his election. . . . They earnestly begged him to accept the election which was harmoniously and canonically performed. They furthermore advised him to send for the cardinals in the castle of St. Angelo so that they could be present at the enthronement.

"In order to be completely certain as to his status, the Archbishop of Bari asked everyone of those present individually whether he had been elected *sincere, pure, et libere et canonice* ['freely and according to the church law'] by all the cardinals, adding that if the election had not been carried out canonically and without compulsion he would not consent to become pope. They answered, 'firmiter et constanter,' that the election was performed freely, canonically, and without compulsion. If he should refuse he would commit a grave sin: for his refusal could easily cause a long vacancy of the papal throne owing to the difficulties of assembling the majority of cardinals in one place.

"The cardinals who had stayed in the castle of St. Angelo, instead of complying with his request to come to the palace, sent a letter, signed by all of them, to the effect that they would approve of everything that was being done as regards the enthronement. When the Senator and the officials heard that the cardinals were frightened to come to the palace because they had not elected a Roman, they themselves went to the castle and gave the cardinals the assurance that they could come to the palace *audacter et secure* ['safely and without fear']: they would not have to fear any public reproach, because the population was in fact satisfied with the election. The cardinals were encouraged by this report and went over to the palace in the afternoon. There they immediately consented to the election and sent the Cardinal of Aigrefeuille to the new pope to ask him to come to the chapel. He came to the cardinals by whom he was elected pope and who received him as such. He and all the other cardinals sat down. The Cardinal of Florence, as spokesman, asked him on behalf of the others whether he accepted the election. He arose from his seat, and being earnestly requested by the cardinals to consent, accepted the election. Thereupon the cardinals intoned the *Te Deum* 'cum magna laetitia,' robed him with the papal vestments, whilst saying the usual prayers, and performed the enthronement. The bells of the palace were rung. He was asked what name he would take, and he replied: 'Urban.' They paid homage to him and with a profound obeisance kissed his pallium [a woolen band signifying papal authority].

Feudal Society

PREFACE

The feudal system had been the bulwark of European social structure, economics, and government for centuries. In one form or another, it had been in existence since perhaps the days of Charlemagne in the eighth century. Now, in the fourteenth century, feudalism was very slowly beginning to disappear. Though it was not quite the all-encompassing system it had been a century or two before, it nevertheless remained influential. An understanding of feudalism is essential for comprehension of the time.

The basic building block of feudal structure was land. Countries were divided into sections of land varying in size and known as fiefs, estates, or manors. Each manor was under the control of a lord. The lord managed the affairs of the manor and provided military protection. Each manor also had its share of peasants, known as vassals or serfs, who tilled the lord's land in exchange for his promise of military protection. As a rule, serfs were also responsible for giving part of the food they produced to the lord. This was sometimes a fixed percentage of the harvest, but it could also be a certain specified amount of food, leading to hardships and even starvation when crops were poor.

The legal relationship of lord and vassal was typically somewhere between that of master and servant and master and slave. In most parts of Europe, serfs had few legal rights. In particular, they had no prospect of appeal if treatment turned brutal or taxation was too high. In some cases, serfs did not even have the right to leave the manor to search for land or work elsewhere; where the law was concerned, a serf who tried to leave his master's service could usually be returned on demand. To protest their living conditions, serfs generally had to work together; often they needed to stage revolts.

For the most part, lords had a similar relationship to national kings as serfs had to the nobles who ran their manors: Like the nobles, the king taxed and offered military protection. There was safety in numbers, so feudal lords tended to band together and establish loyalty to one powerful sovereign. However, in some areas of Europe such homage to a king was not entirely necessary. Independent-minded lords with large enough armies and weak enough kings could sometimes maintain a degree of self-government, especially as long as they did not actively oppose the throne. During the fourteenth century, countries such as England and France typically had relatively powerful central governments, but Germany was an example of a nation in which power was concentrated more in the hands of the lords. Of course, in times of succession the multiplicity of fiefs and nobles encouraged civil warfare, as groups of lords shifted their loyalties from one claimant to the crown to another. As the phrase goes, feudal lords were truly kingmakers.

The decline of feudalism in the fourteenth and fifteenth centuries stemmed from several factors. One was an increasing tendency toward centralization. With better communication and transportation systems, kings were increasingly able to hold a larger amount of territory; more and more, nobles ceased to be independent as they had been earlier. Another important factor was the midcentury outbreak of bubonic plague. This so-called Black Death killed so many people that many fiefs were left without lords, and many surviving lords were left without serfs to work the fields, requiring a different way of structuring society. Finally, the never-ending series of brutal grudge wars between various lords that defined the century not only resulted in the deaths of many knights but also helped spark the peasant revolts that dominated the second half of the period. There were other causes, too; historians debate the importance of each. Whatever the specific reasons, by the year 1399 the feudal system was clearly on its way toward extinction.

The Nobles

Charles Seignobos

A professor at the University of Paris, Charles Seignobos wrote *The Feudal Régime*. It has value as a clear and short description of feudal life in the period that began drawing to a close in the fourteenth century. In this excerpt from Seignobos's book, he describes the social hierarchy of the nobility during this period. While some of the text refers specifically to earlier centuries, the conditions and ideas Seignobos describes applied to the social organization of the early fourteenth century as well.

In all the Europe of the middle ages, those that were rich enough not to have to work formed a privileged class, sharply separated from the rest of society. All who were in this upper class, except the clergy, were warriors by profession.

Charlemagne already had required that all the free men of his empire should bear arms. The necessity of defending oneself, the taste for idleness and adventure, and the prejudice in favor of the warrior's life led in all Europe to the formation of an aristocracy of men of arms. There was no need of the State's higher authority to impose military service. The life of war being alone esteemed among laymen, each one sought to lead it; the class of men of arms included all who had the means to enter it.

The first condition was to be able to equip oneself at one's own expense. Now, from the ninth century, almost all combat was on horseback; accordingly the warrior of the middle ages called himself in France *chevalier,* in southern France *caver*, in Spain *caballero*, in Germany *Ritter*. In the Latin texts the ancient name of the soldier, *miles*, became synonymous with *chevalier*.

In all Europe, war was carried on under the same conditions and

Excerpted from *The Feudal Regime* (New York: Henry Holt & Co., 1902) by Charles Seignobos, translated by Earle W. Dow. Copyright © 1902 by Henry Holt & Co., Inc.

the men of arms were equipped in about the same way. The man completely armed for battle—the *chevalier*, or knight—had his body protected by armor. Down to the end of the eleventh century this was the byrnie, a tunic of leather or cloth covered with metal scales or rings; then the byrnie was everywhere replaced by the hauberk, a coat of metal mail with sleeves and a hood, opening at the top in such fashion that it could be put on like a shirt. The hauberk at first came down to the feet; when it was shortened to the knee the legs were covered with greaves of mail, which protected the feet and to which was fastened the spur, of the form of a lance-point. The hood concealed the neck and the head, and came up to the chin, allowing simply the eyes, nose and mouth to show. At the moment of combat the knight covered his head with the helm, a steel cap in the shape of a rimmed cone, topped by a circular knob of metal or glass, the crest, and provided with a blade of iron which protected the nose, the nasal. This helm was laced to the hauberk with leather strings. Only in the fourteenth century appear the armor of metal plates and the visored casque [helmet], which were to last down to the seventeenth century. . . .

To parry blows, the knights carried the écu, a buckler of wood and of leather bound together by bands of metal, provided in the center with a buckle of gilded iron (whence the name buckler). The écu, after having been round, became oblong, and lengthened out in a manner to cover a man on horseback from his shoulder to his foot. It was carried suspended from the neck by a wide strap; at the moment of combat it was swung to the left arm by means of handles placed on the inside. It was on the écu that the arms which each family had adopted as its emblem were painted, beginning with the twelfth century. The offensive arms were the sword, ordinarily wide and short, with a flat pommel [knob at the end of the handle], and the lance, made of a long thin shaft (of ash or elm), terminated by a lozenge-shaped point. Above the point was nailed a rectangular band of cloth, the gonfalon, which floated in the wind. The lance could be stuck into the ground by the handle, which ended in an iron point.

Thus covered and armed, the knight was well-nigh invulnerable; and his armor was brought nearer and nearer perfection, rendering him like a living fortress. But in consequence he was so heavy he had to have a special horse to carry him in battle. He was provided with two horses: the palfrey, which he rode when on a journey, and the *dextrarius*, led along by a valet. The moment before combat the knight put on his armor, mounted his *dextrarius* and went forward, holding his lance before him.

The knights were looked upon as the only real men of arms; the accounts of combats speak only of them; they alone formed the battle-lines. But other cavaliers went with them on their expeditions, who were covered with a tunic and a bonnet, provided with a lighter and less costly equipment, armed with a small buckler, a narrow sword, a pike, an axe or a bow, and mounted upon horses of less strength. They were the indispensable companions of the knight; they led his battle-horse, carried his buckler, helped him put on his armor the moment before combat and mount into the saddle. In consequence they were ordinarily called valets or squires; in Latin, *scutifer* or *armiger* (he who carries the shield or the armor). For a long time the knights kept these valets of arms at a distance; even at the end of the eleventh century the Chanson de Roland speaks of squires as of an inferior class. They kept their head shaved, like servants, and at table they were served a coarser bread. But little by little the brotherhood of arms brought the knights and the squires together. In the thirteenth century they formed one class, the highest in lay society, and the ancient Latin name of noble (*nobilis*), which designated the first class (in German *edel*), was given to them all.

Degrees of Nobility

To lead the life of a warrior it was necessary to have the means to live without working. In the middle ages no one was noble unless he had a revenue sufficient to support him. Ordinarily this revenue was furnished by a landed estate: the noble possessed a domain; and as he did not cultivate it himself (honor forbade that), he had it cultivated by his tenants. In this way the noble usually exploited at least a few families of villains [villeins, or serfs], in relation to whom he was a seigneur (in Latin *dominus;* whence the Spanish *Don*). But while a sufficient revenue was the practical condition in order to be a noble, there were inequalities of possession among the nobles, glaring inequalities which established a series of degrees, from the squire to the king. The people of the time saw these degrees clearly enough, and even distinguished them by names.

In the highest grade were the princes who had some titled dignity (kings, dukes, marquises, counts), sovereigns of an entire province, possessors of hundreds of villages, who could take several thousand knights to war.

Then came the higher nobles, ordinarily possessors of many villages, who led a troup of knights to war with them. As they had no official title they were designated by names of common speech, whose meaning was vague and somewhat elastic; names which differed with the country but were used synonymously. The most frequent were: *baron*, in the west and south of France and in the Norman regions; *sire* or *seigneur* in the east. . . . In Lombardy they were called captains, in Spain *ricos hombres* (rich men). In Germany people said *Herr,* which corresponds to seigneur; in England, lord; the translation into Latin was *dominus* (master). Later they were also called bannerets, because, to rally their men, they had a square banner at the end of their lance.

Under these came the bulk of the ancient nobility, the knights (in German *Ritter*, in English knight, in Spanish *caballero*, in Latin *miles*), possessors of a domain which consisted, according to the richness of the country, of an entire village or of a portion of a village. Almost all were in the service of some great seigneur, from whom they held their domain; they followed him on his expeditions. This, though, did not hinder them from making war on their own account. They were sometimes called bachelors, in Lombardy vavasors. Also one finds the striking expression *miles unius scuti*, knight of a single shield, who had no other knight under his orders.

At the bottom of the ladder were the squires. At first simple valets of arms in the service of a knight, they became possessors of lands (of the extent of what we today call a great estate) and in the thirteenth century they lived as masters in the midst of their tenants. In Germany they were designated as *Edelknecht* (noble valet), in England squire (corruption of the word *écuyer*), in Spain *infanzon*. They formed the bulk of the nobility in the thirteenth century, and in following centuries enobled bourgeois proudly took the title of squire.

We can thus distinguish four degrees, which correspond roughly to military grades; the princes, dukes, and counts would be generals, the barons captains, the knights soldiers, the squires servants. But in this strange army, where the groups of which it was composed made war against each other and where wealth decided rank, the community of life finally attenuated differences to the point where all, from the general to the valet, began to feel themselves members of the same class. Then the nobility was definitely constituted, then it came to be a closed and isolated class.

In the thirteenth century it became the custom to divide men rigorously into two classes, the nobles or gentlemen (well-born men) and the not-nobles, who were called in France customary men or subject-men. . . . And these classes became rigorously hereditary. The noble families refused to mix with descendants of not-noble families. A man who was not the son of a noble was not allowed the privilege of becoming a knight, even though he was rich enough to lead the life of a knight; the daughter of a not-noble could not marry a noble; he who consented to marry her made a misalliance and thereby dishonored himself; his wife would not be received in the noble families, and his children would not be treated by the nobles as equals. This heredity, which appears less marked in the documents of the preceding centuries, became the dominant trait of society down to the eighteenth century. In proportion as degrees between the nobles were effaced, the noblesse [nobility] became more separated from the rest of the nation. It was in France and Germany that the aristocratic sentiment established itself most strongly. It was weakened in Spain, especially in the south, by contact with the rich inhabitants of the Moorish towns, and in Italy and perhaps in the south of France by the social influence of the merchants. In England, where habitual warfare ended early, nothing distinguished the squire from the rich peasant; the demarcation was established much higher, between the lords and the rest of the nation, and the privileged class was reduced to a high aristocracy of limited numbers.

Chivalry

The warlike society formed by the knights had its usages to which all were bound. The arms of the knight were difficult to handle; before bearing them, it was necessary to have served an apprenticeship. It was an honor to bear them; before doing so one must have been declared worthy of this honor. No one was born a knight; he was made a knight by a solemn ceremony; the king himself had to be made a knight.

Every young noble began by learning the metier [trade] of a man of arms: to mount a horse, to handle arms, to climb a scaling-ladder. But he could serve his apprenticeship either in his father's house (which especially the sons of great families did) or in that of a stranger (apparently the more usual procedure). Ordinarily the father sent his son to a seigneur richer than himself, who took the young man into his service and brought him up. . . . Apprenticeship was complicated with the service of squire; but with this service of a valet of arms was joined the service of a valet de chambre [of domestic service], a characteristic of chivalry customs. The squire assisted his seigneur in dressing and undressing; he brought in the courses and served at table; he made the beds. These duties, which the ancients regarded as debasing and imposed upon their slaves, were honorable in the eyes of the nobles of the middle ages. . . . During this period, which lasted from five to seven years, the young noble, called a squire or page (little seigneur), did not have the right to bear arms.

When he had finished his apprenticeship, ordinarily at from eighteen to twenty years old, if he was rich enough to lead the life of a knight, he entered into knighthood by a martial ceremony. . . . The young man first went through a bath, then donned the hauberk and helmet. A knight, sometimes his father, more often the seigneur who had brought him up, girded with him the sword which he was thenceforth to carry. This was called dubbing and was the essential act. Ordinarily the knight struck the young man a blow of the fist upon the back of the neck: this was the accolade. Afterward the new knight mounted his horse, took a lance, and did an exercise in galloping and in striking at a manikin prepared in advance: this was the quintain. Such was the ceremony of making a knight in the twelfth century. It was sometimes even reduced to a single act, the *colée*, the blow upon the neck: this was a means of avoiding expense. [Medieval French writer] Beaumanoir speaks of an inquest which, to be valid, called for a fixed number of knights. As one was lacking to their number they forthwith made a knight of a gentleman present. One of them gave a blow and said to him: "Be thou a knight."

Later the clergy introduced acts which turned the entrance into knighthood into a complicated religious ceremony. After a fast, the young man passed the night preceding the dubbing in prayers: this was the vigil of arms. In the morning he went to mass; the sword was laid upon the altar, as if to consecrate it to the service of God; the priest blessed it: "Lord, hear my prayers and deign to bless with Thy majestic hand this sword which Thy servant . . . desires to gird upon him." Then came a sermon, in which his duties toward the church, the poor and the widowed were recalled to the future knight.

They usually chose for the ceremony either the great feast-days, especially Easter and Pentecost, or some exceptional event, the marriage or baptism of a prince; or even the occasion of a battle. In that case they dubbed a whole troop of new knights at the same time.

Only the rich became knights. Men of gentle rank who were poor did not care to bear the cost of the ceremony and the expense of the knight's life; they preferred to remain squires. There were consequently two sorts of squires, those who were not old enough and those who were not rich enough to become knights. In England, where knighthood was useless, almost all gentlemen ceased to have themselves received into knighthood and were content to remain squires.

Court Life

Gervase Mathew

In this excerpt, historian Gervase Mathew describes court life in the time of England's Richard II. Mathew uses primary source documents, especially contemporary poetry, to describe the clothing, jewelry, and entertainments popular in royal courts at the end of the fourteenth century. The names mentioned in the text are largely court people, particularly poets and minor nobles, and the titles which come up here and there are mainly poems popular during the time, especially long, book-length ones which have survived to the present.

Court dress seems first to have become magnificent in the early years of Richard's personal rule. In 1388 Sir Simon Burley owned a tabard [tunic] of cloth-of-gold embroidered with roses and lined with green tartarine, a scarlet tabard embroidered with the sun and with golden letters, a white leather coat embroidered with the Burley badge of the Stakes and ornamented with 54 gold buttons, an ermine cape and a cloak of pure minever [white fur]. Such display was financially possible since rich dress was portable capital and money could be raised in its security [that is, it could be used as collateral for loans]. In 1387 and 1388 Simon Burley had raised money from six London citizens on the security of his clothes and of his beds.

There were rapid developments in dress. . . . [A 1389 poem] complains of the new fashions of skin-tight hose and of long pointed shoes, of padded shoulders and high collars. Perhaps the most noticeable changes were the replacement of the cloak by a long-sleeved gown or 'houpelande', the replacement of the hat by a loose hood often shaped like a turban, and a profusion of jewellery that went with a delight in vivid colours.

Excerpted from *The Court of Richard II*, by Gervase Mathew. Copyright © 1968 by Gervase Mathew. Reprinted with permission from John Murray Publishers, Ltd.

It is possible to reconstruct in some detail the costume of a successful courtier about the year 1394. He would have worn a shirt and short drawers ('braies') made of fine linen. Household accounts suggest that linen from Paris and Rheims and Dinant was specially prized, but linen from Brabant [a region of Belgium] was also used. He would then put on close-fitting hose covering the feet, legs and thighs, including a cod-piece—perhaps for the first time. Then there was the under doublet, the 'gipon', worn presumably for warmth, ending at the hips and fastened to the hose, and ornate leather shoes with pointed toes. The art of the tailor was shown in the cote hardie and the houpelande. The cote hardie was the upper doublet and by now the custom was to embroider it with heraldry or badges; it had close-fitting sleeves to the wrist and was worn with a tight girdle, metal-clasped and increasingly jewelled. The houpelande was a long high-necked gown with wide sleeves that fell to the knees and at times almost to the ankles. It was noted in [the 1399 poem] *Richard the Redeless:* 'the slevis slide on the erthe'. The purpose of the tailor's art was to emphasise the four points most prized in men: long arms and legs, broad shoulders and a slender waist. . . .

The cote hardies and houpelandes were of many different colours. In about 1411 Thomas Hoccleve describes a meeting with an elderly man who looked back on the days when he held an 'office lucratyffe' [lucrative] and possessed gowns of scarlet, of sangwyn murrey [red mulberry color], of dark and light blue, of green and of the faire vyolet. The illuminations of Harleian MS. 1319 show blue houpelandes embroidered with different patterns in gold and silver, and Hoccleve describes a scarlet houpelande edged with fur which cost more than £20.

Both the hems of the cote hardie and the sleeves and collar of the houpelande could be set with precious and semi-precious stones. Richard is stated to have owned a dress valued at more than a £1000; if so, it was perhaps not too dissimilar from that worn by Youth in the *Parlement of Thre Ages*, [a contemporary poem], which was of green patterned in gold thread:

> Embroddirde alle with besants and beralles full riche
> His colere with calsydoynnes clustrede full thike
> With many dymande full dere dight one his sleves
> The semys with saphirs sett were full many
> With emeraudes and amatistes appon iche syde
> With full riche rubyes raylede by the hemmes.

Jewellery and Women's Fashions

The use of the white hart badge and of the royal collar may be studied as part of the jewellery of dress. As worn by a magnate [that is, a noble] the white hart could be a jewel: John Holland, Duke of Exeter, possessed a 'livery of the Hart' set with three rubies and two sapphires. Richard had used it as personal ornament before he distributed it as a badge; three brooches of the white hart set with rubies were among the King's jewels in September 1380. It seems likely that he chose it to be his badge because it was already a favourite personal ornament, and that it was a favourite ornament because a white hind had been the emblem of his mother, Joan of Kent. When worn as a badge the white hart would be sewn on the left breast; it was of white silk, and since the royal crown round the neck and the chain attached to it are described as of gold they must have been worked in gold thread.

In contrast to the white hart there is no evidence that the collar was ever distributed as a badge by the King. In the Wilton Diptych there are wreaths of broom [a flowering shrub] around the harts. The white hart, the broom, and the rising sun are the three emblems on Richard's effigy. Two broomscod collars [collars with the design of these shrubs] are known to have belonged to the King; one was ornamented with four rubies, three sapphires and twenty-seven pearls and the other with twenty-three pearls and a ruby.

There is evidence that the use of jewellery was common among the greater magnates, and so too, was the use of cloth-of-gold, but it is likely that the intricacies of fashion were only followed within the court circles. Thomas Hoccleve records of John of Gaunt that 'his garnements [garments] were not fulle wide'. The invention of the linen handkerchief was for the King's personal use and failed to establish itself in late medieval England. . . .

For women, fashion was more conservative than it was for men, presumably since it was not affected by the changing dresses of the King. Yet the presence of great numbers of court ladies was a distinctive mark of the Household of Richard II. The fourth clause of Thomas Haxey's Petition on the 1st of February, 1397, complained of the excessive cost to the realm due to the presence at the court of so many ladies with their retinues. It should be possible to reconstruct a list of women with court influence: Lady Luttrel and Lady de Mohun and probably Lady Burghersh; Lady Swynford, for over twenty years the mistress and for three years the wife of John of Gaunt; her young daughter, Lady Ferrers, who was afterwards Countess of Westmorland; probably the Duchesses of York and of Albemarle; certainly the Duchess of Exeter. Each would be attended by demoiselles [female servants]. This can be paralleled at the Court of Paris; a mark of the new international court culture was the presence of many women and the elaborate dances that this made possible. . . .

Such dances led to a fresh demand for songs. For the women and men either sang as they danced ('caroled'), or danced to a song (a 'conduit'), or joined in the refrain of the song they danced to (a 'virelay'). Even the ballade, though it established itself as a separate literary form, can be considered as a dance-song.

Poetry

Yet besides this demand for lyrics there was a court public for narrative poems. There was now a large sophisticated audience of women as well as of men who needed to be entertained by stories. Convention determined that these stories should be in verse and fashion would have suggested that they should be new. Often such stories would be recited serially. In *Le dit dou Florin* [French poet and chronicler Jean] Froissart states that he read his romance *Meliador* for the first time at the court of Foix in the winter of 1388/9. He read it aloud nightly and it lasted for ten weeks; since there are nearly 31,000 lines in *Meliador*, perhaps he read about 480 lines a night. The lines would obviously have been read slowly. *Palamon and Arcite* is clearly a court story, incorporated later in the *Canterbury Tales*; it reaches its appropriate ending 'and God save al this faire company' in 2,249 lines, but it is divided into three parts. *Troilus and Criseyde* and *The Legend of Good Women* are easily serialized. But *The Parlement of Foules* is a poem for Valentine's day which must always have been recited as a unit, and it is in 699 lines. If the *Canterbury Tales* were read, then each, with the exception of the Knight's, must have been recounted without a break.

Perhaps during the winter months there was need for longer indoor entertainment. Dinner seems to have begun between eleven and twelve. The time between dinner and vespers was set aside for the Royal Audience. The dancing and the story telling would have taken place between vespers (perhaps about three) and the supper of wine and spiced cakes that closed the day.

There were still minstrels—Robert de Vere had four in his household in 1388—but they were becoming outmoded, and in the new court culture they had been supplemented by authors who declaimed their own verse. These had a prestige the minstrel lacked; in Naples, Paris and London they were often courtiers of established rank like Eustache Deschamps and Geoffrey Chaucer. . . .

It is also probable that at times poems and stories would be read aloud by equerries [male servants] or by demoiselles. In a bi-lingual court such readings would take place both in French and English. In 1390 the most prominent courtiers who were also poets were Sir John de Montacute and Sir John Clanvowe. John de Montacute who was later to become Earl of Salisbury and a knight of the Garter composed his rondeaus and ballades in French. The *Cinkante Balades* of John Gower were also intended for a court audience. I would consider it possible that there were also lost French ballades and virelais by Chaucer. Owing to the fifteenth century transmission of texts it would be natural that much more of the French court literature should be lost than of the English.

But Sir John Clanvowe, who was one of Richard's Chamber Knights, wrote his *Book of Cupid* in English. This is more commonly known as *The Cuckoo and the Nightingale*. It contains an echo from the *Knight's Tale,* and influenced Hoccleve. It is clearly a court poem.

> Under a maple that is fayr and grene
> Before the chambre window of the Quene.

It is probable that English was becoming increasingly predominant as a court language and that this affected the whole course of English poetry and prose.

But though poetry had become fashionable it would be easy to overestimate its small share in the ordinary life of the court.

The Serfs

George Holmes

In feudal society, knights, lords, and nobles owned most of the land and held most of the political power. However, they would never have attained such status if it had not been for the great mass of serfs, or villeins, who did most of the actual work. This selection, from George Holmes's *The Later Middle Ages,* describes the circumstances of a serf's existence. Holmes discusses the reasons for the serf system, the possibility of a serf moving upward in society, and the daily life of a serf. His emphasis is on the early years of the fourteenth century and the decade just preceding it, though much of what Holmes has to say applies to later years of the century as well.

T he manor can properly be regarded as the normal unit of medieval rural life. Men thought of it as such themselves and had a clear enough idea of what it typically contained, as can be seen from the contemporary treatises on husbandry and from the set of instructions used by royal officials for describing estates called the "Extent of a manor": this typical manor had a court, tenants both free and servile holding lands and paying rents and services for them, common lands, tenant lands, and land retained in the lord's personal possession.

The land which the lord kept in his own hands, the "demesne" to distinguish it from tenant holdings, was the core of the manor's economic function as the court was of its jurisdiction. In an open-field village the demesne, like other land, was divided into strips but it was exploited directly by and for the lord. The day-to-day organisation was commonly done by a reeve, who was elected annually from among the unfree tenants and was responsible to the lord during his term of office for the profitable working of the demesne and collection of rents. In addition to money rents some of the tenants owed unpaid

Excerpted from *The Later Middle Ages,* by George Holmes. Copyright © 1962 by George Holmes. Reprinted with permission from Thomas Nelson & Sons, Inc.

labour services, perhaps a certain number of days' work each week throughout the year ("week work"), or annual services at the busy times of ploughing, mowing, and reaping. Usually some wage labour was employed, often a great deal, but the manor was sometimes a compact economic unit, consisting of demesne, with tenants who supplied the labour for it as well as working their own holdings.

One basic distinction, dividing Englishmen into two very broad classes, was to be found everywhere. "All men are either freemen or serfs," was a legal maxim. The serf or villein was subject to the lord not only in being his man and owing suit to his court but also in being his personal property. He could be bought and sold with his descendants, his "sequela" as they were called; he could not leave the manor or even marry without permission; and his servile status was inherited by his children. Here again the historian must acknowledge wide regional variations, stemming from geographical differences and distinctions of custom going back to the first English settlements, and perhaps beyond, when peoples with different social systems had settled in different areas. In Kent there were few villeins. In East Anglia there was a high proportion of freemen with extensive lands and little connection with manors, but also a number of large manors whose villeins owed heavy labour services. Moderately sized manors, with small demesnes and generally light services, were characteristic of the Midland counties. But the essential distinction of free and unfree and the institution of labour services are to be found in varying degrees almost everywhere.

In the manor of Borley in Essex in 1308, to take a concrete example, there were 300 acres of arable [land] in demesne plus meadow and pasture, 7 free tenants holding varying acreages and paying money rents, 6 *molmen*, probably the descendants of men who had been freed from villeinage, owing money rents and some services, and 28 *custumarii* holding villein land. The villeins nearly all held land in multiples of 5 acres (5, 10, or 20), and they owed standard services to be performed on the lord's demesne: three days' work each week from Michaelmas (29th September) to St Peter in Chains (1st August) except Christmas, Easter, and Whitsun weeks, the ploughing of 4 acres, carrying manure, weeding corn, mowing the meadow, 24 reaping "works" between 1st August and 29th September, and so on. It is evident that in origin these men and their holdings descended from servile tenants, settled on standard plots with obligations to provide a substantial amount of the work needed for the demesne. The lord's arrangements no doubt explain the origin of villein land and villein status. At Wilburton in Cambridgeshire in the late thirteenth century, to take another example, there were three groups of tenants: freeholders who held tenements varying in size between 6 and 22 1/2 acres, owing moderate services and very small rents; 15 1/2 standard villein units paying a small rent and heavy labour services of 3 days' week work and 5 days in harvest time; and 10 1/2 small cottage units paying a small rent and moderate services. By no means all manors had such symmetrical arrangements, but many had, and the land shortage of the thirteenth century made it fairly easy for the lord to maintain the system if he wished. In the Hundred Rolls, the documents which contain the results of inquiries by Edward I's officials into tenures in [certain regions of England] in 1279, about half the tenants mentioned had free or villein holdings of the standard "virgate" [a fourth of an acre] (or "yardland") or of half-virgates; about one-third had very small holdings of less than a quarter of a virgate; only about 3 per cent had more than a virgate.

Social Change over Time

At the end of the thirteenth century both the geographical differences and the customary distinctions between classes in individual villages were being blurred by the effects of fairly rapid social change and economic progress. Tenements were sometimes divided between heirs who inherited jointly. Pieces of land were being bought and sold. Sometimes lords found it convenient to "commute" the labour services of their tenants by changing them into money rents. Plots of villein land, originally held by serfs and still burdened with customary labour services, were sometimes held by free men who had to arrange for the labour to be done even though their own personal status was unchanged. Conversely it was possible for a villein, with all the personal disabilities of his class, to become a holder of free land as part of quite a large holding and to better himself by marriage and investment. Here is an example of such a man, as near as we shall ever get to the biography of a medieval villein:

> His name was Stephen Puttock, and he lived on the prior of Ely's manor of Sutton at the end of the thirteenth and the beginning of the fourteenth century. There can be no doubt about his villeinage: he was described as *nativus* [belonging to the manor] in a charter; he paid a fine for the lord's licence to marry both his wives, as did his sister when she married (and leyrwite [the fine for immorality by a villein] as well). There can be no doubt that he owed labour services, for he was amerced [i.e. fined] from time to time for carrying them out with less than proper care. Yet he was an important man in the village. Almost certainly he held a full land [i.e. full peasant holding] at least. . . . He was . . . reeve [manager of the manor] in 1310, a chief pledge for a quarter of a century, ale-taster more than once, a frequent member of inquest juries. Like others of his kind he was a sheep farmer. . . .

> But above all he was a great buyer of land. In 1300 he bought three-quarters of an acre without licence. A charter of 1303 recording the purchase of an unspecified parcel from another villein, is still extant. In 1304, he took up Northcroft (containing 8 1/4 acres) from the prior. In 1305 he bought 2

acres from the prior's former bailiff and in 1307 a parcel of meadow from
a free tenant. . . . In 1310 he bought 6 acres of arable for 20 silver marks.
. . . Such a man was thriving into the yeomanry.

Thirteenth-century society included many people like Stephen Put-
tock. But, although the rigidity of social structure was mitigated in this
way, the supremacy of the manorial lord and the essential distinction
between free and unfree were unquestioned.

Nearly everywhere the maintenance of the lords' supremacy was
made easier by one basic fact of English life in 1272 and for half a century after: the scarcity of land. In the thirteenth and early fourteenth
centuries a rapidly growing population, living by simple forms of agriculture, was occupying the land of England to the limits of possibility. There are today few country villages, as the churches show, which
did not exist in the Middle Ages; some have disappeared since 1300.
New townships were being established by English colonists in the
Welsh Marches, sometimes still recognisable from their names, such
as New Radnor. The bishops of Winchester were attracting settlers to
their new boroughs at Burghclere and Hindon and elsewhere in Hamp-
shire and Wiltshire. The monks of Christ Church, the cathedral priory
at Canterbury, were draining Romney Marsh. Peasants were enclos-
ing and cultivating for the first time the fenlands on the edge of the
Wash in Lincolnshire and Cambridgeshire. The denes [valleys for
farming] were being cut out of the ancient forest of the Weald and in
many other parts of England "assarts" were being cleared in the woods
to add to the village fields. It is unlikely that during the period there
were revolutionary changes in technique to improve the yield of existing arable land, though landlords certainly brought seedcorn from
other areas and paid attention to marling and loaming [caring for soil],
and some villages were able to increase their turnover by the change
from a two-field system (the land lying fallow every other year) to a
three-field system (two crops in every three years), which gave more
frequent crops from the same area. A fourteenth-century abbot of
Fountains in Yorkshire, for instance, appointed a group of tenants with
their consent "to ordain the best way that they can to lay out the field
in three parts so that one part shall be fallow each year." The tendency
everywhere was to use more land, more intensively, in the old ways.
Prices of grain rose throughout the thirteenth century to an unprecedented height in its last years. The great floods and famines of
1315–17 and the other calamities of Edward II's reign brought to an
end a period of expansion in which the extraordinary increase of population had driven men beyond the margins of good arable land and
given some areas a settlement more dense than they were to see again
until the eighteenth century.

Peasants in the Hundred Years' War

Nicholas Wright

Many military histories focus on political aspects and on questions of strategy. Less common, perhaps, are books that focus on the role of the ordinary soldier or the bystanders through whose territory the war was fought, often with disastrous results. That is especially true for the medieval period, when few peasants could write and recordkeeping was heavily weighted to the concerns of the nobility.

This excerpt, from British professor Nicholas Wright's *Knights and Peasants: The Hundred Years' War in the French Countryside*, discusses what happened to the French peasants who got in the way of the armies. Their property was destroyed and their livelihoods were wrecked. Moreover, each army frequently indulged in the mass murder of peasants. Killing peasants helped eliminate a possible source of new soldiers. Doing so could also be a way of exacting revenge on the other side: Though the nobility did not always consider the peasants of great importance as people, one lord might respond to the loss of his serfs or soldiers in a battle by attempting to wipe out the opposing lord's subjects. The peasants, of course, had little political power. Their function was to be used as pawns by both kings. The Hundred Years' War is as much their story as the story of the kings and the commanders.

*Editor's Note: In the autumn of 1359 the English King Edward III landed
at Calais, France, together with his sons and a large and powerful army.
Over the next few months they made their way across the French countryside toward Paris, meeting with little opposition along the way. The campaign was bloody and destructive. The English laid waste to farms and those
towns that were not well defended. They spent roughly two weeks encamped
outside the city walls of Paris; their campfires are referred to in the first sentence of the excerpt. Though the army moved easily through most of the
countryside, the campaign was not a success for the English. Paris, Rheims,
and a few other cities proved to be too well fortified, and bad weather the
following spring brought an end to the attempt. In May 1360 the two sides
signed a temporary peace treaty, and Edward returned to England.*

The lumbering advance of a large army, like that of Edward III, the
smoking evidence of which could be seen from the walls of Paris
during the winter of 1359, usually gave sufficient warning of its approach: time enough for the village children who kept watch from the
church towers to sound the alarm so that an orderly evacuation could
be organized. There were occasions, however, as during this campaign,
when peasants placed too much confidence in the strength of their fortified parish church, and they were caught, with catastrophic consequences to themselves, in the deadly embrace of an army equipped for
larger prey. In the single Easter week of 1360, according to the testimony of [chronicler] Jean de Venette, one hundred inhabitants of the
village of Orly were slaughtered by the English and no less than nine
hundred other peasants were burned to death or slaughtered at Châtres
as their church-refuges were reduced to smouldering rubble. The church
at Orly was taken by storm on Good Friday 1360, after the destruction
of its walls. That of Châtres, the lower windows and doorways of which
had been firmly blocked up, was bombarded by stone missiles from the
nearby hill but was eventually lost because of disagreements between
the captain of the place and the peasant refugees. As the flames took
hold so that even the tower and the bells were consumed, the peasants
tried to let themselves down from the windows by ropes, but were "brutally slaughtered" by the English who jeered at their self-inflicted catastrophe. It may be doubted, however, if the attackers benefited much
from the "large supply of food," the "household goods and utensils and
tools," the "crossbows, lead, stones and other instruments of war" which
had been crammed into the fortress.

By the 1380s, the French high command had learned its lesson, and
[French chronicler Jean] Froissart reports the advice given by certain
French veterans to the king of Castile as they assisted him against the
invading army of John of Gaunt.

> We have been told that the people of your kingdom fortify churches and
> bell-towers and use them as refuges for themselves and their goods. You

must know that this will be to the great loss and injury of your kingdom, for, when the English ride out, these little fortresses in churches and bell-towers will not hold out against them. Rather will they be sustained and nourished by what they find within them.

The *chevauchée* strategy [fast-moving raids into enemy territory for the purpose of destruction], employed by the English Crown during much of the fourteenth century, was different only in scale from the strategies operating in the multitude of private wars which were waged, usually by nobles, throughout this period in the teeth of frequent royal prohibitions. The objectives of punishing the enemy in "head and members" for his denial of justice, of compensating oneself for perceived injuries, and of demonstrating one's power were very much to the fore. Both kinds of war were likely to have peasants as important targets. In January 1375, two knights, Gilles of Verlette and his son, acknowledged their part in one of the many private wars which straddled the Franco-imperial border, and which, as they admitted, involved the burning and destruction of houses, the capture of men, women and children for ransom, the killing of men and the plundering of their property, and "all other acts of war." One of their opponents was Pierre de Bar, son of the lord of Pierrefont. He had learned well from his association with such notorious captains of the Companies as Arnaud de Cervole, known as the "Archpriest," and Yvain de Galles, and he, too, admitted to his part in the killing of people, the destruction of houses by fire, the raping of women, and the taking of all manner of goods "by way of vengeance and act of war." No-one doubted that this litany of atrocities described proper acts of war. The only question was whether these were proper wars.

The killing of large numbers of peasants, as an act of war, and the systematic destruction of their property only took place, as a rule, within those restricted areas which had the misfortune to come within the range of one of these marauding armies. It is true that an army of this sort, which could be several thousands strong, and divided into two or three battle-groups each surrounded by its own busy cloud of foragers, could have a devastating effect upon a wide area. Such an army, minute though it may have been by the standards of more modern ones, had the logistical requirements of a medium-sized town and depended almost entirely on its foragers. Edward III reported that his army moving through the Cambrésis in the winter of 1339 burned and destroyed "commonly" a track of between "twelve or fourteen leagues" (up to fifty kilometres) in width. The armies of Edward III, with captains such as Jean de Fauquemont and comprising anything from 2% to 12% of convicted criminals, many of them murderers seeking royal pardons in return for military service, never lacked soldiers unsqueamish enough for this sort of work. Robert Knolles, about to embark in 1370 on a march from Calais into the Ile-de-France, requested and received royal pardons for fifty-five named criminals who had contracted to serve him. Forty-three of these were murderers and the rest were rapists and thieves. Nevertheless, campaigns on this scale were rare during the Hundred Years' War. Of the sixty-three years between 1337 and 1400, there were major campaigns in only eighteen. More frequent were the private wars conducted on a smaller scale by an aristocracy which was largely untamed by the endless royal prohibitions against this tradition; also by the passage of companies of freebooters in search of opportunities to exercise their talents. Even when we include these, usually minor, military enterprises, it must have been a rare catastrophe for a French peasant to find himself caught in their paths.

Ransom and Torture

The killing of peasants by soldiers and the destruction of their property were much more "normal" in situations of reprisal and terrorization, where soldiers were attempting to negotiate collective and individual ransoms and were encountering resistance. Indeed the activities of entire armies on campaign in enemy territory cannot be treated as an entirely separate category from those of garrison soldiers attempting to secure their sources of supply. Both were enmeshed in the trade of protection in return for payments. Henry V, who struggled vigorously to protect his own peasant subjects, was not at all merciful to those of his enemy who failed to offer provisions to his armies and he routinely used the threat of fire to enforce contributions. . . . Maltreatment of noble prisoners in order to obtain a ransom from them annulled their obligation to pay it and entitled them to escape if they could. On the other hand, protection against such tortures which the law of arms usually afforded to the captive man-at-arms was certainly not available to the peasant, and Jean Juvenal des Ursins was not the first to complain about the "new kinds of torment used to extract money from poor people." The discharged soldiers of the [English] Black Prince had a fearful reputation for the "injuries and inhuman tortures" which they were known to use against their prisoners. Those who refused to pay *patis* [money for protection] to the garrison of Pierre Perthuis in Burgundy during the late 1360s had their houses burned down and their ears chopped off. Raymond of Turenne, whose wars in the county of Provence had forced Honoré Bouvet to abandon his priory in Selonnet for the relative security of the royal court in Paris, was accused in the Paris *parlement* of having imprisoned "poor labourers"; of having killed some of them directly and of having left others to starve in obscure dungeons. . . .

Long periods of imprisonment awaiting ransom were not as common for non-noble as for noble prisoners. A nobleman might survive ten or more years of close imprisonment, as did Louis de Chalon after he had been captured at the battle of Auray in 1364. Peasants, on the other hand, either paid up or perished, and [historian] Thomas Basin describes how the peasants of Lower Normandy who were captured by French and English soldiers in the aftermath of the 1435 rebellion either paid their ransoms on the spot or were strangled or drowned. It is true that these actions were part of the general repression of peasant revolt which, as we have already noted, always prompted the most brutal treatment. Such conduct was not, however, unique to those circumstances. In the catalogue of acts of war committed by members of the garrisons which surrounded the town of Bergerac, between February 1379 and May 1382, 168 non-combatants were taken prisoner and forced to pay ransoms in gold coin and in goods.Their average value was pitifully small; ten thousand times less than the sixty thousand gold francs demanded of Louis de Chalon; yet the pressure placed upon them to pay was at least as great. No less than sixteen of them were described as having been tortured "with great blows," and some died under this treatment. A wretched individual who was captured by a pillager of the Bourc d'Espagne in 1382, and taken to the castle of Bouglon (Lot-et-Garonne), was later retrieved, presumably by relatives, "quite dead." Some nine years later, a varlet who had been in the service of the English knight, Robert Chesnel, was captured by Jean le Mercier. When questioned by officers of the Châtelet court in Paris, he admitted that his job had been to beat prisoners either until he was exhausted or until they had agreed to a ransom which his master felt to be adequate. He confessed to having been party to the deaths of no less than sixty Frenchmen, by close imprisonment, by starvation, and by beating them "too much." The threat of such treatment and of the burning of houses in reprisal raids, known as *courses,* was usually enough to persuade the persuadable; and there were always alternatives to ransoms in hard cash for those who had none of this commodity.

Wat Tyler's Rebellion of 1381

Jean Froissart

Jean Froissart was a French historian, priest, and poet who was born in 1337 and died in about 1401. An intensely curious person, Froissart spent much of his life wandering across Europe in search of information and good stories. He soon became an authority on the geography and history of much of England and France. Froissart attached himself to the royal courts in both countries and set down the history of each nation as he saw and heard about it. His *Chronicles* cover the years from 1326 to 1400 and include most of the important events of the time.

This excerpt tells of the Wat Tyler Rebellion of 1381. Tyler was a peasant from the English countryside who believed that the system of taxation was dramatically skewed against the poor. He gathered a number of other peasants and led them on a journey toward London, sacking monasteries and killing tax collectors. The rebellion was eventually put down—though not without many anxious moments for the nobility—and Tyler, with the other ringleaders, was killed. Tyler's was just one of many similar revolts that took place throughout Europe during the 1300s. Though not all were caused by unfair taxation, most were born of frustration with the feudal system and the peasantry's general lack of rights.

[In 1381] there fell in England great mischief and rebellion of moving of the common people, by which deed England was at a point to have been lost without recovery. There was never realm nor country in so great adventure as it was in that time, and all because of the

Excerpted from *The Chronicles of Jean Froissart in Lord Berners' Translation*, edited by Gillian and William Anderson. Copyright © 1963 by Centaur Press, Ltd. Reprinted with permission from Centaur Press, Ltd.

ease and riches that the common people were of which moved them to this rebellion; as sometime they did in France, the which did much hurt, for by such incidents the realm of France hath been greatly grieved. It was a marvellous thing and of poor foundation that this mischief began in England, and to give ensample [example] to all manner of people, I will speak thereof as it was done, as I was informed, and of the incidents thereof.

There was a usage in England and yet is in divers countries, that the noblemen hath great franchises over the commons and keepeth them in service, that is to say, their tenants ought by custom to labour the lords' lands, to gather and bring home their corns, and some to thresh and to fan, and by servage to make their hay, and to hew their wood and bring it home. All these things they ought to do by servage, and there be more of these people in England than in any other realm. Thus the noblemen and prelates are served by them and specially in the counties of Kent, Essex, Sussex and Bedford. These unhappy people of these said countries began to stir, because they said they were kept in great servage, and in the beginning of the world they said there were no bondmen [serfs], wherefore they maintained that none ought to be bond, without he did treason to his lord, as Lucifer did to God. But they said they could have no such battle,* for they were neither angels nor spirits, but men formed to the similitude of [that is, equal to] their lords, saying, why should they then be kept so under like beasts, the which they said they would no longer suffer, for they would be all one; and if they laboured or did anything for their lords, they would have wages therefor as well as other. And of this imagination was a foolish priest in the country of Kent, called John Ball, for the which foolish words he had been three times in the Bishop of Canterbury's prison. For this priest used oftentimes on the Sundays after mass, when the people were going out of the minster, to go into the cloister and preach and made the people to assemble about him, and would say thus, 'Ah! ye good people, the matters goeth not well to pass in England, nor shall not do till everything be common, and that there be no villeins nor gentlemen, but that we may be all united together, and that the lords be no greater masters than we be. What have we deserved, or why should we be kept thus in servage? We be all come from one father and one mother, Adam and Eve: whereby can they say or show that they be greater lords than we be, saying by that they cause us to win and labour for that they dispend? They are clothed in velvet and camlet furred with grise, and we be vestured with poor cloth. They have their wines, spices and good bread, and we have the drawing out of the chaff, and drink water. They dwell in fair houses, and we have the pain and travail, rain and wind in the fields;

---

* Lord Berners' text had "bataille" instead of "taille"—nature.

and by that that cometh of our labours they keep and maintain their estates. We be called their bondmen, and without we do readily them service, we be beaten; and we have no sovereign to whom we may complain, nor that will hear us nor do us right. Let us go to the king, he is young, and show him what servage we be in, and show him how we will have it otherwise, or else we will provide us of some remedy. And if we go together all manner of people that be now in any bondage will follow us, to the intent to be made free, and when the king seeth us we shall have some remedy, either by fairness or otherwise.' Thus John Ball said on Sundays when the people issued out of the churches in the villages, wherefore many of the mean people loved him, and such as intended to no goodness said how he said truth. And so they would murmur one with another in the fields and in the ways as they went together, affirming how John Ball said truth.

The Archbishop of Canterbury, who was informed of the saying of this John Ball, caused him to be taken and put in prison a two or three months to chastise him. Howbeit it had been much better at the beginning that he had been condemned to perpetual prison, or else to have died, rather than to have suffered him to have been again delivered out of prison: but the bishop had conscience to let him die. And when this John Ball was out of prison, he returned again to his error as he did before. Of his words and deeds there were much people in London informed, such as had great envy at them that were rich and such as were noble. And then they began to speak among them and said how the realm of England was right evil governed, and how that gold and silver was taken from them by them that were named noblemen. So thus these unhappy men of London began to rebel and assembled together, and sent word to the foresaid countries that they should come to London, and bring their people with them, promising how they should find London open to receive them and the commons of the city to be of the same accord, saying how they would do so much to the king that there should not be one bondman in all England.

This promise moved so them of Kent, of Essex, of Sussex, of Bedford, and of the countries about, that they rose and came towards London to the number of sixty thousand. And they had a captain called Water Tyler and with him in company was Jack Straw and John Ball. These three were chief sovereign captains, but the head of all was Water Tyler and he was indeed a tiler of houses, an ungracious patron.

When these unhappy men began thus to stir, they of London, except such as were of their band, were greatly afraid. Then the Mayor of London and the rich men of the city took counsel together, and when they saw the people thus coming on every side, they caused the gates of the city to be closed and would suffer no man to enter into the city. But when they had well imagined, they advised not so to do, for they thought they should thereby put their suburbs in great peril to be burnt, and so they opened again the city; and there entered in at the gates in some place a hundred, two hundred, by twenty and by thirty. And so when they came to London they entered and lodged, and yet of truth the third part [three-fourths] of these people could not tell what to ask or demand, but followed each other like beasts, as the shepherds did of old time, saying how they would go conquer the Holy Land [during the time of the Crusades], and at last all came to nothing.* In likewise these villains and poor people came to London a hundred mile off, sixty mile, fifty mile, forty mile and twenty mile off, and from all countries about London, but the most part came from the countries before named. And as they came they demanded ever for the king. The gentlemen of the countries, knights and squires, began to doubt, when they saw the people began to rebel, and though they were in doubt, it was good reason: for a less occasion they might have been afraid. So the gentlemen drew together as well as they might.

The same day that these unhappy people of Kent were coming to London, there returned from Canterbury the king's mother, Princess of Wales, coming from her pilgrimage. She was in great jeopardy to have been lost, for these people came to her carriage and dealt rudely with her, whereof the good lady was in great doubt lest they would have done some villainy to her or to her damosels. Howbeit, God kept her, and she came in one day from Canterbury to London, for she never durst tarry by the way. The same time King Richard her son was at the Tower of London. There his mother found him, and with him there was the Earl of Salisbury, the Archbishop of Canterbury, Sir Robert of Namur, the Lord of Gommegnies and divers other, who were in doubt of these people that thus gathered together and wist not what they demanded. This rebellion was well-known in the king's court or [before] any of these people began to stir out of their houses, but the king nor his council did provide no remedy therefor, which was great marvel. And to the intent that all lords and good people, and such as would nothing but good, should take ensample to correct them that be evil and rebellious, I shall show you plainly all the matter as it was.

To Rochester and Canterbury

The Monday before the feast of Corpus Christi, the year of our Lord God a thousand three hundred and eighty-one, these people issued out of their houses to come to London to speak with the king to be made free, for they would have had no bondman in England. And so first they came to Saint Thomas of Canterbury, and there John Ball had thought to have found the Bishop of Canterbury, but he was at Lon-

---

* a reference to the Pastoureaux of 1320, destroyed at Aigues-Mortes on their way to the Holy Land

don with the king. When Wat Tyler and Jack Straw entered into Canterbury, all the common people made great feast for all the town was of their assent. And there they took counsel to go to London to the king, and to send some of their company over the river of Thames into Essex, into Sussex, and into the counties of Stafford and Bedford, to speak to the people that they should all come to the farther side of London, and thereby to close London round about so that the king should not stop their passages, and that they should all meet together on Corpus Christi day. They that were at Canterbury entered into Saint Thomas' church and did there much hurt, and robbed and brake up the bishop's chamber. And in robbing and bearing out their pillage they said, 'Ah! this Chancellor of England hath had a good market to get together all this riches. He shall give us now account of the revenues of England and of the great profits that he hath gathered since the king's coronation.'

When they had this Monday thus broken the abbey of Saint Vincent, they departed in the morning and all the people of Canterbury with them, and so took the way to Rochester and sent their people to the villages about. And in their going they beat down and robbed houses of advocates [attorneys] and of the procurors [administrators] of the king's court and of the archbishop, and had mercy of none. And when they were come to Rochester, they had there good cheer, for the people of that town tarried for them, for they were of the same sect. And then they went to the castle there and took the knight that had the rule thereof: he was called Sir John Newton. And they said to him, 'Sir, it behoveth you to go with us and you shall be our sovereign captain, and to do what we will have you.' The knight excused himself honestly and showed them divers considerations and excuses, but all availed him nothing, for they said unto him, 'Sir John, if ye do not as we will have you, ye are but dead.' The knight seeing these people in that fury and ready to slay him, he then doubted [suspected] death and agreed to them, and so they took him with them against his inward will. And in likewise did they of other countries in England, as Essex, Sussex, Stafford, Bedford, and Norfolk even to Lynn, for they brought the knights and gentlemen into such obeisance that they caused them to go with them whether they would or not, as the Lord Morley, a great baron, Sir Stephen of Hales and Sir Thomas of Cosington and other.

Now behold the great fortune. If they might have come to their intents, they would have destroyed all the noblemen of England, and thereafter all other nations would have followed the same and have taken foot and ensample by them and by them of Ghent and Flanders, who rebelled against their lord. The same year the Parisians rebelled in likewise and found out [armed themselves with] the mallets of iron, of whom there were more than twenty thousand, as ye shall hear after in this history, but first we will speak of them of England.

When these people thus lodged at Rochester departed and passed the river and came to Dartford, always keeping still their opinions, beating down before them and all about the places and houses of advocates and procurors, and striking off the heads of divers persons; and so long they went forward until they came within a four mile of London, and there lodged on a hill called Blackheath. And as they went, they said ever they were the king's men and the noble commons of England. And when they of London knew that they were come so near to them, the mayor, as ye have heard before, closed the gates and kept straitly all the passages: this order caused the mayor, who was called William Walworth, and divers other rich burgesses of the city who were not of their sect, but there were in London of their unhappy opinions more than thirty thousand. Then these people thus being lodged on Blackheath determined to send their knight to speak with the king, and to show him how all that they have done or will do is for him and his honour, and how the realm of England hath not been well governed a great space for the honour of the realm nor for the common profit by his uncles and by the clergy, and specially by the Archbishop of Canterbury his chancellor, whereof they would have account. This knight durst do none otherwise but so came by the river of Thames to the Tower. The king and they that were with him in the Tower, desiring to hear tidings, seeing this knight coming, made him way, and was brought before the king into a chamber. And with the knight was the princess his mother and his two brethren, the Earl of Kent and the Lord John Holland, the Earl of Salisbury, the Earl of Warwick, the Earl of Oxford, the Archbishop of Canterbury, the Lord of Saint John's, Sir Robert of Namur, the Lord of Vertaing, the Lord of Gommegnies, Sir Henry of Senzeille, the Mayor of London and divers other notable burgesses. This knight Sir John Newton, who was well known among them for he was one of the king's officers, he kneeled down before the king and said, 'My right redoubted lord, let it not displease your Grace the message that I must needs show you, for, dear sir, it is by force and against my will.' 'Sir John,' said the king, 'say what ye will, I hold you excused.' 'Sir, the commons of this your realm hath sent me to you to desire you to come and speak with them on Blackheath, for they desire to have none but you. And, sir, ye need not to have any doubt of your person, for they will do you no hurt, for they hold and will hold you for their king; but, sir, they say they will show you divers things the which shall be right necessary for you to take heed of when they speak with you, of the which things, sir, I have no charge to show you. But, sir, an [if] it may please you to give me an answer such as may appease them, and that they may know for truth that I have spoken with you, for they have my children in hostage till I return again to them and without I return again they will slay my children incontinent.' Then the king made him an answer and said, 'Sir, ye shall have an answer shortly.' Then the king took counsel what was best for him to do, and it was anon determined that the next morning the king should go down the river by water, and without fail to speak with them. And when Sir John Newton heard that answer he desired nothing else, and so took his leave of the king and of the lords and returned again into his vessel, and passed the Thames and went to Blackheath where he had left more than threescore thousand men. And there he answered them that the next morning they should send some of their council to the Thames, and there the king would come and speak with them. This answer greatly pleased them, and so passed that night as well as they might. And the fourth part [four-fifths] of them fasted for lack of victual, for they had none, wherewith they were sore displeased, which was good reason.

All this season the Earl of Buckingham was in Wales, for there he had fair heritages [properties] by reason of his wife, who was daughter to the Earl of Northumberland and Hereford; but the voice was all through London how he was among these people, and some said certainly how they had seen him there among them. And all was because there was one Thomas in their company, a man of the county of Cambridge, that was very like the earl. Also the lords that lay at Plymouth [harbor] to go into Portugal were well informed of this rebellion, and of the people that thus began to rise, wherefore they doubted lest their viage should have been broken, or else they feared lest the commons about Southampton, Winchester, and Arundel would have come on them. Wherefore they weighed up their anchors and issued out of the haven with great pain, for the wind was sore against them, and so took the sea and there cast anchor abiding for the wind. And the Duke of Lancaster, who was in the marches of Scotland between Moorlane and Roxburgh entreating with the Scots, where it was showed him of the rebellion, whereof he was in doubt, for he knew well that he was but little beloved with the commons of England. Howbeit, for all those tidings yet he did sagely demean himself as touching the treaty with the Scots.

The Earl Douglas, the Earl of Moray, the Earl of Sutherland and the Earl Thomas Erskine, and the Scots that were there for the treaty knew right well the rebellion in England, how the common people in every part began to rebel against the noblemen; wherefore the Scots thought that England was in great danger to be lost, and therefore in their treaties they were the more stiffer against the Duke of Lancaster and his council.

Now let us speak of the commons of England and how they persevered.

"Let Us Go to London"

In the morning on Corpus Christi day King Richard heard mass in the Tower of London, and all his lords, and then he took his barge with the

Earl of Salisbury, the Earl of Warwick, the Earl of Oxford, and certain knights, and so rowed down along Thames to Rotherhithe, whereas was descended down the hill a ten thousand men to see the king and to speak with him. And when they saw the king's barge coming they began to shout and made such a cry as though all the devils in hell had been among them. And they had brought with them Sir John Newton, to the intent that if the king had not come they would have stricken him all to pieces, and so they had promised him. And when the king and his lords saw the demeanour of the people, the best assured of them were in dread, and so the king counselled by his barons not to take any landing there, but so rowed up and down the river. And the king demanded of them what they would, and said how he was come thither to speak with them. And they said all with one voice, 'We would that ye should come a-land, and then we shall show you what we lack.' Then the Earl of Salisbury answered for the king and said, 'Sirs, ye be not in such order nor array that the king ought to speak with you'; and so with those words no more said. And then the king was counselled to return again to the Tower of London, and so he did. And when these people saw that, they were inflamed with ire and returned to the hill where the great band was, and there showed them what answer they had and how the king was returned to the Tower of London.

Then they cried all with one voice, 'Let us go to London,' and so they took their way thither. And in their going they beat down abbeys and houses of advocates and of men of the court, and so came into the suburbs of London, which were great and fair, and there beat down divers fair houses, and specially they brake up the king's prisons, as the Marshalsea and other, and delivered out all the prisoners that were within and there they did much hurt. And at the bridge foot they threat[ened] them of London because the gates of the bridge were closed, saying how they would burn all the suburbs and so conquer London by force, and to slay and burn all the commons of the city. There were many within the city of their accord, and so they drew together and said, 'Why do we not let these good people enter into the city? They are our fellows and that that they do is for us.' So therewith the gates were opened, and then these people entered into the city and went into houses and sat down to eat and drink. They desired nothing but it was incontinent brought to them [that is, everything they asked for was given to them], for every man was ready to make them good cheer and to give them meat and drink to appease them.

Then the captains, as John Ball, Jack Straw and Wat Tyler, went throughout London, and a twenty thousand with them, and so came to the Savoy in the way to Westminster, which was a goodly house and it pertained [belonged] to the Duke of Lancaster. And when they entered they slew the keepers thereof and robbed and pilled [pillaged] the house, and when they had so done, then they set fire on it and clean destroyed and burnt it. And when they had done that outrage, they left not therewith but went straight to the fair hospital of the Rhodes called Saint John's, and there they burnt house, hospital, minster and all. Then they went from street to street and slew all the Flemings that they could find, in church or in any other place: there was none respited from death. And they brake up divers houses of the Lombards and robbed them and took their goods at their pleasure, for there was none that durst say them nay. And they slew in the city a rich merchant called Richard Lyon, to whom before that time Wat Tyler had done service in France; and on a time this Richard Lyon had beaten him while he was his varlet, the which Wat Tyler then remembered, and so came to his house and struck off his head and caused it to be borne on a spear-point before him all about the city. Thus these ungracious people demeaned themselves, like people enraged and wood, and so that day they did much sorrow in London.

And so against night they went to lodge at Saint Katherine's before the Tower of London, saying how they would never depart thence till they had the king at their pleasure, and till he had accorded to them all that they would ask accounts of the Chancellor of England, to know where all the good was become that he had levied through the realm; and without he made a good account to them thereof, it should not be for his profit. And so when they had done all these evils to the strangers all the day, at night they lodged before the Tower.

Ye may well know and believe that it was great pity for the danger that the king and such as were with him were in. For some time these unhappy people shouted and cried so loud, as though all the devils of hell had been among them.

In this evening the king was counselled by his brethren and lords, and by Sir William Walworth, Mayor of London, and divers other notable and rich burgesses, that in the night-time they should issue out of the Tower and enter into the city, and so to slay all these unhappy people while they were at their rest and asleep, for it was thought that many of them were drunken, whereby they should be slain like flies; also of twenty of them there was scant one in harness [armed and ready to fight]. And surely the good men of London might well have done this at their ease, for they had in their houses secretly their friends and servants ready in harness. And also Sir Robert Knowles was in his lodging, keeping his treasure, with a sixscore ready at his commandment. In likewise was Sir Perducas d'Albret, who was as then in London, insomuch that there might well [have] assembled together an eight thousand men ready in harness.

King Richard has Wat Tyler beheaded for his insolence in revolting against the injustices of the English government.

Howbeit there was nothing done, for the residue of the commons of the city were sore doubted, lest they should rise also, and the commons before were a threescore thousand or more. Then the Earl of Salisbury and the wise men about the king said, 'Sir, if ye can appease them with fairness, it were best and most profitable, and to grant them everything that they desire: for if we should begin a thing the which we could not achieve, we should never recover it again, but we and our heirs ever to be disherited.' So this counsel was taken and the mayor countermanded, and so commanded that he should not stir; and he did as he was commanded, as reason was. And in the city with the major there were twelve aldermen, whereof nine of them held with the king and the other three took part with these ungracious people, as it was after well-known, the which they full dearly bought.

And on the Friday in the morning, the people being at Saint Katherine's near to the Tower, began to apparel themselves and to cry and to shout and said, without [unless] the king would come out and speak with them, they would assail the Tower and take it by force and slay all them that were within. Then the king doubted these words, and so was counselled that he should issue out to speak with them. And then the king sent to them that they should all draw to a fair plain place, called Mile End, whereas the people in the city did sport them in the summer season, and there the king to grant them that they desired. And there it was cried in the king's name that whosoever would speak with the king, let him go to the said place, and there he should not fail to find the king.

Then the people began to depart, specially the commons of the villages, and went to the same place. But all went not thither, for they were not all of one condition; for there were some that desired nothing but riches and the utter destruction of the noblemen, and to have London robbed and pilled: that was the principal matter of their beginning, the which they well showed, for as soon as the Tower gate opened and that the king was issued out with his two brethren and the Earl of Salisbury, the Earl of Warwick, the Earl of Oxford, Sir Robert of Namur, the Lord of Vertaing, the Lord Gommegnies and divers other, then Wat Tyler, Jack Straw, and John Ball and more than four hundred, entered into the Tower and brake up chamber after chamber; and at last found the Archbishop of Canterbury, called Simon, a valiant man and a wise, and chief Chancellor of England, and a little before he had said mass before the king. These gluttons took him and struck off his head, and also they beheaded the Lord of Saint John's, and a friar minor, master in medicine pertaining to the Duke of Lancaster. They slew him in despite of his master and a sergeant-at-arms, called John Leg. And these four heads were set on four long spears and they made them to be borne before them through the streets of London and at last set them a-high on London Bridge, as though they had been traitors to the king and to the realm. Also these gluttons entered into the princess' chamber and brake her bed, whereby she was so sore afraid that she swooned, and there she was taken up and borne to the waterside and put into a barge and covered, and so conveyed to a place called the Queen's Wardrobe. And there she was all that day and night, like a woman half dead, till she was comforted with the king her son, as ye shall hear after.

Chapter

3

Life and Culture in Fourteenth-Century Europe

In the opinion of many historians, the fourteenth century was some-thing of a cultural wasteland. It is certainly true that the century sits squarely between two periods of notable cultural production: It came significantly after the High Middle Ages of the twelfth century but be-fore the beginnings of the Renaissance in the 1400s. Moreover, the names of the greatest artists, writers, philosophers, and musicians of the age do not match similar lists from many surrounding centuries.

Still, fourteenth-century Europe had its cultural high points. Great writers such as Giovanni Boccaccio, Petrarch, and Geoffrey Chaucer lived during this period. The Italian artist known as Giotto completed many of his best works during the fourteenth century, as did the Dutch painter Hubert van Eyck, and the Frenchman Guillaume de Machaut was an active musician and composer in this time as well. Though few of these are instantly recognizable names today, each of these Europeans made important contributions to the world of art. The 1300s did not see a total neglect of cultural life.

The period was perhaps somewhat more impressive where religious thought and philosophy were concerned. The 1300s were a time of ques-tioning, experimenting, and reshaping the ideas of earlier generations. Thinkers such as William of Ockham, John Wycliffe, and Meister Eck-hardt challenged orthodoxies; in doing so, they not only changed the theological landscape of their time but also set the stage for future philosophers who would take their notions one step further. In a time when religion and politics were tightly connected, too, these thinkers had an important influence on government, although again one that would take several more centuries to be entirely understood and applied.

There were no doubt many reasons for this burst in philosophy. One important reason, however, was the general state of Europe during the time. The 1300s were a difficult period, an era of great hardship and de-privation. Suffering seemed universal. Wars took their toll on young sol-diers and innocent bystanders alike; nobles and peasants died in the fight-ing, and serfs could only look on in dismay as their homes were burned and their crops destroyed by enemy forces. Famines affected the food supply. Diseases ran rampant through villages and across national bound-aries. The Black Death killed millions of Europeans in a few short years, and many others died of measles, pneumonia, and other diseases tamed or eradicated altogether in our time. In the face of such disaster, it is easy to see why philosophers might have wanted to reevaluate the ideas that previous centuries had held dear.

The Famine of 1315–1322

William Chester Jordan

The early years of the fourteenth century were marked by a widespread famine that affected much of northern Europe. Crops either failed or never began to grow. Thousands of people died; thousands more suffered from severe malnutrition, which in turn weakened them and made them susceptible to fatal diseases. Though the era was a good deal less disastrous than the Black Death that was to follow, the years nevertheless earned the name "the Great Famine."

This excerpt comes from William Chester Jordan's book *The Great Famine: Northern Europe in the Early Fourteenth Century*. Jordan bases his account on a wide variety of sources, from scientific examinations of the weather during the period to the records of contemporary chroniclers.

The epoch of the Great Famine saw some of the worst and most sustained periods of bad weather in the entire Middle Ages and that this was particularly unanticipated, given the mild thirteenth century.

Two indexes prepared by [historian Pierre] Alexandre on the severity of winters and the incidence of rainy summers help make the point with greater clarity. For reports of a continuous series of exceptionally cold winters there was nothing like the period 1310–1330. While the series of winters from 1160 to 1170 may have been the worst on record, that fact would have been ancient history to people in 1315. Moreover, for sheer length of time the succession of miserably cold winters in the years 1310–1330 was incomparable; and 1320–1330 was perhaps the second worst period for severe winters in the entirety of the Middle Ages.

Alexandre's index of the incidence of rainy summers also identifies the years 1310–1320 as one of the four worst intervals in the period from 1150 to 1420. Indeed, though it is difficult to be precise on relative rankings, the years 1310–1320 appear to be the second worst period for severe, sustained summer downpours for the Middle Ages as a whole.

Pierre Alexandre's conclusions can be tested against the independent evidence of dendrochronology [the study of tree-ring growth]. Mary Lyons has examined the northern Irish evidence of oaks, whose growth is very sensitive to rainfall. On the basis of tree-ring growth, it would appear that oak growth was 7 percent above normal in 1315 and 10 percent above normal in 1316. The year 1317 saw a growth rate near average (perhaps 2 percent below), which would suggest a tapering off of the rains in Ireland, a conclusion that, as we shall see, the chroniclers support. But in Ireland at least, the year 1318 saw another extraordinary spurt of tree-ring growth in oaks, 8 percent above normal. By contrast, the 1320s—based simply on dendrochronological evidence—appear to have been a period of attenuated growth, suggesting severe prolonged drought. The year 1324 witnessed tree-ring growth 22 percent below normal, and at least three other years in the 1320s had growth rates more than 10 percent below normal. Study of oak-tree growth in Hesse [Germany] on the Continent reveals similar patterns: the years 1310 to 1320 provide evidence of a devastating weather cycle.

Striking and persuasive as are the general conclusions of Alexandre's, Lyons's, and other studies, they pale before the reports in narrative sources. We are not as fortunate as our Enlightenment forebears in terms of numbers of surviving chronicles, but what does survive fully supports their impressions. Texts as disparate as the Nuremberg *Annals*, a Flemish rhymed account for 1315, and a Breton chronicle for 1314 and 1315 declaim the unmitigated severity of the weather. Others identify or dwell on specific aspects of the unfavorable weather. Nearly all contemporary or near contemporary authors emphasize the abnormal persistence of the rains in the opening years. They had already begun, at least in England and perhaps in Germany, in the summer of 1314. Followed by a harsh winter and, of course, expected late-winter rains, which in this instance only compounded the problem, the unseasonable downpours recommenced in earnest in late spring and brought flooding in their wake. These rains, with unusually deafening thunder and terrible displays of lightning in Scandinavia, were steady . . . from Pentecost 1315 on in England, from mid-April in France, and from May Day in the Low Countries, and were heavy throughout the summer in Germany and elsewhere, including Ireland. The winds and overcast skies made the whole summer abnormally cool. . . . In October the rains were still falling in

Britain: four mills on the usually gentle Avon, now swollen and clogged with debris, succumbed to flooding in that one month.

The year 1316 was equally bad or worse. It probably began with another severe winter during which ships were immobilized by ice as the Baltic froze over. The chroniclers make clear that the rains following the severe winter weather came so frequently that the effects of the downpours could not be contained. Spring, summer, fall: they came when the seed had just been scattered, when what seeds remained in place sprouted and the shoots broke through the surface of the earth, and they came with equal severity at harvest. "The whole world was troubled," wrote one chronicler from Salzburg [Austria], which had been at the southeastern geographical limit of the ruinous weather the year before. Yet the chronicler could say the "whole world" in 1316 because as far as he knew, the devastation had spread far to the south and east, to Styria [in Austria], for example, which suffered catastrophic flooding that swept away at least fourteen bridges on the river Mur.

The downpours were somewhat less ubiquitous in 1317: western Germany was hard hit; its periphery less so—in agreement with the dendrochronological evidence already presented. But the amelioration of conditions was brief. The harshest winter of all was 1317/1318. In a *récit* by a French chronicler, winter was said to have been not only severe but interminable, with bitter cold continuous "from the feast of Saint Andrew [30 November] or thereabouts until Easter." To an English observer it was the worst winter in a millennium: "A thusent [thousand] winter ther bifore com nevere non so strong." No more benumbing punishment had ever been inflicted: "Com nevere wrecche into Engelond that made men more agaste."

According to a number of chroniclers, improvement in conditions was more common after April 1318, but local conditions—those in Ireland, for example—were to make 1318 as bad a year in many villages as any of the years in which the disastrous rains were more widespread. And though never again as general or as sustained as in the first three years of the famine, conditions so often degenerated over large regions from 1319 to 1322 that it is no exaggeration to link these years with the earlier years of the catastrophe. Normandy was ripped by devastating windstorms in 1319, the equivalent of nor'easters on the Atlantic seaboard of North America, with the inevitable impact on flocks, herds, and fruit trees. Flanders was repeatedly punished by floods that hobbled the economy and caused major property damage especially in 1320 and 1322. Elsewhere—in England and on the Continent, as, for example, in the region around Aachen [Germany]—sustained periods of bad weather (sometimes compounded, the chroniclers tell us, by lengthy droughts) extended the famine conditions even beyond 1322. But a reasonable closing date for the long series of catastrophes is the winter of 1321/1322. It saw terrible and sustained cold, with the

Baltic and parts of the North Sea frozen over and ships immobilized in icy prisons. Norman chroniclers remarked the snow. It was everywhere; it was deep; it would not melt. . . .

The Effects of War

This tragic period was made more so by war. Although it cannot be said that war caused the famine, it intensified the deprivation by expanding a production crisis into a distribution crisis as well. . . . Here we need only enumerate the conflicts and address a few of their most obvious and general consequences at the regional level in the principalities affected by the persistently bad weather.

In the north a tangle of complicated dynastic struggles kept the kingdoms of Norway, Denmark, and Sweden at one another's throats in various alliances all through the famine, but especially until 1319. These wars also had a disruptive, though not necessarily entirely unprofitable, effect on German-speaking towns and principalities all along the southern rim of the Baltic. Desperately needed resources were being diverted to military needs like castle building at the height of the famine.

Among Germans proper the situation was no better. Locally severe flooding in 1312 and exceptional cold in 1313 had produced regional shortages and high prices in a number of places in the empire. Exacerbating these conditions, war broke out between Ludwig of Bavaria and Duke Frederick of Austria in late 1314 after the so-called double election to the German throne. In the Frankfurt area one chronicler describes how a "great multitude of men and horses" of the duke's army were already perishing from shortages in 1314. Another delighted in observing in real life the topos [morals] learned from stories about knights, in this case hard up from the artificially induced shortages caused by marauding armies and siege warfare, selling their mounts in order to get food and drink. There is a mocking, tongue-in-cheek quality to the latter's report—on the eve of a dearth that would make the conditions he was describing seem almost desirable—and the tone betokens the naive character of expectations about the weather and war: "And what a wonder! Some knights who were sitting on a magnificently outfitted horse gave the horse and their weapons away for cheap wine; and they did this because they were so terribly hungry."

As the wars and the famine conditions persisted, the time for mockery passed. There were numerous treaties, alliances, truces, regulations of tolls, and agreements with respect to suppressing disorder and modifying payments of debts to Jews in the years 1315–1322, especially in the Rhineland and southern Germany. It is probably wrong to conclude from this evidence that the country was in utter turmoil, since such agreements among towns, churches, and lay lords occurred at many other times as well. Nevertheless, most historians seem convinced that the combination of wars and harvest failures convulsed the empire.

An on-again, off-again war in Flanders in which French troops tried to bring the Flemings under their suzerainty bracketed the three major early years of the famine in that region and would be invoked by commentators as one factor (along with the taxation imposed in the preparation for and fighting of the war) that made an already difficult situation more difficult. Even as the Franco-Flemish war affected the famine, the natural conditions that helped provoke the famine made the fighting of the war more arduous. In 1315 the steady, inundating rains ("the ugly weather") turned the roads into quagmires, trapped the riding and cart horses ("there was mud up to their knees"), immobilized wagons, and made supply of troops nearly impossible, as what seems like an infinite number of chroniclers relate. And we are informed monotonously that the distress—and the postponement of combat which it necessitated—saddened the commanders, including Louis X, the king of France . . . who craved nothing so much as a decisive victory in a war whose roots went back twenty years. To the rebellious Flemings, of course, the ceaseless rains that stymied the king were the act of a beneficent God; the belief became a cliché, constantly repeated down the centuries in sources originating in the region.

In the British Isles, too, war was everywhere. The Scots, in the aftermath of the famous battle of Bannockburn (1314) began to ravage large areas on the English borderlands and did long-lasting damage whose precise parameters, given the nature of the evidence, are difficult to assess with precision but appear to have been extensive and massive. The English, in retaliation, were nearly as effective in ravaging the countryside of southern Scotland; but the army that led the way in the raids was far less successful in fulfilling its major mission of bringing the Scots to heel. The difficulty of provisioning the army, together with disease, is said to have led to a greater number of casualties than did battle. Moreover, in both countries border localities that were spared ravaging were affected in other ways as productive resources drained to the battle-scarred areas and the needs of the contending armies grew. . . .

Ireland and Wales, as intimated, also suffered from wars fought on their soil. The spring of 1315 saw the arrival of Scottish forces in Ireland led by Edward Bruce (brother of Robert Bruce); this was a kind of second front in the continuing war between England and Scotland already being played out on the borderlands of the two countries. The mutual violence of the Scots and the Anglo-Irish lords and their supporters aggravated the evil conditions then beginning to be felt after the failure of the winter wheat harvest. The disruptions continued through 1317 as the Scots, failing to enlist sufficient Irish support against English domination to overcome their enemy, went about hungry and harrying the island. Killing in war, terrorism, and dying from the effects of the subsistence crisis went together. Seizures of already much reduced crops are reported.

In southern Wales, following the death at Bannockburn of the great English magnate and power in the Welsh March Gilbert de Clare, the earl of Gloucester, "men raised hostile insurrection in the form of war." Such a power vacuum as that left by the earl's death might have served to persuade Welsh lords (in this case Llywelyn Bren) to rise, but most historians agree that it was the crop failures of 1315 which triggered the revolt against the English. The economic effects of this rebellion were to be felt even in north Wales. If we could not guess as much from what we know of their commitments against the Scots on the borderlands and in Ireland, chronicle evidence assures us that the English found their resources stretched to the limit by the insurrection. It was to the great good fortune of the crown that the rebellion did not evolve into a general rising of the Welsh people and did not see the invasion of north Wales by Scots from Ireland, an invasion that Edward and Robert Bruce briefly contemplated.

Causes as People Saw Them

The weather, then, provoked a production crisis and complicated distribution. Wars and their destruction immediately before and during the onslaught of bad weather compounded the problems, especially that of distribution, in a major way. [There are also] other contributory explanations for the intensity and duration of the famine (some, like inordinate taxation, implicit in what has already been written). . . . Yet probably none of these explanations would have entirely satisfied most medieval men and women. For them, it was God who was unquestionably bringing famine in order to mete out the legitimate recompense for sin. . . . Sin, hatred of the visible Church, empty faith, and lack of loyalty offended God and explained why He permitted the foul weather to linger for such a length of time. It could only be God, as we are informed by one version of the English poem "On the Evil Times of Edward II" (ca. 1320), who apportioned weather "so cold and unkynde"—out of its kind in the sense of rupturing the natural order. As punishment for human pride God "sente derthe [dearth, or scarcity] on erde [earth]." The text "he . . . sendeth rain on the just and the unjust" (Matt. 5.45) confirmed this view: the punishment richly deserved by the unjust had to be endured by the righteous as well, in the same way that sunlight warmed both the wicked and the good. So, too, sickness came on the battered and bewildered population of saints and sinners by God's own ordinance in the "plaga divina."

A merciful God, it must be added, gave fair warning of the disaster. One schoolman, William of Wheatley, who had studied at Paris and later became master of the grammar schools of Lincoln in England, claimed that from things he had seen in the kingdom a good twenty years before the time of high prices and hunger (1315, 1316, and 1317) he could have predicted the catastrophe. He had seen similar signs again, he wrote, while he studied in Paris fifteen years before the famine. William made these claims in a treatise he later composed on the art and science of the interpretation of signs. Unfortunately, the part of his treatise where he begins to talk about the particular signs that pointed to the famine was never completed.

Other observers were more revealing. The years 1315 and 1316 saw a comet appear in the night sky. (Observed not only in the West, the phenomenon in question is also reported in the Chinese Annals as having been visible from 28 November 1315 through 12 March 1316.) This heavenly manifestation was a clear counsel, as readers of earlier northern European chronicles would have been led to believe, of the specter of prolonged famine and death. The Low Country chronicler Lodewijk Van Velthem, who recorded that the comet was visible beginning on 21 December 1315 and whose narrative ended in late 1316 when he put down his quill, was most insistent on this interpretation, adding civil strife and widespread destruction to the litany of expected horrors. Of course, a few chroniclers saw in the comet other portents (the death of Louis X in 1316, the general suffering of France) or nothing at all.

Besides the comet other signs manifested themselves. Swedes observed splashes of scarlet light in the heavens resembling showers of blood; these were allegedly a herald of pestilence. To the English this light, if indeed the same light, made a ruby-red cross of blood as a token of future battle deaths. The traditional signs of the times also included a lunar eclipse (1 October 1316) and two earthquakes (1316 in northern and 1317 in western France).

Like signs in general, the significance of the comet of 1315 and early 1316, the vermilion skies of that year or slightly later, and the other wonders could hardly have been determined with genuine confidence until the disasters themselves became evident: deeper want, pestilence, more casualties of war. For embedded in the political economy of salvation was the notion that the power of the sign, whose *potential* significance was predictable from the memory of past patterns duly recorded, could be reversed by acts of contrition on the part of a sinful humanity. Had the years from 1316 to 1322 been bountiful ones, the comet and the reddened canopy of heaven would have been regarded as that stimulus to conversion which brought disaster to a quick end, reconfirming at the same time the covenant between God and people. Yet Lodewijk Van Velthem was certain when he finished the narrative portion of his chronicle in late 1316 that contrition would be too little and too late; the end of the world was near. At least this is the impression one gets from the fact that the terrible descriptions of 1315 and 1316 furnished by Lodewijk are followed by two long appended books on signs and miracles in which the chronicler-turned-exegete [interpreter] ruminates on the apocalyptic visions of the Book of Daniel. Of course, as it turned out, Lodewijk was wrong. The great Day of Judgment did not come. Nonetheless, a severe punishment was inflicted by the Lord Most High for five more very long years—or so most men and women surely came to believe.

Childhood in the Fourteenth Century

Barbara Hanawalt

This excerpt from Barbara Hanawalt's *Growing Up in Medieval London* describes the daily routine of a typical urban child during the fourteenth century. Hanawalt, a historian who has published many articles on social history and medieval England, describes the chores, entertainment, and family life of children during the time. She also includes information on the costs of having children and on the seamier side of life in medieval London. Of course, there were many variations on the basic pattern that Hanawalt describes. Boys and girls had different experiences; so did the rich and poor.

Children were to arise, as did their elders, "betimes"—that is, at "six of the clock at the farthest." Only seven hours of sleep were recommended for children, although adults were advised to sleep for eight or nine hours:

> Seven hours for a child is temperate and good,
> If more, it offendeth and hurteth the blood.

All manuals urge some devotion or prayers upon arising. Then the children were to sponge and brush the clothing intended for the day's wearing, clean their shoes, comb their hair, and wash both hands and face. Nails were to be pared if they needed it, and teeth were to be cleaned by washing or by scrubbing with an ivory or a wooden stick. Children were advised to take care to dress neatly and according to the social rank to which they belonged, with the collar at the neck, with no seams split, and with the girdle fastened about the waist. Prudent youth were to have a clean napkin that they could use "for cleaning the nose of all filthiness." They were to make their bed if they had one or to fold up the bedding neatly if they slept in the hall or on the shop floor.

Children were not to be allowed to choose their own clothing because they would want clothing of fantastic cut and color, "their foolishness is beyond measure" and parents who indulged them were no better. Instead, children were to be clothed modestly and decently, according to their social rank, in good, sturdy, clean clothing. Clothing in disrepair was to be mended, and worn shoes replaced.

Diet likewise concerned the moralists. In a society in which beer and wine were the common drinks at meals, moralists realized that a child might succumb to drunkenness early in life. A child was not to start a meal with drink and was not to have drink after eating hot broth or milk. Parents were advised to allow a child only two or three drinks of wine or beer during a meal because those beverages deformed their minds and caused an unreasonable diet. Parents were also told to teach their children to eat in moderation and to wait to be fed.

Expectations set by the mayor and the chamberlain for those caring for city orphans seemed to reflect the moderate course set out in the books of advice. Guardians were to find food, linen and woolen clothing, shoes, and other necessities. In the case of an orphan, John, son of William Hanyngtone, these necessities included a furred gown and matching tunic, four pairs of linens, shoes, a bed, and 1*d*. [1 pence] a week for room and board. Records for expenses were carefully kept, either by a tally stick or in written records, so that the officials could be sure that the money remaining was given over to the orphan when she or he reached the age of majority. Gilbert de la Marche, a potter, had guardianship of the property of William, son of Sara la Feyte, but John de Linlee acted as the infant's guardian and provided nourishment, for which the potter gave him 40*s*. [shillings] by tally.

The amounts spent on children's upkeep varied greatly. In 1376, the cost of keeping John, son of John Gartone, was committed to John Bas, a draper, whose daughter the boy had married at the tender age of nine. When the young wife died, her husband was still a minor, and the father-in-law rendered account for expenses that amounted to 2*s*. a week. The care of an invalid daughter of a cordwainer [shoemaker] for six and a half years in the 1380s cost about 12*s*. a year, or about 3 1/2*d*. a week. Obviously, she lived less well than the draper's daughter. Other guardians reported paying amounts of £1 [1 pound] a year, 6*d*. a week, 1/2 mark a year, and 66*s*. 8*d*. annually, to a high of £7 19*s*. 3*d*. for a five-year-old goldsmith's daughter over a two-year period. The social status of the orphan, rather than his or her sex, seemed to determine the amount spent, so that, in accordance with the advice books, the children were maintained according to their station.

After rising and washing, now soberly and cleanly clothed, the children made their first public appearance of the day. On proceeding to the hall, they were expected to greet their parents or master—young men, by removing their caps—showing respect and humility. Breakfast consisted of good meat and drink, consumed after grace had been said. The drink might have been milk, but was equally likely to have been "small beer," a low-alcohol beer made from a second brewing.

The morning routine varied with the age and plans for the children. Boys might go to school in the morning, or they might play in the streets. Apprentices, of course, worked in the shops. Moralists recommended Mass each morning, and, no doubt, youths did attend Mass on some mornings. Deportment in church was to be attentive and reverent. Talking with others (even the clergy), looking about, and laughing were, of course, in bad taste.

Demeanor and Disaster

Appearances were to be kept up in the street as well. "Symon's Lesson of Wisdom for All Manner of Children" not only gave the usual counsel to young boys to keep their heads up, doff their caps to their betters, and greet people courteously, but elaborated on the bad things that boys might do instead. The author no doubt had observed that boys were likely to throw sticks and stones at dogs, horses, and hogs and to imitate the behavior of women and men behind their backs. They were warned not to fight, swear, get their clothing dirty, or lose their books, caps, and gloves.

The moralist was concerned not only about demeanor in the streets, but about the potential for accidents:

> Look thou keep thee from fire and water.
> Be ware and wise how thou look
> Over any brink, well, or brook.
> And when thou standest at any schate [fence]
> Be ware and wise that thou catch no stake;
> For many child without dread,
> Through evil heed is deceived or dead.

Symon had a tender worry about the accidents that happened to children. Perhaps he had served on coroners' juries and knew about accidents firsthand. Thomas, son of Alice de Westwyk, was only six when he was walking alone at dusk and fell into a tub of scalding water. On a June evening, Robert, son of Ralph de Leyre, went to Fishwharf to bathe, but he drowned. The same fate occurred to a sixteen year old who was bathing in a ditch. Water claimed the lives of nine-year-old Mary, daughter of Agnes de Billingesgate, who went to get water from

the Thames in an earthen pot, and of another girl who fell in while fill-
ing water jugs. . . . House fires also claimed the lives of children.

Although young boys were told to look people in the eye in the
streets and to greet them courteously, the "Good Wife" taught her
daughter to keep her eyes cast down:

> And when thou goest on thy way, go thou not too fast,
> Brandish not thy head, nor with thy shoulders cast,
> Have not too many words, from swearing keep aloof,
> For all such manners come to an evil proof.

On the whole, it was better to remain at home:

> Dwell at home, daughter, and love thy work much,
> And so thou shalt, my lief [dear] child, wax the sooner rich.

Women seemed to obey the injunction to stay in their homes. . . .
The young girls, however, sometimes felt cooped up at home. Eleven-
year-old Juliana, daughter of John Turgeys, was so desirous of seeing
what was going on in the High Street that she stood in an open window in a solar [sunroom] and fell out trying to get a better view.

Many exciting events occurred in homes, of course. Alice, daughter of John de Markeby, was at home after curfew when her father got
drunk and began leaping about the house until a knife that he had on
his girdle wounded him in the leg.

Food and Mealtimes

The main meal was a midday dinner. If the courtesy books are correct,
this was a meal taken with considerable ritual. But we must assume
that such was not the case in all London households. The polished
young man, however, was instructed to enter the hall, and say "God
be here," and speak courteously to those present. Many houses had a
holy-water strop by the entrance, and the guests were to dip their fingers in and cross themselves when they entered. . . .

The better houses had basins and jugs for washing the hands before
eating, along with a quantity of towels, napkins, tablecloths, pitchers,
bowls, and magnificent salt cellars. Missing from the list of goods found
in the pantry or buttery were plates, forks, and knives other than those
used for carving. The guests, both men and women, always had their
own knives on their girdles (thus explaining the tragedy of John de
Markeby). People ate with their fingers; for that reason, washing the
hands and keeping the nails clean were important aspects of good table
manners. Rather than using a plate, four-day-old bread or a rough bread
was carved into a trencher [a plate] from which to eat. The trenchers were
collected at the end of the meal and given to the poor, with the sauces of
the rich man's table soaked into the bread. Soups were served in bowls,
and the host was expected to provide spoons. Silver spoons were prized
items and a common gift to a godchild, so that even relatively modest

houses might have them. Failing silver, wooden or horn spoons sufficed.

The young male social climber was expected to stand and chat respectfully with his elders until the host indicated the seats for his guests, according to their degree. It was impolite to dispute the designated seating arrangement. The host sat in front of the salt cellar and placed the most respected guests by him. Those of lesser degree, including most youths, sat below the salt.

Diners ate in pairs, sharing the beer or wine cup and the meat. Thus the moralists instructed the young to "be fellowly and share with him that sits by you." As a practical matter, they also advised wiping the edge of the cup with a napkin after drinking, wiping knives on the trencher rather than on the tablecloth, dipping only a clean knife into the salt cellar, and putting meat scraps in a voider rather than back on the serving dish. Contrary to our perception of diners in the Middle Ages, the refined did not throw their bones to dogs. As the author of "The Young Children's Book" says: "Make neither the cat nor the dog your fellow at the table." And, of course, diners were admonished not to "make a noise as you sup as do boys" or scratch themselves lest people think they had fleas or pick their noses or let a pearl form on the end of the nose or run their hands through their hair lest people think they had lice. "Whether you spit near or far, hold your hand before your mouth to hide it." Guests were to praise the meal, sit up straight, talk courteously, and have a good time without laughing too loud.

But did society really expect this sort of behavior? A case against an apprentice indicates that only a few code words were necessary to paint a picture of disreputable behavior. Maud Fattyng claimed that her apprentice "beat her, her daughter, and her household, despised his food, tore his linen clothes," and owed her money. It took a jury to confirm that he was not such a boor as to beat his mistress, complain about his food, or destroy his clothing, but he had to pay the money back.

Evening Meals and Leisure

We may assume, however, because the moralists dwelt so long on behavior at the table, that ordinary eating was not as refined as they portray it. Most youths would not have been raised in the usual course of their lives to behave correctly at such a meal. The city had many taverns and places to buy prepared food, so many Londoners must have had a pint of beer and a meat pie on the go. Most families would have shared a one-pot meal, accompanied by bread and beer. And, too, there were all those paupers munching on stale trenchers in the streets.

Dinner, especially if it had been the elaborate repast that the moralists describe, might be followed by a postprandial nap for the diners. Servants, of course, had more than enough work to clear up from the dinner. Most artisans returned to their shops to take advantage of the daylight hours. Schoolboys probably returned to school; girls worked on embroidery or other needlework or helped with the household chores.

On Sundays and feast days, excursions outside the walls might while away the holiday. The court records give us some idea of these outings. On a Sunday in August 1337, "Walter de Mordone and his whole family were playing in the fields after dinner."

The evening meal was a light one and was usually followed by leisure activities. London law prohibited evening work, so evenings could be devoted to visiting and entertainment. While the moralists would have had the youth safely at home and early to bed, the evenings sometimes turned into riot. . . . Even the drinking at home could get rowdy. Londoners were more at risk in their leisure than they were at work. . . . Drinking, gaming, and visiting harlots occupied the time of unruly youth. These activities could lead to violence and homicide or careless accidents caused by drunkenness.

One young woman spent a terrifying evening in the tavern of her guardians, Gilbert de Mordone, a stockfishmonger, and his wife. Walter de Benygtone came with seventeen companions to the brewhouse with stones in their hoods, swords, knives, and other weapons. They drank four gallons of beer while they lay in wait to "seize and carry off" Emma, daughter of the late Robert Pourte, who was Gilbert's ward. Gilbert's wife realized that there would be trouble and, together with the brewer, "prayed" Walter and his companions to leave. They refused, saying that they would stay and spend their money there since it was a public house. Gilbert's wife "seeing their folly returned to her chamber taking the said Emma with her." Walter and his companions were so angered by this maneuver that they attacked the brewer and the other people of the house, one of whom fled into the High Street when he was hit by stones to raise the hue and cry. Walter was right behind him, with a knife in one hand and a dagger in the other. A crowd gathered and asked Walter to surrender. When he would not, someone grabbed a staff and bashed him over the head.

For other children . . . evening was a time for begging and for seeking a warm, dry place to sleep. Not all young people had the luxury of sleeping in a bed with thoughts of rising early to brush their clothes and make up their beds.

Games and Play

London adults knew that children must and would play. . . . We may think these games bloodthirsty and unfit for children: on Shrove Tuesday, schoolboys brought fighting cocks to their masters, and they all watched the cock fights. They also played ball in the London fields, with the scholars of each school having a team. London adult males went out on horseback to recall the days of their youth. Many of the games were unorganized, with the children taking the opportunities that lay in their parish to create diversions. They played ball and tag, ran races, played hoops, and imitated adult ceremonies such as royal entries, Masses, marriages, and the giants Gog and Magog. Again, Symon proves to be the moralist with some of the shrewdest observations!

> Child, climb not over house nor wall,
> For no fruit, birds nor ball.
> Child, over men's houses no stones fling,
> Nor at glass windows no stones sling. . . .
>
> And child, when thou goest to play,
> Look thou come home by light of day.

His lessons were very perceptive, as the coroners' inquests confirm. John atte Noke fell to his death when he climbed out a window to retrieve a ball that had landed in the gutter when he was playing. Seven-year-old Robert, son of John de St. Botulph, was playing with two other boys on pieces of timber when a piece fell on him and broke his right leg. Richard, son of John de Wrotham, would have done well to heed Symon's advice about getting home in daylight, for he went to a wharf on the Thames at vespers in October, fell in the river, and drowned. Six-year-old Philip, son of John de Turneye, was walking by a ditch after sunset and slipped and fell in.

Although it was unlikely that children of this age would use weapons in their bird hunts, their stone throwing could be as destructive as the games that older youth played. The city proclaimed in 1327 "against shooting pigeons and other birds perched on St. Paul's or on the houses of citizens, with stone bows and arbalests [a type of bow], because the missiles frequently break the windows and wound passers-by."

Children also participated in games of the "sad and wise," such as horse racing. Being of light build, lads of twelve or thereabouts acted as jockeys to put horses through their paces at Smithfield. In York, two Londoners set a wager about which of two horses would arrive at a cross called "grymstone cross," standing midway between York and Hull. A child was to ride each horse—one starting at Hull and the other at York—always keeping to the right of way. But the man starting off one of the horses put his hands on it and sent it off to the fallow, thus throwing the child rider and breaking the rules of the race. The child was not hurt, but the wager was lost. In general, the boys must have enjoyed such opportunities to ride a swift horse. In the countryside, they seem to have delighted in watering the plow horses after a day's work in the fields.

The urban environment of many cities, including London, provided a number of parades and pageants . . . that involved children and certainly entertained them. In addition, some celebrations were reserved for children. The most notable was that of the boy bishops, whose festivities coincided with the Christmas season, beginning on

St. Nicholas's Day (December 6) and ending on Holy Innocents (December 28) or the Feast of St. William (in honor of the boy said to have been murdered by the Jews of Norwich [January 7]). St. Nicholas's association with young scholars goes back to a legend about two young boys on their way to Athens to study. Their father had instructed them to visit Bishop Nicholas in Myra, but they decided to see to the arrival of their goods and rest for a visit the next day. The landlord, seeing their wealth, killed them and cut them into little pieces to sell as pickled pork. Bishop Nicholas (later a saint) had a vision about the disaster and hurried to the inn. He reprimanded the innkeeper and sought his forgiveness from heaven. His wish was granted, and the pieces of the boys emerged from the brine tub and reassembled. The bishop then sent the boys off, amid great rejoicing, to their studies in Athens.

The oddity of the boy-bishop celebration was that it disassembled the bishop, rather than the boys. The best or most favored scholar was elected from the school to impersonate the bishop as *Episcopus Puerorum*. The rest of the boys formed his dean and prebends [assistant clergy]. The boys took over the church or cathedral for the services and the sermon, ousting the real bishop. It was one of those medieval, world-turned-topsy-turvy events. The boys, whose life seemed all discipline, were given a taste of the power to discipline. They also got to travel in style with their "clergy," stopping at parish homes and religious houses to ask for alms and offerings. They progressed with fine ceremonial copes, rings, and crosses. Like any bishop, they expected a gracious meal and gifts. They sat with the host above the salt and discussed matters of papal dispensations and finer points of philosophy. A sample of their wisdom is preserved in a few of their sermons. What insufferable young twits these boys must have been for a fortnight at Christmas! At least it gave them a chance to taste the power they might someday have and to let off some of the aggressions that had built up under severe discipline during the year. The boys could be rather cute as well. London parishes were reluctant to see the celebration abolished during the Reformation and restored it under Mary Tudor.

Catherine of Siena

Phyllis McGinley

Despite humble origins, Catherine of Siena (1347–1380) was one of the leading figures of the fourteenth century. As a young woman, she opted for a religious life. Her ideas and strong personality soon made her known across Italy; she corresponded with kings, princes, and even the pope himself. During the Great Schism, she was a tireless advocate of Pope Urban's claim to the papacy. She was canonized, or officially declared a saint, in 1461.

This selection comes from Phyllis McGinley's book *Saint-Watching*, which is a compendium of information about various saints through the ages. McGinley is a novelist and poet known for her books on many different subjects.

The most shining name of [the fourteenth] century . . . is that of Catherine, Siena's saint and still most famous citizen. And she was neither noble nor a scholar. She at whose bidding princes put down their arms and popes changed their ways of life was born in 1347, the youngest of the twenty-five children of Giacomo Benincasa, a dyer, and his wife Lapa. Poor Lapa. She has not come off very well at the hands of biographers. They make her out a temper-ridden woman, cross and sharp-tongued. But having to cope with twenty-five lively children as well as a disobedient mystic seems to me excuse enough for a hard word now and then.

Actually, her only faults appear to have been that same quick tongue and the perfectly natural ambition that her yellow-haired Catherine should make a good marriage. She was no visionary but a mother, and she could not for the life of her understand why her daughter should be plagued with extravagant holiness. One fancies her saying to herself, "Adolescents! Forever dramatizing themselves! We'll see what a bit of discipline will do for those day dreams."

So she nagged the girl to marry until Catherine in a gesture of defiance cut off all her beautiful hair. Any mother might well be annoyed at that, and Lapa did her best to exorcise what she thought of as the devil out of her stubborn child. She set her doing the hardest work of the household, deprived her of her bedroom, and forced her to wait on the rest of the family like a servant. Catherine, however, was a match for her peppery parent. She simply did as she was told so charmingly that in frustration her father and finally her mother gave way in everything. Catherine was allowed to lead her own extraordinary life—to shut herself up to prayer and meditation in a little cell of her own. Almost all saints begin so. They spend an early time of physical inactivity and mystical exercise, like athletes preparing for a contest. Indeed, that is what they are: athletes of the spirit. Catherine was a prodigy, and long before she was twenty her preparations were done and she left her cell to begin a mission to the world.

At first she went into the hospitals and the houses of the poor. A plague swept Italy, and she nursed the sick with the same single-mindedness she had expended on her prayers. The sweetness of her nature and the success of her work so endeared her to Siena that in a year or two she became the center of a group of notable disciples. This fellowship, called the Caterinati, consisted of "old and young, priests and laymen, poets and politicians," most of whom she had rescued from lives of illness, idleness, or vice. One of them was the artist Andrew Vanni, who painted the portrait we still have of her. Another was Neri de Landoccio, the poet. The rest followed a dozen different professions. They were united only as followers of this indomitable girl whom they affectionately called "Mama" although she was younger than any of them.

From Siena her fame spread to all of Italy and eventually to the rest of Europe. She advised kings. She intervened between political war parties. She helped draw up treaties of peace. At this time the Pope was living in exile in Avignon, and Rome had nearly fallen apart for lack of central government. Catherine performed the tremendous feat of coaxing a timorous pontiff back to his proper see in the face of hostility and the arguments of France, which preferred that the Pope live in its sphere of influence. Although Catherine never learned to write, she did learn to dictate, and her letters, addressed to half the great of Europe, are famous for their persuasive skill and boldness of insight. She also composed two books, *The Dialogues of Catherine* and *A Treatise of Divine Providence*, which theologians for years discussed and pondered.

She died at thirty-three, so renowned that she has been called "the greatest woman in Christendom." The whole world wept for her. Her character was so original and inflexible that she does not come through to us so delightfully as does, say, [Saint] Teresa. But her political and moral triumphs were as enormous as her personal prestige. The historian who belittles feminine talent before the eighteenth century is unwise to overlook her.

A Medieval Play

Author unknown

Theater in the fourteenth century was quite different from theater today. Few stages and indeed few structures were dedicated to drama. Typically, strolling troupes of players traveled through cities and towns and performed in public buildings and squares. Advertising was by word of mouth, and admission was a donation. Poor donations in a community simply meant that the troupe would go elsewhere the next year. The troupes were small and performed with minimal costumes and props. Usually the same people served in both acting and technical capacities, and the same actor might play two, three, or more parts.

The repertory of these medieval companies varied. Since comparatively few of the plays they performed were ever written down, most are known to us today only through their titles—if indeed their titles were noted anywhere. Most of what survives from fourteenth-century Europe has a strong religious connection: either retellings of biblical stories, such as the Creation or Noah and the Flood, or plays that use biblical figures to make moral points. There were some more secular plays, too, especially ones designed for comic effect, but even these often had equal doses of humor and morality.

This excerpt is a version of a fourteenth-century play. "The Play of St. George," sometimes called "St. George and the Dragon." While the language, cast of characters, and the length of the play may vary depending on the specific version presented, the basic idea of the drama remains the same: a struggle between St. George, patron saint of England, and a host of fourteenth-century enemies, real and imagined. It is an excellent example of drama in the 1300s.

Excerpted from *The Play of St. George* (13th to 15th Century) by author unknown, reconstructed from memory by Thomas Hardy.

Characters

FATHER CHRISTMAS
SAINT GEORGE
VALIANT SOLDIER
TURKISH KNIGHT
DOCTOR
THE SARACEN [Arabian knight]

[*Enter* FATHER CHRISTMAS. *He walks round swinging his club and clearing the room.*]
FATHER CHRISTMAS. Here come I, old Father Christmas;
Welcome or welcome not,
I hope old Father Christmas
Will never be forgot:—
Although it's Father Christmas I've a short time to stay,
But I've come to show you pleasure before I pass away!
Make room, make room, my gallants, room,
And give us space to rhyme;
We've come to show Saint George's play
Upon this Christmas time.
And if you don't believe my words, I straight call out, Walk in,
Walk in, O Valiant Soldier, and boldly now begin!

[*Enter the* VALIANT SOLDIER]
VALIANT SOLDIER. Here come I, the Valiant Soldier,
Slasher is my name,
With sword and buckler by my side
I hope to win the game.
One of my brethren I've seen wounded,
Another I've seen slain,
So I will fight with any foe
Upon this British plain.
Yes, with my sword and with my spear
To 'fend the right, I'll battle here!

[*Enter the* TURKISH KNIGHT.]
TURKISH KNIGHT. Here come I, the Turkish Knight,
Come from Turkish land to fight;
I'll fight Saint George and all his crew,
Aye, countryfolk and warriors too.
Who is this man with courage bold?
If his blood's hot, I'll make it cold!
VALIANT SOLDIER [*coming forward*]. If
thou art called the Turkish Knight,
Draw out thy sword, and let us fight!

I am the friend of good Saint George,
I've fought men o'er and o'er,
And for the sake of good Saint George
I'd fight a hundred more.
    [*They fight. The* VALIANT SOLDIER *falls.*]
To slay this false Knight did I try—
'Tie for the right I have to die! [*Dies.*]
    TURKISH KNIGHT [*marching round*]. If Saint George but meet me here,
I'll try his mettle without fear!

        [*Enter* SAINT GEORGE.]
    SAINT GEORGE. Here come I, Saint George, the Valiant man,
    With glittering sword and spear in hand,
Who fought the Dragon boldly, and brought him to the slaughter,
By which I won fair Sabra, the King of Egypt's daughter.
    So haste away, make no delay,
    For I can give some lusty thumps,
    And, like a true born Eriglishman,
    Fight on my legs or on my stumps!
What mortal man would dare to stand
Before me with my sword in hand?
    TURKISH KNIGHT [*advancing*]. Make not so bold, Saint George, I pray;
Though thou'rt all this, thou'rt one I'll slay!
    SAINT GEORGE. My blood is hot as any fire,
    So I must say thee Nay,
For with my trusty sword and spear
    I'll take *thy* life away!
    TURKISH KNIGHT. Then thou and I will battle try.
    SAINT GEORGE. And if I conquer thou shalt die!
So give me leave, I'll give thee battle,
And quickly make thy bones to rattle!
        [*They fight. The* TURKISH KNIGHT *is wounded and falls upon*
        one knee.]
    TURKISH KNIGHT. Can there a doctor come to me
From anywhere in this countree?
    FATHER CHRISTMAS [*looking about*]. Is there a doctor to be found?
To cure this man of his deadly wound?
For whatsoever wrath you feel
Toward your foeman, we must heal.

    [*Enter the* DOCTOR, *a bottle strapped under his arm.*]
    DOCTOR. Yes, there's a doctor to be found
To cure this man of his deadly wound.
With this small bottle that you see
I cure all evils there can be;

The phthisic [tuberculosis], the palsy and the gout,
If the devil's in I'll blow him out.

FATHER CHRISTMAS. Doctor then, O what's thy fee,
For doing of this great merc-y?

DOCTOR. Fifty pound is my fee,
But ten pound less I'll take of thee.

FATHER CHRISTMAS. What dost say, eh? Half a crown?

DOCTOR. No. I tell thee forty poun'—
A small sum that to save a man,
And you've the money in your han'.

FATHER CHRISTMAS. Try thy skill; it must be so,
Whe'r I pay thy fee or no.
Small money have I, but do thy best,
And trust the victors for the rest.

> [*The* DOCTOR *restores the* KNIGHT *by giving him a draught
> from the bottle he carries. Exit* DOCTOR. *The fight is resumed.
> But the* TURKISH KNIGHT *sinks by degrees, and is at last killed
> by* SAINT GEORGE.]

SAINT GEORGE. The first one, Father, now is dead:
Call in the second, that Champion whom I dread.

> [FATHER CHRISTMAS *looks about, but nobody appears. Pause.*]

Where is the Saracen? He doth so long delay,
That hero of renown, I long to show him play!

[*Enter the* SARACEN *with a loud strut.*]

SARACEN. The Saracen behold in me:
I am the man who'll conquer thee!
My head is cased in iron, my body in steel;
I'll fight with thee, Saint George, and make thee feel! [*Looks at the
dead bodies.*]
O see what blood Saint George has spilled in fight;
I'll vanquish him before I sleep this night.

SAINT GEORGE. Since then 'tis not against thy will,
Nor yet against thy might,
If thou canst battle with Saint George
Draw out thy sword and smite.

> [*They fight. The* SARACEN *falls wounded.*]

Tremble, thou tyrant, for thy sin that's past,
Tremble to think to-night shall be thy last;
My conquering arm shall send thy fire and fume
By one more stroke to thy eternal doom;
Aye, I, despite the steel thou boastest so,
Dispatch thee now to where the wicked go.

SARACEN. O pardon me, Saint George. Thy pardon now I crave,
O pardon me this night, and I will be thy slave!

SAINT GEORGE. I never will pardon thee, thou Saracen,
But rise, and draw, and we will fight again!

[*The* SARACEN *rises. They fight. The* SARACEN *is killed and his head cut off.*]

FATHER CHRISTMAS [*advances*]. To greet our ears, O what wild moans
Throughout this fight, and what deep groans!
Is there a doctor to be found
That can raise dead men from the ground,
So as to have them for to stand
And walk again upon this land?
I've heard of a mill that grinds old people young
But not of a leech to give these dead men tongue!

SAINT GEORGE. Yes, that same doctor can be found
To raise these dead men from the ground,
So as to have them for to stand
And walk again upon the land.

FATHER CHRISTMAS. Then, Doctor, Doctor, prithee come,
And raise these men now dead and dumb:
Saint George, thyself hadst better call him here,
To save these corpses from the dreadful bier.

SAINT GEORGE. I warrant he'll answer to my call;
[*Calls.*] Doctor, haste here and save them all!

[*Enter* DOCTOR *slowly.*]

FATHER CHRISTMAS. Ha, Doctor, is it in thy skill
To cure dead men as if but ill?

DOCTOR. Being a doctor of great fame
Who from the ancient countries came,
And knowing Asia, Afric-ay,
And every mystery out that way,
I've learned to do the best of cures
For all the human frame endures.
I can restore a leg or arm
From mortification or from harm,
I can repair a sword-slit pate,
A leg cut off—if not too late.

FATHER CHRISTMAS. But, Doctor—

DOCTOR. Yea, more; this little bottle of alicumpane [*Touches the bottle.*]
Will raise dead men to walk the earth again!

FATHER CHRISTMAS. That is, forsooth, a strange refrain!
Try thy skill on these men slain.

DOCTOR. A hundred guineas is my fee
And nothing less I'll take of thee.

[FATHER CHRISTMAS *starts astonished.*]

SAINT GEORGE. Such money I will freely give
If that thou mak'st these men to live.
DOCTOR [*advancing to the fallen men*].
I put a drop to each soldier's heart. [*He holds his bottle to the lips and to the heart of each, adding slowly.*]
Rise—Champions—and—all—play—your—part!
> [*They rise inch by inch*, FATHER CHRISTMAS, SAINT GEORGE *and the* DOCTOR *singing a slow song or chant as they rise. A lively song follows from the whole company, walking round. Exeunt omnes, except* FATHER CHRISTMAS.]

FATHER CHRISTMAS. You needs will have confest [confessed]
That our calling is the best,
But now we won't delay, lest tediousness befall.
And I wish you a Merry Christmas, and God bless you all!
> [*Exit* FATHER CHRISTMAS.]

Food in the Fourteenth Century

Reay Tannahill

Examining a culture's food tells a great deal about the way ordinary people lived their lives and how their lives differed from those of the nobility. In this excerpt, Reay Tannahill, a British writer and one of the world's leading authorities on food throughout history, takes a close look at the fourteenth century's menus, cookery, and techniques for preserving food—all very different from the world of today.

Most of what is known about medieval food comes from court catering records or the kitchen account books of monasteries and noble households, which are informative about raw materials, prices and quantities. For recipes and general culinary lore there is a handful of works on cookery and etiquette. All of them, with the notable exception of the domestic manual compiled by a fourteenth-century Parisian merchant known as the *Ménagier,* have one serious historical failing—they relate to the kitchens and dining halls of the great nobles and landowners.

From the historical point of view these manuscripts also have other failings. Still, as of old, the recipes are carefree about quantities, seldom specify whether salted or fresh meat should be used and never trouble to spell out heat intensities or cooking times. Not that the authors can be criticized for this. Such manuscripts were originally intended as *aides-mémoire* [memory aids] for the cooks (usually royal) who wrote them, or for assistants or successors who would know without having to be told not only how to deal with the preliminaries when salted or dried foods were being used, but also most of the other essentials necessary to the production of dishes with which they were already, in general terms, familiar. What the cooks' manuals do, in effect, is supply the details of medieval food preparation without the guiding principles.

The first principle, of course, was to ensure—in days when an instruction to "soak in several changes of water" involved some scullion [kitchen servant] in numerous trips to the well—that salt meat and fish were as thoroughly desalted as soaking could make them. That this first principle was often flouted is shown by the number of remedies in the medieval cook's armoury.

The basic expedient was to hang a linen bag of oatmeal in the cauldron to absorb some of the excess, but the cook commonly ensured that the menu as a whole had a salt-neutralizing bias. Some dishes were routinely offered as accompaniments to others for that very reason.

Where potatoes or rice might be used today as side dishes that help to soak up the salt without themselves becoming salty, the Middle Ages relied on dried peas, dried beans, breadcrumbs or whole grain. Puréed beans with bacon was the standard combination in poorer households, but the rich preferred frumenty, mortrews or blamanger—the forerunners of today's bread sauce.

By medieval times frumenty had become a thick pudding of whole wheat and almond milk sometimes enriched with egg yolks and coloured with saffron. It was the standard accompaniment for venison. Mortrews, which took its name from the mortar in which the ingredients were pounded, was made by mixing boiled and puréed white meat or fish with breadcrumbs, stock and eggs, and then reducing it over the fire; a sprinkling of pepper and ginger added the finishing touch. For blank mang or blamanger (the scarcely recognizable ancestor of the modern blancmange) shredded chicken was mixed with boiled rice and almond milk, then seasoned with sugar and salt; aniseed and fried almonds were the correct garnish.

The cook's other recourses were to employ spices or fruit to offset saltiness, and/or creamy sauces to smooth it out. Some medieval recipes look almost as fearsome as Roman ones, with unspecified quantities of ginger, pepper, saffron, cinnamon, cloves and mace, but although these may, in truth, have been no more than the equivalent of "a pinch of mixed spice," it seems as if medieval cooks may have used rather more than a pinch. The starches and creams that reduce saltiness also reduce the intensity of the spices themselves, and in some types of dish the spices would scarcely have been discernible unless they were used generously. Nor had the medieval host any more desire to hide his expensive spices under a bushel than his Roman predecessors had done.

"Pumpes," for example (which, except for the choice of meat, sound very much as if they might have come from a kitchen in Baghdad) were a fairly typical dish, and made as follows:

"Take and boil a good piece of pork, and not too lean, as tender as you may; then take it up and chop it as small as you may; then take cloves and mace, and chop forth withall, and also chop forth with raisins of Corinth; then take it and roll it as round as you may, like to small pellets, at two inches about, then lay them on a dish by themselves; then make a good almond milk, and blend it with flour of rice, and let it boil well, but look that it be quite runny; and at the dresser, lay five pumpes in a dish, and pour the pottage thereon. And if you will, set on every pumpe a flower, and over them strew on sugar enough and mace: and serve them forth. And some men make the pellets of veal or beef, but pork is best and fairest."

Game and Fish

Much of the rich man's time was taken up with hunting. He enjoyed the exercise as much as the game he came home with, and for the cook game was certainly less trouble all round, although even the finest roast had to be accompanied by one or more spicy dipping sauces. The dipping sauce was so generally useful that in Paris the professional saucemaker had become a familiar figure by the fourteenth century. Included in his repertoire were "yellow sauce," in which ginger and saffron predominated; "green sauce," with ginger, cloves, cardamom and green herbs; and "cameline sauce"—the great fourteenth-century favourite—in which cinnamon was the essential ingredient.

According to Guillaume Tirel, cook to Charles V of France and compiler of the 1375 cookery book *Le Viandier de Taillevent,* cameline was made as follows. "Pound ginger, plenty of cinnamon, cloves, cardamom, mace, long pepper if you wish, then squeeze out bread soaked in vinegar and strain all together and salt it just right." The English version had one or two additional refinements. "Take raisins of Corinth, and kernels of nuts, and crust of bread and powder of ginger, cloves, flour of cinnamon, pound it well together and add it thereto. Salt it, temper it up with vinegar, and serve it forth."

Dried fish, the other mainstay of the menu, was a pallid food that needed to be livened up with mustard or vinegar or disguised with spices or fruit. It was one of the greatest challenges to the cook's ingenuity during periods when the Church took a firm stand on fasting. Then, meat, eggs and dairy products were forbidden on Wednesdays, Fridays, Saturdays and the whole of Lent—half the days of the year.

One masterly way of dealing with stockfish was "lenten ryschewys," a kind of fruity rissole [deep-fried cake filled with meat or fish] encased in batter. "Take figs and boil them up in ale; then take when they be tender and pound them small in a mortar; then take almonds, and shred them thereto small; take pears and shred them thereto; take dates and shred them thereto; and take [dried haddock or ling] that is well soaked and shred thereto." The resulting paste was shaped, floured, dipped in batter and fried in oil. . . .

The Menu

There is a dismal monotony about the peasant menu across the continents and across the centuries that is probably more apparent than real: in China rice, vegetables and perhaps a mouthful of pork; in India rice, vegetables and a spicy sauce; in Mexico maize pancakes or beans, with tomatoes and peppers; in northern Europe dark bread, cabbage, beans or salt pork from the stockpot, with curds to round off the meal.

These, however, were only the basics, and because they sound dull it is too easy to assume that they *were* dull. Yet there must have been good cooks in the fourteenth century, as in the twentieth, cooks who knew how to make use of the seasonal bounty of the countryside. Some peasants in some places may have eaten consistently well.

Even so, the servants in the castles and fortified houses of the countryside were more reliably catered for. Most of their meals might consist of pease pudding, salt herring or dried cod, followed by cheese and washed down with ale brewed on the estate, but their bread was a decent maslin and occasionally they had beef or goose to eat with it, or even a few leftover delicacies from the lord's table (though the beggar at the gate had first call on these).

By the fourteenth century, however, there was a new class in the population, still closer to the peasantry than to the nobility, but with a positive identity of its own. In the dinners given by its members, especially the prosperous town merchants, the particular character of the medieval cuisine is displayed more clearly than in the banquets of the great.

The menu at this time bore very little resemblance to today's. It was as if *table d'hôte* [a fixed-price full course meal] and *à la carte* [a separate price for each menu item] were one and the same thing, with the alternative dishes in each course all being placed on the table at the same time. A "course" was a more or less haphazard assortment, its only real consistency that it offered a wide choice within itself; not until the sixteenth century did there emerge some degree of unity. The diner surveyed what was on offer, and made his own choice—some of this, some of that—with no compulsion to take a platterful of everything, even if the option existed.

In Paris in 1393 a merchant's guests might have been offered the following.

First Course	Second Course
Miniature pastries filled with cod liver or beef marrow	"The best roast that may be had"
	Freshwater fish
A cameline "brewet" —pieces of meat in a thin cinnamon sauce	Broth with bacon
	A meat tile
Beef marrow fritters	Capon pasties and crisps
Eels in a thick, spicy purée	Bream and eel pasties
Loach in a cold green sauce flavoured with spices and sage	Blank mang (blamanger)
Large joints of meat, roasted or boiled	Third Course
Saltwater fish	Frumenty
Fritters	Venison
Roast bream and darioles	
Sturgeon	Lampreys with hot sauce
Jellies	

After the meal the board was cleared to make way for dessert, which encompassed a variety of sweet and spicy confections. Either then or later, spiced wines and wafers were served, as well as dry whole spices "to help the digestion."

It is the menu rather than the individual dish that divides the fourteenth century so irrevocably from the twentieth. A "meat tile," for example—pieces of sautéd chicken or veal, with a spiced sauce of pounded crayfish tails, almonds and toasted bread, and a garnish of whole crayfish tails might be quite acceptable at a modern table if the rest of the meal were light and fresh-flavoured. But balance was lacking from the medieval menu.

On the tables of the rich there would be fewer fish dishes (except on fast days) and more game birds and beasts. The overall number of dishes would also be much greater than those offered on the middle levels of society. But where the aristocratic table differed most strikingly was in presentation. The medieval world, still only marginally literate, compensated by being intensely visual, and its delight in architecture, painting, silverware and costume overflowed onto the rich man's table in the form of gilded swans, peacocks in all their plumage and extravagant "soteltes" (subtleties)—sweets, jellies or pastries moulded into splendid and fanciful representations of lions, eagles, crowns or coats of arms. When sugar became readily available in the sixteenth century, Italian confectioners won a high reputation for the intricacy of their spun-sugar sculptures.

As the Middle Ages merged into the Renaissance and became fascinated by Classical antiquity, even more exotic conversation pieces were invented. . . .

To make pies that the birds may be alive in them
and fly out when it is cut up

Make the coffin [piecrust] of a great pie or pasty. In the bottom thereof make a hole as big as your fist, or bigger if you will. Let the sides of the coffin be somewhat higher than ordinary pies. Which done, put it full of flour and bake it, and being baked, open the hole in the bottom and take out the flour. Then, having a pie of the bigness of the hole in the bottom of the coffin aforesaid, you shall put it into the coffin, withal put into the said coffin round about the aforesaid pie as many small live birds as the empty coffin will hold, besides the [small] pie aforesaid. And this is to be done at such time as you send the pie to the table, and set before the guests: where, uncovering or cutting up the great lid of the pie, all the birds will fly out, which is to delight and pleasure show to the company. And that they be not altogether mocked, you shall cut open the small pie.

Petrarch

Francesco Petrarch

Francesco Petrarca (1304–1374), or Petrarch as he is known in the English-speaking world, was a scholar and a poet. He is perhaps best known for a series of love poems and for his work to popularize classical literature. However, Petrarch was also an enthusiastic writer of letters and a philosopher. His effect on literature and thought was enormous. For his rejection of medieval ideas of poetry, he has been called the first modern poet; for his forward-thinking philosophy, he has been termed the first poet of the Renaissance. He wrote in both Latin and Italian. This selection encompasses nearly all of Petrarch's "Letter to Posterity," which serves as a brief autobiography of the first part of his life. At some point in the writing he broke off and never finished the work. The excerpt gives a sense of Petrarch's playfulness, wit, and attention to details—such as specific times—not necessarily valued by people of his period.

You may perhaps have heard something about me—although it is doubtful that my poor little name may travel far in space and time. Still, you may by chance want to know what sort of man I was or what was the fate of my works, especially of those whose reputation may have persisted, or whose name you may have vaguely heard. There will be various opinions on this score, for most people's words are prompted not by truth but by whim. There is no measure for praise or blame. But I was one of your own flock, a little mortal man, neither of high nor base origin, of an old family—as Augustus Caesar says of himself—and by nature not evil or brazen, except as contagious custom infected me. Youth led me astray, young manhood corrupted me, but maturer age corrected me and taught me

by experience the truth of what I had read long before: that youth
and pleasure are vain. This is the lesson of that Author of all times
and ages, who permits wretched mortals, puffed with vain wind, to
stray for a time until, though late in life, they become mindful of
their sins.

In my youth I was blessed with an active, agile body, though not
particularly strong. I can't boast of being handsome, but in my
greener years I made a good impression. I had a fine complexion,
between light and dark, ardent eyes, and a vision that was for many
years very sharp. (But it failed me unexpectedly when I was over
sixty, so that I was forced reluctantly to the use of spectacles. Old
age suddenly took possession of my body, which had always been
perfectly healthy, and assailed me with its usual train of illnesses.)

I have always been a great scorner of money—not that I shouldn't
like to be rich, but because I hated the labors and cares that are the
inseparable companions of wealth. I escaped the trouble of giving
sumptuous feasts; but I led a happier life with a simple diet and common foods than all the successors of Apicius with their gourmet dinners. I never liked so-called banquets, which are mere festivals of
gluttony, hostile to sobriety and good manners. I have always
thought it tiresome and useless to invite others formally, and no less
so to be invited by others. But I have always been happy to take a
meal with friends, so that I have never found anything pleasanter
than their unannounced appearance; and I have never willingly sat
down without a friend. Nothing annoyed me more than display, not
only because it is bad in itself and the enemy of humility, but because it is troublesome and disturbing.

When I was young I was racked by an overwhelming love affair—but it was pure and it was my only one. I should still be racked
by it, had not death, bitter but providential for me, extinguished the
flames when they were already cooling. Certainly I wish I could say
that I have been free from lusts of the flesh, but if I should say so I
should be lying. But this I can surely say, that when I was drawn to
them by the ardor of my age and by my temperament, I always in-
wardly detested their vileness. When in fact I was nearing forty and
my vigor and impulses were still strong, I renounced not only that
obscene act but the very recollection of it, as if I had never looked
at a woman. I number that among my highest blessings, and I thank
God, who freed me when still sound and vigorous from that vile
servitude, always odious to me.

But let me change the subject. Pride I recognized in others, not in
myself; and though I was a person of small account, I was of even
less account in my own esteem. As for wrath, it often did harm to
me, never to others. I may frankly say, since I know I am telling the
truth, that though I have a touchy spirit, I readily forget offenses and

well remember benefits received. I have been very desirous of honorable friendships and have faithfully cherished them. It is the torture of the elderly that they must so often mourn the death of those dear to them. I was lucky enough to be intimate with kings and princes and to hold the friendship of nobles, to the point of arousing envy. But I held aloof from many of whom I was very fond; my love of freedom was so deeply implanted in me that I carefully shunned those whose high standing seemed to threaten my freedom. Some of the greatest kings of our time have loved me and cultivated my friendship. Why I don't know; that is their affair. When I was their guest it was more as if they were mine. I was never made uncomfortable by their eminence; I derived from it many advantages.

My mind was rather well balanced than keen, adept for every good and wholesome study, but especially inclined to moral philosophy and poetry. I neglected poetry in the course of time, finding my pleasure in sacred literature, wherein I discovered a hidden sweetness which I had previously despised, and I came to regard poetry as merely decorative. I devoted myself, though not exclusively, to the study of ancient times, since I always disliked our own period; so that, if it hadn't been for the love of those dear to me, I should have preferred being born in any other age, forgetting this one; and I always tried to transport myself mentally to other times. Thus I have delighted in the historians, though troubled by their disagreements. In case of doubt I decided either according to verisimilitude [the appearance of truth] or the authority of the writer.

People have said that my utterance is clear and compelling, but it seems to me weak and obscure. In fact in my ordinary speech with friends and familiars I have never worried about fine language; I am amazed that Caesar Augustus took such care about it. When, however, the subject matter or the circumstances of the hearer seemed to demand something else, I have taken some pains with style, I don't know if effectively or not. Those to whom I spoke must decide. If only I have lived well, I make small account of how I have spoken. To seek reputation by mere elegance of language is only vainglory.

Early Years

My parents were worthy people, of Florentine origin, middling well-off, indeed, to confess the truth, on the edge of poverty. As they were expelled from their home city, I was born in exile in Arezzo [an Italian city southeast of Florence], in the 1304th year of Christ's era, at dawn on a Monday, the 20th of July.

Either circumstances or my own choices have thus disposed my life up to now. Most of my first year was spent in Arezzo, where Nature had brought me to birth; the six years following in Incisa, the home of my paternal ancestors, fourteen miles from Florence. (My mother had had her exile remitted.) The eighth year was spent in Pisa, the ninth and later years in Transalpine Gaul, on the left bank of the Rhone. The city's name is Avignon, where the Roman Pontiff kept, and still keeps, the Church of Christ in shameful exile [a reference to the Great Schism]. . . .

So there on the banks of that windy river I spent my boyhood under the care of my parents, and my youth under the direction only of my own vanities. There were, however, considerable breaks, for at that time I spent a full four years in Carpentras, a small city not far to the eastward. In both these places I learned a little grammar, dialectic, and rhetoric, fitted to my age. And how much one commonly learns in the schools, or how little, you know well, dear reader. Then I went to study law at Montpellier for four years, and then to Bologna, where I took a three-year course and heard lectures on the whole body of civil law. Many asserted that I would have done very well if I had persisted in my course. But I dropped that study entirely as soon as my parents' supervision was removed. Not because I disliked the power and authority of the law, which are undoubtedly very great, or the law's saturation with Roman antiquity, which I love; but because law practice is befouled by its practitioners. I had no taste for learning a trade which I would not practice dishonestly and could not honestly. If I had been willing to practice, my principles would have been ascribed to incompetence.

Thus at twenty-two I came home. Since custom has nearly the force of nature, I call "home" that Avignon exile, where I had lived since childhood. I was already beginning to be known there, and my acquaintance was sought out by important people. Why, I now admit I don't know, and I wonder at it; but then I did not wonder at all, because, in the manner of young men, I thought I was most worthy of every honor. I was especially welcomed by the eminent and noble Colonna family, which then attended, or better, adorned the Roman Curia [the body governing the Catholic Church]. I was received by them, and honored in a way that might possibly be justified now, but certainly was not so then. I was taken to Gascony by the illustrious, the incomparable Giacomo Colonna, then Bishop of Lombez, whose like I doubt if I have ever seen or ever shall see. In the shadow of the Pyrenees I passed an almost celestial summer, with host and companions in a common mood of high spirits. Returning, I was attached to his brother, Cardinal Giovanni Colonna, for many years, not as if to an employer but as to a father, or rather as to a very affectionate brother. I was practically independent, in my own home.

At that time my youthful curiosity tempted me to visit France and Germany. And although other reasons were alleged to gain the approval of my superiors for this journey, the real reason was my ardent desire to see something new. In that excursion I first saw Paris, and I took pleasure in finding out what was true and what fabulous in the tales of that city. After my return I made a trip to Rome, which I had longed to see from childhood on. There I paid my court to the great-spirited father of the family, Stefano Colonna, a man cast in the antique mold, and I was so warmly welcomed by him that one would say he made no distinction between me and one of his own sons. This excellent man's affectionate good will persisted until the end of his life, and it is still vivid in my spirit, and will not fade until I cease to be.

Back again, I could not bear the congenital irritation and disgust I feel for all cities, but most of all for that abhorrent Avignon. Seeking some haven, I discovered a very narrow valley, but solitary and delightful, called Vaucluse [Closed Valley], fifteen miles from Avignon, where the Sorgue, king of all fountains, has its source. Captured by the charm of the place, I transported my books and myself thither when I had passed my thirty-fourth birthday. It would make a long story if I should tell what I did there, through many a year. In a nutshell: almost all my little works were either completed or begun or conceived there; they were so abundant that even to the present they keep me busy and worn out. My mind was like my body, marked more by agility than strength; thus I easily conceived many projects which I dropped because of the difficulty of execution. The very aspect of my retreat suggested my undertaking my *Bucolicum carmen*, a book about life in the woods, and two books of my *De vita solitaria*, dedicated to my friend Philippe [de Cabassoles]. He was always a great man, but then he was the insignificant Bishop of Cavaillon. Now he is a cardinal and the great Bishop of Sabina, and the last survivor of all my old friends. He loved me, and still loves me, not episcopally [as a bishop], . . . but as a brother.

Africa and Other Concerns

One Good Friday, as I was wandering in the hills, a compelling inspiration came to me to write an epic poem about that first Scipio Africanus [a Roman general], whose glorious name had been dear to me since boyhood. I called it *Africa*, after its hero. By some good fate, whether the book's or my own, it was acclaimed even before publication. I began it with a great burst of enthusiasm, but soon, distracted by various concerns, I put it aside.

While I was leading my retired life there, in a single day . . . arrived letters from the Roman Senate and from the Chancellor of the University of Paris. They summoned me, as if in competition, to receive the laurel crown of poetry in Rome and in Paris. With youthful exultation I thought myself worthy of the honor that men of such standing proposed. I measured my own merit by the testimony of others. But I hesitated a little as to which invitation I should heed.

So I wrote to the aforementioned Giovanni Colonna, asking his advice. He was nearby; I wrote to him late in the day, and I had his answer by nine the next morning. I followed his advice, and decided that the prestige of Rome was to be preferred to all else. (I still have the two letters containing my query and his approval.) So I went to Rome. And although, as is the way of youth, I was a very kindly judge of my own affairs, I was uneasy about accepting my own estimation of myself and that of my proposers. But they surely would not have made the offer if they hadn't thought me worthy of the honor.

I decided therefore to visit Naples first. I presented myself there to that noblest of kings and philosophers, Robert, illustrious in his government and in literature. He is the only king of our times who has been a friend of learning and of virtue. I asked him to examine me according to his own lights. Today I wonder—and I think you too, reader, will wonder, if you are well informed—at the warmth of his judgments and of his reception. When he learned the reason for my coming, he was delighted and amused at my youthful self-confidence. And perhaps he reflected that the honor I sought redounded to his own credit, since I had chosen him from all mortal men to be my only qualified critic. To be brief, after endless conversations on all sorts of subjects I showed him my *Africa*, which pleased him so much that he asked me to dedicate it to him. Naturally I could not and would not refuse. He then set a day to deal with my examination, and he kept me at it from noon to evening. And since the time was too short, with one thing leading to another, he did the same on the two following days. Thus, after sounding my ignorance for three days, he decided on the third day that I was worthy of the laurel. He wanted me to receive it in Naples and he begged me earnestly to agree; but my love for Rome was more mighty than the honorific instances of even so great a king. Finding that my purpose was inflexible, he gave me letters and escorts to the Roman Senate, whereby he benevolently stated his recommendation.

This royal judgment was echoed by many others and especially, in those days, by myself. But today I can't accept the unanimous verdict. There was more affection and encouragement to youth in it than conscientiousness.

Anyway, I went to Rome; and, unworthy as I was, bolstered by the royal judgment, I, who had been merely a raw student, received the poet's laurel crown, to the great joy of the Romans who could attend the ceremony. There are some letters of mine about this also, both in prose and in verse. The laurel did not increase my knowledge, though it did evoke a great deal of envy. But that is a longer tale than I can tell here.

From Rome I went to Parma, and spent some little time with the

Correggi, very worthy men and very generous to me, but much at odds with each other. They gave their city such a good government as it had never had within man's memory, and such as it is not likely to have again. I was very conscious of the honor I had just received and worried for fear that I should seem unworthy of it. Then one day I was climbing in the high hills beyond the Enza River in the Reggio region, and I came to a wood called Selvapiana. Suddenly struck by the beauty of the site, I was moved to pick up my interrupted *Africa*. My creative fervor roused from its torpor, and I wrote a little that very day, and somewhat more every day thereafter. Returning to Parma and finding there a secluded, quiet house (which I later bought and still own), I completed the work in a short time with so much ardor that today I am still amazed at it.

I then returned to the fountain of the Sorgue and to my transalpine solitude.

Religious Thought in the Fourteenth Century

Robert E. Lerner

As Robert E. Lerner argues in this selection from his book *The Age of Adversity*, a hodgepodge of religious movements gained importance in the fourteenth century. In some ways these ideas were new, in others they were simply a reworking of older philosophies; but in each case, as Lerner reports, they seemed to contradict much of what thirteenth-century theologians and philosophers had believed. This led to religious and civil conflict. Lerner argues that the ideas and the response of the Catholic Church to them presaged the Protestant Reformation of the sixteenth century.

The epitaph of a certain thirteenth-century theologian sums up a dominant intellectual attitude of the age. It said of him simply that "he knew all that there is to be known." The men of the thirteenth century felt so sure of themselves and their capacity to understand and make general statements about the nature of the world around them that there was no danger of this being taken as a jest. Such magnificent self-confidence, moreover, seemed to be fully justified by imposing achievement. Gothic cathedrals soared to the skies and dominated horizons in sharp contrast to earlier, earthbound structures. The sculpture and the glass of these awe-inspiring buildings told the whole story of men from the Creation to the Last Judgment and provided, as has often been said, an encyclopedia in pictures for those who could not read. For those who could read, encyclopedias in words were both plentiful and imposing, encompassing such subjects as history, natural history, law, and morals. Perhaps most impressive of all was the *Summa theologica* of St. Thomas Aquinas, a great summary of theology which endeavored to ask and answer, by the exercise of human reason, a huge number of bewildering metaphysical questions.

But in cultural matters, just as in economic and political life, the thirteenth century may have pushed too far too fast. While settlers, hungry for profits, tried to cultivate marginal lands, and kings, thirsting for power, demanded increasing obedience from their subjects, cathedrals toward the end of the century were built so high that they were either left unfinished or, as at Beauvais [France], actually collapsed. St. Thomas died at the height of his powers, and one account reports that shortly before his death he abandoned work on the *Summa*, saying "I cannot do it." The harmonious and majestic reconciliation that had given meaning and form to mediaeval civilization began to crumble just as men found themselves struggling for survival in the physical disarray of their society brought on by famine, plague, and war. Disillusioned by the moral and spiritual disintegration of the age, they sought security and salvation with desperate energy and ingenuity.

Modern readers tend to view the self-confidence of the thirteenth century with admiration and nostalgia, even to the extent, on the part of a few, of deeming the thirteenth the greatest of centuries in our entire tradition. This is probably because the idea of knowing all that can be known is totally foreign to our own intellectual powers or pretensions. In this attitude of mind we resemble the fourteenth century. During that period of economic and political instability, men seldom found the traditional answers adequate to meet the crushing new problems that seemed to arise on all sides. The change in mental attitude is graphically illustrated by the fact that the *summa* or summary, which had been a favorite compositional form of the thirteenth century, was replaced in the fourteenth century by the tract. This characteristic form of writing was addressed to particular, often practical, questions and written from all conceivable points of view, conservative and progressive. In certain respects the age indeed gives the impression of being intensely conservative and progressive at the same time. Yet even reactionary approaches frequently arrived at conclusions that were new, and with hindsight the fourteenth century can be seen as a period of gestation for some distinctly modern ideas. Such a view will be taken [here], but with a warning to the reader to bear constantly in mind that most "modern" movements were still minority movements and that the diversity of the age defies most attempts at formulation.

Having said this, one must reiterate that the men of the fourteenth century remained wholly mediaeval—which is to say profoundly religious. This does not mean that they were moral or pious, but that good or bad, weak or strong, they accepted unquestioningly the ultimate superiority of spiritual values in life. For this reason the humiliation of the papacy and the abuses of the clergy were traumatic. Their need for faith in God was if anything increased, with the result that the fourteenth century was a period of religious innovation in which many sought solace and salvation outside the established church. Those who did had the effective choice of attempting either to substitute intuitive religious experience (mysticism) for organized religious service or to develop their own personal formulation of necessary belief (heresy) in place of established dogma.

Mysticism

Mysticism [which supposed a direct link between the individual and God] had a long history within the development of Christianity. St. Augustine's *Confessions*, for example, radiate a mystical outlook, and the twelfth century produced one of the greatest mystics of all time in the person of St. Bernard. In the thirteenth century, however, mysticism was less prevalent because the mystic's search for God is intuitive and the age was fundamentally rational, preferring reason to intuition. The opposite was true of the fourteenth century, when rationalism was often questioned and mysticism became a dominant strain of European religiosity.

The first and greatest of the fourteenth-century mystics was the German Meister Eckhart (ca. 1260–1327), who, like St. Thomas Aquinas, was a member of the Dominican order [of monks]. Eckhart was trained in the scholasticism of St. Thomas but went beyond scholasticism to the study of Neoplatonism [the idea that the word is simply an emanation of God]. As [writer Solomon Katz] has explained, "the Neoplatonists sought to be in touch with the absolute, with the eternal, which they conceived as lying behind all phenomena." This striving for the union of the individual soul with the absolute became the major preoccupation of Meister Eckhart. Eckhart taught that by Divine Grace the essence of the soul, or "spark" as he called it, could be unified with God so long as the individual was prepared to dedicate himself entirely to this goal. Such an emphasis on the possibility of union between God and his creatures, however, verged dangerously near to pantheism [the belief that God is everywhere and everything] and as a result Eckhart was condemned for heresy by the papal court at Avignon. This judgment has become the source of some controversy. Few scholars would deny that Eckhart's language was so paradoxical and ambiguous that it might have disquieted orthodox theologians. Yet it also seems clear that despite his startling language Eckhart had no heretical intentions.

Eckhart's German disciples, Johann Tauler (ca. 1300–1361) and Heinrich Suso (ca. 1295–1366), were more cautious. Suso, speaking constantly about the sorrows of Christ, placed himself in the center of the orthodox tradition. Both Suso and Tauler avoided Eckhart's ambiguous references to the Trinity; they also divorced themselves from suspicions of pantheism by attacking pantheist heretics with great vigor, if not vituperation. A similar course was taken by mystics in other parts of Europe. In Flanders the great mystic Jan Ruysbroeck (1293–1381) followed the general pattern of Eckhart's thought but made a sharp and open break with pantheism, while in the South, mystics like the famous St. Catherine of Siena (1347–1380), acting without any direct relationship to the mysticism of the North, also pursued a more strictly orthodox and militant course.

The influence of this mystical current was manifold. Unlike earlier mystics, those of the fourteenth century were not content with pursuing their vision in seclusion and isolation. Eckhart and his followers had a message that they burned to share, and their most constant activity was the preaching of this message to as many people as would listen to it. Thus the most characteristic expressions of the movement were sermons composed and delivered in the German vernacular. These sermons take a pre-eminent place in the history of German culture because the constant use of German to express a complicated and ecstatic vision enriched the vernacular and helped to shape the course of German prose.

The spread of mysticism also resulted in an important movement for moral reform. Because the mystics insisted that union with God could be achieved only by the pure in heart, people became concerned with problems of morals and ethics. In Germany this concern helped to give purpose to life during a period of social incoherence. In addition, the practical aspect of the movement affected the course of education. Through the influence of Ruysbroeck, a community was established in Holland which educated the young in the so-called *Devotia moderna*, or new devotion. This Dutch community was to train some of the leading thinkers of future generations including the great [early sixteenth-century] Christian Humanist Erasmus. Mysticism also had an indisputable link with the Protestant Reformation. While men like Suso and Tauler were careful to insist upon their orthodoxy, their message stressed an inner response which by implication could easily be extended to a contempt for outward forms such as the sacraments. Tauler himself referred to the "inward-looking man" and declared that "churches make no man holy, but men make churches holy." The perpetuation of such sentiments helped to foster a gradual alienation from the Church and cultivated the harvest that was later to be reaped by Martin Luther.

Heresy

Most of the fourteenth-century mystics remained in the orthodox camp and were generally careful to avoid conflict with Church dogma.

But criticism, of course, went further and frequently resulted in heresy. Indeed, throughout the century heresy posed a great problem and challenge for Church discipline and Christian life.

The most radical challenge was offered by the heresy of the Free Spirit. This movement had existed in the thirteenth century, but became truly dangerous only after the papacy had moved to Avignon. There is not much accurate information regarding the beliefs of the devotees of the Free Spirit because most of their writings were efficiently consigned to the flames. Yet the major outlines of the heretical program are clear. The fundamental tenet was that man could achieve deification by his own decision and without the aid of Divine Grace. Free Spirit heretics claimed godlike powers and declared that they had reached a state of sinlessness which rendered traditional morality irrelevant. This doctrine was probably the most radical attack on tradition that the Middle Ages had ever known. Standard moral precepts were turned upside down as Free Spirit heretics proclaimed unrestrained sexual license and tried to justify idleness and theft. Whether the Free Spirit heretics actually practiced what they preached is a question that is nearly impossible to answer, but merely preaching such a doctrine was a sufficient threat to orthodoxy. Furthermore, its followers were surprisingly well organized and were able to spread their ideas from France to Austria and from Holland to Italy. Naturally the Church did its best to uproot this growth and by the fifteenth century had largely succeeded. But the initial success of the movement was a significant symptom of the times and an important harbinger of the future.

Entirely different from the heresy of the Free Spirit was the English heresy of John Wyclif (ca. 1330–1384). In his early career as a professor at the University of Oxford, Wyclif was known only as a scholar who enjoyed complicated theological arguments. If he had lived in another, happier age he might have spent his life in dry, scholarly disputes. But in the late fourteenth century England was becoming a hotbed of anticlericalism. For one thing, the client popes of the French monarchy were making constant and exigent demands for money. By no means eager to meet these papal exactions, the English aristocracy challenged the authority of the Avignonese papacy and sought support in latent anticlericalism and such a potent spokesman as Wyclif.

Wyclif based his attacks on the clergy on a position diametrically opposed to that of the Free Spirit heresy. While the latter argued that man could become divine by his own decision and without intervention of Grace, Wyclif stressed the saving power of Grace and the fundamental sinfulness of man. According to Wyclif, no man could claim absolute power or dominion without the gift of Grace. This limitation he extended even to the priestly office and priests, including popes; those who were not in a state of Grace were according to Wyclif no priests at all. With the popes in Avignon and the clergy becoming more and more embroiled in secular affairs, this doctrine attracted much favorable attention and support. But as Wyclif grew older he became more radical. In his later writings he attacked the very existence of Church government, not just its unworthy servants, and argued that true Christian life depended on a return to the literal rather than the customary allegorical interpretation of the Bible, which meant, in this context, the elimination of the clerical hierarchy. Finally, just before he died, he attacked the doctrine of the Eucharist, which conferred on priests, worthy or not, the exclusive right to administer this central sacrament of the Church, a monopoly for which he found no authority in the records of the apostolic tradition. From a plea for radical reform Wyclif had moved to a direct challenge of the most fundamental dogma of the church. His influential supporters, hardly prepared for open heresy, began to be disaffected. If he had lived longer he might have faced severe penalties, but he died unharmed before the tide had fully turned against him.

The heresy of Wyclif was notable for a number of reasons. Before the late fourteenth century, England had been a stronghold of orthodoxy and was remarkably immune from heretical infection. Thus Wyclif's successful career in the most orthodox of countries was an impressive testimony to the weakening of Church discipline and the burgeoning criticism of traditional standards and dogmas. More specifically Wyclif's insistence on a literal interpretation of the Bible led to a translation of the Bible into English. The vernacular Wyclifite Bible was copied frequently and had an important influence on the development of the English language as well as on the development of English piety.

If Wyclif's growing intransigence toward the end of his life cost him his aristocratic support, it earned him a sizable following among the lower classes. After his death, these followers, known as "Lollards," were persecuted and went underground until they were able to take up their criticism openly once more during the time of the Protestant Reformation. Wyclif's views were also carried by Czech scholars to Bohemia, where they had more obvious success. Transplanted in Bohemia, Wyclif's example stimulated and encouraged John Hus (1370–1416) in developing the heresy which exerted a great influence on central Europe throughout the fifteenth century and which was another important forerunner of the Protestant Reformation.

Nominalism

Beside the introspective reformism of the mystics, the radical reformism of the Free Spirit heretics, and the near Protestant reformism of the Wyclifites, the remarkable diversity of fourteenth-century thought and criticism was rounded out by the logical reformism of the nominalist movement. The major tenets of nominalism [a belief that abstractions do not exist beyond the minds of humans, separating faith and reason in a way unacceptable to many orthodox thinkers of the time] were no more new to the fourteenth century than were the other previously mentioned movements. What was new was the rigor with which they were driven to their ultimate conclusions and the train of highly significant consequences which this procedure produced.

The great fourteenth-century exponent of nominalism was an English Franciscan by the name of William of Ockham (ca. 1295–1349). In the later Middle Ages, the Franciscans competed openly and often passionately with their rival order, the Dominicans. In the realm of philosophy, this meant that Franciscan scholars tended to exploit the inherent contradictions in the magnificent theoretical edifice of the Dominican school. Brought to its greatest perfection by St. Thomas Aquinas in his *Summa theologica*, it was organized on the principle that human reason is generally compatible with faith. For example, St. Thomas tried to demonstrate that such a basic proposition of Christian faith as the existence of God could be proved by human reason. Ockham, on the other hand, contended that a sharp division had to be made between reason and faith. According to him, human beings could only be certain about knowledge obtained by direct experience received through intuition or the senses and that such experience could only perceive particulars and not general categories. For Ockham, therefore, the great scholastic categories were mere names (in Latin, *nomina*, whence the term nominalism) and could not—as his opponents maintained—be made the subject of human science. The most important of these general categories was, of course, the idea of God; and Ockham, following his argument to its logical conclusion, insisted that knowledge of God could properly be sought not through human science but only in revealed theology. Human science, that is, should no more concern itself with theology or metaphysics than theology should interfere with such human sciences as grammar, logic, or physics. By this simple but devastating formula, the elaborate synthesis constructed by St. Thomas was torn down and reduced to fragments.

Self-evident as Ockham's view will seem to us—since it is axiomatic to modern science—nominalism never became more than a minority movement in the fourteenth century. Its ramifications, however, were frequently far more widespread and important than the number of its followers would suggest, and its implications often seemed to be reflected in some of the characteristic tendencies of the age. Nominalism, for example, with its stress on earthly knowledge susceptible of dispassionate proof, might seem to provide little place for mysticism; but its very insistence that knowledge of God was irrational and could not be approached by human science left this ultimate problem to the subjective methods cultivated by the mystics. In this context it is interesting to point out that Martin Luther, who—

though no mystic—was to affirm the subjectivity of religion and to denounce the teachings of St. Thomas, was to be educated in the nominalist University of Erfurt and to refer to William of Ockham as his "dear master."

Nominalism also had a great influence on the development of political theory. Ockham himself was not content to pass his life within the confines of a university. He became actively engaged in politics and took the side of the Franciscans in their attacks on papal worldliness. As a result he was condemned and forced to flee to the court of the Pope's leading enemy, Emperor Louis of Bavaria, where he joined other refugees from papal wrath who served as propagandists for the imperial cause. One of the most original and effective of these was Marsiglio of Padua (ca. 1275–1343), whose ideas were similar to Ockham's but whose writing was less obscured by difficult language and whose conclusions were far more revolutionary.

Marsiglio of Padua's major work was the *Defensor pacis (Defender of the Peace)*, written in collaboration with the Parisian scholar John of Jandun in 1324. Probably the most significant contribution to political theory written in the later Middle Ages, it attacked the theory of a united Christian community ruled over by the pope. As Ockham had argued for a separation between the spheres of faith and human science, so Marsiglio argued for a separation between spiritual and secular authority. Marsiglio, however, did not rest with the theory of two coordinate powers, but went on to insist that the Church should be subordinated to the state. The clergy, according to Marsiglio, were simply members of the state whose special function was to teach and interpret scripture. In all other matters he considered them to be no different from other classes in society and claimed that they should therefore be subject to secular authority.

In addition to defending the superiority of the secular to the spiritual, Marsiglio also developed some striking constitutional ideas about the nature of the state itself. The ultimate source of authority, he declared, rested among the better citizens of the state, who should shape the laws. It was the function of the monarch merely to enforce them; and if he failed in this responsibility or exceeded his authority, he was simply to be replaced. In modern terms this meant that Marsiglio wanted the executive to be placed in a position subordinate to the legislature.

Geoffrey Chaucer

S.S. Hussey

One of the great literary figures of the fourteenth century was English
poet Geoffrey Chaucer (c. 1342–1400). Best remembered for *The Canterbury Tales*, a series of poems about various late fourteenth-century
characters, Chaucer produced a wide variety of other works as well.
This excerpt from S.S. Hussey's *Chaucer: An Introduction* briefly describes what we know about Chaucer's life and the circumstances under which his works were written.

These circumstances were very different from what prevails today.
As Hussey explains, Chaucer was not a professional poet, and there
were few if any professional writers during this time. Literacy was
much less widespread; even people who were able to read liked to hear
poems told orally at least as much as they liked to read them on their
own. Books were much less common, too; Chaucer lived before the invention of the printing press, and copies of books had to be made labo-
riously, one at a time. Finally, the language was different. Chaucer wrote
in what we now call late Middle English. He used spellings unfamiliar
to us today and grammatical constructions we no longer use; similarly,
his vocabulary is not always our vocabulary, and many words since his
time have disappeared or changed meanings. As a result, Chaucer's language is barely accessible to readers today and needs frequent glossing
to be intelligible. Nevertheless, Chaucer stands as a great poet, one of
the finest of any era to write in English.

For most people English literature still begins with Chaucer. This
is not simply because of the language barrier of Old English and
the (occasionally deceptive) ease of understanding Chaucer's late
Middle English, but because we feel that here is a man who wrote a

Excerpted from *Chaucer: An Introduction,* by S.S. Hussey. Copyright © 1971 by S.S. Hussey.
Reprinted with permission from Taylor & Francis Books, Ltd.

good deal, with an evident feeling for style, and who accepted the permanent worth of what he had written, placing it, with all due modesty, in the classical tradition. . . .

Although tributes to his reputation almost all come from after his death, there seems little doubt that he was regarded as a first-class poet by his contemporaries, and that, despite the occasional assertions of his own inferiority that appear in his works, he knew that he was a success with them.

Yet he was not a professional poet; probably no one was in the fourteenth century. It is not surprising, therefore, that we know much more about his life than we know about how and when he wrote his poems. Medieval audiences, in any case, would seem to have been interested chiefly in the story and less in the personality of its poet. Plagiarism was no sin, and many of Chaucer's stories, like Shakespeare's, are borrowed from other writers. As [British poet] T.S. Eliot said, one test of a great poet is what he does with his borrowings, and in Chaucer, as again in Shakespeare, much is transformed in the process. Consequently, in medieval poetry, sheer originality is at a much lower premium than it is nowadays, and the sense of tradition is correspondingly strong. . . . In the records we have, then, Chaucer appears as courtier, diplomat and civil servant, but hardly ever as poet.

We do not know exactly when he was born. At a trial in 1386 at which he was a witness, he confessed to being then "forty years old and more," so that it is usual to put his birth about 1343. He was a Londoner, and his father was a well-to-do wine merchant who enjoyed some minor royal patronage. The family was reasonably prosperous without being gentry, and their fortunes were perhaps in the ascendant—which augured well for young Geoffrey. His education may well have been at St Paul's cathedral school, but this is by no means certain. Wherever it was, it would have involved much learning by heart and dictating from the master's book, for books were expensive and in short supply and there was an almost complete absence of reference books. Chaucer, therefore, had to memorize, but even so his memory was clearly remarkable, and it served him in good stead throughout his poetic career. Unfortunately we have neither a contemporary map nor a detailed description of the London in which Chaucer grew up, although a good deal of information about life in the city can be obtained from the records. As a boy, he probably lived in Upper Thames Street, near the river and wharves, not far either from St Paul's (then a great social as well as a religious centre) or from Lombard Street and the markets of Cheapside. Medieval London was still a place in which it was possible to move about quickly, and it was easy to walk out of the city into the surrounding countryside. Its population in the later fourteenth century may have been between 50,000 and 60,000.

The first mention of Chaucer's name shows him in 1357 in the service of Elizabeth, Countess of Ulster, wife of Prince Lionel, one of the sons of Edward III. The accounts of Elizabeth's household include payments for a short cloak, red and black breeches, a pair of shoes, and twenty shillings "for necessaries at Christmas." This suggests that he was a page in Elizabeth's (and later in Lionel's own) service where he would begin to acquire the fashionable code of courtly manners and to further his study of French and Latin. Offices, pensions and other means of financial security were in the gift of heads of households, whether royal or noble, and indeed medieval government was, to a large extent, carried on through households and not through committees. As yet there was no professional intelligentsia to counteract the influence of the nobility, and society was governed by comparatively few men, all of whom would know one another. Most of them would seem to us young for their responsibilities; their expectation of life was shorter than ours, and, for Chaucer's generation, growing up in mid-century, had been reduced still further by plague, the notorious Black Death of 1348–9. 1359–60 finds Chaucer fighting in France, perhaps with Lionel. He was taken prisoner, but the fact that the king contributed to his ransom money might suggest that he had already come under the notice of either Edward or of his famous son, the Black Prince. There follows an annoying gap between 1360 and 1366. Lionel was in Ireland from 1361 to 1366. The records for this expedition are quite full but do not include Chaucer's name. A more probable conjecture is that he was a student at the Inner Temple during those years, but the records for this period have unfortunately disappeared. Although he would have received some legal instruction there, his studies would by no means have been confined to law, since a training of this kind was a natural preparation for a career in public affairs, such as Chaucer's was. In late medieval England, the legal schools were beginning to break the church's earlier monopoly of education.

Adult Life

In 1366 Chaucer's father died and his mother remarried. Chaucer himself also probably married in this year. We know next to nothing about his married life—a few wry jokes in his works about shrewish wives need not be taken personally—but his wife Philippa was in the queen's service and her sister was first the mistress and then the third wife of John of Gaunt, the most powerful of Edward III's sons, especially after the death of the Black Prince in 1376. Chaucer had clearly made an advantageous marriage, although he may already have been regarded as a coming young man. It may have been his marriage that brought about his transfer to the king's service in which he is described as a valet in 1367 and as a squire in the following year. He may possibly have gone to Spain with the Black Prince in 1366 (a safe conduct for travel in Spain was granted him in that year), and more probably to France again in 1369, with Gaunt this time. He was abroad in 1368 and 1370 on diplomatic or commercial business for the king. He surely continued in these years his acquisition of both the code of courtly manners and poetic technique. (We know that he wrote many short poems, some perhaps lost, and several of these are probably early work.) He also made some translations and adaptations from French in the 1360s. His first major poem, *The Book of the Duchess,* can be confidently dated 1368–9. A good comment on these years is the portrait of the Squire on the Can-

terbury pilgrimage: twenty years old, already with campaign experience, lover, fashionable dresser, good horseman and dancer, composer of songs which he could accompany on the flute, and always courteous and willing to serve— blending . . . "literature and the arts with his warlike studies." By 1370, Chaucer had already, in the modern phrase, "arrived."

1370–86 were crowded years. He visited Italy twice, in 1372–3 and 1378. It is after *The Book of the Duchess* that the influence of [Italian writers] Boccaccio, Dante and Petrarch shows in his poetry, and he may well have first become acquainted with their work in Italy.

Geoffrey Chaucer

At home he obtained a rent-free house above Aldgate, in the city of London, in 1374, and he kept it for twelve years. He was appointed Controller of Customs and Subsidies on Wools, Skins and Hides in the Port of London in 1374—he uncovered a smuggling plot in 1376 and received the whole value of the merchandise as a reward—and Controller of the Petty Customs on wines and merchandise in 1382. In 1385 he became a Justice of the Peace for Kent and in 1386 Knight of the Shire (MP) [member of parliament] for the same county. But in 1386 he gave up his Aldgate house, both controllerships at the customs, and was not re-elected MP in 1387. Perhaps these retirements were connected with the absence from England and the partial eclipse of his patron, John of Gaunt. Philippa Chaucer died in 1387. Edward III, too, was dead, and the new king, Richard II, was a minor and not yet in control of affairs of state. In London there was opposition, which was to grow stronger later in Richard's reign, to the court party. Two of his acquaintances, Nicholas Bembre and the writer Thomas Usk, were executed in these years. On the other hand, the withdrawal from public service may have been welcome: 1386–7 are the years generally assigned to the *General Prologue* and the drawing up of the scheme of *The Canterbury Tales*. From 1370 to 1386, therefore, Chaucer was a successful diplomat and civil servant, and in his poetry new Italian influences supplemented (but did not replace) the French conventions noticeable from the beginning of his writing.

In 1389 Chaucer was back in public life again—if he had ever been really out of it. Gaunt returned from Spain in 1389, and in the same year Richard announced that he was of age and intended to assume full royal powers. From that year until 1391 Chaucer was Clerk of the King's Works at Westminster, the Tower of London, Eltham and Sheen (the latter two palaces he mentions in *The Legend of Good Women*) and other royal residences, eight in all. His duties also included supervising the survey of walls, sewers, ditches and bridges along the Thames and the construction of seating for tournaments. (In *The Knights Tale* he describes a magnificent amphitheatre for a tournament which seems, like those in London, to have been a considerable social event.) In 1391 he was appointed sub-forester of the royal forest of North Petherton in Somerset—which may or may not have been a sinecure [a job with few responsibilities]—and the appointment was renewed in 1398. This is the last regular office he is known to have held. From 1395 onwards he may have been enjoying the favour of John of Gaunt's son, Henry, Earl of Derby, who became Henry IV in 1399. But Chaucer may not have been altogether happy during these years. We find him borrowing money from the Exchequer [government treasury]. In his occasional poems he complains he is getting old and that his scribe will not copy accurately, but these may be no more than half-humorous remarks. In 1399 he leased a house in the garden of Westminster Abbey, but did not live long to enjoy it, for he died in October 1400, not yet sixty. He is buried in the Abbey, but as a resident in the precincts [of the district], not as a poet.

Religious Life

Eileen Power

One of the most famous fictional characters to come out of the fourteenth century was a woman named Madame Eglentyne. Madame Eglentyne was a prioress, or the head nun in a convent, in a book by English writer Geoffrey Chaucer. In this excerpt, British historian Eileen Power uses Madame Eglentyne's fictional life as a springboard for investigating the realities of life in a convent. If there were a real Madame Eglentyne, Power asks, what would her background have been like—and what would she have thought of her surroundings?

Power was a professor of history at several English colleges and universities during the first half of the twentieth century, a time when very few women served in those capacities. She was known for her lively writing style and her thorough research. While Power occasionally cites examples from earlier and later centuries, the composite "Madame Eglentyne" that she draws is made up primarily of real nuns from the fourteenth century.

In the Middle Ages all the nunneries of England, and a great many of the monasteries, used to be visited at intervals by the bishop of their diocese—or by somebody sent by him—in order to see whether they were behaving properly. It was rather like the periodical visitation of a school by one of Her Majesty's inspectors, only what happened was very different. When Her Majesty's inspector comes he does not sit in state in the hall, and call all the inmates in front of him one after another, from the head mistress to the smallest child in the first form, and invite them to say in what way they think the school is not being properly run, and what complaints they have to make against their mistresses and which girl habitually breaks the rules—all

Excerpted from *Medieval People* (London: Methuen, 1924) by Eileen Power.

breathed softly and privately into his ear, with no one to overhear them. But when the bishop came to visit a nunnery, that is precisely what happened. First of all, he sent a letter to say he was coming, and to bid the nuns prepare for him. Then he came, with his clerks and a learned official or two, and was met solemnly by the prioress and all the nuns, and preached a sermon in their church, and was entertained, perhaps, to dinner. And then he prepared to examine them, and one by one they came before him, in order of rank, beginning with the prioress, and what they had to do was to tell tales about each other. He wanted to find out if the prioress were ruling well, and if the services were properly performed, and if the finances were in good order, and if discipline were maintained; and if any nun had a complaint, then was the time to make it.

And the nuns were full of complaints. A modern schoolgirl would go pale with horror over their capacity for tale-bearing. If one nun had boxed her sister's ears, if another had cut church, if another were too much given to entertaining friends, if another went out without a licence, if another had run away with a wandering fluteplayer, the bishop was sure to hear about it; that is, unless the whole convent were in a disorderly state, and the nuns had made a compact to wink at each other's peccadilloes [small offenses]; and not to betray them to the bishop, which occasionally happened. And if the prioress were at all unpopular he was quite certain to hear all about her. "She fares splendidly in her own room and never invites us," says one nun; "She has favourites," says another, "and when she makes corrections she passes lightly over those whom she likes, and speedily punishes those whom she dislikes"; "She is a fearful scold," says a third; "She dresses more like a secular person than a nun, and wears rings and necklaces," says a fourth; "She goes out riding to see her friends far too often," says a fifth; "She-is-a-very-bad-business-woman-and she-has-let-the-house-get-into-debt-and-the-church-is-falling-about-our-ears-and-we-don't-get-enough-food-and-she-hasn't-given-us-any-clothes-for-two-years-and-she-has-sold-woods-and-farms-without-your-licence-and-she-has-pawned-our-best-set-of-spoons; and no wonder, when she never consults us in any business as she ought to do." They go on like that for pages, and the bishop must often have wanted to put his fingers in his ears and shout to them to stop; especially as the prioress had probably spent half an hour, for her part, in telling him how disobedient and ill-tempered, and thoroughly badly behaved the nuns were.

All these tales the bishop's clerk solemnly wrote down in a big book, and when the examination was over the bishop summoned all the nuns together again. And if they had answered "All is well," as they sometimes did, or only mentioned trivial faults, he commended them and went his way; and if they had shown that things really were in a bad way, he investigated particular charges and scolded the culprits and ordered them to amend, and when he got back to his palace, or the manor where he was staying, he wrote out a set of injunctions, based on the complaints, and saying exactly how things were to be improved; and of these injunctions one copy was entered in his register and another was sent by hand to the nuns, who were supposed to read it aloud at intervals and to obey everything in it. We have in many bishops' registers these lists of injunctions, copied into them by the bishops' clerks, and in some . . . we have also the evidence of the nuns, just as it was taken down from their chattering mouths, and these are the most human and amusing of all medieval records. It is easy to see what important historical documents visitation reports are. . . .

Madame Eglentyne

Let us see what light the registers will throw upon Madame Eglentyne, before Chaucer observed her mounting her horse outside the Tabard Inn. Doubtless she first came to the nunnery when she was quite a little girl, because girls counted as grown up when they were fifteen in the Middle Ages; they could be married out of hand at twelve, and they could become nuns for ever at fourteen. Probably Eglentyne's father had three other daughters to marry, each with a dowry, and a gay young spark of a son, who spent a lot of money on fashionable suits.

> Embroidered . . . as it were a mede
> All ful of fresshe flowers white and rede.

So he thought he had better settle the youngest at once; and he got together a dowry (it was rarely possible to get into a nunnery without one, though Church law really forbade anything except voluntary offerings), and, taking Eglentyne by the hand one summer day, he popped her into a nunnery a few miles off, which had been founded by his ancestors. . . . Then he had to give Eglentyne her new habit and a bed, and some other furniture; and he had to make a feast on the day she became a nun, and invite all the nuns and all his own friends; and he had to tip the friar, who preached the sermon; and, altogether, it was a great affair. But the feast would not come at once, because Eglentyne would have to remain a novice for some years, until she was old enough to take the vows. So she would stay in the convent and be taught how to sing and to read, and to talk French . . . with the other novices. Perhaps she was the youngest, for girls often did not enter the convent until they were old enough to decide for themselves whether they wanted to be nuns; but there were certainly some other quite tiny novices learning their lessons; and occasionally there would be a little girl like the one whose sad fate is recorded in a dull law-book, shut up in a nunnery by a wicked stepfather who wanted her inheritance (a nun could not inherit land, because she was supposed to be dead to the world), and told by the nuns that the devil would fly away with her if she tried to set foot outside the door. However, Eglentyne had a sunny disposition and liked life in the nunnery, and had a natural aptitude for the pretty table manners which she learnt there, as well as for talking French, and though she was not at all prim and liked the gay clothes and pet dogs which she used to see at home in her mother's bower, still she had no hesitation at all about taking the veil when she was fifteen, and indeed she rather liked the fuss that was made of her, and being called *Madame* or *Dame,* which was the courtesy title always given to a nun.

The years passed and Eglentyne's life jogged along peacefully enough behind the convent walls. The great purpose for which the nunneries existed, and which most of them fulfilled not unworthily, was the praise of God. Eglentyne spent a great deal of her time singing and praying in the convent church, and, as we know,

Ful wel she song the service divyne,
Entuned in hir nose ful semely.

The nuns had seven monastic offices to say every day. About 2 A.M. the night office was said; they all got out of bed when the bell rang, and went down in the cold and the dark to the church choir and said Matins, followed immediately by Lauds [prayers intended for the morning]. Then they went back to bed, just as the dawn was breaking in the sky, and slept again for three hours, and then got up for good at six o'clock and said Prime. After that there followed Tierce, Sext, None, Vespers, and Compline, spread at intervals through the day. The last service, Compline, was said at 7 P.M. in winter, and at 8 P.M. in summer, after which the nuns were supposed to go straight to bed in the dorter, in which connexion one Nun's Rule ordains that "None shall push up against another wilfully, nor spit upon the stairs going up and down, but if they tread it out forthwith!" They had in all about eight hours' sleep, broken in the middle by the night service. They had three meals, a light repast of bread and beer after prime in the morning, a solid dinner to the accompaniment of reading aloud in the middle of the day, and a short supper immediately after Vespers at 5 or 6 P.M.

From 12 to 5 P.M. in winter and from 1 to 6 P.M. in summer Eglentyne and her sisters were supposed to devote themselves to manual or brain work, interspersed with a certain amount of sober and godly recreation. She would spin, or embroider vestments with the crowned monogram M of the Blessed Virgin in blue and gold thread, or make little silken purses for her friends and finely sewn bands for them to bind round their arms after a bleeding. She would read too, in her psalter or in such saints' lives as the convent possessed, written in French or English; for her Latin was weak, though she could construe *Amor vincit omnia* [Love conquers all]. Perhaps her convent took in a few little schoolgirls to learn their letters and good manners with the nuns, and when she grew older she helped to teach them to read and sing; for though they were happy, they did not receive a very extensive education from the good sisters. In the summer Eglentyne was sometimes allowed to work in the convent garden, or even to go out haymaking with the other nuns; and came back round-eyed to confide in her confessor that she had seen the cellaress [official in charge of the convent's provisions] returning therefrom seated behind the chaplain on his nag, and had thought what fun it must be to jog behind stout Dan John.

Except for certain periods of relaxation strict silence was supposed to be observed in the convent for a large part of the day, and if Eglentyne desired to communicate with her sisters, she was urged to do so by means of signs. The persons who drew up the lists of signs which were in use in medieval monastic houses, however, combined a preternatural ingenuity with an extremely exiguous sense of humour, and the sort of dumb pandemonium which went on at Eglentyne's dinner table must often have been more mirth-provoking than speech. The sister who desired fish would "wag her hands displayed sidelings in manner of a fish tail"; she who wanted milk would "draw her left little finger in manner of milking"; for mustard one would "hold her nose in the upper part of her right fist and rub it"; another for salt would "fillip [hit] with her right thumb and forefinger over the left thumb"; another desirous of wine would "move her forefinger up and down the end of her thumb afore her eye"; and the guilty sacristan [person in charge of the equipment for masses], struck by the thought that she had not provided incense for the Mass, would "put her two fingers into her nostrils." In one such table drawn up for nuns there are no less than 106 signs, and on the whole it is not surprising that the rule of the same nuns enjoins that "it is never lawful to use them without some reason and profitable need, for ofttimes more hurt hath an evil word, and more offence it may be to God."

Monotony and Carelessness

The nuns, of course, would not have been human if they had not sometimes grown a little weary of all these services and this silence; for the religious life was not, nor was it intended to be, an easy one. It was not a mere means of escape from work and responsibility. In the early golden age of monasticism only men and women with a vocation, that is to say a real genius for monastic life, entered convents. Moreover, when there they worked very hard with hand and brain, as well as with soul, and so they got variety of occupation, which is as good as a holiday. The basis of wise [monastic founder] St Benedict's Rule was a nicely adjusted combination of variety with regularity; for he knew human nature. Thus monks and nuns did not find the services monotonous, and indeed regarded them as by far the best part of the day. But in the later Middle Ages, when Chaucer lived, young people had begun to enter monastic houses rather as a profession than as a vocation. Many truly spiritual men and women still took the vows, but with them came others who were little suited to monastic life, and who lowered its standard, because it was hard and uncongenial to them. Eglentyne became a nun because her father did not want the trouble and expense of finding her a husband, and because being a nun was about the only career for a well-born lady who did not marry. Moreover, by this time, monks and nuns had grown more lazy, and did little work with their hands and still less with their heads, particularly in nunneries, where the early tradition of learning had died out and where many nuns could hardly understand the Latin in which their services were written. The result was that monastic life began to lose that essential variety which St Benedict had designed for it, and as a result the regularity sometimes became irksome, and the series of services degenerated into a mere routine of peculiar monotony, which many of the singers could no longer keep alive with spiritual fervour. Thus sometimes (it must not be imagined that this happened in all or even in the majority of houses) the services became empty forms, to be hurried through with scant devotion and occasionally with scandalous irreverence. It was the almost inevitable reaction from too much routine.

Carelessness in the performance of the monastic hours was an exceedingly common fault during the later Middle Ages, though the monks were always worse about it than the nuns. Sometimes they "cut" the services. Sometimes they behaved with the utmost levity, as at Exeter in 1330, where the canons giggled and joked and quarrelled during the services and dropped hot candle wax from the upper stalls on to the shaven heads of the singers in the stalls below! Sometimes they came late to Matins, in the small hours after midnight. This fault was common in nunneries, for the nuns always would insist on having private drinkings and gossipings in the evening after Compline, instead of going straight to bed, as the rule demanded—a habit which did not conduce to wakefulness at 1 A.M. Consequently they were somewhat sleepy at Matins and found . . . difficulty in getting up early. Wise St Benedict foresaw the difficulty, when he wrote in his rule: "When they rise for the Divine Office, let them gently encourage one another, because of the excuses made by those that are drowsy.". . . There was a tendency also among both monks and nuns to slip out before the end of the service on any good or bad excuse: they had to see after the dinner or the guest-house, their gardens needed weeding, or they did not feel well. But the most common fault of all was to gabble through the services as quickly as they could in order to get them over. They left out the syllables at the beginning and end of words, they omitted the dipsalma or pause between two verses [of psalms], so that one side of the choir was beginning the second half before the other side had finished the first; they skipped sentences, they mumbled and slurred what should have been "entuned in their nose ful semely," and altogether they made a terrible mess of the stately plainsong.

The Black Death

PREFACE

One of the most disastrous events of this or any century was the arrival of the bubonic plague. Cutting a wide swath through Europe—and indeed much of Asia as well—the plague killed perhaps one out of every three people living between India and the Atlantic coast of Europe. The disease left behind not only millions of corpses but also a shattered and broken society.

Today we know that the bubonic plague is carried by rats and is transmitted to humans by fleas. Infected rats passed the disease on to the fleas that bit them. The fleas, in turn, could give the plague to the humans they bit. The plague, in humans, ran its course alarmingly quickly: A healthy person who contracted the disease could die from it in a matter of hours, a few days at the most. And most who caught the plague did die from it. Estimates are that only about 10 percent of the plague's victims survived it.

The first sign of infection was usually the appearance of enlarged lymph glands, called buboes. Infected people quickly came down with high fevers and developed dark hemorrhages under their skin—hemorrhages whose color gave the disease the name the Black Death. Worse, the victims' lungs became infected. A sneeze, a cough, even deep breathing, scattered plague bacteria through the air. Those in the same room as a plague patient could breathe in the bacteria—and contract the illness themselves.

The plague struck Europe with very little warning. In 1346 the Black Death abruptly arose in a port near the Black Sea. The following year it struck London, carried by rats who lived on trading vessels; by 1348 it had spread so widely that scarcely a town anywhere in Europe had still managed to escape the disease. No country, ethnic group, or class was exempt, although the plague did attack some areas and peoples more ferociously than others. Still, for every community that suffered only a few deaths to the pestilence, another was virtually wiped out. Families abandoned stricken relatives; the whole population of some villages packed up at the first sign of plague and headed for what they hoped would be safety in the next town. Even doctors and members of the clergy, concerned for their own safety, began to refuse to treat the sick and provide services to the dying.

The causes of the plague, however, were not well understood. Many believed that the Black Death was sent from heaven as punishment for human sins. Others searched for a scapegoat. Few made the necessary connections between rats, fleas, and the disease. Pope Clement VI, in a vain attempt to earn God's favor, declared that 1348 would be a holy year in which Christians were invited to come to Rome for prayers and devotion. Clement hoped that a show of piety would turn away God's wrath, but, of course, his proclamation had the opposite effect. Plague shot quickly through the tightly packed mob of people who descended on Rome; by one estimate, 90 percent of the pilgrims died of the plague.

The worst of the Black Death was over by 1351. But the damage had been done. In a five-year period, millions upon millions of people had died, a disaster of almost unimaginable proportions. And the plague was not finished. Several times during the rest of the century, the Black Death would return to kill those who had escaped the first round of infection—or those who had not yet been born. Each time, the world watched in terror and in sorrow and did its best to pick up the pieces afterwards.

The Plague and the *Decameron*

Giovanni Boccaccio

One of the greatest literary works to come out of the Black Death was the *Decameron* by the Italian writer Giovanni Boccaccio (1313–1375). Writing during the plague years 1348 to 1353, Boccaccio used the plague as a framing device for a series of short stories that make up the heart of the book. The stories are told by a group of fictional Italians who left the city of Florence for the countryside in an effort to escape the disease.

While the stories contained in the *Decameron* are an unquestioned literary masterpiece, the introduction is valuable in its own right. Boccaccio's description of the plague and its effect on Florence bring home for the reader the horror and drama of the disease. His emphasis is not merely on the deaths that resulted from the plague, but also on the ways that the social system broke down in the face of disaster.

In the year of Our Lord 1348 the deadly plague broke out in the great city of Florence, most beautiful of Italian cities. Whether through the operation of the heavenly bodies or because of our own iniquities which the just wrath of God sought to correct, the plague had arisen in the East some years before, causing the death of countless human beings. It spread without stop from one place to another, until, unfortunately, it swept over the West. Neither knowledge nor human foresight availed against it, though the city was cleansed of much filth by chosen officers in charge and sick persons were forbidden to enter it, while advice was broadcast for the preservation of health. Nor did humble supplications serve. Not once but many times they were or-

Excerpted from *The Decameron* (New York: The Limited Editions Club, 1930) by Giovanni Boccaccio, translated by Frances Winwar. Copyright © 1930 by The Limited Editions Club.

dained in the form of processions and other ways for the propitiation
of God by the faithful, but, in spite of everything, toward the spring
of the year the plague began to show its ravages in a way short of
miraculous.

It did not manifest itself as in the East, where if a man bled at the
nose he had certain warning of inevitable death. At the onset of the
disease both men and women were afflicted by a sort of swelling in
the groin or under the armpits which sometimes attained the size of a
common apple or egg. Some of these swellings were larger and some
smaller, and all were commonly called boils. From these two starting
points the boils began in a little while to spread and appear generally
all over the body. Afterwards, the manifestation of the disease changed
into black or livid spots on the arms, thighs and the whole person. In
many these blotches were large and far apart, in others small and
closely clustered. Like the boils, which had been and continued to be
a certain indication of coming death, these blotches had the same
meaning for everyone on whom they appeared.

Neither the advice of physicians nor the virtue of any medicine
seemed to help or avail in the cure of these diseases. Indeed, whether
the nature of the malady did not suffer it, or whether the ignorance of
the physicians could not determine the source and therefore could take
no preventive measures against it, the fact was that not only did few
recover, but on the contrary almost everyone died within three days
of the appearance of the signs—some sooner, some later, and the majority without fever or other ill. Moreover, besides the qualified medical men, a vast number of quacks, both men and women, who had
never studied medicine, joined the ranks and practiced cures. The virulence of the plague was all the greater in that it was communicated
by the sick to the well by contact, not unlike fire when dry or fatty
things are brought near it. But the evil was still worse. Not only did
conversation and familiarity with the diseased spread the malady and
even cause death, but the mere touch of the clothes or any other object the sick had touched or used, seemed to spread the pestilence.

What I am going to relate is indeed a strange thing to hear—a thing
that I should hardly have dared believe and much less write about,
though I had heard it from a trustworthy witness, had I not seen it with
my own eyes, and in the presence of many others. So active, I say, was
the virulence of the plague in communicating itself from one person
to another, that not only did it affect human beings, but, what is more
strange, it very often proceeded in an extraordinary way. If an article
belonging to one sick of the plague or who had died of it was touched
by an animal outside of the human species, the creature was not only
infected, but in a very short time it died of the disease—a fact which
among others I observed one day with my own eyes, as I said before.
The rags of a poor fellow who had died of the plague, had been

thrown into the public street. Two hogs came across them and, according to their habit, first they went for them with their snouts and then, taking them in their teeth, began shaking them about their jaws. A little while later, after rolling round and round as though they had swallowed poison, both of them fell down dead upon the rags they had found to their misfortune.

Dealing With the Plague

Because of such happenings and many others of a like sort, various fears and superstitions arose among the survivors, almost all of which tended toward one end—to flee from the sick and whatever had belonged to them. In this way each man thought to be safeguarding his own health. Some among them were of the opinion that by living temperately and guarding against excess of all kinds, they could do much toward avoiding the danger; and forming a band they lived away from the rest of the world. Gathering in those houses where no one had been ill and living was more comfortable, they shut themselves in. They ate moderately of the best that could be had and drank excellent wines, avoiding all luxuriousness. With music and whatever other delights they could have, they lived together in this fashion, allowing no one to speak to them and avoiding news either of death or sickness from the outer world.

Others, arriving at a contrary conclusion, held that plenty of drinking and enjoyment, singing and free living and the gratification of the appetite in every possible way, letting the devil take the hindmost, was the best preventative of such a malady; and as far as they could, they suited the action to the word. Day and night they went from one tavern to another drinking and carousing unrestrainedly. At the least inkling of something that suited them, they ran wild in other people's houses, and there was no one to prevent them, for everyone had abandoned all responsibility for his belongings as well as for himself, considering his days numbered. Consequently most of the houses had become common property and strangers would make use of them at will whenever they came upon them even as the rightful owners might have done. Following this uncharitable way of thinking, they did their best to run away from the infected.

Meanwhile, in the midst of the affliction and misery that had befallen the city, even the reverend authority of divine and human law had almost crumbled and fallen into decay, for its ministers and executors, like other men, had either died or sickened, or had been left so entirely without assistants that they were unable to attend to their duties. As a result everyone had leave to do as he saw fit.

Many others followed a middle course, neither restricting themselves in their diet like the first, nor giving themselves free rein in lewdness and debauchery like the second, but using everything to sufficience, according to their appetites. They did not shut themselves in, but went about, some carrying flowers in their hands, some fragrant herbs, and others divers kinds of spices which they frequently smelled, thinking it good to comfort the brain with such odors, especially since the air was oppressive and full of the stench of corruption, sickness and medicines.

Still others, of a pitiless though perhaps more prudent frame of mind, maintained that no remedy against plagues was better than to leave them miles behind. Men and women without number, encouraged by this way of thinking and caring for nobody but themselves, abandoned the city, their houses and estates, their own flesh and blood even, and their effects, in search of a country place—it made no difference whether it were their own or their neighbor's. It was as if God's wrath in seeking to punish the iniquity of men by means of the plague could not find them out wherever they were, but limited itself to doom only those who happened to be found within the walls of the city. They reasoned as though its last hour had struck, and therefore no one ought to be there.

Although the members of these different factions did not all perish, neither did they all escape. On the contrary, many in each group sickened everywhere, and since they themselves had set the example to those who had been spared, they were abandoned to their lot and perished altogether.

Let alone the fact that one man shunned the other and that nobody had any thought for his neighbor; even relatives visited their folks little or never, and when they did, they communicated from a distance. The calamity had instilled such horror into the hearts of men and women that brother abandoned brother, uncles, sisters and wives left their dear ones to perish and, what is more serious and almost incredible, parents avoided visiting or nursing their very children, as though these were not their own flesh.

As a result, the only help that remained to the many men and women who sickened was either the mercy of friends, who were rare, or the covetousness of servants who agreed to nurse them at the prospect of ridiculously exorbitant wages. Even at that, however, these servants were scarce and of the run of coarse-grained men and women, unused to such services and whose chief duty was perhaps to reach the patients whatever they called for, or to watch them die. Often their occupation brought them to perdition, together with their profits. From this neglect of the sick by neighbors, relatives and friends, and from the scarcity of servants, an almost unprecedented custom arose. Once sick, no woman, however charming, beautiful or well-born, hesitated to engage a man in her service, no matter whether he was young or old, high-born or low, or to reveal any part of her naked body to him if the disease required it, as if he had been of her own sex—all of which later resulted in immodesty in those who were cured. It followed also that many who might perhaps have lived if they had been tended, perished of this neglect. So great was the multitude of those who died in the city night and day, what with lack of proper care and the virulence of the plague, that it was terrible to hear of, and worse still to see. Out of sheer necessity, therefore, quite different customs arose among the survivors from the original laws of the townspeople.

Burials

It used to be common, as it is still, for women, friends and neighbors of a dead man, to gather in his house and mourn there with his people, while his men friends and many other citizens collected with his nearest of kin outside the door. Then came the clergy, according to the standing of the departed, and with funereal pomp of tapers and singing he was carried on the shoulders of his peers to the church he had elected before death. Now, as the plague gained in violence, these customs were either modified or laid aside altogether, and new ones were instituted in their place, so that, far from dying among a crowd of women mourners, many passed away without the benefit of a single witness. Indeed, few were those who received the piteous wails and bitter tears of friends and relatives, for often, instead of mourning, laughter, jest and carousal accompanied the dead—usages which even naturally compassionate women had learned to perfection for their health's sake. It was a rare occurrence for a corpse to be followed to church by more than ten or twelve mourners—not the usual respectable citizens, but a class of vulgar grave-diggers who called themselves "sextons" and did these services for a price. They crept under the bier and shouldered it, and then with hasty steps rushed it, not to the church the deceased had designated before death, but oftener than not to the nearest one. Usually they walked behind five or six members of the clergy, with little light and sometimes with none at all. Then, with the help of these "sextons" the priests, without exhausting themselves with too long or too solemn a service, lowered the dead into the first unoccupied grave they came across.

More wretched still were the circumstances of the common people and, for a great part, of the middle class, for, confined to their homes either by hope of safety or by poverty, and restricted to their own sections, they fell sick daily by thousands. There, devoid of help or care, they died almost without redemption. A great many breathed their last in the public streets, day and night; a large number perished in their homes, and it was only by the stench of their decaying bodies that they proclaimed their death to their neighbors. Everywhere the city was teeming with corpses. A general course was now adopted by the people, more out of fear of contagion than of any charity they felt toward the dead. Alone, or with the assistance of whatever bearers they could muster, they would drag the corpses out of their homes and pile them in front of the doors, where often, of a morning, countless bodies might be seen. Biers were sent for. When none was to be had, the dead were laid upon ordinary boards, two or three at once. It was not infrequent to see a single bier carrying husband and wife, two or three brothers, father and son, and others besides.

Times without number when a couple of priests were walking, carrying a cross before a corpse, they were soon followed by two or three sets of porters with their respective biers. And, where the holy men had thought to be burying one man, they found seven or eight on their hands, sometimes more. Nor were these dead shown the respect of candles, tears or mourners. Death had become so common that no more attention was given to human lives than would be given to goats brought to slaughter nowadays. It clearly proved that the wisdom which a natural course of events, with its trivial and infrequent trials, had not been able to impress upon men of understanding—that is, to bear evil patiently—had become an open book to the most unthinking by the very magnitude of their miseries, causing them to expect and accept them for what they were worth.

So many bodies were brought to the churches every day that the consecrated ground did not suffice to hold them, particularly according to the ancient custom of giving each corpse its individual place. Huge trenches were dug in the crowded churchyards and the new dead were piled in them, layer upon layer, like merchandise in the hold of a ship. A little earth covered the corpses of each row, and the procedure continued until the trench was filled to the top.

City and Country

But I shall not linger over the details of our city's past afflictions, for while such bitter times were upon it, the country round about was not spared. In the castles which were as miniature cities compared to the large towns, through the scattered hamlets and in the fields the wretched, poverty-stricken peasants and their families died helpless and untended. On the wayside, in the tilled fields, about their houses, indifferently by day or night they fell dead, more like animals than human beings; whereupon those who remained, growing lax in their habits like the city folk, and careless of their duties, lived as though every day were their last. Perversely they did their best, not to help improve the products of their beasts and of the soil over which they had sweated, but to consume whatever was within their reach. The animals, oxen, asses, sheep, goats, pigs, fowls—all of them ran wild. The very dogs, known for their faithfulness, were driven from their houses, and went straying as they pleased through the fields, where the neglected wheat crop drooped, ungarnered and uncut. Sometimes the undisciplined beasts went back to their homes at night like rational creatures, for they had had enough food all day, and returned well-satisfied.

To go back to the city—what more can be said? Such was the cruelty of heaven and to a great degree of man, that between March and the following July it is estimated more than a hundred thousand human beings lost their lives within the walls of Florence, what with the ravages attendant on the plague and the barbarity of the survivors toward the sick. Who would have thought before the plague that the city had held so many inhabitants?

What vast palaces, what beautiful houses and noble dwellings once full of lords and ladies remained deserted to the least servant! Alas! How many memorable families, how many vast heritages, how many notable fortunes were left without a lawful heir! What brave men and lovely ladies, what charming youths whom [classical physicians] Galen himself and Hippocrates and Aesculapius would have pronounced in the soundest health dined in the morning with their relatives, only to sup that very night with their dead in the other world!

But I am weary of dwelling on such miseries.

Medicine and the Plague

Robert S. Gottfried

Europeans knew virtually nothing about the plague's cause and transmission, making the disease impossible to combat. Most medieval doctors were ineffective in treating the disease. In many cases, their methods actually made things worse.

In this excerpt, history professor Robert S. Gottfried surveys fourteenth-century medicine and its attempt to cope with the plague. He also explains how the plague helped to change old ideas and move Europeans slowly toward a more effective model of disease and a more efficient way of treating patients. Gottfried has written extensively on epidemics and medieval Europe.

The basis of preplague medicine was the theory of humors. The human body had four humors—blood, phlegm, yellow bile, and black bile—which, in turn, were associated with particular organs. Blood came from the heart, phlegm from the brain, yellow bile from the liver, and black bile from the spleen. [Classical doctors] Galen and Avicenna attributed certain elemental qualities to each humor. Blood was hot and moist, like air; phlegm was cold and moist, like water; yellow bile was hot and dry, like fire; and black bile was cold and dry, like earth. In effect, the human body was a microcosm of the larger world.

When one's bodily humors were in equilibrium, one was in good health; this was called *Eukrasia*. When one's humors were not in balance, one was sick, a condition called *Dyskrasia*, and it was the physi-

Excerpted from *The Black Death: Natural and Human Disaster in Medieval Europe,* by Robert S. Gottfried. Copyright © 1983 by The Free Press. Reprinted with permission from The Free Press, a division of Simon & Schuster, Inc.

cian's job to find the means to restore the proper balance. Rest was usually the first prescription, but if the body's innate curative powers proved to be insufficient, the doctor went to work. First, the patient's diet was altered. For example, if he were too hot, various foods were prescribed to make him cooler or, in some cases, hotter still, to purge the infection. If this failed, the physician might recommend bloodletting, phlebotomy, cautery, or cupping [cures involving the drawing of blood or the burning of the flesh]. The belief that the object of medicine was to restore *Eukrasia* helps to explain the reaction of physicians to the Black Death. By modern standards, medieval plague remedies often seem ludicrous, but, given the state of medicine in the mid–fourteenth century, they were rational and well-advised. The Greeks and their Islamic commentators were fine theoreticians and, by their own standard, competent physiologists, but they based their ideas on theory rather than direct, clinical observation and experience. Medieval physicians . . . were poor anatomists, pathologists, and epidemiologists, and were able to do little to fight the plague.

By the fourteenth century, Europe had six principal medical schools, located in Salerno, Montpellier, Bologna, Paris, Padua, and Oxford. The school in Salerno was the first to reach prominence, in the late eleventh century, and it benefited from contacts with nearby Arabic and Byzantine doctors. As a result of these contacts, its faculty stressed the teaching of anatomy. Unfortunately, the anatomy was based on the dissection of pigs. By the thirteenth century, the medical school in Salerno had grown moribund and lost its ascendant position to the school in Montpellier, which prided itself on its connection with leading Jewish physicians from Spain and North Africa. Jews were barred from other medical schools, and Montpellier was their only alternative. . . .

The medical schools at Bologna and Paris came into prominence in the thirteenth century. Bologna was unique among medieval universities in that it specialized in higher, or graduate, degrees rather than undergraduate ones. Its law school was probably the finest in Europe, but the medical school was justly famous as well, with a particular reputation for being innovative. The best known of its professors was the surgeon William of Saliceto, a pioneer in the methods of cautery, who stressed the importance of surgical classes. Indeed, Bologna's most innovative feature was the prominence it gave to surgery, a subject not even on the curriculum of most of the other European schools. Dissection of human cadavers was begun in the 1260s and popularized in the early fourteenth century, when a Bolognese professor, Mondino de'Liuzzi, published his *Anatomia*, a fairly accurate text based on human dissection. It remained the standard text in Europe for almost a hundred years. Mondino described anatomy in clear and simple language: "After the muscle, the bones. Now the bones of the chest are many and are not continuous in order that they may be expanded and contracted, since it [the chest] has to be ever in motion."

By the time of the Black Death, the medical school at the University of Paris was generally considered to be the most prestigious in Europe. It was, at the very least, the biggest and richest medical school, part of the biggest and richest university, primarily because of the lavish patronage of the king of France, the bourgeoisie of Paris, and the French church. . . . The medical school in Paris was not as innovative as the one in Bologna, but because it was so well-supported and paid its faculty good salaries, it had the most famous and influential, if not necessarily the best, professors. It was to the faculty of the medical school of Paris that the pope would go for advice on the Black Death.

If university-trained physicians were at the top of the medical profession, surgeons stood second. They had a professional standing of sorts, were incorporated into the university program in southern European medical schools, and were granted some recognition in the schools of the North. Before the Black Death, surgeons were clearly second-class medical citizens, regarded primarily as skilled craftsmen best-suited to bleeding and closing wounds. Many of them were literate and had some textbook training, but most of their knowledge was based on experience. Unlike physicians, who often never touched their patients, surgeons performed operations, including trephining (a kind of medieval brain surgery), phlebotomy, and cautery, and did much of the bone setting that is basic to medicine. While university-trained physicians were accounted the social equal of wealthy merchants (though not the equal of great bankers and long-distance traders) and lawyers, surgeons were rated at a lower level, with notaries and goldsmiths.

Barber-surgeons were distinct from surgeons proper and made no pretense of being an elite. Most were illiterate, none went to a university, and their training came entirely from practice during apprenticeship. They did some of the same things as surgeons, including phlebotomy and cautery, often directed by a physician or surgeon. More commonly, they performed rather menial tasks such as cupping, setting simple fractures, and applying poultices. They had less knowledge of infection and sanitary practices than did physicians and surgeons, and the traditional barbers' pole of red and white probably comes from the time when barber-surgeons hung out their bloody surgical rags to dry. Virtually all barber-surgeons were part-time doctors, shaving and cutting hair to augment their medical fees, and were sometimes joined in their casual practice by the butcher-surgeon. Barber-surgeons were generally organized in craft guilds, but their medical activities were usually regulated by local physicians or surgeons, who otherwise kept their distance. They had no knowledge of pathology, physiology, or epidemiology, and their principal attraction was the comparatively low fees that they charged.

Apothecaries were more difficult to classify. They were, above all, pharmacists, which gave them an important place in the medical hierarchy, since pharmacy was a major part of the physician's cure. But apothecaries did more than just fill prescriptions and therein lies the problem of trying to place them in late medieval Europe's medical hierarchy. Many apothecaries prescribed drugs, and hence treatment, which made it difficult to distinguish their public role from that of the physician, who rarely touched the patient. Apothecaries' training, if they had any, was as herbalists, and they doled out their prescriptions as if following cookbooks, with little understanding of the human body or infectious disease. . . .

Finally, there was a group of unlicensed or nonprofessional medical practitioners, people with no formal training, organization, or regulation. The role of the nonprofessionals, like that of the apothecaries, is difficult to assess, but this is not because of ambiguity about their roles. Rather, little evidence of their activities survives. The nonprofessionals probably did a bit of everything, or at least attempted to, for without formal training they learned whatever they knew through trial and error. The appeal of the nonprofessionals lay in their fee schedules; they stood at the bottom of the doctors' social scale and charged the lowest rates. The nonprofessionals were not very common in cities or large towns, but were found primarily in rural areas, where professionals did not venture. Generally speaking, there was a correlation between the size of a settlement and the amount of education its doctor had. There was another important feature of the nonprofessional practitioners. A fairly high proportion of

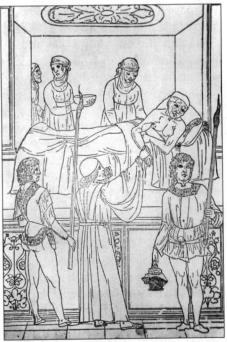

The failure of medieval medicine to curb the plague brought about drastic changes in the study of medicine.

them, perhaps 15% to 20% judging from English sources, were women and a lot of these were older women. Barred from the other areas of practice, women with medical inclinations were forced to work outside the formal hierarchy.

This, then, was Europe's medical community in the fourteenth century. It was slowly becoming more professional. Medical schools and municipal guilds provided strict regulation, and it seems that most doctors took their jobs seriously. But preplague medicine was firmly rooted in the Greek theoretical-philosophical past. Despite some limited gains, its corpus of knowledge was based on texts hundreds of years old and was completely inadequate in the face of the new diseases that came to Europe in the fourteenth century. Most physicians had little formal training in anatomy and pathology, and most surgeons had no theoretical background. Epidemiology was based on Galen's *Book of Fevers*, which was a thousand years old by 1347. It is little wonder that in 1348, when King Philip VI of France asked the medical faculty of the University of Paris for an opinion on plague, its advice was virtually useless. . . .

Possible Causes of the Plague

It is surprising that virtually all of the medical observers failed to make the connection between plague and the plethora of dead rodents that preceded an epidemic. A few commentators, including Avicenna, did claim that one of the portents of pestilence's coming was "when mice and animals living under the earth fled to the surface and were disturbed, as if they were drunk." Further, the Swedish bishop Bengt Knuttson, author of a popular fifteenth-century treatise, claimed that filth, "fleys," and vermin brought plague. But these comments and others like them were made only in a general sense, without a true understanding of the connection of insects, rodents, and *Y. pestis* [the plague].

Most of the [fourteenth-century medical] treatises [on the plague] were divided into three sections. The first considered the causes of plague, the second dealt with preventive measures, and the third proposed cures. A number of causes were suggested; the most popular ones derived from astronomy and astrology. For example, the doctors at the University of Paris, who took their theory from Avicenna, claimed that on 20 March 1345, at 1:00 P.M., a conjunction of three higher planets—Saturn, Jupiter, and Mars—in the sign of Aquarius caused a corruption of the surrounding air. This portent of famine, pestilence, and high mortality was explicable in terms of the accepted humoral theory. Jupiter was believed to be a warm and humid planet, dominated by earth and water. Mars, being excessively hot and dry, set those elements aflame. No one was quite sure what Saturn had or did, but most experts felt that its combination with anything was bad.

The differing geographic effects of the Black Death were due to regional variations in the intensity of rays from the planets. . . .

A second popular explanation was environmental. Its chief proponents were Spaniards. . . . In some cases, the environmental theory was linked with the astral one by connecting the causes of natural phenomena, such as earthquakes, to the planetary conjunctions. Eurasia did suffer a series of earthquakes from 1345 to 1347, and many doctors believed that this released noxious fumes from the earth's core; some even claimed that the devil was behind it all. Neither Galen nor Avicenna spoke of earthquakes, and the theory seems to have originated in the fourteenth century.

A second environmental theory stressed changes in the earth's temperature. Its advocates claimed that climatic changes brought warmer, damper weather and severe southerly winds that carried plague. These scholars predicted plague by the colors of the evening sky, heavy rains, persistent mists, violent winds, cloud formations, and less probable phenomena such as raining multitudes of reptiles, frogs, and toads. Certain kinds of weather conditions are known to influence rodent and insect life cycles and could be considered as factors in the spread and frequency of pandemic plague, a relationship suggested by Avicenna, who believed that most epidemic diseases were brought by winds from the equator. Appropriately enough, two of the principal proponents of climatic causes for plague were the Spanish Muslims Ibn Khātimah and Ibn al-Khatib.

Some theorists, basing their arguments primarily on Galen, claimed that whether the cause of plague be astral or environmental, its transmission between men could be explained by miasmacontagion, or corruption of the air. Galen had claimed that miasma was a disease substance that invaded an organism from the outside, while contagion was the disease substance actually generated within that organism and carried about by the corrupted air. Corruption was either partial or total. Partial corruption was the deterioration, but not the complete destruction, of the element air; in total corruption, the basic component was so contaminated that air was no longer recognizable in its elemental form. In the late fourteenth century, many doctors claimed that foul odors were another source of air corruption. Such odors could come from decaying matter, manure, corpses on a battlefield, or just about any spoilage of humans or animals. Since bad smells were common in the Late Middle Ages, this theory would account for plague's omnipresence.

Among the fourteenth century doctors who stressed the role of corrupt air were Ibn Khātimah, Gentile of Foligno, the German physician John Hakr, and the medical faculty of the University of Montpellier, who hastily threw together a tractate lest their Parisian counterparts be accepted as the sole authority. The Montpellierians believed that the deadly vapors came from the South, and they advised that doors and windows on houses be given Northern exposures. It was believed that air was deadliest in the summer and early autumn—in fact, the peak time for flea-borne, and not air-borne, plague in most of northern Europe—because the hot weather opened the pores of the body, making individuals more susceptible to attack. This theory about open pores explains the general medical opposition to bathing and vigorous exercise during epidemics, and the varying vulnerability of individuals. . . . It was thought that the breath, clothing, bedding, or even stare of an infected individual, could pass on the deadly plague.

A few medical authorities added further causes, ranging from "lust with old women" to overeating, but, in dealing with the origins of plague, most finished the opening parts of their tractates by addressing susceptibility and immunity. Why did some people get it while others did not? Most doctors claimed that the answer rested in the theory of the four humors. Persons of hot, moist temperament were most likely to succumb. If those unfortunate types were also young and slightly corpulent and, even worse, passionate, sensual, *and* female, they were particularly vulnerable. So, too, were big eaters and drinkers, athletes, and the younger, more active members of society in general. The predominance of humors that gave them their youthful, active personalities also made them vulnerable to plague.

Prevention

The second section of most plague treatises was devoted to prevention and resistance. On a strictly practical note, preventive steps were always urged, since doctors realized the inadequacies of their curative abilities. The best preventive measure was prayer, and both Christian and Muslim writers suggested the wearing of religious charms. Christians wore crosses, while Muslims favored little gold lions, an astrological protector symbolizing a favorable period of the year. Christian and Muslim writers disagreed on the role of flight in preventing plague. Christian writers thought it was the second best prophylaxis. Flight was urged from any place with plague, and from places with low elevation, marshes, stagnant waters, southern exposures, or coastal areas to cool, dry, and/or mountainous environs. If flight were not possible, the conditions of the "safe" areas (e.g., mountains) were to be emulated as closely as possible. People were advised to stay in during the day, glaze or cover over any brightly lighted windows, and try above all to stay cool.

Islamic writers disdained flight for religious reasons. Like their Christian counterparts, most Muslim authorities believed that the ultimate cause of the Black Death was the wrath of God. But, to the Muslims, Allah's will was inevitable, and flight was useless and unnecessary. For the true believer, death from plague was actually a mercy, a gift from God, a release from the travails of life, and a ticket to paradise. It was only the infidel who needed to flee for, to him, death from plague meant damnation.

On the other aspects of preventive medicine, Christians and Muslims generally agreed. Pleasant smells were important, for they drove away noxious plague fumes. Those threatened by plague were urged to burn aromatic softwoods such as juniper and ash. Oak, pine, rosemary, aloe, amber and musk were other good smells. Hands and feet were to be washed regularly and lightly sprinkled with rose water and vinegar, but bathing was to be curtailed because it opened the pores and thus made the body more vulnerable to attack. Exercise was not advised for the same reason, and also because fatigue made one more susceptible to the plague.

There was a school which advocated preventive pharmacy. Figs, filberts, and rue [a type of herb], all before breakfast on an empty stomach, were recommended. The best spices to ward off plague were myrrh, saffron, and pepper, all to be consumed later in the day, along with the best vegetables—onions, leeks, and garlic. These remedies were not to be used in excess since they might make the humors too hot and thus make one more vulnerable to plague. Readers were urged to keep gardens so that they would have a ready supply of the crucial herbs and spices close at hand.

There were additional ways in which the body could be readied to fight plague. Among the steps recommended was purgation through laxatives, diuretics, phlebotomy, and cautery. In the context of late medieval physiology, phlebotomy was quite rational and "scientific." Particular veins were linked with astral signs and the humors in order to change the flow of heat and fluids in the body. The proper humoral balance, maintained through bleeding, was essential to ward off plague.

Diet was important, too. Here, medieval doctors followed Aristotle's advocacy of moderation in all phases of life, saying that a balanced diet helped to maintain the humors at peak efficiency. It was recommended that meals be light and be eaten very slowly with each bite well-chewed, so that one always would rise from one's meal still hungry. Meat, dairy products, and fish, all of which could spoil fairly quickly and hence begin to smell bad, were to be avoided. Bread, eggs, fruit, and vegetables were best, the latter two because they aided digestion. Desserts were forbidden, except for nuts, since it was believed that they also helped in digestion. Wine and clean water were the only safe drinks.

Too much sleep was bad, especially right after eating or during the middle of the day. Further, one was advised never to sleep on one's back, since this allowed potentially pestilential air to run down the nostrils and into the lungs. Rather, the experts advised sleeping on one's side and shifting back and forth, as this aided digestion and

excretion, both crucial to a healthy balance of the humors and opti-
mum strength for avoiding the plague. Much of this preventive lore
was summed up in the early fifteenth century in the popular poem
"Dietary and Doctrine for the Pestilence" by the English monk John
Lydgate:

> Who will be whole and keep him from sickness
> And resist the stroke of pestilence
> Let him be glad and void of all heaviness
> Flee wicked aire, eschew the violence
> Drink good wine and wholesome meats take
> Walk in clean air, eschew mists black.

Treatments and Cures

The third section of most plague treatises dealt with treatments and
cures. This was invariably the briefest section, since doctors were
rarely able to offer positive help. Some authorities wrote of general
cures to be used against all fevers, but most recognized the unique
nature of plague and the necessity for trying to deal with it in a novel
way. Islamic doctors, drawing on Avicenna, stressed bloodletting.
Ibn Khātimah claimed: "After people learned this [phlebotomy], and
saw its effects they began to have bloodletting done for themselves,
without medical prescription, several times a month, without consideration or fear, without feeling harm or weakness, and without
contracting sickness in consequence." Islamic doctors also suggested
lancing the buboes [swollen lymph glands] and then applying an
ointment made from Armenian Clay, an iron-rich oxide whose healing properties were much praised by Galen. Other poultices, especially those made from violets, were recommended. These were to
be rubbed into the lanced buboes while the patient drank fruit juices.

Some Christian doctors were often more scientific when discussing cures. Some of them believed that plague was carried
through the body by the veins, or even by wormlike organisms, so
they based their treatments on the bleeding of veins. Before discussing the cure, they described plague's symptoms: coughing, pains
in the chest, shortness of breath, fever, buboes, and the vomiting of
blood. The physiology of treatment usually followed the position of
the University of Paris faculty. The Parisians claimed that the body
needed natural heat to maintain itself. Under normal circumstances,
air circulating through the lungs was thought to do this. But when
plague attacked the pulmonary system, the body juices broke down,
air stopped circulating, and eventually the victim died. The heart occupied the crucial position because the body's juices flowed from it.
Accordingly, one effective way to treat plague was to bleed veins
close to the heart. If the buboes appeared near other major organs
such as the liver or the spleen, the veins leading to them were bled.

In general, Christian doctors believed that pain and the appearance of buboes revealed where the body was being attacked and they began treatment at that point.

Beyond purgatives, bleeding, and the latter's allied treatments, cautery and cupping, there was little advice. Pharmaceuticals were occasionally prescribed for cures, but most authorities believed that they were more effective as a preventive measure. . . . The fourth day after infection was believed to be the crucial one. Consequently, most medicines were designed to carry the patient until that day, when it was hoped the person's "natural restorative powers" would take over.

There were a few other cures, including proper nursing, bed rest, the drinking of a lot of fluid, and the application of herbal salves and ointments. Some physicians, adhering to the theory of the crucial fourth day, advised a wait-and-see attitude. But virtually all authorities believed that there was no sure cure, and this understanding, which served in part to change medical practice, was one of the most important legacies of the Black Death. The medical profession had been charged with maintaining the health of society. Its failure was widely noted, discussed, and criticized. Organized medicine, particularly the university-trained physicians, suffered a blow to its prestige and confidence. Medieval science, rooted as it was in a false Galenic base, was unable to change and respond successfully to its greatest challenge. Medical education, based on textual analysis rather than on clinical investigation and hypothesis, had ceased to progress by the thirteenth century and could not respond to the crisis of the fourteenth century. The result was collapse, rethinking, and reorganization.

Long-Term Effects of the Plague on Society

J.N. Hays

European society was forever changed by the Black Death. The population nosedived, work came to a stop, and whole families and villages were wiped out. The changes were far-reaching. They affected the European social structure, economic systems, governments, and—perhaps most importantly—the European view of the world. Some of the changes were certainly for the better; others were not. In this excerpt, historian J.N. Hays discusses the effects of the plague on society. This article is drawn from Hays's book *The Burdens of Disease*, which covers epidemics in the West over a period of two thousand years.

The Black Death of 1347–1350 seriously reduced the population of Europe. Mortality, it is now generally agreed, was in the range of 30 to 40 percent, in some places higher, in some places lower. But the plague's impact on the European population did not end in 1350. Although controversy continues about just when the population began to grow again, much local evidence suggests that repeated visitations of plague in the years after 1350 contributed to holding populations down. The population of Cuxham [England] in 1377 had reached only one-third of its 1348 level. Many writers, in fact, see no real recovery of growth in the European population until the end of the fifteenth century. For this remarkable period of declining or stagnant populations the plague bears at least some responsibility. Once plague established itself in the 1340s it remained an almost constant menace for over three hundred years, in what may be properly called a prolonged plague pandemic. [Researcher] Jean-Noël Biraben has compiled tables which claim that plague was present somewhere in Europe every year between 1347 and 1670. The most serious and widespread episodes followed on the heels of the great Black Death; thus the epidemics of the early 1360s and middle 1370s, though overshadowed by the 1347–1350 catastrophe, rank as demographic disasters in their own right. Such massive aftershocks hampered the recovery of population levels late in the fourteenth century; and although the intervals between major plague waves seemed to have lengthened in the fifteenth and sixteenth centuries, the disease could still be a powerful brake on growth in some localities.

The social and economic consequences of the great decline in population between the mid-fourteenth and the late fifteenth centuries have been much discussed, and some points remain controversial. . . . Europe in the early 1300s manifested many signs of a society with cheap labor and expensive land. To some extent the Black Death reversed that picture; Europe, now population-short, experienced rising labor costs and falling land costs. Especially in western Europe, the drastic depopulation forced landlords to lower rents, to replace fixed-term rents with share-cropping arrangements, to offer higher wages for agricultural labor, and to commute the traditional labor services demanded of peasants by lords. Considerable regional variation in such effects could be found; in some cases, for example, deaths among the tenantry enabled landlords to let out lands on new terms that freed them from long-term customary arrangements favorable to a tenant family. But in many places in western Europe the lives of peasants improved as the obligations of manorialism fell away. [Researcher] Emmanuel LeRoy Ladurie's classic study of the peasants of Languedoc [France] shows them enjoying the results of abundant and cheap land and high wages in the second half of the fourteenth century and the fifteenth century.

For many European landowners the serious depopulation of 1347–1350 created problems: lower rent receipts, a shortage of tenants, perhaps higher wages to pay, perhaps lower prices for the produce of their lands as demand for those products fell. Landlords had several options. They could join employers everywhere in attempts to hold wages down by statutes that could be enforced with state power, or to use other legislative or judicial means to control labor (such as restricting the laborers' geographical mobility). Several European states adopted such measures in the years after 1348—for example, the English Statute of Labourers of 1349—and serious social and political grievances often resulted.

Another possibility for the landowner was greater efficiency. Labor apparently became more productive, if only because (in agriculture) it was possible to abandon the cultivation of marginal lands and concentrate on richer soils. Still other landlords converted their fields from arable to pasture and thus reduced their labor costs. That point relates to a subtle but significant shift: that in the years after the great epidemic, what we may loosely call "luxury" products and crops prospered, at least in relation to more "staple" items. Several likely factors combined to cause this trend. Survivors of the Black Death possessed greater per capita wealth than they enjoyed before 1348, for such sources of wealth as land, tools, or plate [precious metals] did not vanish in the same proportion as the people who shared them. Survivors also perhaps enjoyed marginally higher incomes, if land costs fell while wages rose. With both greater wealth and greater income came marginally higher disposable income, and items that had been unimaginable luxuries might become desirable possibilities.

Producers—large and small—might respond to this new situation. The demand for grain products fell with the fall in population; half the population will not eat twice the bread it had eaten even if the price falls in half (that is, the demand for such "necessities" as bread is relatively inelastic, or constant regardless of price). The years after 1348 were therefore difficult for producers of grain, caught between higher labor costs and declining absolute demand for their products. For some, the answer lay in the production of goods for which demand might be more elastic, goods that appealed to the new wealth and higher level of disposable income. And so in Spain and England the importance of pasture for wool increased. More land, proportionally, was also given over to crops from which drink could be made: barley for beer in England and Germany, grapes for wine in France, northern Italy, and southern Germany. More varied fruits and vegetables appeared, especially in France and Spain, while the demand grew for exotic substances such as sugar. Crops from which industrial materials came prospered: dyestuffs, flax and hemp, mulberry trees (for silkworms). Meanwhile, areas that had lived by the export of grain, such as Sicily and southern Italy, suffered hard times. Finally, the position of smallholding peasants in this changed market might be mixed; as subsistence farmers they benefited from lower land costs, but as producers for a market they might lose.

The Black Death and subsequent plague assaults may have eased the lives of surviving peasants in western Europe, making their land cheaper, increasing their wages, and decreasing the traditional labor services expected of them. But the general experience of the peasantry of eastern Europe should make us wary of the power of the plague as an overwhelming historical cause. At least in theory the same change in the positions of laborers and landlords occurred there, although it is possible that the plague's incidence and hence mortality was lower in eastern Europe. Perhaps more eastern peasants survived, but that point remains speculative; certainly the position of the eastern landlords strengthened. They seized opportunities that made the east increasingly the supplier of large-scale agricultural products to the more developed western European economies. A different political milieu made it possible for landowners to tighten the bonds of serfdom on the large estates on which they pursued those profitable activities. Disease and its resulting depopulation is clearly not the single determinant of social, economic, and political change.

The industries of towns likewise found a different climate in the post-plague era. Without doubt the great epidemic caused tremendous short-run disruption, as the social mechanisms of markets, transportation, money institutions, and production collapsed in varying degree; a sudden dearth of artisans, or merchants, or seamen might each bring their trade to a standstill, with effects that rippled through an entire local economy. In the somewhat longer term, urban industries shared some—but not all—of the circumstances that affected the rural economy. A peasant in the countryside could benefit immediately from more or better land after 1348; an urban artisan did not have those advantages. Productivity of urban crafts may have declined per capita, at least temporarily, owing to the loss of hard-to-replace skills. But some evidence suggests that such a decline was very temporary, and that both productivity and prices rose in the years after 1350. For that prosperity both demand for manufactured goods and greater efficiency of production may have been responsible. The same factors that promoted the sale of "luxury" agricultural products also applied to manufactures; with more disposable income, consumers demanded more clothing (or fancier clothing, involving silks and dyestuffs) and the products of skilled artisans. Not all manufacturers profited; wool cloth made in Florence declined relative to the luxurious silk, and hard time for some artisans (also facing competition from wool producers elsewhere) resulted. Certainly contemporary observers noticed that conspicuous consumption was a common reaction among survivors of the Black Death.

In the century after the great epidemic, Europe embarked on one of its seminal periods of technological innovation. The sternpost rudder and the ship outfitted with both square-rigged and lateen sails expanded the possibilities of ocean navigation, and Europeans simultaneously adopted compasses from Asian civilizations. By about 1450 the various technologies involved in printing by movable type had been brought together. In the 1400s the use of firearms made headway; what in the 1300s had been a battlefield curiosity became before the end of the 1400s a decisive weapon of war. These technological changes are dramatic and well known, but others of great importance

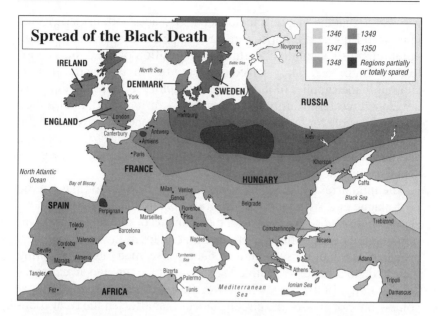

also appeared in the late 1300s and the 1400s. Especially significant were the spinning wheel and the rapid spread of such instruments of power as water- and windmills (especially the latter) in industrial processes. In some manner we may see all of these technological changes as "labor saving," whether printing presses that save the labor of copyists, mills that save the labor of fullers [people who shrink and thicken cloth], or cannon that save the labor of battering-ram carriers. Is it too much to wonder whether the scarcity of labor in the century after 1350 encouraged such innovations?

Plague and the European Spirit

The great epidemic had serious consequences for "authority" in several respects. The landed class had dominated European social, economic, and political life for centuries. On balance in western Europe, the Black Death damaged its economic position, especially in respect to the peasantry which it had exploited for so long. Its power over the peasantry did not end in 1350, but in the later medieval centuries its authority did gradually weaken. Many factors contributed to that immense change in social relationships, including the changing power of towns and trading wealth, the growing authority of central political leaders such as kings, and the development of military technology that supplanted the armored horseman. Although it would be foolish to claim that the Black Death ended the power of the western European landed class, it would also be foolish to assert the epidemic's irrelevance.

The institutional authority of the Church received several blows. To the extent that it depended on learned and administrative talents, it suffered. Such talents and learning could not be quickly replaced, and the death of a parish priest, for example, sometimes resulted in the rapid ordination of a replacement with little training or vocation. Such a circumstance might worsen an already bad situation if the deceased priest had shirked his pastoral duties while the plague raged. Many did (as many did not) and contemporaries held the secular clergy up to unfavorable comparison with the mendicants; some members of the clergy had abandoned their flocks, and others had enriched themselves in the crisis. And even if a clergyman remained devoted to his parish in its travail, his powerlessness was manifest; the extent to which members of the clergy commanded respect because of their "superhuman" qualities was weakened by their inability to stem the disease, and by their own vulnerability to it.

The epidemic touched off long-simmering resentments against the Church as well as against other symbols of authority. The direction taken by the Flagellant movement [a sect that believed in punishing themselves physically for their sins] in Germany provides an illustration. Flagellant processions, especially in Germany, quickly passed out of clerical hands and control. The Flagellants were often highly organized groups, under the direction of a master—a layperson—who heard confessions and imposed penances, thus seemingly poaching on the preserves of the clergy. A millennium was thought to be at hand, in which Christ (perhaps accompanied by the Emperor Frederick Barbarossa, awakened from his mountain tomb) would come again, slay the priests who oppressed the people, and take from the rich to give to the poor. Flagellants saw themselves as armies of saints. In some horrific cases the coming of such an army ignited savage massacres of the Jews, the most obvious outsiders who might serve as scapegoats for the tragedy of the epidemic; thus the Jewish populations of Frankfurt, Mainz, Cologne, and Brussels were put to the sword as a part of the mass hysteria. . . .

These plague-inspired popular movements fed other, later fourteenth-century currents. For while the epidemic may have weakened the institutional authority of the Church, it did not diminish the piety of the population. Although "piety" is hard to measure (as is "authority"), the same civilization that denounced the laxity of the clergy left bequests to churches for prayers and buildings, went on pilgrimages, and manifested signs of intense personal piety that found an outlet in such movements of the laity as confraternities [religious-based organizations]. By the late fourteenth and early fifteenth centuries such expressions of lay piety boiled over in what the Church judged to be heresy, as with the Lollards [followers of John Wycliffe] in England and the Hussites [followers of Jan Hus] in Bohemia.

Did public morality decline during and after the epidemic? Some witnesses claimed that the horror of the plague loosened the bonds of behavior. [Italian writer Giovanni] Boccaccio reported: "Others . . . maintained that an infallible way of warding off this appalling evil was to drink heavily, enjoy life to the full, go round singing and merry-making, gratify all one's cravings whenever the opportunity offered, and shrug the whole thing off as one enormous joke. Moreover, they practiced what they preached to the best of their ability." But the same author also told of those who lived abstemiously in the hope of avoiding plague, and it is possible as well that the plague overstimulated moralists to find "sin" everywhere to explain the catastrophe. The drastic mortality laid the basis for conspicuous consumption by the survivors, nevertheless, and there were those who adopted a tonight-we-drink-for-tomorrow-we-die attitude. And as we have seen, in some cases the social fabric was badly torn by revolutionary movements and hysterical massacres of innocents.

As hard to measure as "piety," "authority," and "morality" is the notion of a civilization obsessed with death and its images. [Scholar] Johan Huizinga, in a famous book written in 1924, drew a memorable picture of a post-plague world of extreme contrasts, of silences and noises, a highly strung civilization quick to violence and outward displays of emotion, one in which the smell of blood mixed with that of roses. Millard Meiss, who studied Florentine and Sienese art in the wake of the plague, showed that art grew more "religious" and "conservative," perhaps from a general desire for intense personal religious expression in painting, but perhaps a reflection of the typical *arriviste* [new and uncertain] tastes of those enriched by the changed circumstances.

Certainly much evidence says that Europeans reacted to the Black Death with mingled guilt and fear: convinced that their sins had brought on God's wrath, fleeing in terror when and where they could, and savagely turning on scapegoats. To many Europeans the Apocalypse seemed at hand. [Scholar] Michael Dols's study of the same epidemic's effects on another civilization both offers interesting contrasts and reinforces the view of European guilt and fear. Dols found that Mamluk Egypt, where the mortality in 1348 rivaled that experienced in Europe, was generally free of most of the hysterical reactions found in Europe. According to Dols, differences in religious background and ideas account for the different reactions. A plague epidemic . . . had ravaged the Middle East in the earliest years of Islam, so that the faith's original writings discuss the plague specifically and with (for Muslims) enormous authority.

Muslims regarded the plague as God's gift, not his scourge—"a mercy and a martyrdom" for the faithful. Flight was therefore wrong, for it was flight from God and God's will (although there was some theological disagreement about that point, Dols admits). Because plague came directly from God, Muslim thinkers more consistently held to a heaven-sent miasma as the immediate cause; doctrines of "bad air" did not slide into ideas of contagion, as they did in the Christian world. Hence Muslims did not turn on alien minorities who might be blamed for contagion. More generally, the Muslim tradition lacked the Christian emphasis on original sin, which lay behind both the guilt felt by Christians and the punishment which Christians believed that someone deserved. Mamluk Egypt, Dols argues, reacted with reverent resignation to the disaster of the Black Death.

The Fourteenth Century Outside Europe

PREFACE

Europe has dominated the historical record of many recent centuries. From scientific discoveries to the age of geographic exploration, from experiments in democracy to world wars, the events, ideas, and peoples of Europe have been particularly influential through time. That dominance, however, was certainly not the case in the 1300s. Many of the fourteenth century's cultural high points were to be found in Asia, Africa, and the Americas.

Certainly, few parts of the world could rival Asia during the fourteenth century for political intrigue, military might, and achievement in the arts. In Japan, for example, infighting among various clans led to political unrest that lasted most of the century—and civil war that was waged on and off through much of it. In China, the century was best known for the replacement of the ruling Mongol emperors with the rule of the native Chinese Mings. And farther east, in India, the emergence of the Muslim Tughluq dynasty was another major political story of the century.

Indeed, the largest of the Asiatic empires dwarfed the territory held by most European kings and queens. The Central Asian ruler Timur, for instance, controlled much of the western part of the continent from his base in Samarkand, a city in modern-day Uzbekistan. His empire lapped up against eastern Europe and parts of Africa as well. The military might of the Turkish Ottoman Empire could not be matched by Europeans of the time, either; under a succession of commanders, the Ottoman army advanced well into southeastern Europe during this time. Population figures are hard to come by, and estimates of fourteenth-century numbers are notoriously unspecific, but it seems likely that the Tughluqs in India and the Ming in China both ruled many more people than did even the most powerful of European leaders.

The situation outside Asia was less striking but similar. Several great civilizations arose in the New World during this period, unknown to Europeans and Asians alike. The Aztecs of Mexico were a prime example. An imperialist empire with a thriving cultural life and military strength that would have been the envy of England or France, the Aztecs constructed their capital city of Tenochtitlán, present-day Mexico City, in the early fourteenth century. Other strong societies grew up in Africa, where the Mali Empire held sway over much of the western part of the continent.

Except for a few neighboring cultures such as the Ottomans, Eu-

ropeans of the fourteenth century had little to do with the world outside their boundaries. Nevertheless, many of the same themes repeat themselves from one continent to the next. The political arguments in Japan or India were quite similar to the political squabbles
created by the feudal system in Europe, for instance. The appetite
for power and control of a Timur or a Mansa Mūsā in Mali was
matched, if somewhat less successfully, by the kings who fought
for dominance during the Hundred Years' War. And the enthusiasm
with which China threw over its Mongol rulers was similar to the
enthusiasm of the European peasant revolts of the time. Political
change and violence marked the period, whether in Europe or outside it.

Tensions in Japan

John Whitney Hall

This excerpt, taken from an article by historian John Whitney Hall, describes the infighting that took place among Japanese rulers in the early and middle fourteenth century. Godaigo, the emperor, had done a great deal early in his tenure to reestablish the powers of the king. He had been exiled by political opponents, and had returned with the help of a general named Takauji, a member of the powerful Ashikaga family. The two were successful in their attempt to wrest power from Godaigo's original opponents, but soon became enmeshed in difficulties of their own. Many of the names mentioned in the text are of powerful families or clans that ruled sections of Japan during medieval times. The Hōjō, the Minamoto, and the Hosokawa all fit into this category.

G odaigo returned to the capital intent on setting himself up as a true monarch. To that purpose he activated the records office and established an awards commission (*onshō-gata*). Through these and other organs of government, he began to make appointments to central and provincial posts and to distribute titles to landholdings. Almost immediately there was a falling out with Takauji. Although they had fought to destroy the Hōjō and to return Emperor Godaigo to the throne, neither Takauji nor his followers were prepared to go along with the emperor's plan to create a government centered on the throne in which military leaders would be of equal or lower rank than the court nobles, men without experience in warfare or statecraft. Takauji personally was well treated by Godaigo. Designated "first to be rewarded," he received the fourth court rank junior grade, the privilege of using one of the characters from the emperor's private name, the governorships of two provinces and the position of

Excerpted from "The Muromachi Bakufu," by John Whitney Hall in *Warrior Rule in Japan*, edited by Marius B. Jansen. Copyright © 1995 by Cambridge University Press. Reprinted with permission from Cambridge University Press.

shugo [political official] of another, and numerous landholdings. Takauji, however, had already petitioned for the posts of *seii tai shōgun* (literally, "barbarian-subduing generalissimo)" and *sōtsuibushi* (constable general), the positions that would give him the authority to establish a new bakufu [military headquarters]. Although Godaigo did name Takauji *chinjufu shōgun* (general of the northern pacification command) and, later, *sei-tō shōgun* (general of the eastern pacification command), he refused during his lifetime to grant Takauji's request. Instead, he successively named his sons, the princes Morinaga and Norinaga, to the post, thus giving form to a polity in which civil authority would outrank or displace the military.

Godaigo's conception was bold, but the execution of his plan was inept and highly prejudiced. As the [fourteenth-century chronicle] *Taiheiki* records, although men like Takauji and [military leader Nitta] Yoshisada received special attention, "the offices of *shugo* and governor in more than fifty provinces were received by nobles and court officials; likewise confiscated estates and great estates were given them until they became . . . rich and powerful. . . ." Following the destruction of the Hōjō, a considerable amount of vacated land and a large number of provincial posts were available for award to those who had assisted in Godaigo's return to the throne. But by including court nobles among the recipients, the emperor ran out of resources with which to reward his military supporters. Among those poorly treated were local leaders such as Akamatsu Norimura, who, once having been appointed *shugo* of Harima, later had the appointment withdrawn. Such arbitrary action led to a general disillusionment among military leaders in the provinces. Takauji, aspiring chief of the military estate and potential shogun, became the most prominent alternative to Godaigo. But he was not alone, as his rivalry with Nitta Yoshisada was to prove.

In 1333, after crushing the Hōjō in Kyoto, Takauji set up a secretariat (*bugyō-sho*) to administer the city. . . . As the winning general, Takauji assumed the right to reward his followers with grants of confiscated landholdings and to make appointments to the posts of *shugo* and *jitō*. Obviously there was a conflict of authority and jurisdiction here that could not long remain unresolved. During most of 1334 Takauji and Godaigo managed a precarious coexistence in Kyoto. The emperor publicly announced his plan, called the Kemmu restoration, and established various organs of central government. Takauji did not take office in any of these, nor did he disband his own secretariat. When Godaigo dispatched his young son Prince Norinaga to Kamakura in an effort to assert the imperial presence in the Kantō, Takauji had his brother Tadayoshi appointed military guardian to the prince. When Takauji complained to Godaigo that the newly appointed shogun, Prince Morinaga, was plotting his death, the emperor had Morinaga sent to Kamakura to be placed in Ashikaga Tadayoshi's custody.

In 1335, Hōjō remnants recaptured Kamakura and drove out Tadayoshi and Prince Morinaga. In the confusion, Tadayoshi had Prince Morinaga killed. Takauji now led his own army, without imperial orders, to the Kantō and quickly retook Kamakura. This time Takauji remained in Kamakura for a year and began to put on the mantle of shogun, giving out land patents and confirmations. When it was clear that Nitta Yoshisada was siding with Godaigo, Takauji declared Nitta's lands confiscated and began to distribute them to his followers. Godaigo retaliated by declaring Takauji an "enemy of the throne" (*chōteki*) and stripping him of his titles and honors. He commissioned generals loyal to his cause, among them Nitta Yoshisada and Kitabatake Akiie, to recapture the Kantō.

Takauji was now in full rebellion against Godaigo, and his break with rival military leaders like Yoshisada was complete. Taking to the field again, he fought his way back to Kyoto in the second month of 1336, against heavy opposition from forces supporting Godaigo's cause. Takauji managed to hold the city for only four days before being driven out toward the western provinces. His retreat was not complete until he had reached the island of Kyushu.

Although Kyushu and the western Honshū provinces were not areas in which the Ashikaga had many direct military connections, Takauji used to his advantage a commission of chastisement against Nitta Yoshisada that he obtained from the retired emperor Kōgon-in, head of the senior branch of the imperial house. Also, by representing the Minamoto cause and professing to champion basic warrior interests in the event of his becoming shogun, Takauji was able to build up a considerable following along the path of his retreat. When possible, he found opportunities along the way to place his collateral followers in favorable positions, promising the most powerful local families and the heads of Ashikaga collateral branches who supported him the military governorships of various provinces and districts, depending on the success of his cause. To the Hosokawa he promised the entire island of Shikoku; to the Imagawa, Bitchū; to the Akamatsu, Harima; and to the Niki, Tamba. By the time he arrived in Kyushu, TakaUji had already won over most of the local military lords, such as the Shimazu, and only a brief military campaign was needed to gain the support of the remainder.

By the fifth month of 1336, with some of his house retainers and collateral commanders and contingents led by his newly won allies from western Japan, Takauji began the countermarch toward Kyoto. His forces moved by both land and water. At the critical battle of Minatogawa in Settsu, the Ashikaga won a decisive victory, forcing

Nitta back to Kyoto and Emperor Godaigo to take refuge with the monks of Hieizan. Takauji entered Kyoto in the company of Prince Yutahito, the brother of Kōgon-in who had previously given Takauji his imperial mandate. Takauji generously endowed the Kōgon–in faction with lands and guarantees of protected income. Somehow the imperial regalia was obtained from Godaigo. These emblems, which were given to Prince Yutahito, became the basis for his installation as Emperor Kōmyō. Takauji began the construction of a new imperial palace, the first permanent one in many years, which was completed the following year. Takauji had now played the supreme role of having installed an emperor with his military power. He further legitimized himself by taking high court rank and adopting the role of chief of the warrior estate. The secretariat he had established three years before had remained in operation and was now turned into a bakufu in all but name. Takauji's public posture was further enhanced when he promulgated the Kemmu *shikimoku* (the Kemmu injunctions), making public the policy he proposed to follow when named shogun. But the appointment did not come until 1338.

There was work yet to be done. Kyoto was still not safely in Ashikaga hands, nor would the enemies of the new bakufu leave the field. Godaigo, claiming that he had given up only replicas and that he still possessed the authentic regalia, kept his cause alive from the mountainous region of Yoshino. There he set up a court in exile, which, because it was located south of Kyoto, was called the Southern Court. The court that remained in Kyoto, which served to legitimate the Ashikaga shogun, was, by the same token, called the Northern Court. Fighting in the name of these two courts continued until 1392, when a settlement was arranged. The existence of two imperial courts, each claiming legitimacy, each calling on the warrior houses throughout Japan to fight for its cause, justified the resort to arms, often for purely private objectives. The basic motivations were not always apparent, but in the years to follow intense rivalries for power among the most powerful military houses in the provinces were fought out.

Takauji's two primary military rivals from the beginning were Nitta Yoshisada and Kitabatake Akiie, both of whom had their largest bases of support east and north of the capital. Although both men were killed in battle in the summer of 1338, and despite Godaigo's death in the summer of 1339, the fighting did not end. Godaigo's son Prince Norinaga succeeded to the "junior" line under the name Gomurakami. In the central provinces, Kusunoki Masatsura, *shugo* of Kawachi, kept the Ashikaga forces on the defensive. In Kyushu, Godaigo's other son, Prince Kanenaga, succeeded in establishing himself at Dazaifu as the chief agent of the capital. The divided polity and the civil war it engendered continued. But the main issue regarding the establishment of a bakufu in Kyoto had been settled. . . .

In 1350, events took another sudden turn, this time brought on by conflicts within the Ashikaga leadership. For several years, a rift over basic policy had been growing between Takauji and his brother Tadayoshi. This was the consequence of the division of responsibilities that had been worked out between the two men. The division was a natural one to make: Takauji was responsible for military strategy and personnel, and Tadayoshi concerned himself with the bakufu's administrative and judicial organs. But policy differences soon developed between the brothers. Takauji, more sensitive to the interest of the local military houses on whose support he depended, tended to be soft regarding the military encroachment on civil estates. Tadayoshi was more inclined to permit the bakufu courts, staffed to considerable extent by hereditary legal experts, to support the proprietary interests of the capital elite. Eventually factions among the Ashikaga collaterals formed behind the brothers.

In 1349, Takauji, having been persuaded of Tadayoshi's disloyalty, dismissed his brother from his bakufu assignments, withdrawing the expectation that he would be next to inherit the title of shogun. The next year Takauji was forced to take to the field against Tadafuyu, his own troublemaking natural son who had been adopted by Tadayoshi.

In the winter of 1351–2, Tadayoshi was captured and killed, presumably by poisoning on Takauji's orders. But Tadayoshi's death only increased the anti-Takauji sentiment in the Kantō. It was not until the spring of 1355 that Takauji, after perhaps the most destructive battle of the civil war, in which several sections of the city were destroyed, retook Kyoto conclusively.

Takauji died in 1358 and was succeeded as head of the Ashikaga house and shogun by Yoshiakira, then in his twenty-eighth year. As might be expected, the second shogun at first had trouble keeping the Ashikaga forces in line, but the intensity of the civil war had subsided. The most powerful *shugo* houses capable of opposing the Ashikaga—the Shiba, Uesugi, Ōuchi, and Yamana—had settled their differences and had joined forces with the bakufu. Yoshiakira died in 1368, to be succeeded by his ten-year-old son Yoshimitsu.

The Tughluq Dynasty in India

Stanley Wolpert

Over the years, the story of southern Asia has frequently been the story of cultural and religious clashes. India and its neighbors have seen struggles pitting Hindu against Muslim, Hindu against Hindu, Muslim against Muslim, and much more. The fourteenth century was no exception. The Tughluqs, who governed much of the region during most of this time, were a Muslim dynasty with a base in the north Indian city of Delhi. Over time, and with decidedly mixed results, the Tughluqs tried to tighten control over several surrounding areas: notably Madura and the Deccan regions of southern India and Bengal to the east. At the same time they attempted to hold off local cries for change, especially those from Hindu leaders. This excerpt from Stanley Wolpert's *A New History of India* describes the Tughluq years and sets them into the context of their time.

For most of the fourteenth century, the Tughluqs ruled Delhi. The founder of this third Muslim dynasty in India was Ghiyas-ud-din Tughluq, the son of a court Turkish slave and a Hindu Jat woman, who ruled mildly for five years. In 1325, Ghiyas-ud-din and his favorite son were both killed when a victory pavilion erected by his other son and successor, Muhammad (r. 1325–51), suddenly collapsed. Catapulted to power over the corpses of his father and brother, Muhammad Tughluq's long reign may be read as a search for religious expiation of this guilt by a man of not inconsiderable sensitivity and talent. The Muslim world traveler Ibn Battuta, who journeyed through Asia and Africa from 1325 to 1354, served for a while as chief judge (*qazi*) at Muhammad's court and recalled how strict the sultan was about compelling "the people to master the ordinances for ablutions, prayers, and the principles of Islam." He could not, however, succeed in teaching others to do what he personally ignored, and rebellion was widespread throughout this era. In a grandiose attempt to subdue southern resistance to his rule by establishing a second capital in the Deccan, Muhammad Tughluq forced many nobles and officials to abandon their homes in Delhi in 1327 and journey south over five hundred miles, across the Vindhya-Satpura divide to Daulatabad (Devagiri). Many died in that arduous journey. For those who survived, moreover, Deccan heat and lack of perennial river water made Daulatabad an inhospitable site for the sultanate's secondary capital.

In 1329–30, Muhammad Tughluq attempted another surprising innovation, the issue of new currency. Possibly hoping to emulate the imperial Chinese, whose use of paper currency was quite successful, the sultan issued brass or copper tokens that were proclaimed to be the equivalent of the increasingly rare silver *tanka* (140 grains). The scheme was apparently as well motivated as any paper currency issue and might have worked were it not for the fact that foreign merchants refused to take tokens for their goods, even though they used them readily within India. What is more, Indians were permitted to turn in their coppers at the royal mint for silver or gold, and they did so more vigorously each month. Indeed, most Indians seem to have become kitchen coppersmiths in the wake of this "reform," and mountains of Tughluq copper tokens were subsequently said to have remained lying for a century outside the sultanate's treasuries. Within three or four years, the sultan was obliged to withdraw his special coins because of the heavy loss of public treasure. From 1335 to 1342, India suffered one of its most severe and prolonged periods of drought and famine. Although all accounts of foreign travelers make note of the plaintive suffering at that time, the sultanate made no concerted effort to assist its subjects by general tax relief or food distribution. Widespread economic discontent led to rebellions throughout the sultanate, which proved most effective in the south. In 1335, an independent Sultanate of Madura was established by the Tughluq governor Ahsan Shah. When Muhammad's army moved south to subdue that fire, others raged in Lahore and Delhi, forcing the sultan to return north. Hindu chiefs, noting the success of Muslim officers in their Tamilnad rebellion, raised similar banners of independence from Delhi. Muslim intrusion into the Deccan had driven many Hindu warriors south of the Tungabhadra River, where a new Hindu kingdom arose in 1336, named for its capital, *Vijāya-nagar*, "City of Victory."

Harihāra I (r. 1336–57), founder of Vijāyanagar, had converted to Islam in order to serve the Tughluqs as a governor in his southern homeland, but he reconverted to Hinduism and quickly became leading tributary overlord of the southern Deccan. Winning the support and allegiance of the most powerful local landholders (*nāyakas*), Harihāra conquered the domain of the Hoysala overlord, Balāla III, and developed his urban capital as the most "important place" in the region of peninsular India. By 1343 Vijāyanagar claimed sovereignty over all lands hitherto tributary to the Hoysalas, but was less successful later in seeking to extend its control north of the Tungabhadra. Rebellion against Muhammad Tughluq's reign broke out in Daulatabad and other Deccan cities in 1345, led by discontented Muslim nobles, among whom was Hāsan Gangu, who proclaimed himself sultan of the Deccan in 1347. Taking as his title-name Ala-ud-din Bahmān Shah, Hasan founded the Bahmāni dynasty, the mightiest and longest-lived Muslim dynasty of the Deccan, which remained united for some two hundred years and survived in fragmented form for a century after that. For the last half of the fourteenth century and all of the fifteenth, the Bahmāni dynasty fought a series of ten indecisive but bloody wars against Vijāyanagar over the fertile *doab* [strip of land between two rivers] soil between the rivers Krishna and Tungabhadra, which marked their disrupted boundary. South India was thus effectively removed from the control of Delhi's sultanate, which had reached its peak of power and entered a phase of rapid deterioration following the death of Muhammad Tughluq.

Bengal and a New Emperor

Bengal declared its independence from Delhi in 1338. Following a deadly struggle among the region's leading *māliks* ("nobles"), Mālik Hāji Ilyās emerged victorious, assuming the title of Sultan Shāms-ud-din (r. 1339–59) and founding the Ilyās Shāhi dynasty, which ruled over Bengal from its capital at Lakhnawati for almost a century. Bengali independence from West Indian Muslim rule was thus asserted early and maintained until the sixteenth-century Mughal conquest. Nor was it language and political independence alone that differentiated the region of Bengal from the rest of North India in this era, for even the form of Islam predominantly practiced there was peculiarly attuned to its cultural character and ancient heritage. Sufism, Islam's mystic thread, which evolved primarily as a legacy of Persian influence upon Islamic orthodoxy, struck a responsive chord in the mass of Bengal's population, especially among the lowest class of Hindu outcastes and former Buddhists, who were left without a priesthood to turn to for spiritual guidance after 1202; it appealed as well to many Muslims, for whom it revitalized the message of Islam.

Three orders of Sufi saints had appeared in India by the thirteenth century: the Chishtī Suhrawardi, and Firdawsi, all of which appealed to the same mystical yearning for union with God, experienced by so many Hindus as well as Muslims and other "God-intoxicated" seekers the world over. The fervent love of God, which played so important a role in the passionate yearnings for "the mother goddess" that had characterized Bengali religious consciousness from time immemorial, may well have its roots in the same lush alluvium [soil], fed by torrential monsoons which gave birth to "golden" jute, the premier crop of Bangladesh. The ineffable blend of love and sorrow, of human frailty and poverty amid the awesome forces of nature's lush wealth, helped fashion the uniquely sensitive, passionate, and mercurial temperament characteristic of Bengal; it seems also to have predisposed millions of Bengalis to the ardent appeal of Islamic mysticism. The wandering *pirs* (Sufi preachers), who went into Bengal's remote villages to bring their message of divine love to impoverished peasants, sounded much the same as Hindu *bhakti* ("devotional") saints offering salvation through worship of the mother goddess, or Mahayanist Buddhists bearing the promise of divine salvation by grace of a Bodhisattva's [the savior of Mahayanist Buddhism] blessing. Bengali translations of epic Sanskrit literature were encouraged by court patronage during this era of independent Muslim rule, serving at once both to weaken the grip of Brahman pundits over the people and to provide the national mortar of a literary vernacular language to this culturally fecund region. Under a succession of independent Muslim dynasties, Bengal was to retain its sovereign status, free of interference from Delhi, till the peak of great Mughal power and Akbar's conquest in 1576.

When Muhammad Tughluq was killed fighting rebellion in Sind in 1351, his orthodox cousin, Firuz, ascended the throne of Delhi, from which he reigned for thirty-seven years (1351–88). Famed for his abolition of torture, his passion for building, and his lifelong adherence to the tenets of Islamic orthodoxy, Firuz was blessed with a reign of good monsoons and abundant harvests. He sought in vain to reconquer Bengal, but soon contented himself with building a new capital instead of carrying on futile wars. The new Delhi constructed in his name, Firuzabad, was replete with gardens as well as mosques and colleges. His generous patronage of the *ulama* [Islamic learned men] gave Firuz the best "historic press" of all the sultans of Delhi, and he is credited with having constructed no fewer than forty mosques, thirty colleges, a hundred hospitals, and two hundred new towns in the environs of the capital. He was also attracted by various irrigation schemes, supporting the construction of some fifty dams and reservoirs and bringing hitherto barren land into productive use. Less suspicious, perhaps, than his predecessors, Firuz cut down on the royal spy corps, investing more heavily in productive enterprises. He seems to have been one of the most intelligent, if not enlightened, monarchs of the sultanate, although his orthodoxy led him to a number of hostile actions against the Hindus, which ultimately alienated the majority of his subjects. Brahmans [a class of Hindu priests] felt particularly persecuted, since they had hitherto generally been exempt from paying the *jizya* [a personal tax] (as they were from the payment of all taxes) but were now obliged to do so. Many nonbrahmans converted to Islam during Firuz's reign, thus escaping the poll tax entirely, though they were still faced with the obligation of paying the less onerous Muslim *zakat* (alms).

Firuz was the last of the strong sultans of Delhi. Within a decade of his death, half a dozen transient monarchs held tenuous sway over the precarious fortunes of that fast-declining kingdom. While rival factions fought among themselves in Delhi, the Central Asian armies of Timur the Lame (Tamerlane), waiting beyond India's northwestern gates, swooped down through the passes to plunder the Punjab and in 1398 entered Delhi itself. The death and plunder of Old Delhi by Timur's forces left "towers built high" with the heads and ravaged bodies of Hindus. Tens of thousands of slaves were dragged away as living booty, and the great mosque at Samarkand was later to be rebuilt by the stonemasons of Delhi. Timur abandoned the Indian plains before the hot weather in 1399, leaving a trail of blood and torture behind him as he moved north to his homeland.

Ibn Battuta

Ross E. Dunn

Ibn Battuta (1304–1368) was one of the great travelers of the medieval world. Unlike many so-called travelers whose texts are lined with imagined events and impossible creatures, Ibn Battuta was a careful, reliable, and thorough observer of the world around him. His accounts are a prime source of information on a multitude of places, peoples, and cultures of the time. This description of Ibn Battuta's life and importance comes from the introduction to Ross E. Dunn's *The Adventures of Ibn Battuta: A Muslim Traveler of the Fourteenth Century.*

A bu 'Abdallah ibn Battuta has been rightly celebrated as the greatest traveler of premodern times. He was born into a family of Muslim legal scholars in Tangier, Morocco, in 1304 during the era of the Marinid dynasty. He studied law as a young man and in 1325 left his native town to make the pilgrimage, or *hajj*, to the sacred city of Mecca in Arabia. He took a year and a half to reach his destination, visiting North Africa, Egypt, Palestine, and Syria along the way. After completing his first *hajj* in 1326, he toured Iraq and Persia, then returned to Mecca. In 1328 (or 1330) he embarked upon a sea voyage that took him down the eastern coast of Africa as far south as the region of modern Tanzania. On his return voyage he visited Oman and the Persian Gulf and returned to Mecca again by the overland route across central Arabia.

In 1330 (or 1332) he ventured to go to India to seek employment in the government of the Sultanate of Delhi. Rather than taking the normal ocean route across the Arabian Sea to the western coast of India, he traveled north through Egypt and Syria to Asia Minor. After touring that region, he crossed the Black Sea to the plains of West Central

Asia. He then, owing to fortuitous circumstances, made a westward detour to visit Constantinople, capital of the Byzantine Empire, in the company of a Turkish princess. Returning to the Asian steppes, he traveled eastward through Transoxiana, Khurasan, and Afghanistan, arriving at the banks of the Indus River in September 1333 (or 1335).

He spent eight years in India, most of that time occupying a post as a *qadi*, or judge, in the government of Muhammad Tughluq, Sultan of Delhi. In 1341 the king appointed him to lead a diplomatic mission to the court of the Mongol emperor of China. The expedition ended disastrously in shipwreck off the southwestern coast of India, leaving Ibn Battuta without employment or resources. For a little more than two years he traveled about southern India, Ceylon, and the Maldive Islands, where he served for about eight months as a *qadi* under the local Muslim dynasty. Then, despite the failure of his ambassadorial mission, he resolved in 1345 to go to China on his own. Traveling by sea, he visited Bengal, the coast of Burma, and the island of Sumatra, then continued on to Canton. The extent of his visit to China is uncertain but was probably limited to the southern coastal region.

In 1346–47 he returned to Mecca by way of South India, the Persian Gulf, Syria, and Egypt. After performing the ceremonies of the *hajj* one last time, he set a course for home. Traveling by both land and sea, he arrived in Fez, the capital of Morocco, late in 1349. The following year he made a brief trip across the Strait of Gibraltar to the Muslim kingdom of Granada [in present-day Spain]. Then, in 1353, he undertook his final adventure, a journey by camel caravan across the Sahara Desert to the Kingdom of Mali in the West African Sudan. In 1355 he returned to Morocco to stay. In the course of a career on the road spanning almost thirty years, he crossed the breadth of the Eastern Hemisphere, visited territories equivalent to about 44 modern countries, and put behind him a total distance of approximately 73,000 miles.

Early in 1356 Sultan Abu 'Inan, the Marinid ruler of Morocco, commissioned Ibn Juzayy, a young literary scholar of Andalusian origin, to record Ibn Battuta's experiences, as well as his observations about the Islamic world of his day, in the form of a *rihla*, or book of travels. As a type of Arabic literature, the *rihla* attained something of a flowering in North Africa between the twelfth and fourteenth centuries. The best known examples of the genre recounted a journey from the Maghrib [northwestern Africa] to Mecca, informing and entertaining readers with rich descriptions of the pious institutions, public monuments, and religious personalities of the great cities of Islam. Ibn Battuta and Ibn Juzayy collaborated for about two years to compose their work, the longest and in terms of its subject matter the most complex *rihla* to come out of North Africa in the medieval age. His royal charge completed, Ibn Battuta retired to a judicial post in a Moroccan provincial town. He died in 1368.

Ibn Battuta's *Rihla*

Written in the conventional literary style of the time, Ibn Battuta's *Rihla* is a comprehensive survey of the personalities, places, governments, customs, and curiosities of the Muslim world in the second quarter of the fourteenth century. It is also the record of a dramatic personal adventure. In the four centuries after Ibn Battuta's death, the *Rihla* circulated, mostly in copied manuscript abridgments of Ibn Juzayy's original text, among people of learning in North Africa, West Africa, Egypt, and perhaps other Muslim lands where Arabic was read.

The book was unknown outside Islamic countries until the early nineteenth century, when two German scholars published separately translations of portions of the *Rihla* from manuscripts obtained in the Middle East. In 1829 Samuel Lee, a British orientalist, published an English translation based on abridgments of the narrative that John Burckhardt, the famous Swiss explorer, had acquired in Egypt. Around the middle of the century five manuscripts of the *Rihla* were found in Algeria following the French occupation of that country. These documents were subsequently transferred to the Bibliothèque Nationale in Paris. Two of them represent the most complete versions of the narrative that have ever come to light. The others are partial translations, one of which carries the autograph of Ibn Juzayy, Ibn Battuta's editor. Working with these five documents, two French scholars, C. Défrémery and B.R. Sanguinetti, published between 1853 and 1858 a printed edition of the Arabic text, together with a translation in French and an apparatus of notes and variant textual readings.

Since then, translations of the work, prepared in every case from Défrémery and Sanguinetti's printed text, have been published in many languages, including Spanish, Italian, German, Russian, Polish, Hungarian, Persian, and Japanese. In 1929 Sir Hamilton Gibb produced an abridged English translation and began work on a complete edition of the work under the auspices of the Hakluyt Society. The last of the four volumes in this series is still in preparation. However, English translations of various portions of the *Rihla* have appeared [since the eighteenth] century as books or as articles in anthologies and scholarly journals.

The numerous translations of the *Rihla*, together with the extensive corpus of encyclopedia articles, popular summaries, and critical commentaries on Ibn Battuta and his career that have accumulated since the eighteenth century, are a tribute to the extraordinary value of the narrative as a historical source on much of the inhabited Eastern Hemisphere in the second quarter of the fourteenth century. The book has been cited and quoted in hundreds of historical works, not only those relating to Islamic countries but to China and the Byzantine empire as well. For the history of certain regions, Sudanic West Africa, Asia Minor, or the Malabar coast of India, for example, the *Rihla* stands as the

only eye-witness report on political events, human geography, and social or economic conditions for a period of a century or more. Ibn Battuta had no professional background or experience as a writer of geography, history, or ethnography, but he was, as [one historian] de-
clares, "the supreme example of *le géographe malgré lui*," the "geo-
grapher in spite of himself."

The Western world has conventionally celebrated Marco Polo, who
died the year before Ibn Battuta first left home, as the "Greatest Traveler in History." Ibn Battuta has inevitably been compared with him
and has usually taken second prize as "the Marco Polo of the Muslim
world" or "the Marco Polo of the tropics." Keeping in mind that neither man actually composed his own book (Marco's record was dic-
tated to the French romance writer Rusticello in a Genoese prison),
there is no doubt that the Venetian's work is the superior one in terms
of the accurate, precise, practical information it contributes on medieval
China and other Asian lands in the latter part of the thirteenth century,
information of profound value to historians ever since. Yet Ibn Battuta
traveled to, and reports on, a great many more places than Marco did,
and his narrative offers details, sometimes in incidental bits, sometimes
in long disquisitions, on almost every conceivable aspect of human life
in that age, from the royal ceremonial of the Sultan of Delhi to the sexual customs of women in the Maldive Islands to the harvesting of co-
conuts in South Arabia. Moreover his story is far more personal and
humanely engaging than Marco's. Some Western writers, especially in
an earlier time when the conviction of Europe's superiority over Islamic civilization was a presumption of historical scholarship, have
criticized Ibn Battuta for being excessively eager to tell about the lives
and pious accomplishments of religious savants and Sufi mystics when
he might have written more about practical politics and prices. The
Rihla, however, was directed to Muslim men of learning of the fourteenth century for whom such reportage, so recondite to the modern
Western reader, was pertinent and interesting.

As in Marco's case, we know almost nothing about the life of Ibn
Battuta apart from what the autobiographical dimension of his own
book reveals. Aside from three minor references in Muslim scholarly
works of the fourteenth or fifteenth century that attest independently
to the Moroccan's existence and to his achievements as a traveler, no
document has ever come to light from his own age that mentions him.
To understand his character, his aspirations, his social attitudes and
prejudices, his personal relations with other people and, finally, the
way he "fits" into fourteenth-century Muslim society and culture, we
must rely almost exclusively on the *Rihla* itself. Fortunately, by ex-
pressing here and there in its pages his reactions to events, his an-
noyances, his animosities, and the details of his personal intrigues, he
reveals something of his own character.

Western writers have sometimes characterized Ibn Battuta as a brave explorer like Marco Polo, risking his life to discover *terra incognita* and bring knowledge of it to public attention. In fact Ibn Battuta's experience was drastically different from that of the Venetian. Marco traveled as an alien visitor into lands few Europeans had ever seen and whose people knew little, and cared to know little, about Europe. He was an oddity, a "stranger in a strange land," who was given the opportunity to visit China only because of the very special political circumstances that prevailed for a short time in the thirteenth and early fourteenth centuries: the existence of the great Mongol states of Asia and their policy of permitting merchants of all origins and religions to travel and conduct business in their domains. Marco does indeed herald the age of European discovery, not because the peoples of Asia somehow needed discovering to set themselves on a course into the future, but because his book made an extraordinary and almost immediate intellectual impact on a young Western civilization that until that time had a cramped and faulty vision of what the wider world of the Eastern Hemisphere was all about.

Ibn Battuta, by contrast, spent most of his traveling career within the cultural boundaries of what Muslims called the Dar al-Islam, or Abode of Islam. This expression embraced the lands where Muslims predominated in the population, or at least where Muslim kings or princes ruled over non-Muslim majorities and where in consequence the *shari'a,* or Sacred Law, of Islam was presumably the foundation of the social order. In that sense Islamic civilization extended from the Atlantic coast of West Africa to Southeast Asia. Moreover, important minority communities of Muslims inhabited cities and towns in regions such as China, Spain, and tropical West Africa that were beyond the frontiers of the Dar al-Islam. Therefore almost everywhere Ibn Battuta went he lived in the company of other Muslims, men and women who shared not merely his doctrinal beliefs and religious rituals, but his moral values, his social ideals, his everyday manners. Although he was introduced in the course of his travels to a great many Muslim peoples whose local languages, customs, and aesthetic values were unfamiliar in his own homeland at the far western edge of the hemisphere, he never strayed far from the social world of individuals who shared his tastes and sensibilities and among whom he could always find hospitality, security, and friendship.

The Rise of the Ottomans

M. Philips Price

The fourteenth century has been called an era of disaster for Europe. People most often use this phrase to refer to internal struggles such as the bubonic plague, the frequent famines, the peasant revolts, and the constant battles among European countries. But the fourteenth century was a time when Europe was under serious attack from outside as well. The Islamic Ottoman Empire, which originally covered approximately present-day Turkey, spent much of the century gradually moving into southeastern Europe.

Being conquered by the English or the French was bad enough, but for many Europeans, being conquered by Muslims was far worse. Only a century or two earlier Christian knights had gone on crusades into Muslim territory, fighting to reclaim the land for Christianity. Now it was Islam's turn to do the invading. As journalist M. Philips Price explains in this excerpt, the Ottoman leaders Osman, Orhan [also known as Orkhan], and Murad were successful for several reasons, not the least of which was a tolerance for other religions and ways of thinking.

The Osmanlis [Ottomans, called "Osmanlis" after their leader Osman], being pagans, for they had not yet accepted Islam, were tolerant of all customs and religions. But they were not impressed by the Christianity that they saw, and Arab missionaries who came to them early in the fourteenth century easily induced them to accept Islam. Their conversion to Islam welded the Osmanlis together. Gradually they began to absorb even some of the Greeks into their system. Thus

Excerpted from *A History of Turkey* (New York: Macmillan, 1956) by M. Philips Price.

began that great fusion which laid the foundations of the Ottoman Empire. The physically strong and vigorous Turks combined with the witty and intelligent Greeks. The East and West began to fuse and create something which proved of value to posterity. The Turks provided physical strength and a practical, if not very profound, outlook on life. Through the Greeks, the Turks came in contact with the art and culture of the ancient world. In architecture it was Greek influence that produced the early Osmanli buildings, at Brusa. The Turkish mosques were based on the style of the Byzantine churches. The only original Turkish conception in architecture were the minarets [thin towers], which have certainly provided a very striking feature of the mosques of Turkey. The two great civilisations of this period of history in the Middle East were the Arab and the Byzantine. The Arab was ruined by the Mongol invasion, the Byzantine was ruined by the Fourth Crusade and the Latin occupation. A decadent Hellenism [Greek culture], however, now came into contact with the young and vital energies of the Osmanli Turks, and it was the Turkish role in history to pick up what survived of Hellenic civilisation and incorporate it into the system they were now to create.

During the reign of Osman (1290–1326) the Turks had practically no contact with their eastern neighbours, the Emirates of Anatolia and the powerful Karamanli. Their contacts were entirely with their western neighbours, the Greeks of the Kara Su and Sakaria valleys. In 1326 Osman turned his attention towards the Greek town of Brusa. He wanted it to round off his territory. The Greek commander of Brusa, Evrenos, disgusted with the lack of support which he got from Constantinople and with the sordid intrigues in the capital, agreed to surrender the place to Osman. Later he became a Moslem and a commander in Osman's army. His example was followed by others, and thus the Turks absorbed more and more of their Greek neighbours. The simple faith of Islam appealed to many Greeks, who were tired of the controversies, both religious and political, which constantly racked the Byzantine capital. The Greek Orthodox Church had fallen on difficult times since the Latin occupation. It was too conservative to undergo anything like a Reformation. The only change possible for those who were discontented was to embrace the faith of Islam. Thus Osman created, where [Central Asian conquerors] Genghiz Khan and Timur destroyed. He did not build up ephemeral power which collapsed at his death. He absorbed his adversaries by tolerance and by using their ideas and capabilities. Consequently the work of the Osmanli Turks endured, whereas that of the Mongols and the Tartars vanished. In Western Asia at this time it was easy for Mahomed to succeed Christ, and the words "I believe in one God and Mahomed is His Prophet" became the new creed that could be heard repeated now in the city of Nicene Creed.

Osman died soon after taking Brusa, and was succeeded by his son, Orkhan, who developed Brusa as the capital of the Osmanlis, and here, with the aid of Greek architects and artists, he erected many fine buildings. Orkhan attracted many upper-class Greeks to his service by rewards and emoluments [other payments]. Those Greeks that helped him in his campaigns he rewarded with grants of land. But land under the Osmanlis was held as a military fief and carried with it the obligation for further service, and the land had to be relinquished if he left the service of the Emir. Thus from the first the Turks built up a land system without a hereditary nobility.

The eyes of Orkhan and of his son Murad, who succeeded him in 1359, were fixed on the West. They were attracted by the wealth and superior culture of the Greeks, and soon after he became ruler Orkhan married a Byzantine princess. Soon the Osmanlis were thinking of contacting the Slav civilisation across the Aegean Sea to the west of the Byzantine Empire. Then Turkish forces began to cross the sea and land in Thrace [in extreme southeastern Europe]. They were invited to go over by the Byzantine Emperor, Cantacuzemos, who wanted to use the Osmanlis in the civil war that he was fighting with the rival dynasty of the Palaeologi. This internal disruption within the Byzantine Empire greatly facilitated the Osmanlis' expansion into Europe. By the beginning of the reign of Murad, the Osmanlis were securely planted on the coasts of Thrace, taking full advantage of the civil war among the Greeks. Thus long before the Turks had any status in Asia Minor they were beginning to become a power in Europe. The Turks were advancing into the Balkans at a time when the greater part of Asia Minor was held by quite different branches of the Turkish-speaking people. The Osmanlis were set on becoming Europeanised Turks from the outset. In 1360 Murad took Adrianople from the Byzantines. This was the next most-important city of the Empire after Constantinople. Rulers of Europe, who up to now had paid no attention to the Osmanlis when they were an insignificant tribe in Asia Minor, began to get alarmed at their progress in military and political power in Europe. But there was little that they could do, because there was no united force to oppose them. In 1389 Murad pushed forward against the Serbians, and at the battle of Kossovo destroyed Serbian independence. In spite of the Turkish victory, however, Murad was killed either in action or by assassination. The evidence of what happened is conflicting.

Reasons for the Success

Meanwhile jealousies and quarrels between Serbians, Bulgars and Hungarians made easy the Turkish advance. The Bulgars actually gladly accepted Turkish suzerainty in order to save them from their Christian neighbours! The Turks also were assisted by the deep hatred existing at that time between the Eastern and the Western Christian

Churches. Orthodox Christians of the Balkans, and some of the heretical sects like the Bogomils, accepted Turkish rule because they knew they would receive greater toleration than they would get from the [Catholic civil rulers] Hapsburgs or the Roman Catholic prelates.

Murad was one of the greatest of the Osmanli leaders of the early days. His successful military campaign in Thrace and the Balkans made him the real founder of the Ottoman Empire. But he was not just a ruthless conqueror. He was a very astute diplomat whose wise actions and tact enabled him to secure the submission of whole communities without striking a blow. He laid the foundations also of a policy which enabled his successors to solve the problem of creating a multi-racial empire where more than one religious belief also prevailed. While the Osmanlis were in Asia Minor on the eastern borders of the Byzantine Empire, they were able to absorb their Greek neighbours easily into their political system. But when they rapidly acquired vast territories in South-east Europe, they found they were not numerous enough to absorb the Christian Slavs and Greeks and had to come to some accommodation with them. So Murad adopted a new tactic which was ruthless but effective. He offered the Christian population full Turkish citizenship if they would become Mahommedans [Muslims]. Those who would not be converted became second-class citizens. The Turkish soldiers were allowed to make slaves of the males of conquered Christians who would not become Mahommedans and concubines of the women in campaigns where Turkish arms were resisted. Other Christians were allowed freedom of their religion and their laws regulating family life, but had to pay special taxes. This led to many conversions and also to a great mixing of the races, so that the Turkish blood was soon swamped into the flood of the new Greek and Slav citizens of the European provinces. In the reign of Murad, too, a beginning was made in the creation of the Corps of Janissaries. These were a military force recruited from Christian youths who were taken from their families early in life and given special privileges and free education and taught absolute loyalty to the Sultan. They became a praetorian guard, devoted to the Ottoman State and for centuries one of the pillars of its strength.

The Turkish Army in the fourteenth century, when the drive into Europe was taking place, developed tactics and training which gave it advantage over others. The Turks probably learnt from the Byzantines, with their traditions of the Roman legion, the art of using well-trained infantry.

Murad had the wisdom to see that the Christians were better educated than the Turks, and that their incorporation into the Ottoman State, if it could be achieved, would ensure administrative ability and organising capacity for the political system. If some of the Christian Slavs and Greeks of the Balkans and Thrace could be got to help to build up an empire which was Moslem but was one in which, though Christians, they could, if they wished, rise to the highest posts, then this empire could turn round and from its centre in European Thrace could recross into Asia Minor and subdue the other Turkish emirates of that sub-continent. And that, in fact, happened. Murad, before he met his end at Kossovo and before he had completed his conquest of Serbia, decided to invade Asia Minor and start to subdue the Turkish emirates there. In 1377 he absorbed by purchase and arrangement the small emirates of Hamid and Tekke, and from this vantage-point he set out to attack the powerful Karamania Emirate. And he took with him in this campaign important contingents of Christians, both Serb and Greek, who had elected to join his army. They were, in fact, very efficient troops, and fought well for their Moslem lord, because they were well treated. But the campaign was not very successful. In a battle with the Karamanian Turks near Konia no decision was reached, both sides retiring, and the Osmanli Turks, fresh from their victories in Europe, found that their kinsmen, the Turks of Asia Minor, were a tougher proposition than the Greeks and Slavs of the Balkan peninsula. The Osmanlis therefore remained for a while yet an empire based largely on South-east Europe and with large non-Moslem communities within it.

Strength of an Empire

When Murad died on the battlefield of Kossovo, his son Bayazid became Emir of the Osmanlis. He made it a point of doing all he could to conciliate the Serbs. He gave them full autonomy, and married Despina, the daughter of the Serbian prince. He incorporated Serbian troops into his army with the same rights as his Moslem troops. It is doubtful if the Serbs in those days felt the defeat at Kossovo as a serious disaster. Their incorporation into the Osmanli Empire gave them security from their Christian neighbours, the Bulgars and the Hungarians, from whom they had in the past suffered much. It is probable that only in later times, when Turkish rule in the Balkans became corrupt and oppressive, did the Serbs begin to look on Kossovo as a national humiliation. In fact, soon after the battle both Osmanli and Serbian troops were together invading Bosnia in order to secure its submission to the Empire.

Secure then, as it seemed, in Europe, Bayazid was the first Turkish ruler to seriously tackle Asia Minor and the problem of securing the submission of the other Turkish emirates. In 1390 he moved south from the Osmanli territories in north-west Asia Minor and occupied Ephesus. Then he took Aidin and reached the lower Aegean, but was not able to build up a naval force because he could not get the craftsmen and engineers. In the following year he attacked the powerful Karamanian Turks, and for the first time defeated them at Ak Chai and entered Konia, their capital. He went on to occupy Samsun on the Black Sea, Kastamuni and Sinope. But he failed to assimilate the Turks of these regions into his political system. Before he could seriously tackle this problem, Sigismund, leading an Hungarian army, marched south into Bulgaria and threatened the Turkish acquisitions in Europe. Hurrying back from Asia Minor, Bayazid attacked the invaders at Tirnovo in Bulgaria, drove them out and incorporated Bulgaria into the Empire. Bulgarian independence and autonomy disappeared and the Bulgarian Church was put under the Greek Patriarch. Bayazid then turned his attention to Constantinople. For the first time a Turkish ruler sought to besiege and take the great city of the Byzantines, the second Rome. His motives were not clear, because the Greeks had not given him any trouble at that time. Possibly he thought the time had come when the plum was ripe to fall into his lap. The siege went on for some time. The Osmanlis built a fort on the Bosphorus, and at one time actually got into Galata. But Constantinople held out, and ultimately the city was relieved by Genoese and Venetian naval forces. It was possibly the absence of Turkish naval forces that prevented Bayazid from taking Constantinople this time. Bayazid, too, was showing signs of deterioration. He had taken to a life of ease, and was leaving the army command to others.

In 1402, however, he was galvanised into action. He had to give up further plans for the siege of Constantinople in order to meet a much more serious danger than the poor Byzantine Emperor. For Timur Tamerlane, the last of the great Central Asian Tartar conquerors, had entered Asia Minor, had taken Sivas by storm and was marching west. Timur claimed descent from Genghiz Khan through the latter's son, Djagatai. Like the Mongols, he just set out to conquer lands without any idea what to do with them when he had conquered them. He had built up a powerful military force, with strong cavalry formations whose movements were rapid and who lived on the country. It is by no means certain that Timur was really interested in Asia Minor. Actually he seemed more interested in the richer lands of Syria and Egypt, where better loot could be obtained than in Asia Minor. Probably Bayazid could have diverted Timur if he had been tactful. But instead he sent him insulting letters which was further evidence that he was deteriorating and had not the wisdom of his earlier years. So the Turkish and Tartar armies met at Ankara in July 1402. Bayazid again showed a complete lack of caution. Instead of withdrawing into the hills to rest his men after a long march, he put them on the plain and attacked Timur's forces entrenched on higher ground. He put Tartar mercenaries in front who at once deserted to Timur, and within a short time the Osmanlis were completely routed. Bayazid was taken prisoner and died the following year. The battle of Ankara was memorable because it was the only defeat which the Ottoman armies suffered for the first three centuries of Turkish history. But it had no historical significance and was merely a temporary reverse in a general advance. And Timur's invasion of Asia Minor was of the nature only of a raid. After a year he retired to Samarkand in Central Asia again, and died soon after, leaving the condition of Asia Minor fundamentally unchanged. The Anatolian emirates re-established their independence once more, and the Osmanlis went on with the building of their Empire, based on South-east Europe. One interesting fact emerged at this time which showed the strength of the Osmanli regime. At the moment of the Osmanlis' greatest weakness, after the defeat of Bayazid, the Greek and Slav Christians of the Balkans and the Christian levies in the army showed no sign of wanting to throw off their rule. Nothing is more indicative of the fundamental soundness of the regime than that.

Timur

Bertold Spuler

Few leaders in history, let alone the fourteenth century, have been as feared as Timur (1336–1405), also known as Tamur, Tamburlaine, and Tamerlane. A Central Asian who made his name through a combination of courage, cruelty, and a knowledge of human nature, Timur began as an obscure local chieftain but soon became lord of an enormous area that included nearly all of western Asia. This excerpt, from German historian Bertold Spuler's *The Mongols in History*, describes Timur's career.

A mong all the troubles which paralysed public life in Transoxania [the territory between the Central Asian rivers Amu Dar'ya and Syr Dar'ya] and Persia towards the end of the fourteenth century, a new military genius began slowly but surely to exercise control. This was Timur, the chief of a small Turkic tribe. The son of Taragai, chief of the Tatar tribe of Barlas, he was born in 1336. In his youth he had sought the company of influential chieftains and generals until such time as he was able to assemble an army of his own. By 1360 he had played a part in local fighting which, although fierce, had no lasting significance and his reputation had increased. It is not clear whether the wound which caused him to limp and gained him the nickname Leng ("the Lame") was sustained during this fighting, or during a sheep-stealing escapade; but thereafter Europeans called him Tamerlane (Timur Leng). Disputes with his former friends led to his control of [the Central Asian territories] Kashgar and Khorazm, and he collected a considerable army mainly of Turks with whom were included the remains of some Mongol tribes. In deference to the traditional sentiments of his new subjects, Timur had a descendant of Chengiz [Genghis] Khan nominally elected as Khan, while he himself adopted the modest title of Beg, or Emir.

Excerpted from *The Mongols in History* (Paris: Payot, 1961) by Bertold Spuler, translated by Geoffrey Wheeler. Copyright © 1961 by Payot.

Timur's seizure of power did not bring peace to central Asia, for he was fully occupied in other parts of his empire. In the Qypchaq [Central Asian region] he was able to install as ruler his favourite, Tokhtamysh, and in 1379 he crossed the Amu-Dar'ya in order to conquer Persia. The incredible cruelty of his troops, who erected pyramids and towers built from the skulls and bodies of soldiers killed in combat or executed after victory, spread terror throughout Western Asia and contributed much to overcoming—or at least weakening—all resistance. Timur did not rely entirely on strategy for success; in critical situations, he always tried to establish contact with those of his enemies whom he considered might be susceptible to inducement; and on many occasions such approaches brought about the desertion of numbers of enemy soldiers at the crucial point of a battle. His victories cannot, therefore, be attributed solely to his military genius.

His life consisted of a ceaseless round of wars and surprise attacks whose cruelty equalled, if it did not surpass, that of Chengiz Khan's expeditions; since his military operations followed no general plan, a detailed account of them would serve no purpose. Chengiz Khan and his successors at least proved their ability to build a well-organized empire, and to develop its economy and civilization by uniting widely differing regions. They also early showed some appreciation of the worth of advanced civilization; while Timur, who was uneducated but had a developed inborn intelligence, regarded the arts and sciences simply from the point of view of their practical utility, without considering their real spiritual value. His achievements had no effect whatsoever on the development of civilization in Asia, and many of his undertakings were little more than freebooting expeditions. It will be enough, therefore, to confine ourselves to the bare description of the more important of his military operations.

Between 1379 and 1385 Timur succeeded in bringing the whole of eastern Persia under his sway. He overcame a number of native rulers, including the very able Kurt dynasty whose capital was at Herat [in present-day Afghanistan], and crushed the repeated revolts against him. It was Tokhtamysh's rebellion that drew Timur's attention towards Western Asia; his former favourite had been attempting to effect an alliance against his erstwhile protector [Timur]. Between 1385 and 1387, after Tokhtamysh had occupied Tabriz, Timur's troops pillaged [the southwestern Asian territories of] Azarbaijan, Georgia, Armenia and northern Mesopotamia, expelled Tokhtamysh's troops from the Caucasus [the area between the Black and Caspian Seas in Asia], and slew tens of thousands of the inhabitants. A convinced Muslim, Timur considered it his first duty to tackle the Christians of these countries, who were therefore inhumanly tortured by his troops. The conqueror then marched on [the Iranian cities of] Esfahan and Shiraz, where he overthrew the ruler and repeated his atrocities, particularly at Esfahan. An invasion by Tokhtamysh and a series of revolts in Transoxania brought Timur home. He crushed the revolts and then began a campaign against Tokhtamysh which led him from Central Asia to the banks of the Volga [river flowing from Russia into the Caspian Sea]. The decisive action at Kandurcha [in southwestern Asia] did not take place until 1391; Tokhtamysh was forced to flee, leaving the field open to Timur.

He now returned once more to Samarkand [Timur's capital city in present-day Uzbekistan, Central Asia] which he had rebuilt as his winter residence, having adorned it sumptuously for his own glorification. Only in the rebuilding of Samarkand did Timur show any interest in literature and the arts. He erected magnificent buildings which he staffed with scholars, artists and craftsmen from all the lands which he had conquered, with the object of enhancing his prestige. However, he never stayed in Samarkand for long. In 1392 and 1393 again he invaded Persia and Mesopotamia, and attacked Syria, overthrowing all those local rulers who refused to do him homage. In 1395 he finally destroyed the power of Tokhtamysh, and became master of the entire territory stretching to the shores of the Mediterranean and the frontiers of Asia Minor.

Further Attacks

To gain further loot for his troops, and at the same time satisfied that his earlier conquests were safe, he launched an attack on India where, he believed, the Muslim princes were not doing enough to propagate Islam. His advance across the Indus towards Delhi brought disaster to the country. Innumerable prisoners were taken and killed, and on 18 December 1398, as a result of a trivial dispute between his troops and some Indian soldiers, Delhi was laid waste, a mishap that brought the city fresh consequences for many decades. Greatly enriched by the spoils of India, Timur determined to attack the Turkish Sultan Bayezid I, who had for some time been sending him annoying messages. Before beginning a campaign, he protected his left flank by conquering Syria, the Egyptians who help the country hesitated to defend their territories, and consequently the fall of the fortresses of Aleppo and Damascus was inevitable.

In order not to be deflected from his main objective, Timur did not attack the valley of the Nile itself; he realised that the most risky battle of his life awaited him in Asia Minor. Bayezid neglected to take the necessary precautions, and Timur was able to advance as far as Ankara [in present-day Turkey] before he met with the Turkish army, which had just besieged Constantinople. On this occasion too, Timur managed to induce some of the enemy forces to betray their commander. The battle of 1402 thus turned in his favour, and the Sultan himself, who had refused to escape, fell into the hands of the conqueror. He was imprisoned [according to legend, in an iron cage] (the famous iron cage may simply have been a wire-net litter), and died the following year.

The whole of western Asia was now under Timur's control, and he could regard himself as solely dominating an empire of an extent roughly equal to that of Chengiz Khan. Many rulers established relations with him; there arrived at his court even an ambassador from the king of Castille [in present-day Spain], Clavigo, who has left us an interesting description of his voyage.

But his restless warrior's blood did not allow Timur to administer or govern his possessions effectively. Regardless of the weariness of his army and of the indignation of most of his commanders, who wanted to enjoy the riches they had acquired, Timur planned a new campaign, this time with the object of conquering China. Shortly after his departure, however, he fell ill, and on 19 January 1405 he died at Otrar on the banks of the Syr-Dar'ya. The empire he left behind him was not as well-founded as that of Chengiz Khan, and the absence of a uniform organization was immediately felt. The futility of his conquests became apparent, and the fatal consequences for the Near East and Muslim civilization, and for the Caucasus and the Christians of the East stood out in even stronger relief. For all of these Timur's conquests meant nothing but total ruin and final destruction; his death brought no such positive advantage to humanity as the opening up of communications and the exchange of civilizations characteristic of the time of Chengiz Khan.

The Aztec Empire

Robert Ryal Miller

Many of the greatest civilizations of the fourteenth century were unknown to Europeans. Among these was the Aztec civilization of the New World. Once only one of a number of diverse peoples who populated central Mexico, the Aztecs slowly built an empire. By the beginning of the fourteenth century, the Aztecs dominated the immediate region, and their influence stretched throughout Central America. In the 1320s they started to construct the city of Tenochtitlán, later known as Mexico City.

Politically, the Aztec civilization lasted only until the early part of the sixteenth century, when the Spanish, led by Hernán Cortés, defeated the empire. However, many aspects of Aztec culture persist in Mexican and Central American life today. This excerpt, from *Mexico: A History* by historian and professor Robert Ryal Miller, describes some of the social, religious, and political customs of Aztec civilization. The excerpt begins with a discussion of human sacrifice, a custom widespread among many cultures at many different periods through history and a ritual practiced frequently by the Aztec civilization. As Miller makes clear, the sacrifice of captives, criminals, and others was not simply a mark of brutality but instead had political and religious significance.

The Aztec practice of human sacrifice was an indispensable part of their religion. Through the terror that it generated it also helped them consolidate their power and prevent subject people from rebelling. Besides war captives the victims included convicted criminals whose offenses called for capital punishment. Sacrificial techniques varied: rain rituals involved slaying of children with the hope that their tears would assure plentiful rainfall; the rite of spring was celebrated by priests who donned the skins of flayed victims; and other ceremonies were associated with shooting arrows into captives who were lashed to a scaffold. All military prisoners were sacrificed. Some of them had a gladiatorial role in which they were tied to a gigantic stone and forced to defend themselves with a wooden club against an Aztec warrior armed with an obsidian-edged sword. But by far the most common method of sacrifice was to march or drag male captives up the steps to the summit of a pyramid, where each man was stretched across a sacrificial stone while four priests held his limbs and another priest plunged an obsidian knife into his chest and tore out the palpitating heart, which he offered to the appropriate god.

The rationale for all this bloodshed was that human blood was the proper nourishment for gods. To assure plentiful crops the rain god and earth goddess had to be appeased or regularly presented with divine food, and if there was a drought or flood, additional sacrifices were made. It was believed that the sun, especially, needed human blood in order to assure its continuance. The fact that it rose pale each morning after cosmic battle during the night was proof of its frailty, according to Aztec priests. Huitzilopochtli, the Mexican tribal god imposed on the Aztec world, had several manifestations—sometimes he was Tonatiuh, the Sun God; at other times he was a war god or patron of war. In either guise he demanded human hearts and human blood.

Aztecs perceived an intimate relationship between religion and war. Huitzilopochtli, who spoke to them through oracles, insisted that only continuous warfare and human sacrifice could maintain the sun in the sky. The Aztecs believed that there had been four previous worlds, or suns, each of which had suffered a cataclysmic end. The current Fifth Sun was doomed to destruction in a great earthquake, but that final day could be postponed by human sacrifice. Thus war was a sacred duty, and all able-bodied males received military training to become soldiers in time of war. There was no standing army, but the frequency of military campaigns gave ample opportunity for youths to prove themselves in battle. Warriors, whether they brought prisoners to the sacrificial stone, were themselves killed in battle, or were captured and sacrificed by the enemy, performed the highest service to church and state. These "men with hearts of stone" were idealized by the Aztecs; their final reward was an elevated place in the hereafter, a warrior's paradise.

Three groups dominated Aztec society: the warrior elite (*teteuctin*), the hereditary nobility (*pipiltin*), and the high priests. The warrior elite, or knights, were those of noble birth who had proved themselves in battle by capturing prisoners. They were eligible for membership in the military lodges: Eagle Knights, Jaguar Knights, and Knights of the Arrow. A *teuctli* warrior had a number of privileges—he could wear an

Tenochtitlán was a splendid complex of cities, lakes, and canals that served as the center of Aztec civilization.

elaborate costume, participate in war councils, acquire former enemy property and slaves, have a harem, and eat human flesh. Portions of sacrificial victims, cooked with squash and flowers, were served to warriors. This was "divine food," for it was believed that the victim had become a demigod once sacrificed. The knights were not allowed to keep the victim's heads; these were skewered on public skull racks. There were several of these racks in Tenochtitlán, each with many thousands of skulls accumulated over the years.

Because the Aztecs had so many religious festivals and more than two hundred deities, there was a need for many priests. By the sixteenth century, some five thousand officiated in Tenochtitlán alone. These religious leaders, virtually all of whom practiced celibacy, were organized into a hierarchy and were supported by their own properties as well as by tribute. Their functions varied—some were in charge of temples, sacrifices, or festivals; others were soothsayers or custodians of tribal lore. By learning to read and write pictographic codices [manuscipt books] priests preserved and extended knowledge in various fields, including astronomy, mathematics, theology, medicine, law, history, and oral literature. Many priests served the state as government advisors, medicine men, or as teachers in the schools for noble youths.

Aztec nobles (*pipiltin*) were part of the ruling class and as such enjoyed specific prerogatives. They wore distinctive clothing, had their own courts, were permitted polygamous marriages that were advantageous in politico-economic terms through family alliances, and their children could attend the *cálmecac* school that was a prerequisite for obtaining the highest positions in church and state. Nobles had hereditary lands from which they received tribute. Although the nobles had contempt for the commoners, a few of the latter who performed outstanding service, usually in war, were rewarded with non-inheritable noble status.

The Lower Classes and Women

Commoners (*macehualtin*) were the largest segment of the empire's population. Their basic socio-economic unit was the *calpulli*, something akin to a clan or a ward, which owned the agricultural land, assigned the use of the land to its members, and paid tribute or taxes as a unit. Each *calpulli* had its own elected officers who regulated local affairs, supervised communal storehouses, kept tribute records, controlled the armory, and in wartime commanded the unit's military forces. They also maintained for teen-aged boys a barracks school, the *telpóchcalli*, which offered instruction in citizenship, military training, religion, and crafts.

Serfs (*mayeques*), who tilled landholdings that belonged to the nobility and clergy, composed almost one-third of the Aztec population. Tied to the land and dispersed throughout the empire, they were not organized into *calpulli* and thus did not have the advantages or tribute responsibilities of the commoners. Their status was fixed; they could not expect to move up in society.

Among the lowest members of the social scale were day laborers (*tlalmaitl*), who were not members of a *calpulli*; and at the very bottom were slaves (*tlacotin*) who constituted about 5 percent of the population. There were several categories of slaves, depending on the circumstances of enslavement. Male captives taken in warfare were usually sacrificed, but not the many enemy women and children who were enslaved through conquest. Contractual slaves were individuals who sold themselves into slavery when they could not pay their debts. Others sold their children into slavery. The punishment for many criminal offenses was slavery, and it was not uncommon for a condemned person to become a slave of his victim's family. Mitigating features of this servitude permitted slaves to own property, maintain families, and, for some, to regain their freedom after their debt or purchase price was repaid. All children born to slaves were free and enjoyed full citizenship rights.

Aztec women formed part of the various social ranks from nobility to slavery. Although they were not eligible for the highest offices of state, some women acted as regents for their minor sons, and of course marriages of a chief's daughters or sisters were important in cementing tribal alliances. For commoners, marriages were arranged through a marriage broker, usually an older woman, who followed tribal customs such as making certain that each partner came from a different clan. The great majority of women were wives and mothers with the usual household duties of food preparation and child rearing. But there were other female occupations: priestesses, temple virgins, midwives, weavers, herbalists, potters, musicians, dancers, prostitutes, and market vendors.

An Aztec woman had definite legal rights, such as those of holding property or entering into contracts in her own name. She could obtain a divorce from her husband if he deserted her, was cruel, or failed to support her or their children. If divorced, she could remarry. Widows could only marry within the clan of their deceased husband. Divorce and remarriage were relatively easy for Aztec males; grounds for legal dissolution included sterility, neglect of household duties, or declaration that a wife was habitually ill-tempered. Married women were expected to be faithful to their husbands, and girls were supposed to be chaste, but a man could have extramarital relations with unmarried females. Women's rights were definitely inferior to those of men, and females had a secondary role in the warrior-dominated and class-conscious society.

Chapter
6

The Mali Empire

PREFACE

The contributions of Africa to the rest of the world have often been neglected over the years. Many historians have dismissed Africa as a backwater: a place on the fringes of the political and cultural trends of the world, a continent where nothing of any importance was ever accomplished. Other historians have tended to focus exclusively on Africa as a victim of historical events such as colonialism, apartheid, and the slave trade. In each case, the effect is the same: The great civilizations of Africa are ignored or relegated to a line or two in a textbook.

In truth, Africa has been the home to several civilizations that rivaled any others of their time. The country of Zimbabwe, for example, was named after a ruined city in the southern part of Africa. The exact origins of the city are shrouded in history, but there is no doubt that the cultures it supported flourished for several centuries. The Songhai and Ghana Empires of West Africa were likewise military powers and cultural leaders; they dominated the trade and government of their regions for years at different times. And although various Egyptian civilizations certainly included many European features, they also contained much that was drawn from the surrounding regions of Africa.

The Mali Empire of West Africa was another of the great African societies. Flowering after the height of the Ghana Empire and before Songhai came into its own, Mali was the unquestioned leader in its time and place. Under leaders such as Mansa Mūsā, Mali was known throughout Africa and the Middle East for its wealth and its art. Mali controlled extensive communications and trade routes throughout North Africa and made excellent use of them. This not only brought goods from the outside world to Mali territory, but it also enabled visitors and emissaries from other nations to observe Mali at its peak.

The Mali Empire was relatively short-lived. It was probably less than a hundred years old when the fourteenth century began, and within another hundred years it had been entirely superseded by the Songhai. Its peak may have lasted only a generation or two, but the peak was certainly memorable.

Mansa Mūsā and the Magnificence of Mali

Lester Brooks

The Mali Empire was the center of trade in northern Africa during the fourteenth century. Mali was also the center of political power for the area, and it was the westernmost outpost of the Muslim world. At its peak, some historians estimate that the empire covered an area the size of Western Europe.

This excerpt, from Lester Brooks's *Great Civilizations of Africa*, describes one of the Mali Empire's most successful and influential periods: the years between 1312 and 1337, in which Mansa Mūsā served as ruler. The name *Mansa Mūsā* means "Emperor Moses"; as Brooks tells the story, he deserved the name. Brooks includes many primary source quotations in his account. A writer with a particular interest in race relations, Brooks was one of the first Americans to publish material on early African achievements for popular audiences.

M ansa Kankan Musa I . . . came to power in 1312 (about twenty years after the first Crusade ended). "Musa" is Arabic for "Moses," and Mansa Musa proved to be just such an inspired leader to the peoples of Western Sudan.

Mansa Musa built Mali into one of the greatest and most famous empires of the world of that time. In his reign of twenty-five years this extraordinary man stamped his personality indelibly on African history. He was, says an Egyptian contemporary, Al Omari, "the most important of the Moslem Negro kings; his land is the largest, his army the most numerous; he is the king who is the most powerful, the richest, the most fortunate, the most feared by his enemies and the most able to do good to those around him."

The greatest challenge he faced was to bring stability to the land. Peace and safety within Mali's borders were urgent needs, and Mansa Musa rapidly established law and order throughout his domain. He then sent his armies into the field to extend the empire. They carried the banners of Mali west into Tekrur, clear to the Atlantic coast; north to the Sahara, taking cities such as Walata; and even across the desert to the salt-mining outpost of Taghaza. They advanced eastward, beyond the cities of Timbuktu and Gao to the borders of Hausaland. To the south Mansa Musa's troops continued Mali's firm grip on the gold-producing regions. At the height of Mansa Musa's power, Mali was (according to Al Omari's report) "square in shape, being four months [of travel] in length and at least as much in breadth. . . ." It measured perhaps fifteen hundred miles by a thousand miles, roughly the size of all of Western Europe.

Governing this mammoth area was a gigantic task that took keen judgment, wisdom and administrative skill. Kankan Musa had all of these. His domains were as varied as their people. At the close of his reign, there were twenty-four semi-independent kingdoms within the empire of Mali. Most of these had tribal chiefs whom Musa had left in power so long as they demonstrated their loyalty to him; the others had governors whom the emperor had placed in power. Some of these governors were generals who had conquered the territories. Mansa Musa made other men governors in recognition of outstanding services to him and the empire.

In addition to these kingdoms, there were territories under the direct control of the Emperor. Within each of these there were further subdivisions into provinces placed under the administration of *ferbas* (governors). The major towns and cities were under *mochrifs* (mayors). *Ferbas* and *mochrifs* were appointed by the Mansa.

Mansa Musa was able to maintain peace throughout his lands—a major accomplishment. It took a huge army to do this. The upkeep on a vast standing army required a good deal of money, but the money was available, thanks to Mansa Musa's efficient tax system and the prosperity of the empire.

Now the caravans of Morocco, Egypt and North Africa came to Mali and the emperor sent his ambassadors and agents to reside in Fez, Morocco's capital, in Cairo, and other important centers. Mansa Musa's capital became a major crossroad of the Moslem world and daily the city was thronged with merchants, traders and scholars from North Africa and Egypt who had come on business or had settled there. As a devout Moslem, Mansa Musa welcomed the men of Islam from whatever quarter they came. It was a time of general expansion for the Moslem world, a time when it led the West in learning, arts and culture. Religion and trade also went together. Mansa Musa recognized these vital elements of Islam and encouraged them to the utmost.

Mansa Musa as Seen by Al Omari

The man proved himself a wise ruler. We have a word picture from Al Omari of the restraint exercised by Mansa Musa in governing his domains. It is a picture of practical statesmanship of the kind needed to rule thousands of diverse peoples scattered over the face of West Africa:

> The sultan of this country [Mali] has sway over the land of the "desert of native gold," whence they bring him gold every year. The inhabitants of that land are savage pagans whom the sultan would subject to him if he wished. But the sovereigns of this kingdom have learned by experience that whenever one of them has conquered one of these gold towns, established Islam there and sounded the call to prayer, the production of gold dwindles and falls to nothing; meanwhile it grows and expands in neighboring pagan countries. When experience had confirmed them in this observation, they left the gold country in the hands of its pagan inhabitants and contented themselves with assuring their obedience and paying tribute.

Al Omari also tells us something about the great emperor and the customs of the court:

> [Mansa Musa] is known to the people of Egypt as the king of Tekrur but he himself becomes indignant when he is called thus, since Tekrur is only one of the countries of his empire. The title he prefers is that of lord of Mali, the largest of his states; it is the name by which he is most known. . . .
>
> The Sultan [Mansa Musa] holds court in his palace on a great balcony called *bembe* where he has a great seat of ebony that is like a throne fit for a large and tall person. On either side it is flanked by elephant tusks turned towards each other. His arms stand near him, being all of gold, saber, lance, quiver, bow and arrows. He wears wide trousers made of about twenty pieces [of material] of a kind which he alone may wear. Behind him there stand about a score of Turkish or other pages bought for him in Cairo. One of them, at his left, holds a silk umbrella surmounted by a dome and a bird of gold: the bird has the figure of a falcon. His officers are seated in a circle about him, in two rows, one to the right and one to the left; beyond them sit the chief commanders of his cavalry. In front of him there is a person who never leaves him, who is his official executioner; also another who serves as intermediary [spokesman] between sovereign and subjects, and who is named herald. In front of them again, there are drummers. Others dance before their sovereign, who enjoys this, and make him laugh. Two banners are spread

behind him. Before him they keep two saddled and bridled horses in case he should wish to ride.

Arab horses are brought for sale to the kings of this country who spend considerable sums in this way. Their army numbers one hundred thousand men of whom there are about ten thousand horse-mounted cavalry; the others are infantry having neither horses nor any other mounts. They have camels in this country but do not know the art of riding them with a saddle. . . .

The officers of this king, his soldiers and his guard receive gifts of land and presents. Some among the greatest of them receive as much as 50,000 *mitqals* of gold a year [1 mitqal = 1/8 oz.], besides which the king provides them with horses and clothing. He is much concerned with giving them fine garments and making his cities into capitals.

It is one of their customs that whenever someone charged with a certain task or important affair reports to the king, the latter questions him on everything that has happened from the time of his departure to the time of his return and in great detail. Legal cases and appeals also go up to the sovereign who examines them himself. Generally he writes nothing but gives his orders, most of the time, orally. He has *qadis* [judges], secretaries, offices.

From this we have a portrait of a man who has the qualities of a great leader: attention to detail, concern for justice, liberal rewards to his loyal servants, availability to his subjects; a person aware of his responsibilities and of his empire and unwilling to see them diminished or slighted by thoughtless word or deed.

Mansa Musa's Pilgrimage

We also see Mansa Musa as a devout, practicing Moslem. This is clear from his pilgrimage to Mecca—a journey of some three thousand miles via Cairo over some of the most infernal territory on the face of the globe. But, as might be expected of so unusual a man, when Mansa Musa made the pilgrimage it became an event of international importance, one of the most famous trips in history. It spread his name far and wide and was a topic of conversation for a century.

Musa's *hajj* [pilgrimage] was the stuff of legend and fable from the outset. It was spectacular in size because the emperor brought along friends, family, doctors, savants, princes, tribal chiefs and governors of the empire. Some of the latter made the journey at Musa's insistence, in part as hostages to prevent attempts to take over the kingdom, in part to allow his son to rule without hindrance during his absence. There are varying reports on the number of people who went with Mansa Musa: One report put the figure at eight thousand; another estimated sixty thousand!

Outfitting thousands of people and animals for a journey of about nine thousand miles for upwards of a year was a monumental task. For months food and supplies were gathered from all over the empire. Gold dust from the royal treasury was divided into three hundred-pound loads—a typical camel burden—and there were one hundred of these! Musa had five hundred slaves with him and each of them carried a staff in which there was gold weighing five hundred *mitqals*. (The *mitqal*, *miskal* or *miscal* was a measure of gold and varied from about 59.7 grains in Tunis to 74 grains in Aleppo. About 4.81 grams seems to have been an accepted standard.)

The Emir [lord], el Mehmendar, tells about Musa's visit to Cairo on the first leg of his pilgrimage in July, 1324:

> When I went out to greet [Mansa Musa] in the name of the glorious Sultan el Malik en Nasir [of Cairo], he gave me the warmest of welcomes and treated me with the most careful politeness. But he would talk to me only through an interpreter [although he could speak perfect Arabic].
>
> I suggested that he should go up to the palace and meet the Sultan. But he refused, saying, "I came for the pilgrimage and for nothing else and I do not wish to mix up my pilgrimage with anything else." He argued about this. However I well understood that the meeting was repugnant to him because he was loath to kiss the ground [before the Sultan] or to kiss his hand. I went on insisting and he went on making excuses. But imperial protocol obliged me to present him [at the Egyptian court] and I did not leave him until he had agreed.
>
> When he came into the Sultan's presence we asked him to kiss the ground. But he refused and continued to refuse, saying, "However can this be?" Then a wise man of his suite whispered several words to him that I could not understand. "Very well," he thereupon declared. "I will prostrate myself before Allah who created me and brought me into the world." Having done so he moved towards the Sultan. The latter rose for a moment to welcome him and asked him to sit beside him. Then they had a long conversation.

Mansa Musa's reluctance to kowtow to a local sultan was understandable pride. In terms of gold and monetary wealth, Mali was incomparably richer than Egypt. And so far as territory was concerned, Musa's realm was many times larger. He was truly the khan of Africa, ruling a vast empire second in the world of that time only to that of Genghis Khan in Asia.

El Mehmendar's description of Mansa Musa's departure from Cairo makes it clear that it was costly to have a rich and powerful guest in those days. Consider the size of Musa's caravan and the requirements of protocol for the host to such an emperor:

> When the time of pilgrimage [departure] arrived, [the Sultan of Egypt] sent [Mansa Musa] a large quantity of *drachmas* [silver coins], baggage camels and choice riding camels with saddles and harness. [The Egypt-

ian Sultan] caused abundant quantities of foodstuffs to be bought for his suite and followers, established posting-stations for the feeding of the animals, and gave to the emirs of the pilgrimage a written order to look after and respect [the Emperor of Mali]. When the latter returned it was I [el Mehmendar] who went to greet him and settle him into his quarters.

This man spread upon Cairo the flood of his generosity: There was no person, officer of the [Cairo] court or holder of any office of the [Cairo] sultanate who did not receive a sum in gold from him. The people of Cairo earned incalculable sums from him, whether by buying and selling or by gifts. So much gold was current in Cairo that it ruined the value of money.

Does history record any other case of a royal host's hospitality being repaid so liberally by his imperial visitor's generosity that the economy of the host's country is ruined? Al Omari, writing in Cairo, provides a footnote to this shower of gold:

Gold in Egypt had enjoyed a high rate of exchange up to the moment of [Emperor Musa's] arrival. The gold *mitqal* that year had not fallen below twenty-five *drachmas*. But from that [arrival] day onward, its value dwindled; the exchange was ruined and even now it has not recovered. The *mitqal* scarcely touches twenty-two *drachmas*. That is how it has been for twelve years from that time, because of the great amounts of gold they [Mansa Musa's entourage] brought to Egypt and spent there.

No doubt Mansa Musa gave substantial amounts of his gold as alms in Mecca, as the pilgrimage was the central purpose of his trip. Perhaps his generosity had similar impact there. An embarrassing moment occurred when the great emperor discovered (as who has not?) that he had spent all his money. Egyptian merchants were eager to loan him enough gold to complete his journey. No one had the slightest doubt about his ability to repay the loans.

Certainly the emperor's trip was the sensation of the Moslem world. It literally put Mali on the map. Maps of Africa after this time almost always show Mali and many have drawings of Mansa Musa. They usually show him as a black emperor with robe, crown, scepter and orb of gold. Mali became fixed in people's minds as the Eldorado—[the legendary] country with limitless gold, and as a result there was an even greater flow of traders, merchants, religious leaders and scholars to the empire.

On his return journey Mansa Musa brought a number of outstanding Moslem scholars to Mali. Among them was a famous poet and architect, Al Saheli of Cordoba, whom Musa engaged to build a palace and a great mosque at Timbuktu. As the huge caravan approached Mali on the return trip, messengers came with news that the major city of Gao, capital of the Songhay people, had been captured. It had been under siege by Musa's troops for many years. Delighted at this news, Mansa Musa made a special visit to the conquered city. He took back to his capital two Songhay princes as hostages to insure Gao's loyalty. But they also were honored as princes of Mali.

Mansa Musa had forged an unprecedented empire in Africa. One the most widely-traveled of the Moslem writers of the Middle Ages, a Berber [North African] named Ibn Battuta, wrote about his visit to Mali and his judgments are instructive.

Among the admirable qualities of the Malians, Ibn Battuta noted several: They abhorred injustice and the Sultan forgave no one who was guilty of it. Peace and order prevailed in the land and no one needed to fear "brigands, thieves or ravishers." If foreigners died in Mali, their possessions were placed with a trustworthy man until they could be claimed by a qualified person. The people of Mali were highly devout. They wore fine white garments on the holy day; they memorized the Koran. "One festival day," says Ibn Battuta, "I visited the *qadi* and saw children [chained] and asked him, 'will you not let them free?' He replied, 'only when they know their Koran by heart.' In short, Ibn Battuta found the people of Mali honest and just, living by laws, Allah-fearing, devout and determined to educate their children in their religion. Of course not all that Ibn Battuta saw pleased him. Several customs he found "deplorable" from his Berber perspective:

> Women go naked into the Sultan's presence without even a veil; his daughters also go about naked. On the twenty-seventh night of Ramadan I saw about a hundred women slaves coming out of the Sultan's palace with food and they were naked. Two daughters of the Sultan were with them and these had no veil either, although they had big breasts.

> The blacks throw dust and cinders on their heads as a sign of good manners and respect.

> They have buffoons who appear before the Sultan when the poets are reciting their praise-songs.

> And then a good number of Negroes eat the flesh of dogs and donkeys.

Mansa Musa is known to have desired to settle in Arabia to meditate at Mecca after his pilgrimage. He expected to install his son formally as his successor and then return to the holy city. But the demands of his mammoth empire prevented this and he never left Mali again. In 1337, the year Edward III of England challenged the French King Philip VI in what became the start of the Hundred Years' War, Mansa Kankan Musa died. His twenty-five years of exceptional leadership had created a phenomenally great empire.

Life and Government in Mali

W.F. Conton

Mali was only one of several strong West African empires that flourished before European colonization. Mali's greatness was preceded by the Ghana Empire and followed by the Songhay, or Songhai. (It should be noted that neither the Mali nor Ghana Empires were precisely where the countries that bear those names today are located.) The Mandingo people had been instrumental in establishing the empire as a powerful force under the first great king, Sundiata, who lived during the thirteenth century.

There are fewer written sources regarding the Mali Empire than there are about European civilizations of the time. Nevertheless, close examination of the sources that do exist give a fairly detailed picture of the empire's social and governmental structures. Some information comes from the writings of such visitors to the kingdom as the Muslim traveler Ibn Battuta, born in Morocco in 1304. Other information comes from trade records, oral history, and archaeological evidence. In this excerpt, West African education officer W.F. Conton sums up what the records reveal about Mali life and government.

L ike the capital of Ghana the capital of Mali occupied different sites at different times. The village of Niani near Bamako was a later site, chosen by Sundiata himself. Niani means "misery," and local tra-

Excerpted from *West Africa in History,* vol. 1, by W.F. Conton. Copyright © 1961 by George Allen & Unwin, Ltd. Reprinted with permission from Taylor & Francis Books, Ltd.

dition confirms that it was built after Sundiata's flight there. Mandingos do not rebuild ruined towns, for they believe that this is to invite a repetition of the tragedy which ruined them in the first place. They move to a new site near by to keep watch over the spirits of their ancestors.

So we can conclude that at least one of the sites of Mali's capital was about 250 miles south of Koumbi Saleh, site of the capital of the Empire of Ghana, which it overthrew. Mali was much more extensive than Ghana. At one time much of modern Guinea, Senegal, Sudan and modern Ghana was subject to the Emperor. . . . Other important towns in this broad domain were Taghaza, Walata, Karsakhun and, further downstream on the Niger, Timbuktu and Gao, which was later to become the capital of the Empire of the Songhai, which overcame Mali. Then there were Muli, the modern Muri, near Niamey, which was the eastern frontier town of Mali, and Yufi. The latter was probably in the area of the modern Nupe between Jebba and Lokoja, and is described as one of the largest of negro towns in the fourteenth century, ruled over by a powerful chief who had placed it out of bounds to all non-negroes.

The Empire of Mali seems to have been even wealthier than that of Ghana. The media of exchange were salt and cowrie shells. The salt was worth 20 to 30 mithqals [1 mithqal was about an eighth of an ounce of gold] a camel-load (two blocks) in the capital in normal times, and 40 when there was a shortage. At Walata, nearer to its source, the salt could be bought for 8 to 10 mithqals a camel-load. 1,150 cowrie shells were exchanged for a gold dinar in the fourteenth century in Mali.

The wealth of the Emperor was based on the trade in gold across the desert. And this wealth was indeed fabulous. [One Mali emperor] Mansa Kankan Musa took 60,000 men to Mecca, and eighty camels each bearing 300 lb. of gold, together with 500 slaves each carrying a golden staff weighing 500 mithqals. Small wonder that Cairo gaped! The famous gold nugget to which . . . the Emperor of Ghana had [once] tethered his horse was now in the imperial treasury at Mali. Gold was obtained from Wangara, and was taken to the capital and other large towns to be exchanged for the salt and other goods brought by the Arabs across the desert. Sometimes the people of Mali would themselves venture into the desert town of Taghaza to buy salt with their gold.

Trade

Taghaza was a rather unattractive town, we read, whose houses were built of blocks of salt, and roofed with camel skins. But it had the vital commodity which the people of Mali needed and could pay well for. So slaves of the negro Massufa tribe lived more or less permanently at Taghaza, digging for salt for their Berber [North African] masters. These slaves lived on the excellent dates which the Arab traders brought them from Sijilmasa, and also on camels' flesh and millet—quite a good diet for slaves anywhere!

Another indication of the wealth of fourteenth-century Mali was the highly organized nature of the trade across the desert. Although, as you can imagine, the journey was dangerous and unpleasant, there was so much coming and going of merchants to and from the capital that something almost like an entire tourist agency had developed, complete with guides. On leaving Taghaza, with its brackish water, and its flies, a caravan would set out on the ten-day journey to Tasarahla. The next stop would be Walata, which was the northernmost outpost of the Empire. From here a takshif (guide) would set out to meet the party four nights out, and lead them into the town. In Walata in Ibn Battuta's day, the Emperor had a Farba or Governor, who sat on a carpet under an arch, with guards carrying lances and bows in front of him, and Massufa headmen behind. The Farba would only speak to strangers through an interpreter, just like a modern West African chief. The food here was good, with water-melon in the shade of the date palms, plenty of mutton, and a good underground water supply. And the people could afford Egyptian cotton.

From Walata the traveller to the capital of Mali found that he need only carry salt, glass ornaments, and spices, in order to be able to barter for his daily needs. The variety of food increased—there was now chicken, pulped lotus fruit, rice, funi (kuskus), haricot beans, and hippopotamus meat cut from animals caught with harpoons. And once in the capital itself, we find descriptions of tremendous wealth. The Emperor's armour bearers had gold and silver quivers, swords ornamented with gold and carried in golden scabbards, and they bore gold and silver lances and crystal maces. But even the ordinary people seem to have been well off. Some of the houses had candles—not common commodities even in Europe in those days.

The women of Mali are described by Arab travellers as beautiful, and given more respect than the men. Lines of inheritance here, as in ancient Ghana, passed through the female line. Although many of them were zealous Muslims, they did not wear veils. Like typical Muslim women elsewhere, however, they never travelled with their husbands. If in Walata they could afford cotton cloth, in the capital the women had a range of even more expensive fabrics available to them—silks, and a "velvety red tunic" out of which the coverings for the Emperor's "bembi" (platform) were made. There was also, however, quite a lot of local weaving done; although perhaps some of it, like the "kente" weaving in modern Ghana, was done with imported thread. . . .

Court Life

Your social position was measured by the number of slaves and maid-servants you had. But all inhabitants, bond or free, were submissive to their Emperor. They swore by his name, and anyone summoned to an audience with him would put on his oldest clothes, and a skull-cap in place of his usual turban. He would raise his clothes and trousers knee-high, and move forward towards the Emperor in an attitude of great respect, hitting the ground with his elbows. He would then listen with bent back to the Emperor on the raised "bembi." If His Majesty saw fit to reply to his petition, his humble subject would uncover his back and throw dust over himself, rather like a chicken. On such occasions many of the petitioners would recount their acts of service and devotion to the Emperor. Those standing around would twang their bow strings as a sign of acclaim for the narrator's words.

These audiences were obviously important social occasions, as well as ceremonial occasions. The "bembi" was in an open square, and the general public would shelter in the shade of the trees to watch the show, whilst the Emperor had his silk canopy surmounted by a golden bird to protect him from the hot sun. We read of magnificent bows and quivers, and gold and silver two-stringed guitars, in the Emperor's retinue. There were also trumpets, drums and bugles, which would sound out to herald his arrival and departure. Two horses and two goats always stood near at hand to protect the assembled company from evil spirits. A special place would be reserved for the emirs [lords], who were probably subject kings, and one of whose duties was to keep the flies off the imperial "bembi." Also in attendance on these splendid occasions were the Emperor's military commanders, chaplain, interpreter, wives, and slave girls with gold and silver fillets through their hair. The linguist or "Dugha" would play an instrument with small calabashes [gourds] at its lower end, which must have resembled the "balangie" still in use in Sierra Leone today. The Dugha's duties were to chant poems of praise to the Emperor for his victories and his other deeds of valour. The women and girls would also sing, and play their instruments. Thirty youths, dressed in red woollen tunics and white skull caps would accompany the girls' singing, beating drums slung from their shoulders. Finally, boys would turn cart-wheels and do nimble acrobatic exercises, and give displays of swordsmanship.

On feast days there was the extra treat of poets, wearing feathers and wooden heads with red beaks, who would recite poems encouraging their Emperor to follow the noble example of his predecessors. Then the chief poet would stand on the steps leading up to the "bembi," lay his head on the Emperor's lap, mount to the "bembi" itself, and then lay his head first on the right then on the left imperial shoulder—a custom we are told was older in Mali than Mohammedanism [Islam].

But just as behind all the pomp and ceremony there lay the military skill to conquer Gao, so also there lay an efficient administrative system for running the internal affairs of the Empire. You could not enter Mali, for example, unless your papers were in order. Ibn Battuta had to write ahead to the semi-permanent non-negro residents of Mali to ask them to get these papers ready for him. He says that otherwise he would have had difficulty in crossing the Sankara River into the capital itself. But neither military skill nor good administrators can have much effect under a bad Emperor. The Mali Emperor during Ibn Battuta's visit was Sulayman, who died in 1359. He was also the last of the able Emperors, and his death plunged the Empire into civil war. Sulayman's son Kamba was slain in a long struggle with a grandson of Mansa Kankan Musa, who became in turn Mansa Mari Jata II. The latter was a cruel and selfish ruler, who even sold the famous gold nugget the Emperor of Mali had won from the Emperor of Ghana. No doubt, therefore, Mari Jata II's subjects were glad when sleeping sickness cut short his life. Musa II, his son and successor, was rather weak and his very able Prime Minister Jata had to struggle hard to keep the crumbling Empire together. Whilst Jata was suppressing a revolt by the Sultan of Bornu in the east, Timbuktu in the north was captured by Tuareg desert tribes. The Fulani were also on the attack. Then the Songhai of Gao rebelled, and it was they who finally replaced Mali in about 1475 as the most important state in West Africa.

The Ming Dynasty

PREFACE

Today the name *Ming* is most likely to conjure up images of expensive vases, detailed portraits, and other artistic artifacts. The picture is quite accurate. The Ming dynasty of China was known during its time for its achievements in the cultural realm, and critical opinion of Ming art today is just as high. The Mings were justly known for the quality of the art their time produced, and they are justly remembered for it several centuries later.

But the Ming years were important for a good deal more than just the production of art. Ming China had a strong worldly side as well. The Mings ruled a powerful political empire that dominated the affairs of eastern Asia. They had a strong commercial presence, too, voyaging to nearby lands and trading goods when possible. But perhaps most important, the Mings restored independence and a sense of national pride to China after years of foreign rule.

The Ming were a series of emperors connected by blood and alliance. Like European kings, the Ming emperors succeeded to their thrones because of who they were, and they kept their titles largely by the threat of violence to those who tried to unseat them. The era of Ming dominance was long by European standards; the dynasty lasted across the space of several hundred years. To be specific, the Ming dynasty began in 1368, when Chu Yüan-chang became the first Ming ruler, and continued until the dynasty fell to the Manchus in 1644. Few ruling groups anywhere on Earth can boast such a long period of dominance in the affairs of one country.

The Ming dynasty came about partly because of dissatisfaction with the ruling Mongols. The country had been in the thrall of Mongol rulers since 1211, when Genghis Khan had successfully invaded China and taken control from the previous dynasty. Foreign rule was nothing new to China—its recent history had been a constant swing between native Chinese dynasties and government by conquerors from outside the country—but the period of Mongol rule was unusually long-lasting. Besides, the quality of rulers had dropped off sharply; since the death of the Mongol ruler Kublai Khan in 1294, the succession of emperors had ignored Chinese concerns and given native Chinese plenty of reason to want a change.

That change was not accomplished without a fight. First, battles were fought between Chinese rebels and the ruling Mongols. Then, when the Mongols had been successfully driven out of the country, the rebels broke down into squabbling factions. Even by the end of the fourteenth century, these issues had not been completely resolved. Despite the civil strife, the economic and cultural growth of China had already begun under native rule. Newly independent, China would continue to be a world power for a number of years to come.

The Establishment of the Ming Dynasty

René Grousset

The establishment of the Mings under Chu Yüan-chang was not particularly difficult, as French historian René Grousset explains in this selection. Incompetent Mongol rulers who followed the thirteenth-century leader Kublai Khan helped. So did the charisma, leadership, and political skills of Chu Yüan-chang. The first emperor, however, only set the stage for what was to come. Several policies and ideas initiated by Chu Yüan-chang continued through the next few decades, most notably the attempt to expand the new empire. Grousset, acknowledged as one of the great European writers on China, therefore extends his summary of the founding of the Ming into the early years of the fifteenth century as well.

In the course of her long history China can number few sovereigns as remarkable as Kublai. By his strong personality, his statesmanlike qualities, his profound wisdom, and the firmness and humanity of his government, this Mongol ranked with the greatest Chinese emperors of former times. His grandson Temur (Ch'eng-tsung, 1294–1307) was also an energetic and conscientious ruler; but after these two emperors the Yüan dynasty rapidly degenerated. Its princes, sunk in debauchery and lacking in willpower, atoned for their vices only by a Lamaist [a type of Buddhist] religious bigotry which gave the Confucian literati a fresh grievance against them. Worst of all, they

Excerpted from *The Rise and Splendour of the Chinese Empire,* by René Grousset, translated by Anthony Watson-Gandy and Terence Gordon. Copyright © 1968 by the Regents of the University of California. Reprinted with permission from University of California Press.

never ceased quarrelling among themselves, and in a few years destroyed the imposing administrative façade which under Kublai had aroused the admiration of Marco Polo. The last emperor of this line, Toghan Temur (Shun-ti, 1333–1368), who took pleasure only in the company of catamites [boy prostitutes] or of Tibetan Lamas, allowed disorder to degenerate into anarchy.

The decadence of the imperial family encouraged Chinese patriots to revolt against foreign domination. The insurrection was organized by secret societies, especially by the White Lotus, a sect which now prophesied the millennium and preached the advent of Maitreya, the Buddhist Messiah. Like the revolution of 1912 (which also appealed to the people to overthrow a foreign dynasty), the movement started on the lower Long River and in the Cantonese region. It began in the year 1352, and from 1355 onwards the revolt spread across the entire south of China—across the former Sung empire. It was accompanied by appalling anarchy, since it was led by numerous chieftains who were half patriots and half bandits, and who fought among themselves at the same time as they waged war against the Mongols.

The rest of these various adventurers were to be eclipsed by the cleverest among them, Chu Yüan-chang, the founder of the Ming dynasty. The son of a poor farm labourer in the province of Anhui, he was seventeen when an epidemic carried off his entire family. In order to live, he entered a monastery; but his Buddhist vocation was evidently very superficial, for when the popular revolt against the Mongols broke out in the south—he was then twenty-five—he discarded his habit and took up arms, leading a revolt on the lower Long River. Although at first he was no more than the simple chieftain of a band like the other rebels, he stood out among them by reason of his political sense and his prudent humanity towards the populace; wisely, he won the people over instead of oppressing them. Whenever he captured a town, he forbade his soldiers to pillage it, with the result that the inhabitants hailed him as a liberator who freed them, not only from the Mongols, but from the other insurgent chieftains. In 1356 he captured Nanking and made it his capital, the seat of a government which established order and put down the anarchy elsewhere prevalent. His principal rival, the son of a simple fisherman, had for his part become master of [neighboring provinces] Hupei, Hunan and Kiangsi. In 1363 Chu Yüan-chang defeated his opponent, killed him, and took possession of his territory. In 1367 and 1368 he occupied the Cantonese region, and so gained possession of the whole of South China. Then he marched against Peking.

It was a triumphal march; for the imbecility of the last Mongols had made the task of the liberator an easy one. Instead of uniting against the insurrection, they continued to quarrel among themselves and thus to divide their forces. On the night of September 10, 1368, the cow-

THE MING DYNASTY   245

ardly Toghan Temur, the unworthy descendant of the great Kublai Khan, fled from Peking to take refuge in Mongolia, and Chu Yüan-chang made his entry into the capital.

In a Peking delivered from the Mongols, Chu Yüan-chang was proclaimed emperor by his army and became the founder of the Ming dynasty. At the age of forty, after a struggle that had lasted thirteen years, this unfrocked monk, who had started life as a pauper, became the liberator of his country and successor to the heritage of [the ancient dynasties] Han and T'ang. This fortunate adventurer was already far better off than the founders of Sung, who had never succeeded in expelling the barbarians from this city of Peking that he himself had captured so easily. Thus he looked back for his examples beyond Sung, to T'ang, the last native dynasty to rule over the entire territory of China; in 1373 he promulgated an administrative code based on that of T'ang. However, he did not move his capital to the north, but continued to live at Nanking. Being himself a native of the lower Long River region, and having expelled the foreign rulers of China with an army composed of southerners, to begin with he employed a government of southerners. Moreover, it must be remembered that the whole of North China had been in Tartar hands for two hundred and forty-two years, while Peking itself had been in their power for four hundred and thirty-two years; during these long centuries the northern provinces had been pervaded by barbarian elements. It was South China that from 1126 to 1279 had served as a refuge for Chinese independence; and it was from there that the new movement of national liberation had started. Thus the south represented the true China, and it was the south that triumphed with the establishment of the Ming dynasty. All the same, the new emperor was too shrewd a politician to accept the preponderance of southerners for very long. In order to bridge the gulf between north and south, a gulf which two and a half centuries of political separation had been steadily widening, and with a view to the spiritual as well as political reunification of China, he decided in 1380 not only to have the north administered by officials from the south, but also to staff the south with men from the north. For the same cause, he did not hesitate in 1370 to proscribe the secret societies of the White Lotus and the White Cloud, even though they had largely contributed to the overthrow of the Mongol domination; times had changed, and moreover the secret societies had previously backed the wrong horse by declaring their support for rivals of the new emperor.

The New Society

The founder of the Ming dynasty sought in all fields to bring about a restoration of values, to bridge the hiatus of the Mongol and Ju-chen [twelfth-century conquerors from the northeast] dominations and link the new China with the far-distant past; doubtless he applied himself to this eminently traditionalist enterprise with a zeal which was all the greater for the fact that he himself had been a nobody. In 1370 he re-modelled the system of examinations for recruiting the mandarinate [certain civil servants of high rank] and re-established the titles of no-bility. The worship of Confucius was solemnly celebrated, and the emperor enlisted the support of the literary academies, which under the Mongol regime had been centres of opposition to Buddhist cleri-calism. Meanwhile this former monk had not forgotten his co-religion-ists. He even continued to surround himself with Buddhist monks, and he soundly castigated any of the literati who attempted to remonstrate with him on these grounds; on one occasion he went so far as to exe-cute a certain Grand Judge for this offence. This incident is sympto-matic; for as the emperor grew older (he lived to the age of seventy) he became increasingly intolerant of remonstrance and lost the popu-lar good-nature which had so largely contributed to his success. He became habitually suspicious, and once had eighteen dignitaries and all their families executed. As the result of a plot, real or imaginary, fifteen thousand people were put to death in Nanking. The former ad-venturer who had become Son of Heaven wished to re-establish ab-solutism before he died.

Chu Yüan-chang's real successor was the next emperor but one, his second son, whose reign-title was Yung-le (1403–1424) and whom we shall refer to as Yung-le-ti. This warrior sovereign had an expan-sive conception of his role. Whereas Kublai had set out to build a Chi-nese empire for the Mongols, Yung-le-ti now attempted to win for China the Mongol heritage of Kublai's descendants. The grand khan Kublai, by his advance from the Yellow River to Tonkin, had obtained the submission of the whole territory of China and had become an au-thentic Son of Heaven. The third Ming emperor set out to conquer Mongolia and play the part of Grand Khan.

It was with this aim in view that in 1409 the emperor transferred his capital from Nanking to Peking. It was he who drew up the im-posing plan of the Imperial City which forms the centre of modern Peking, as well as more detailed plans for the "Violet-purple Forbid-den City" [imperial palace]; it was he who conceived that succession of palaces, marble terraces, throne rooms, gardens and perspectives worthy of the greatest Chinese traditions; he who enlarged the lakes, built the artificial hills, and planted the gardens with the flowers and shrubs of his native Long River Valley. All this was restored and per-fected by the Ch'ing emperors in the eighteenth century, but every-where it still bears the mark of the Ming emperor Yung-le-ti. And it was Yung-le-ti who first built the Temple of Heaven (1420) and the Temple of Agriculture (1422) near the south wall of Peking.

The transfer of the capital to Peking was in itself a declaration of policy. No other purely Chinese dynasty had ever thought of choosing this residence; the historic role of Peking had begun only with the Tartars. In the tenth century the Ch'i-tan [Mongol invaders] established one of their capitals there; they were followed by the Ju-chen in the twelfth century, and by Kublai in 1260. Such a choice by conquerors from the north is easily understood, since Peking lay on the outer fringe of medieval China, being the principal town of one of the frontier marches. Just over the threshold of Shan-hai-kuan lay Manchuria, then untilled; just through the pass of Nan-k'ou lay, then as now, the steppes of Mongolia. Geographically and historically, Peking is a Sino-tartar compromise; the Chinese is still at home there and the Tartar is not yet out of his element. Yung-le-ti, by moving his court from Nanking to the threshold of Mongolia, to Kublai's former capital, was staking a claim to the heritage of Kublai's descendants.

His father, it is true, had set him an example in this direction. Chu Yüan-chang, after expelling the Mongols from Chinese territory, had pursued them into their homeland. In 1372 a column of Chinese troops advanced to the River Tola in Outer Mongolia, and in 1388 a hundred thousand Chinese again crossed the eastern Gobi and fought the tribes to the east of the Buir Nor, between the Khalkha Gol and the Kerulen. However, these incursions were no more than the following up of a victory, expeditions of reprisal intended to inspire the nomads with a salutary fear. The emperor Yung-le-ti, on the other hand, practised a consistent policy in Mongolia, where the authority of the clan of Genghiz had been seriously weakened by the ignominy of their expulsion from China. The emperor sought to incite the chieftains of other tribes, particularly the Eleuths, or Western Mongols, to revolt against them. He intervened on several occasions in the ensuing civil wars in Outer Mongolia, notably in 1410 and 1411, when he led his troops as far as the Upper Onon and the native prairies of Genghis Khan. In this way he helped to transfer the hegemony of Outer Mongolia from the descendants of Genghis to the Eleuth khans; but it was not long before the Chinese had reason to regret the substitution of fresh clans in place of the decadent power whose lack of authority had paralysed the nomadic hordes.

In Indo-China, too, Yung-le-ti sought to resume the great imperial policy of Han and T'ang. In the kingdom of Annam, the legitimate dynasty had been overthrown by a usurper. The emperor made this an excuse to occupy the country, which he divided up into Chinese provinces (1407). But before ten years had passed, the Annamese were beginning a long and exhausting guerilla war against the occupation forces. Four years after the death of Yung-le-ti the leader of the insurgents, Lê Lo'i, captured Hanoi and expelled the Chinese (1428).

Early Ming Wars and Successions

Louise Levathes

Simply removing the Mongol kings from China did not eliminate war-fare from the country. The early Ming Empire was marked by wars against marauding Mongols—and a fiercely contested civil war as well. The passage, from Louise Levathes's *When China Ruled the Seas,* describes some of these battles. The first Ming emperor, Chu Yüan-Chang (called here Zhu Yuangzhang) ruled effectively, if brutally, but the question of who would succeed him was a major issue. One son, Chu Ti (Zhu Di), bravely fought off the Mongols and coveted the throne, but the designated heir was the first emperor's grandson Chu Yün-wen (Zhu Yunwen). Before the end of the century the struggle between the two would-be kings would break out into violence, with Chu Ti the eventual winner.

A s Zhu Yuanzhang rose to power, he took dozens of concubines and consorts, some Mongolian and some Korean, fathering in all twenty-six sons and sixteen daughters. The empress Ma bore no more than four of the sons, although it was rumored that she was barren and may not have given birth to any of the emperor's children. She was certainly not the mother of Zhu Di, who would eventually usurp the throne. According to one legend, he was the son of the last Mongol emperor. When Zhu Yuanzhang entered Daidu, the Mongol capital, the story went, he found a young princess, one of [Mongol ruler] Toghon-temur's wives, who had been abandoned or forgotten by the Mongols when they fled. He took her as his wife, and she did not tell

Excerpted from *When China Ruled the Seas* (New York: Oxford University Press, 1994) by Louise Levathes. Copyright © 1994 by Louise E. Levathes. Reprinted with permission from Louise Levathes.

him she was already pregnant. When she gave birth to Zhu Di, the emperor accepted him as his own son. In fact, Zhu Di was probably the son of one of the emperor's lesser consorts who gave birth prematurely. For that unfortunate happenstance, an insult to the emperor, she was subjected to a Chinese torture called "the iron skirt." Immobilized out in the cold by a suit of iron clothes, the young woman, already weakened from her difficult labor, eventually died of exposure.

Determined to overcome his humble beginnings by establishing a proper imperial court, Zhu Yuanzhang invited four eminent Yuan scholars to Nanjing to serve the fledgling rebel government and to supervise the instruction of the princes and court officials. A Daoist temple was temporarily converted into a miniature palace, where officials learned court etiquette and were tested for three days before an examiner posing as the emperor.

Zhu asked one of the scholars, Song Lian, "What is the most important work to understand the task of ruling?" Song replied that it was a commentary on the Daxue (Great learning) called *Da xue yan yi* by the Song scholar Zhen Dexiu. The emperor had passages from the book copied on the palace walls of the Forbidden City and sometimes gathered his officials around a particular inscription and asked Song to comment on it. Imperial princes also studied the *Shi jing* (Book of poetry), a collection of folk songs that were read as guides to moral behavior, as well as the *Shu jing* (Book of documents), a collection of pronouncements from the sage kings of antiquity that was regarded as a guide to proper conduct of rulers, and the *Chunqiu* (Spring and autumn annals), a history of the ancient dukedom of Lu (present-day Shandong province) edited by Confucius and said to reflect his moral judgments on political behavior.

The strong Confucian principle of filial obligation was taught to the princes through such parables as the story of the stepmother who repeatedly berated her stepson in front of his father. Though the son was mistreated, he nevertheless made every effort to please his stepmother. One day in the middle of winter he took off his clothes and lay down on a frozen lake so that he might melt the ice and obtain fresh fish for her.

Once the emperor became very angry when he discovered that one of his sons had been struck on the head by his tutor for not being attentive. The emperor was on the verge of taking action against the tutor when Empress Ma intervened. She advised her husband that "as brocade in the process of weaving needs shearing, so do children, undergoing instruction, require punishment." Reluctantly, Zhu let the matter drop.

Zhu's unpredictable temper was sometimes directed against his concubines, on whose behalf the empress also intervened. On one occasion she pretended to be more angry at a concubine than her husband was and sent the girl off to a palace official to be punished.

"Why did you interfere with this?" the emperor asked her.

"When you are in a temper, your punishments tend to be excessive," she said. "The staff officials will deal justly with her case. Even a criminal should not be judged by you but should be turned over to the proper authorities."

"And why were you angry with the woman?" he asked.

"To reduce your anger," she replied.

After the death of his oldest son in 1392, the emperor hesitated in appointing his bookish fourteen-year-old grandson, Zhu Yunwen, as his successor over Zhu Di, then thirty-two, whom he considered the most capable of his sons. From an early age, it was said, one could see the difference between the two, but it cannot be determined whether the tales of Zhu Di's superiority are true or simply products of his later attempts to alter official histories. One day, the emperor was supposed to have asked both Zhu Yunwen and Zhu Di to write the second line of a couplet modeled after his opening line: "Wind blows the horse's tail into a thousand strands of thread."

Zhu Yunwen's response was drab: "Rain beats the sheep's wool into a flat piece of felt." But Zhu Di said, "Sun reflects off the dragons' scales into ten thousand bits of gold." If poetry can reveal the soul, a strong, optimistic spirit shone through these lines and impressed the emperor.

But Zhu Yuanzhang's Confucian advisers counseled against favoring Zhu Di. They said it would cause a rift among his other sons and plunge the country into civil war. Still worried about the capabilities of his grandson, Zhu Yuanzhang launched on a campaign in the final years of his life to rid the empire of anyone who might conceivably be a threat to his successor. Fifteen thousand civil officials and loyal military commanders were summarily executed in the emperor's mad purge. Even the faithful [general] Fu Youde came under suspicion and was charged and summoned to Nanjing. According to some accounts, Fu Youde presented the heads of his two sons to the emperor before he slit his own throat in the presence of the astonished court.

After the executions, Zhu Yuanzhang was said to have placed a thorny stick in front of the heir and told him to pick it up. Zhu Yunwen hesitated. "I'm getting rid of the thorns before giving you the stick—is there anything more I can do?" said the emperor. . . .

Like his father before him, Zhu Di was an able soldier, and as it had for his father, this skill would prove essential to his gaining and retaining the throne. Zhu Di's abilities were evident in his very first command, when the emperor entrusted him to stem the southward advance of the elusive Mongol leader Naghachu in the winter of 1390.

Fragments of the outcast Mongol armies expertly launched lightning-fast guerrilla raids on Chinese towns and outposts, followed by equally swift retreats into the security of the endless steppes of Mongolia, where their tracks vanished with the wind. They could live for months off their herds of sheep, moving camp frequently to find pasture and hustling their sturdy ponies from oasis to oasis. The Ming troops, burdened by long trains of supply wagons, were slow, and they frequently exhausted themselves before they had even seen the enemy or engaged in combat. A winter campaign was particularly dangerous and seldom attempted.

When Zhu Di, accompanied by the twenty-year-old [servant] Ma He, moved his army out of Beijing on March 2, he knew Naghachu would think he was secure. It was unseasonably cold, and the Mongols would not expect to be pursued. Indeed, as Zhu Di's troops moved through Gubeikou pass in what is now the Great Wall, uncertainty about the undertaking spread through the ranks. Officers and soldiers alike were reluctant to continue when they saw the barren, windswept plains laid out before them, from horizon to horizon and beyond. It was madness to proceed in such weather, they thought.

The Chinese cavalry wore a Mongolian style of dress: high leather boots, loose trousers, and short red jackets open at the front to facilitate riding. They had tight-fitting steel helmets with red tassels like horsetails and wore triangular-shaped breast plates of iron or copper over their jackets. Their leather shoulder and knee pads and wide leather belts were fashioned in the shape of large animal heads, making them look as if they were possessed by fierce beasts.

Zhu Di pulled his horse to a halt and, gathering his commanders around him, revealed his plan to send scouts ahead to find Naghachu and gather information about his campsite. They would not wander aimlessly looking for him; they would go directly to him—with a carefully planned attack.

As the scouts departed, galloping quickly out of sight, the army pushed on. Before long, the scouts discovered the Mongol chief camped at a place called Yidu, just across the Mongolian border. Zhu Di hastened toward Yidu as snow began to fall heavily, covering the desert with a silver patina. Again the soldiers were apprehensive.

"The weather is so bad the enemy would not dream of our coming," Zhu Di exhorted them. "If we advance quickly in the snow, we can surprise them and win a big victory."

They rode on, and, when they were near the Mongol campsite, Zhu Di ordered his men to hide in the dunes. He had something of a secret weapon, a Mongol officer named Nayira'u, who had been captured by the Chinese some months before and was a close friend of Naghachu's. Zhu Di sent the Mongol officer out to meet the Mongol leader. Naghachu was astonished to see his old friend and wept. As the two embraced and began to talk, Zhu Di ordered his men to close in on the camp.

When Naghachu realized the deception and jumped onto his horse to flee, he was stopped by Nayira'u, who told him of Zhu Di's plan. Seeing no way to escape, Naghachu surrendered. The prince graciously received the Mongol leader like an honored guest and that night prepared a banquet for the entire army and their families. The Mongols feasted, and on the following day many decided willingly to join Zhu Di's army. His bloodless victory won the prince both admiration and apprehension in Nanjing. Proudly, the emperor announced that his worries about the security of the northern border were finally over. Silently, advisers to the heir worried about the prince's growing military power.

Seven years later, in 1398, Zhu Yuanzhang, who had named his reign "Hongwu," meaning "Vast Military Prowess," died at the age of seventy-one. Fearing that his sons might undermine the authority of the heir and fight among themselves if they gathered in the capital for his funeral, he issued orders before his death that they were all to stay in their respective fiefs and not, under any circumstances, to attend his burial. The location of his tomb had been chosen with great care early in his reign. It was finally placed just east of Nanjing, on a slight rise halfway up Purple Mountain, where a small stream flowed in front of it on its way around the mountain. The spirit of the emperor was thus trapped between the mountain and the stream and would not be able to wander after his death, creating insecurity and trouble for his descendants.

Rows of large carved stone animals, soldiers, and civil officials were placed around the base of the mountain leading to the tomb and arranged in double pairs so that one set would always be "on guard." The mile-long path wove and turned to discourage evil spirits, who were believed to travel only in straight lines. His pallbearers were entombed with him along with forty-two of his concubines. The concubines were either buried alive or had their throats cut. Sheep and pigs were also skinned, cooked, and buried as offerings to the spirit of the emperor, who was believed still to have worldly needs.

Civil War

There is much debate about whether Zhu Di was forced into a civil war by his scholarly nephew, now twenty-one years old, or whether he himself provoked a rebellion by increasing the size of his garrison illegally. The truth perhaps lies somewhere in between. Official histories do report that upon ascending the throne, Zhu Yunwen adopted a policy called *xiaofan*, meaning "reducing the feudatories," that is, eliminating the guard forces of his uncles. One by one, Zhu Di's brothers were placed under house arrest and stripped of their powers and military forces. In a rage, Zhu Bo, the prince of Xiang, one of the ablest of Zhu Yuanzhang's sons, refused a summons to appear before the emperor and answer trumped-up charges of impropriety. He set his palace at Jingzhou on fire, burning his family to death, then rode his terrified horse into the flames, killing himself.

By the summer of 1399, a year after Zhu Yunwen acceded to the throne, five of the most powerful princes had been eliminated and two others had died of natural causes. None of the other remaining princes was old enough or influential enough to be of concern to Yunwen, except, of course, the prince of Yan in Beijing. Zhu Di, who had obeyed his father and had not left his fief since the funeral, was now isolated. To give himself time to decide what to do, he feigned madness. He ran through the streets of Beijing screaming and yelling, stealing food and wine, and sleeping in gutters. For days at a time he sank into apparently deep depressions and would see no one. In warm weather he sat by the stove, shivering and complaining of the cold. But it was all a smokescreen, meant to deceive the emperor into thinking he was ill and harmless.

Early that summer Zhu Di asked that his three sons, who were at the emperor's court in Nanjing, be returned to him. So as not to arouse Zhu Di's paranoia, the emperor permitted the sons to travel home. It was Zhu Yunwen's most serious mistake. With his sons by his side, Zhu Di would not hesitate to act if he were provoked. And he was soon provoked.

In July the emperor sent a small force to Beiping [Beijing] to arrest two of Zhu Di's commanders, who were supposed to have been involved in suspicious activities. At first Zhu Di agreed to turn his officers over to Zhu Yunwen's agents, but then, in a daring plan, he convinced the arresting officers to enter his palace alone and seized them, executing them on the spot. Before the court could formally protest this action, the prince of Yan took the initiative and declared his intention to *feng tian jing nan*, that is, "accept Heaven's [command] to quell the troubles [at court]." He spoke not of rebellion but rather of removing the "treasonous" officials around his nephew. He was especially wary of two Confucian advisers, who, he charged, had changed the policies of Zhu Yuanzhang, the founder of the dynasty by leading this attack on the princes. . . .

[The prince] thought he was a worthier choice than Zhu Yunwen to succeed his father. Certainly he was more capable. Had not fortune-tellers told him he had the walk of a dragon and the stride of a tiger? And yes, the thought of rebellion had crossed his mind and the minds of others, particularly his adviser the monk and military strategist Daoyan, who mocked the emperor, saying he was "born with a weak and soft-hearted nature." Secretly, Daoyan had already begun training a special strike force of eight hundred in the palace park. He cleverly filled the park with flocks of honking geese and ducks to mask the noise of their military maneuvers. But, the prince wondered, was this the right moment to strike, or was he acting too hastily?

A bad storm had struck Beiping the night Zhu Di seized the emperor's officers. Tiles were blown off the prince's palace, and Zhu Di thought this was a sign from heaven that he would be defeated. But Daoyan reassured him that it was instead a bad omen for the emperor.

"Has my Lord not heard," he said, "that when dragons fly in heaven, wind and rain accompany them. The falling tiles mean that heaven will change your residence to a yellow-tiled house"—the imperial palace.

At first the emperor did not take the rebellion seriously and went about his business as usual. He was determined to decentralize the government and free it from some of the terrors of his grandfather. Political prisoners held since the early days of the dynasty were released, and some punitive taxes were repealed. But because all of the capable military leaders who could have come to the aid of Zhu Yunwen had been killed in Zhu Yuanzhang's last, frantic purge, the emperor really had no potential allies in his mission to quash the rebellion. The first imperial troops sent to fight Zhu Di in the north suffered defeat at every turn, despite their vastly superior numbers. Out of humanity or naiveté, the emperor ordered his troops not to kill the prince. Zhu Di knew this and took advantage of it.

Again Zhu Di stunned his enemy with surprise raids. Once, in the middle of the night, while the emperor's troops were drinking and celebrating the autumn festival in Hebei province, several thousand of Zhu Di's forces struck and slew eight thousand imperial soldiers. Another ten thousand were captured soon after, when Zhu Di's men, hiding underwater near a bridge and breathing through reeds, surprised the imperial army crossing overhead. Such attacks ultimately crippled and defeated what had been a mighty army of 130,000.

In the late fall, however, a second, larger army of an estimated five hundred thousand men was sent north by the emperor to capture Beiping. But the troops marched out of Nanjing in their summer uniforms and were caught unprepared by the northern snows. Imperial soldiers, freezing in their straw sandals, attacked Beiping, raining arrows over the walls. The prince and his army were on maneuvers outside the city, so the women of Beiping mounted the walls and bravely threw pots down on their attackers until the men arrived to help them. The city stood, and the imperial casualties numbered almost two hundred thousand.

Trade in Early Ming Times

Timothy Brook

Although China was predominantly an agricultural country during the fourteenth century, the early Ming Empire also had a well-developed network of trade routes and systems of manufacturing. Iron, textiles, tea, paper, and many other materials were produced within the empire and were available for sale in markets throughout the nation. Certainly, the industry and commerce of Ming China was a good deal more elaborate than European industry and commerce of the time.

The ancient Chinese philosopher Confucius expressed concerns about the appropriateness of engaging in commerce, concerns that persisted into the Ming period and were evident in the social standing of traders and merchants. However, the need for goods was great and the opportunity to make money appealing, and so commerce was a necessity. In this excerpt, professor and author Timothy Brook discusses the importance of trade in early Ming society and the ambivalence with which society at large accepted it.

The common view of merchant origins in the early Ming was that people took up trade because they couldn't survive by staying at home and tilling the fields as they were supposed to. Faced with starvation, they took to the roads as peddlers and, if they were lucky, moved up to more lucrative trade. Reports from Shanxi province, whose natives earned a strong reputation for commercial acumen in the Ming, reflect this logic: "As Zezhou is stuck in the middle of ten thousand mountains, there is not much land. Even when there is a bumper harvest, people don't have enough to eat." As a consequence, local people "without an inch of land to call their own" became merchants, iron-workers, or salt peddlers. Or again: "Shangdang is in the midst of ten thousand mountains, so merchants rarely go there, yet the land is poor and so people trade. As practically nothing is produced, one in ten takes off." With levels of production too low to support the local population, areas not implicated in prominent commercial networks saw the poorest leave to survive elsewhere by engaging in small-time commerce. Taking up trade with neither example nor experience was an act of desperation. Only the exceptional ever progressed to higher levels of commercial dealing. Most remained within a permanent commercial underclass that facilitated trade but did not direct it, yet it was their itinerant retailing that lubricated the early-Ming economy.

Merchants working at the wholesale level faced the difficulties of long-distance transportation, especially in the early Ming when the infrastructure was still in the process of being rebuilt. Commercial travel took its toll. Biographies of virtuous widows in the early Ming often refer to the accidental deaths of merchant husbands. The biography of a virtuous widow in fourteenth-century Yangzhou says that she became one because "her husband went off to pursue commerce and drowned." She was not the only Yangzhou widow whose husband met this fate: the husband of another is recorded as having drowned going upriver to Nanjing. Death by drowning was sufficiently common in commercial circles, or at least sufficiently feared, that it appears in the standard Ming carpentry manual as one of the outcomes of spells cast by evil housebuilders. "If a boat turned upside-down is hidden in the ground to the north of the house," the manual warns, "one will perish in a river when going out to trade."

The hardship of trade was made heavier by the negative attitude toward commercial gain that Confucianism voiced. To be a merchant was to be in the bottommost and least respected of the ancient "four categories of the people" (*simin*), which descended from gentry (*shi*) to peasant (*nong*) to artisan (*gong*) to merchant (*shang*). This neat and simplifying formula, which dates back at least to the Eastern Han dynasty, was disrupted when the Mongols introduced dozens of new categories for the Chinese they came to rule, but [Ming emperor] Hongwu and his advisors called it back as a template by which to fix the division of labor in society. The founder ordered his Minister of Revenue in 1385 to "inform the realm that each of the four categories of the people should keep to their proper occupations and not go wandering about to gain sustenance." Hongwu was not fixated on using the fourfold classification to limit the occupations among the people or create a caste system, invoking it more as a convenient shorthand for the settled hierarchy that should prevail in local society: a moral rather than a regulatory framework. Everyone realized that lots of people didn't fit the model. The magistrate's handbook *New Mirror for Shepherding the People*, for instance, summarized "the correct occupations of the people" as "officials, soldiers, doctors, diviners, gentry, peasants, artisans, and merchants," which still managed to place the merchants in the lowest position. Hongwu himself departed from the fourfold categorization when it suited him, at times specifying six categories by adding Buddhist monks and Daoist priests after the merchants.

Gazetteer compilers of the early Ming tend to be much more conservative about the occupations they identify and the stigma they place on merchants. Whenever the allegation is credible, they depict local society in terms of the four categories. Best of all was to picture only gentry and peasantry on the local social landscape. Thus a compiler praised Lu'an prefecture in southeastern Shanxi by saying that "the people are hard-working and frugal and devote themselves to agriculture, and the gentry revere good breeding and apply themselves to study." Merchants and artisans simply disappear from this picture. In neighboring Qinzhou, they are mentioned but minimized: "By local custom the people are frugal and simple and devote themselves single-mindedly to plowing and reading; few engage in commerce."

In any but the most backwoods counties, and sometimes even there as well, merchants were on the rise in the early Ming, even if their social prestige was limited and the gentry declined to notice them. Hongwu made mild attempts to keep the public status of merchants relative to other occupations low through sumptuary regulations [laws to prevent extravagance]. [For example, he passed an] edict against merchants wearing silk—which wealthy merchants in any case sidestepped by wearing silk at home and either changing or putting something over it before going out. If the emperor recognized the need for disincentives, this suggests that people were more than willing to give up farming for trade if they had the opportunity. The stigma against commerce was either minor or did not exist, at least among the pragmatic poor.

Markets

Markets were the physical nodes in the expanding network of trade that merchants were constructing in the early Ming. They emerged wherever goods were being moved, collected, or transshipped in volume: most commonly as permanent markets open every day in county seats (only a few interior county seats lacked a permanent market at the beginning of the Ming, and all had one by the turn of the fifteenth century), but also as periodic markets (held at a rate anywhere from three to fifteen days a month) at strategic locations on rivers, along main thoroughfares, or at junctions where roads and rivers crossed. Local magistrates collected taxes at these markets, acted occasionally to oversee them, and involved themselves rarely in setting them up, but otherwise they left the existence and operation of markets to merchants.

A few larger cities like Nanjing had several full-time markets specializing in different types of trade. That city's 1395 gazetteer lists thirteen. The Great Market in the center of the city was a general market for all types of goods, while those outside the city wall specialized. For fruits in season, one went to the Sanshan Street Market; for fish and vegetables, to the New Bridge Market or the North Gate Bridge Market at Hongwu Gate; for textiles, tea, salt, and paper, to the market outside Qingliang Gate; for bamboo, to the Laibin Street Market outside Treasure Basin Gate . . . for charcoal, to the Longjiang Market outside Jinchuan Gate; for grain, to the East Bank Market in the southwestern suburb; for construction timber, to the riverside market outside Yifeng Gate at the northwest corner.

The power of marketing networks to concentrate resources in key regional cities like Nanjing shaped the early-Ming world in ways that the state did not anticipate. Suzhou is a prime example. That city had been the base of Hongwu's arch-rival Zhang Shicheng, as well as a major center of gentry-landlord power under the Mongols. At the start of his reign, the emperor tried to bring Suzhou to its knees by imposing crushing taxes and forced relocations, and to eclipse it by investing heavily in Nanjing and granting it extraordinary prominence as his capital. The plan did not succeed. Because of the strength of its commercialized economy, Suzhou proved able to shoulder the tax burden the emperor placed on it. Indeed, that tax burden may have helped to further stimulate commercialization by forcing people to pursue innovative strategies for making money.

The Yongle emperor abandoned his father's plan. By removing the primary capital to the north, he quickly deflated Hongwu's aspiration that Nanjing should enjoy regional preeminence. Although the Grand Canal linked both Suzhou and Nanjing to Beijing, the southern capital's connection to the canal was a side spur. The main artery flowed through Suzhou. The reopening of the Grand Canal effectively shunted Nanjing to secondary status and ensured that the Suzhou region would prosper as a nexus of interregional integration. By the middle of the fifteenth century, Suzhou had fully recovered the prosperity it had been robbed of at the beginning of the dynasty. Nanjing survived comfortably as an administrative and cultural center, but it lacked the physical integration with surplus-producing regions that Suzhou enjoyed and could compete only in specialized commodities, notably luxuries. . . . The other contender for commercial supremacy in the Jiangnan region was Hangzhou, but it lay another 200 kilometers farther down the Grand Canal and that much farther away from the center of the delta. Hangzhou appears to have served more as a feeder into the Suzhou market than as a competing market center for the region.

CHRONOLOGY

1302
Truce between England and Scotland.

1304
Birth of Petrarch; birth of Ibn Battuta.

1306
Robert Bruce is crowned king of Scotland; Jews are expelled from France.

1307
Dante writes *The Divine Comedy.*

1312
Mansa Mūsā takes the throne of the Mali Empire.

1313
Birth of Giovanni Boccaccio.

1314
Battle of Bannockburn.

1315
Famine strikes much of northern Europe.

1320
Founding of the Tughluq dynasty in India.

1325
Approximate date of the founding of Tenochtitlán in Mexico.

1326
Death of Osman in Turkey.

1327
Edward II is deposed in England and replaced by Edward III.

1328
Birth of John Wycliffe.

1331
Civil war erupts in Japan over succession questions.

1332
Bubonic plague is recorded in India.

1337
Birth of Jean Froissart; start of the Hundred Years' War.

1340
English defeat French in sea battle off Sluys; birth of Geoffrey Chaucer.

1346
French are defeated at the Battle of Crécy.

1347
Black Death comes to Europe.

1348
Boccaccio begins writing *Decameron.*

1351
End of the initial outbreak of the plague.

1352
Ibn Battuta explores the Sahara.

1359
Treaty of London settles some issues of the Hundred Years' War.

1363
Timur begins conquest of much of Asia.

1368
Beginning of Ming dynasty in China.

1369
Founding of the Hanseatic League.

1370
England sacks Limoges in France.

1376
Death of Edward, the Black Prince, of England.

1378
Start of the Great Schism.

1380
Death of Catherine of Siena.

1381
Peasants' revolt in England, led by Wat Tyler.

1387
Chaucer begins work on *The Canterbury Tales.*

1392
Ashikaga family takes control of Muromachi in Japan.

1396
The Battle of Nicopolis.

1398
Timur conquers India.

1399
Richard II is deposed as king of England.

1400
Froissart publishes his *Chronicles.*

FOR FURTHER READING

Adam of Usk, *The Chronicle of Adam of Usk*. Ed. Edward Maunde Thompson. London: John Murray, 1876.

Morris Bishop, trans., *Letters from Petrarch*. Bloomington: Indiana University Press, 1966.

Giovanni Boccaccio, *Decameron*. Trans. Frances Winwar. New York: Modern Library, 1936.

Derek Brewer, *Chaucer in His Time*. Edinburgh, Scotland: Thomas Nelson and Sons, 1963.

Timothy Brook, *The Confusions of Pleasure*. Berkeley and Los Angeles: University of California Press, 1998.

Lester Brooks, *Civilizations of Ancient Africa*. New York: Four Winds, 1971.

W.F. Conton, *West Africa in History*. Vol. 1. London: George Allen and Unwin, 1961.

Thomas B. Costain, *The Three Edwards*. Garden City, NY: Doubleday, 1958.

Ross E. Dunn, *The Adventures of Ibn Battuta: A Muslim Traveler of the Fourteenth Century*. Berkeley and Los Angeles: University of California Press, 1986.

Robert S. Gottfried, *The Black Death*. New York: Free, 1983.

Bernard Grun, *The Timetables of History*. New York: Touchstone, 1982.

Barbara Hanawalt, *Growing Up in Medieval London*. New York: Oxford University Press, 1993.

J.N. Hays, *The Burdens of Disease*. New Brunswick, NJ: Rutgers University Press, 1998.

George Holmes, *The Later Middle Ages.* Edinburgh, Scotland: Thomas Nelson and Sons, 1962.

S.S. Hussey, *Chaucer: An Introduction.* London: Methuen, 1971.

John Jolliffe, trans., *Froissart's Chronicles.* New York: Modern Library, 1967.

William Chester Jordan, *The Great Famine: Northern Europe in the Early Fourteenth Century.* Princeton, NJ: Princeton University Press, 1996.

Robert E. Lerner, *The Age of Adversity.* Ithaca, NY: Cornell University Press, 1968.

Robert S. Lopez, *The Commercial Revolution of the Middle Ages, 950–1350.* Englewood Cliffs, NJ: Prentice-Hall, 1971.

May McKisack, *The Fourteenth Century.* Oxford, England: Oxford University Press, 1959.

Michel Mollat and Philippe Wolff, *The Popular Revolutions of the Late Middle Ages.* Trans. A.L. Lytton-Sells. London: George Allen and Unwin, 1973.

Charles Panati, *Panati's Extraordinary Endings of Practically Everything and Everybody.* New York: Harper and Row, 1989.

Charles Seignobos, *The Feudal Regime.* Tran. Earle W. Dow. New York: Henry Holt, 1930.

Desmond Seward, *The Hundred Years' War: The English in France, 1337–1453.* New York: Atheneum, 1978.

Bertold Spuler, T*he Mongols in History.* Trans. Geoffrey Wheeler. New York: Praeger, 1971.

Barbara Tuchman, *A Distant Mirror.* New York: Alfred A. Knopf, 1978.

Walter Ullmann, *The Origins of the Great Schism.* Hamden, CT: Archon Books, 1967.

Nicholas Wright, *Knights and Peasants: The Hundred Years' War in the French Countryside.* Rochester, NY: Boydell and Brewer, 1998.

INDEX

Adam of Usk, 60
Africa, 227
  see also Mali Empire
Africa (Petrarch), 141–43
Akiie, Kitabatake, 197, 198
Alexandre, Pierre, 107
Al Omari, 230–31
Anderson, Gillian and William, 93
apothecaries, 177
Aquinas, Saint Thomas, 145, 150
art, 105
  influenced by the plague, 190
  Ming, 241
Ashikaga family, 197–98, 199
Asia
  India's Tughluq dynasty, 200–204
  infighting in Japan, 195–99
  Timur's invasions in, 218–20
  travels in, 205–206
  see also Ming dynasty; Ottoman
  Empire
Aztecs, 193
  human sacrifice by, 221–22
  lower classes of, 224–25
  nobles of, 224
  priests of, 224
  on warfare, 222
  warrior elites of, 222–23
  women, 225

Bahmani dynasty, 202
Balkans, 212–13
Ball, John, 94–97, 100, 103
Bannockburn, Battle of, 110
  aftermath of, 31–32
  English attack in, 27–29
  Robert Bruce in battle for, 28
  and Scottish
    vs. English army size for, 25–27
    preparation for, 27

victory in, 29–30
Barbanera, 47, 48
Battuta, Abu'Abdallah ibn, 200–201
  birth of, 205
  compared with Marco Polo,
    208–209
  death of, 206
  in Mali, 234, 239
  travels of, 205–206
    book on, 207–208
Bayazid (emir of the Osmanlis),
  214–15
Béhuchet, Nicholas, 47–48, 50
Bengal, 202–203
Biraben, Jean-Noël, 185
bishops
  and the Black Death, 19–20
  convents inspected by, 157–59
Black Death, the, 105
  burials during, 171–72
  causes of, 165–66, 178–80
  in city and country, 172–73
  compared with other plagues, 19
  and crime, 38
  curing, 168, 182–83
  deaths from, 19, 165
  effects of, 20–21
    on the Church, 188–89
    economic, 185–87
    guilt and fear as, 190
    on industry, 187
    on landed class, 188
    on piety of individuals, 189
    on public morality, 189–90
    technological changes, 187–88
  medical reaction to, 175
  method of transmission, 165
  Muslims on, 190–91
  nursing sick during, 170–71
  people affected by, 19–20, 165

Don de Dios • God's Gift

La Reconciliación
Reconciliation

para programas parroquiales y escolares • *for Parish and School Programs*

LOYOLA PRESS.
UN MINISTERIO JESUITA
A JESUIT MINISTRY

Reconocimientos

Cantos

"Enséñame" (página v). Texto y música por Lorenzo Florián. Copyright © 2004, World Library Publications, Franklin Park, IL. www.wlpmusic.com Todos los derechos reservados. Usado con permiso.

"Amor, amor" (página v). Tradicional.

"Vamos ya", (página v). – "We Go Forth" Texto original en inglés y música por James V. Marchionda. Traducción al español por Peter M. Kolar. Copyright © 2004, 2007, World Library Publications, Franklin Park, IL. www.wlpmusic.com Todos los derechos reservados. Usado con permiso.

La versión en castellano del *Confiteor* ("Yo confieso") está tomada del *Misal Romano* © 2003 Obra Nacional de la Buena Prensa, A.C., Conferencia del Episcopado Mexicano. La versión en castellano del Acto de Contrición está tomada del *Catecismo de la Iglesia Católica*: Compendio © 2005 Librería Editrice Vaticana. La versión en castellano de las palabras de absolución está tomada del *Ritual de la Penitencia* © 2003 Obra Nacional de la Buena Prensa, A.C., Conferencia del Episcopado Mexicano. La versión en castellano de la oración al Espíritu Santo está tomada de *Una Guía de oración para padres de familia* © 2005 Loyola Press. Todos los derechos reservados.

Loyola Press ha hecho todos los intentos posibles por localizar a los propietarios de los derechos de autor de las obras citadas en el presente trabajo a fin de hacer un reconocimiento pleno de la autoría de su trabajo. En caso de alguna omisión, Loyola Press se complacerá en reconocer el crédito en las ediciones futuras.

Acknowledgments

Songs

"Make Us One" (page v). Text and music by James V. Marchionda. Copyright © 2000, World Library Publications, Franklin Park, IL. www.wlpmusic.com. All rights reserved. Used by permission.

"Peace Walk" (page v). Text and music by Julie Howard. Copyright © 1995, World Library Publications, Franklin Park, IL. www.wlpmusic.com. All rights reserved. Used by permission.

"We Go Forth" (page v). Text and music by James V. Marchionda. Copyright © 2004, World Library Publications, Franklin Park, IL. www.wlpmusic.com. All rights reserved. Used by permission.

The English translation of the *Confiteor* ("I confess") from *The Roman Missal* © 2010, International Commission on English in the Liturgy, Inc. (ICEL); the English translation of the Act of Contrition and the Absolution from *Rite of Penance* © 1974, ICEL; the English translation of the Prayer to the Holy Spirit from *A Book of Prayers* © 1982, ICEL. All rights reserved.

Loyola Press has made every effort to locate the copyright holders for the cited works used in this publication and to make full acknowledgment for their use. In the case of any omissions, the publisher will be pleased to make suitable acknowledgments in future editions.

Traducción y adaptación/*Translation and adaptation:* Miguel Arias y Santiago Cortés-Sjöberg/Loyola Press.

Diseño interior/*Interior design:* Loyola Press Ilustración de portada/*Cover art:* Susan Tolonen Diseño de portada/*Cover design:* Loyola Press.

ISBN-13: 978-0-8294-4111-6, ISBN-10: 0-8294-4111-5

Copyright © 2016 Loyola Press

LOYOLA PRESS.
UN MINISTERIO JESUITA
A JESUIT MINISTRY

3441 N. Ashland Avenue
Chicago, Illinois 60657
(800) 621-1008
www.loyolapress.com

Impreso en los Estados Unidos de América.
Printed in the United States of America.

18 19 20 21 22 Web 10 9 8 7 6 5 4 3

Índice

Contents

Al abrir este libro,
recuerdo lo mucho que Dios me ama
y su llamado a unirme a él
y a toda su creación.

Gracias, Dios mío,
por darme el sacramento de la Reconciliación
como señal de tu amor y de tu presencia
en mi vida.

As I open this book,
I remember how much God loves me
and calls me to be one with him
and all creation.

Thank you, God,
for giving me the Sacrament of Reconciliation
as a sign of your love and presence
in my life.

Enséñame

ESTRIBILLO
Enséñame a vivir, enséñame a seguir,
seguirte solo a ti, mi Señor y Salvador.

Señor, tú eres mi Rey, protector y salvador.
Pues un niño soy, Señor; enséñame tu amor.

ESTRIBILLO

Señor, mi amigo serás. Tú me guías por siempre jamás.
Pues un niño soy, Señor; enséñame tu amor.

ESTRIBILLO

Amor, amor

Amor, amor, amor, amor;
hermano mío, Dios es amor.
Ama a todos como hermanos;
Dios es amor.

Vamos ya

Se repite cada línea después del guía:

Al rezar,
vamos ya
en la gracia de Jesús.
Llamados
a vivir
el santo Evangelio.

v

Make Us One

God of love, make us one
And unite us in Christ.
In our hearts, in our minds,
In our souls, and in our spirits,
Make us one, God of love.

Peace Walk

REFRAIN
Come, let us walk in the way of our God,
Let us walk in the way of our God.
(Repeat)

VERSE
Pray for God's gentle peace within.
May the pilgrimage now begin.
Peace abide within our hearts.
All who love God, walk in peace.

We Go Forth

Repeat each line after the leader:

We go forth
From this prayer
With the grace of Jesus.

Called to live
What he taught
In the holy Gospel.

Dios nos llama amigos

Buenos amigos

¡Los amigos son estupendos! Jugamos con ellos, compartimos dulces con ellos y vamos con ellos a distintos lugares. Los amigos hacen que cada día sea un día divertido.

¿Qué cosas divertidas haces con tus amigos?

_____

_____

_____

Oración

Dios, Creador nuestro, tú me has creado y me amas. Ayúdame a ser un buen amigo tuyo.

1

Good Friends

Friends are great! We play with them, share treats with them, and go places together. Friends make each day fun.

What fun things do you do with your friends?

_____

_____

_____

Prayer

God, our Creator, you made me and you love me. Help me be your good friend.

1

La gracia: un don de Dios

Dios existía antes que cualquier otra cosa. Él quería compartir su vida con nosotros. Por eso Dios creó un hermoso jardín. Creó a Adán y a Eva para que disfrutaran del jardín. Dios vino del cielo para caminar con Adán y Eva. Eran felices. Dios les había dado un gran don llamado **gracia**. La gracia es la vida de Dios en nosotros. Nos ayuda a ser amigos de Dios y de los demás.

Dios dio a Adán y Eva una regla: no debían comer la fruta de un cierto árbol del jardín.

Satanás quería que Adán y Eva desobedecieran a Dios y por eso los tentó para que de todas formas comieran de esa fruta. Adán y Eva cayeron en la **tentación**. Perdieron el don de la gracia. Todo cambió.

God's Gift of Grace

God existed before anything else. He wanted to share his life with us. So God created a beautiful garden. He created Adam and Eve to enjoy the garden. God came from heaven to walk with Adam and Eve. They were happy. God had given them a great gift called **grace**. Grace is God's life in us. It helps us to be friends with God and with one another.

God gave Adam and Eve one rule—they were not to eat the fruit of one certain tree in the garden.

Satan wanted Adam and Eve to disobey God, so he tempted them to eat the fruit anyway. Adam and Eve gave in to the **temptation**. They lost the gift of grace. Everything changed.

Adán y Eva ya no eran felices el uno con el otro. Habían desobedecido a Dios. Cuando Dios vino del cielo para caminar con ellos, se escondieron de él. Dios les preguntó si habían comido de la fruta de aquel árbol y ellos le dijeron que sí. Habían dañado su amistad con Dios. Ya no tenían el don especial de la gracia. Tuvieron que abandonar el hermoso jardín.

adaptado de Génesis 2, 3

Adam and Eve were no longer happy with each other. They had disobeyed God. When God came from heaven to walk with them, they hid. God asked them if they had eaten the fruit of that one tree, and they said yes. They had hurt their friendship with God. They no longer had that special gift of grace. They had to leave the beautiful garden.

adapted from Genesis 2, 3

Una mala decisión

Dios creó un jardín
que era muy bonito.
Lo llenó de frutas y flores,
y de toda clase de árboles.

Adán y Eva eran felices;
Dios era su amigo especial.
Pensaban que esta alegría
jamás se acabaría.

Pero Satanás vino a tentarlos,
"Todo saldrá bien", dijo.
"No escuchen lo que Dios dice,
escúchenme a mí".

Hicieron lo que Satanás les dijo,
y después corrieron
y se escondieron.
Perdieron la gracia y la amistad de Dios,
por haber hecho lo que hicieron.

The Wrong Choice

God created a garden
that was beautiful to see.
He filled it with fruit and flowers,
and every kind of tree.

Adam and Eve were happy;
God was their special friend.
They thought these happy times
would never, ever end.

But Satan came to tempt them,
"All will be fine," he said.
"Don't listen to what God says,
listen to me instead."

They did as Satan told them,
and then they ran and hid.
They lost God's grace, his friendship,
because of what they did.

Mmm...

Pienso en esto

Una tentación es un pensamiento o sentimiento que puede llevarme a tomar una mala decisión.

¿En qué momentos has tomado malas decisiones?

Atascados en el camino

Los amigos son muy importantes para nosotros. Pero en ocasiones nos enojamos con ellos. A veces, incluso podemos sentir celos. Puede ser que tomemos algo de ellos que nos gustaría tener, o que decidamos no ayudarlos cuando lo necesiten. Cuando nos comportamos así, estamos cayendo en la tentación.

Quizás sepamos que las cosas que hacemos, o que no hacemos, están mal. Puede que sepamos que dañan nuestra amistad con Dios y con los demás. Nos gustaría dejar de hacerlo, pero no sabemos cómo. Es como si estuviésemos atascados y solo pudiéramos actuar así.

A partir del momento en el que Adán y Eva se alejaron de la amistad de Dios, todas las personas nacen con el **pecado original**. El pecado original es lo que hace que nos sea más difícil ser amigos de Dios y de los demás.

Stuck Along the Way

Friends are very important to us. But sometimes we get angry with our friends. Sometimes we may even be jealous of them. We might take something of theirs that we really want. Or we might choose not to help when one of them needs help. When we do these things, we are giving in to temptation.

We may know that the things we do—or don't do—are wrong. We may know that they hurt our friendship with God and with one another. We would like to stop, but we don't know how. We just seem stuck acting that way.

Ever since Adam and Eve turned away from God's friendship, all people are born in **Original Sin**. Original Sin makes it more difficult for us to be friends with God and with one another.

Hmm . . .

I Think About This

A temptation is a thought or feeling that can lead me to make a wrong choice.

When have you made wrong choices?

La promesa de Dios

La Biblia nos relata la historia de la promesa de Dios de ayudarnos. Dios prometió enviar a un Salvador. Nuestro **Salvador**, Jesús, nos liberaría del pecado original. Nos enseñaría cómo ser mejores amigos de Dios. Él nos **reconciliaría** con Dios.

La Virgen María conocía la promesa de Dios. Rezaba para que el Salvador viniera pronto. Un ángel visitó a María. El ángel le dijo que Dios le pedía a ella que fuera la madre del Salvador. María dijo que sí. Haría lo que Dios le pedía. Ella sería la madre del Salvador prometido por Dios.

Mmm...

Pienso en esto

Reconciliar *significa "unir de nuevo"*.

God's Promise

The Bible tells us the story of God's promise to help us. God promised that he would send a Savior. Our **Savior**, Jesus, would free us from original sin. He would show us how to become closer friends with God. He would **reconcile** us with God.

Mary knew about God's promise. She prayed that the Savior would come soon. An angel came to Mary. The angel told Mary that God was asking her to be the mother of the Savior. Mary said yes. She would do what God asked. She would be the mother of the Savior that God promised.

Hmm...

I Think About This

Reconcile *means "to bring together."*

La historia de nuestra fe

Usa palabras del banco de palabras para completar la historia.

Banco de palabras

sí	Eva	María	Salvador
tentó	pecado	amistad	Jesús

Adán y _____ eran muy felices en el

jardín de Dios. Satanás _____ a Adán

y a Eva. Adán y Eva dañaron su _____

con Dios cuando pecaron. Desde entonces,

todas las personas nacen con el _____

original. Pero Dios prometió a un _____

para ayudarnos. Esa persona es _____.

Su madre se llama _____. Ella le dijo

_____ a Dios.

Escucho la Palabra de Dios

"Él les enviará un salvador y defensor que los libre".
Isaías 19:20

¡Dios está muy feliz de ser tu amigo!

The Story of Our Faith ✏️

Use words from the word bank to complete the story.

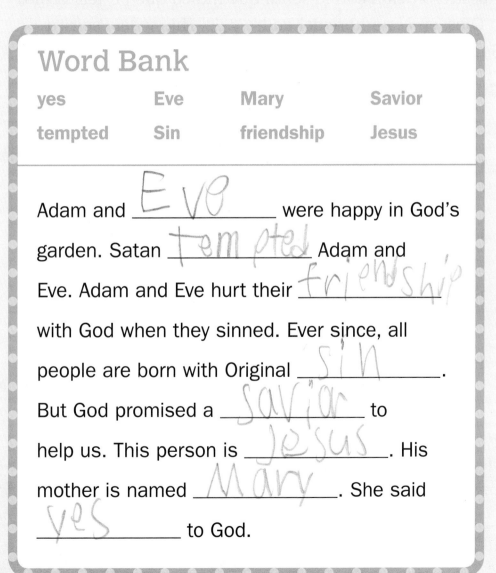

Word Bank

yes	Eve	Mary	Savior
tempted	Sin	friendship	Jesus

Adam and _Eve_ were happy in God's garden. Satan _tempted_ Adam and Eve. Adam and Eve hurt their _friendship_ with God when they sinned. Ever since, all people are born with Original _Sin_. But God promised a _Savior_ to help us. This person is _Jesus_. His mother is named _Mary_. She said _yes_ to God.

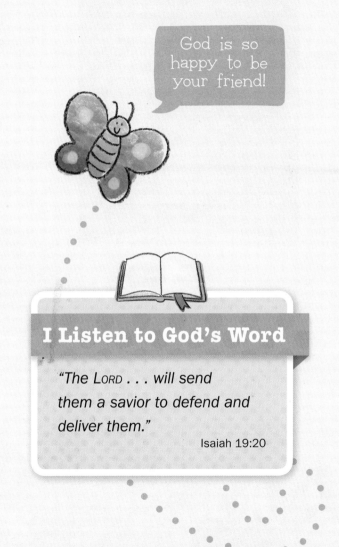

God is so happy to be your friend!

I Listen to God's Word

"The LORD . . . will send them a savior to defend and deliver them."

Isaiah 19:20

Dios cuida de nosotros

Dios nos creó y quiere que seamos felices. Él quiere que seamos amigos de él y de los demás. Dios nos ama en todo momento, no importa lo que hagamos. Él es un amigo que nos cuida y está siempre dispuesto a perdonarnos. Ser amigos de Dios nos ayuda a ser amigos de los demás.

Nuestra amistad con Dios

Guía: Reunidos como amigos de Dios, comencemos nuestra oración con la señal que indica que pertenecemos a Dios: en el nombre del Padre y del Hijo y del Espíritu Santo. Amén.

Guía: Tú creaste el mundo para que viviéramos en él.

Todos: Te damos gracias, Señor.

Tú nos das la gracia para vivir como amigos tuyos.
Te damos gracias, Señor.

Tú nos ayudas cuando somos tentados.
Te damos gracias, Señor.

Tú nos aceptas y das la bienvenida cuando hemos pecado.
Te damos gracias, Señor.

Tú nos enviaste a Jesús para que fuera nuestro Salvador.
Te damos gracias, Señor.

Our Friendship with God

Prayer Leader: Gathered as God's friends, let us begin our prayer with the sign of belonging to God. In the name of the Father, and of the Son, and of the Holy Spirit. Amen.

Prayer Leader: You created the world for us to live in.

All: We thank you, God.

You give us grace to live as your friends.
> We thank you, God.

You help us when we are tempted.
> We thank you, God.

You welcome us back when we have sinned.
> We thank you, God.

You sent Jesus to be our Savior.
> We thank you, God.

God Cares for Us

God made us and wants us to be happy. He wants us to be friends with him and with one another. God loves us at all times, no matter what we do. He is a friend who cares for us and is always ready to forgive. Being friends with God helps us to be friends with others.

Todos: Dios de amor, gracias por el don de tu amistad. Ayúdanos a caminar junto a ti.

Guía: Recordando el amor que Dios nos tiene, recemos juntos la oración que Jesús nos enseñó:

Todos: Padre nuestro, que estás en el cielo,
santificado sea tu Nombre;
venga a nosotros tu Reino;
hágase tu voluntad
en la tierra como en el cielo.
Danos hoy
nuestro pan de cada día;
perdona nuestras ofensas,
como también nosotros perdonamos
a los que nos ofenden;
no nos dejes caer en la tentación,
y líbranos del mal.
Amén.

Cuando celebro

Me uno en oración a la Iglesia extendida por toda la tierra.

When I Celebrate

I join in prayer with the Church around the world.

All: Loving God, thank you for the gift of your friendship. Help us to walk closely with you.

Prayer Leader: Remembering God's love for us, let us pray the prayer that Jesus taught us.

All: Our Father, who art in heaven,
hallowed be thy name;
thy kingdom come;
thy will be done
on earth as it is in heaven.
Give us this day our daily bread,
and forgive us our trespasses,
as we forgive those who trespass against us;
and lead us not into temptation,
but deliver us from evil.
Amen.

Viviendo mi fe

Recuerdo lo que aprendo

- Adán y Eva vivían en la gracia como amigos de Dios.
- Adán y Eva decidieron no seguir a Dios.
- Todas las personas nacen con el pecado original.
- Dios prometió a un Salvador.
- María es la madre de nuestro Salvador.

Comparto con *mi familia*

Conversa con tu familia acerca de nuestra amistad con Dios. ¿Qué pueden hacer como familia para vivir en amistad con él?

Vivo lo que aprendo

Obedezco las reglas de Dios.

Digo sí a Dios.

Doy gracias a Dios por su amistad.

Oración final

Gracias, Dios, por ser mi amigo. Ayúdame a decirte que sí, como lo hizo María.

Conozco estas palabras

Encuentro estas palabras en el *Glosario:*

gracia, p. 76

pecado original, p. 76

reconciliar, p. 76

Salvador, p. 76

tentación, p. 76

Living My Faith

I Remember What I Learn

- Adam and Eve lived in grace as God's friends.
- Adam and Eve chose not to follow God.
- Everyone is born in Original Sin.
- God promised a Savior.
- Mary is the mother of our Savior.

I Live What I Learn

I obey God's rules.

I say yes to God.

I thank God for his friendship.

I Know These Words

I find these words in the Glossary.

grace, p. 76   **Savior,** p. 76

Original Sin, p. 76   **temptation,** p. 76

reconcile, p. 76

I Share with My Family

Talk with your family about friendship with God. What can you do as a family to live in friendship with him?

Closing Prayer

Thank you, God, for being my friend.
Help me to say yes to you as Mary did.

Jesús nos salva

¡Salvados de nuevo!

A veces te olvidas qué tareas tenías para la escuela y llamas a un amigo para que te ayude. O quizás se te olvidó tu almuerzo o el dinero para comprarlo y tienes que pedirle a un compañero que comparta el suyo contigo.

¿Te han pasado algunas de estas cosas? ¿Cómo te sentiste cuando alguien vino a ayudarte?

Oración

Jesús, Salvador nuestro, ayúdame a recordar que tú siempre estás listo para ayudarme.

Saved Again!

Sometimes you forget what to do for homework and have to call a friend for help. Or maybe you forget your lunch or lunch money and have to ask your classmates to share with you.

Have any of these things ever happened to you? How did you feel when someone came to your rescue?

Prayer

Jesus, our Savior, help me to remember that you are always ready to help me.

11

Jesús, nuestro Salvador

José, al igual que la Virgen María, sabía que Dios había prometido salvarnos. Una noche José tuvo un sueño. En su sueño, un ángel le dijo que el hijo de María era de Dios. El ángel le dijo a José que le diera al bebé el nombre de Jesús.

Jesús es el Hijo de Dios. El nombre "Jesús" quiere decir: "Dios salva".

adaptado de Mateo 1:18–21

Jesús creció y aprendió a ser carpintero. Años más tarde, anduvo de pueblo en pueblo enseñando y sanando a las personas.

Jesús enseñó a las personas lo mucho que Dios, nuestro Padre, las quiere. Él quería que todas las personas fueran amigas de Dios. Quería que vivieran una vida santa.

Jesus, Our Savior

Like Mary, Joseph knew of God's promise to save us. One night, Joseph had a dream. In his dream, an angel told him that Mary's baby was from God. The angel told Joseph to name the baby Jesus.

Jesus is the Son of God. Jesus' name means "God saves."

adapted from Matthew 1:18–21

Jesus grew up and learned how to be a carpenter. Later, he went from town to town teaching and healing people.

Jesus taught people about how much God our Father loves them. He wanted all people to be friends with God. He wanted them to live holy lives.

Pero, a causa del pecado original, las personas seguían alejándose de Dios. No les gustaba lo que Jesús enseñaba. Hicieron que lo arrestaran.

Jesús sufrió, murió, resucitó de entre los muertos y ascendió al cielo para salvarnos del pecado. Ofreció su vida para que pudiéramos reconciliarnos con Dios, nuestro Padre. Ofreció su vida porque nos ama.

INRI

But because of Original Sin, people still turned away from God. They did not like what Jesus was teaching. They had him arrested.

Jesus suffered and died, rose from the dead, and ascended into heaven to save us from sin. He offered his life so we could be reconciled with God our Father. He offered his life because he loves us.

Bienvenidos a la familia de Dios

Jesús nos dio los **sacramentos** para estar presente con nosotros hoy. Él nos da su gracia, especialmente en los sacramentos.

La gracia de Jesucristo viene a nosotros en el **Bautismo**. Cuando somos bautizados, recibimos el Espíritu Santo. El Bautismo nos libera del pecado original y de todo pecado personal.

La gracia que recibimos en el Bautismo nos fortalece, mientras tratamos de resistir la inclinación a pecar, nos esforzamos por vivir la ley moral, promovemos la justicia y lo que está bien y crecemos como las personas que Dios nos llama a ser, para que podamos vivir en verdadera libertad.

Diáconos, sacerdotes y obispos realizan los bautizos, pero en caso de extrema necesidad, cualquier persona que tenga la verdadera intención de hacer lo que hace la Iglesia, también puede bautizar. Se hace vertiendo agua sobre la cabeza de la persona que va a ser bautizada, mientras se dice: "Yo te bautizo en el nombre del Padre, del Hijo, y del Espíritu Santo". En ese momento pasamos a formar parte de la familia especial de Dios: la Iglesia católica. Somos hechos hijos e hijas de Dios.

Welcomed into God's Family

Jesus gave us the **sacraments** in order to be present with us today. He gives us his grace, especially in the sacraments.

The Grace of Jesus Christ comes to us in **Baptism**. When we are baptized, we receive the Holy Spirit. Baptism frees us from Original Sin and all personal sin.

The grace we receive in Baptism strengthens us as we resist the inclination to sin, strive to live out the moral law, promote justice and what is good, and grow as the people God calls us to be, so that we might live in true freedom.

Baptism is performed by a deacon, priest, or bishop, but in the case of extreme necessity, it can be performed by any person who has the true intention of doing what the Church does. It is done by pouring water on the head of the person who is going to be baptized, while saying: "I Baptize you in the name of the Father, the Son, and the Holy Spirit." We are then welcomed into God's special family, the Catholic Church. We become children of God.

I Listen to God's Word

Go, therefore, and make disciples of all nations, baptizing them in the name of the Father, and of the Son, and of the holy Spirit, teaching them to observe all that I have commanded you.

Matthew 28:19–20

Hijos de Dios

La gracia es un don que Dios nos da libremente. No tenemos que hacer nada para ganar el amor de Dios. En el Bautismo recibimos la gracia de Dios. El amor y la gracia de Dios son dones que él nos da a todos. Se bautiza a los niños para que entren de lleno en la gracia de Dios como hijos de Dios. Podemos devolver a Dios el amor al compartirlo con los demás.

En el corazón, dibújate a ti mismo compartiendo el amor de Dios con los demás.

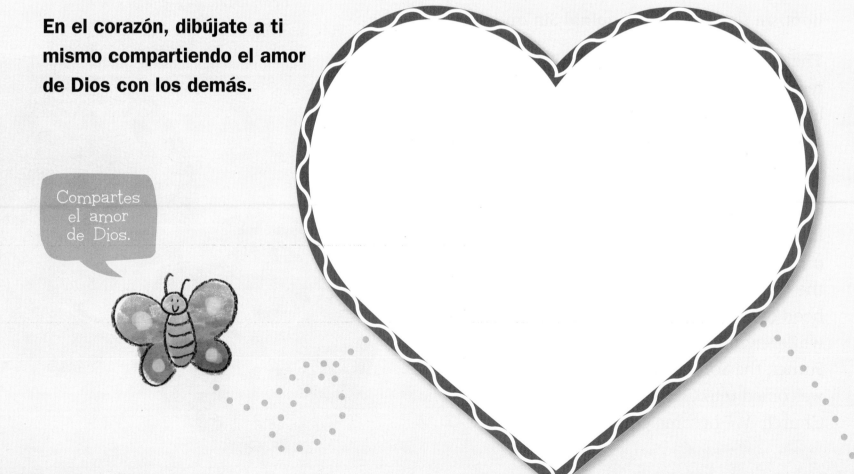

Compartes el amor de Dios.

Children of God

You share God's love.

Grace is a gift of God that he gives us freely. We don't have to do anything to earn God's love. In Baptism, we receive God's grace. God's love and grace is a gift he gives all of us. Children are baptized so that they may share fully in God's grace as children of God. We can return God's love by sharing it with others.

In the heart, draw yourself sharing God's love with others.

Pienso en esto

Los sacramentos de la Iniciación nos hacen miembros plenos de la Iglesia.

Amigos de Dios

A medida que crecemos, Dios continúa ayudándonos con su gracia. Nos ayuda mediante los sacramentos.

Durante la celebración del sacramento de la **Confirmación** somos ungidos con óleo. La Confirmación nos fortalece en la fe. Nos da la fuerza para ser seguidores de Jesús.

Jesús nos da el don de su Cuerpo y su Sangre en la **Eucaristía**. Recibir la Sagrada Comunión nos ayuda a permanecer cerca de él y a crecer en santidad.

El Bautismo, la Confirmación y la Eucaristía son los **sacramentos de la Iniciación**. No todo el mundo recibe los sacramentos de la Iniciación a la misma edad. En la tradición oriental, los tres sacramentos de la Iniciación se administran en una misma celebración: la Confirmación se administra después del Bautismo, seguida de la participación en la Eucaristía, expresando así la unidad de los tres sacramentos.

A veces cometemos **pecados** y nos alejamos de Dios. Celebramos el perdón de Dios mediante el sacramento de la **Reconciliación**.

¿Cuál es una manera en la que puedo decirle a Dios que estoy arrepentido de mis pecados? Puedo rezar el **Acto de Contrición**.

Friends with God

As we grow, God continues to help us with his grace. He gives us help in the sacraments.

During the Sacrament of **Confirmation**, we are anointed with oil. Confirmation makes us stronger in our faith. It gives us the strength to be followers of Jesus.

Jesus gives us the gift of his Body and Blood in the **Eucharist**. Receiving Holy Communion helps us stay close to him and grow in holiness.

Baptism, Confirmation, and the Eucharist are **Sacraments of Initiation**. Not everyone receives the Sacraments of Initiation at the same age. In the Eastern tradition, Baptism, Confirmation, and Eucharist are administered in one celebration, expresing the unity of the sacraments. Confirmation is administered after Baptism, followed by participation in the Eucharist.

Sometimes we **sin** and turn away from God. We celebrate God's forgiveness in the Sacrament of **Reconciliation**.

What is one way I can tell God I'm sorry when I sin? I can pray the **Act of Contrition**.

Hmm...

I Think About This

The Sacraments of Initiation make us full members of the Church.

Estás en camino

Este año celebrarás por primera vez el sacramento de la Reconciliación. Haz un dibujo de tu familia. Ellos te ayudarán a prepararte para celebrar este sacramento.

Esta es mi familia: _____.

On Your Way

You will celebrate the Sacrament of Reconciliation for the first time this year. Draw a picture of your family. They will help you prepare for the sacrament.

This is my family: _____.

La Señal de la Cruz

Se nos dio la bienvenida a la familia de Dios en el Bautismo. El sacerdote trazó una cruz en nuestra frente. Cuando celebramos el sacramento de la Reconciliación el sacerdote nos da la bienvenida en nombre de Dios. Luego, rezamos juntos la Señal de la Cruz. Nos recuerda que somos seguidores de Jesús y miembros de la Iglesia.

Una señal de bienvenida

Guía: Comenzamos nuestra oración con la Señal de la Cruz. Recordamos que pertenecemos a la familia de Dios, la Iglesia.

Tranquilos y en silencio, hablemos con Jesús en nuestro corazón.

Imagínate que estás presenciando el Bautismo de un bebé. Ves al sacerdote trazar un cruz en la frente del bebé. Cuando el sacerdote o el diácono bautiza al bebé con agua en el nombre del Padre y del Hijo y del Espíritu Santo, tú sabes que este bebé pertenece ahora a la familia de Dios. La cruz es una señal de bienvenida y demuestra que pertenecemos a la familia de Dios, la Iglesia.

1 • • • • • ▶   2 • • • • • ▶

A Welcoming Sign

Prayer Leader: We begin our prayer with the Sign of the Cross. We remember that we belong to God's family, the Church.

Be still and talk with Jesus in your heart.

Imagine that you are at the Baptism of a baby. You watch the priest trace a cross on the baby's forehead. When the priest or deacon baptizes the baby with water in the name of the Father, and of the Son, and of the Holy Spirit, you know this baby now belongs to God's family. The cross is a sign of welcome and shows that we belong to God's family, the Church.

The Sign of the Cross

We were welcomed into God's family at our Baptism. The priest traced a cross on our forehead. When we celebrate the Sacrament of Reconciliation, the priest welcomes us in God's name. Then we pray the Sign of the Cross together. It reminds us that we are followers of Jesus and members of the Church.

3 ·······▶ **4** ·······▶ **5**

Cuando rezo

No siempre necesito usar palabras. Dios sabe lo que hay en mi corazón.

Tú también quieres darle la bienvenida al bebé. Acércate. ¿Qué mensaje de bienvenida desearías compartir con él?

Pide a Jesús que bendiga al bebé y a todos los que son bautizados en su nombre. Quédate tranquilo junto a Jesús, y deja que le hable a tu corazón, de amigo a amigo.

Que el Dios que te creó y te dio la bienvenida a su familia esté en tu mente y en tu corazón, ahora y siempre. Te lo pedimos . . .

Todos: . . . en el nombre del Padre y del Hijo y del Espíritu Santo. Amén.

You want to offer a welcome to this baby too. Come close. What welcoming message would you like to share?

Ask Jesus to bless this baby and all who are baptized in his name. Be still with Jesus, and let him speak to your heart, friend to friend.

May the God who created you and welcomed you into his family be in your mind and heart, now and forever.

We ask this . . .

All: . . . in the name of the Father, and of the Son, and of the Holy Spirit. Amen.

When I Pray

I don't always need to use words. God knows what is in my heart.

Viviendo mi fe

Recuerdo lo que aprendo

- El nombre *Jesús* significa "Dios salva".
- Recibí una vida nueva en el sacramento del Bautismo.
- Soy fortalecido en el sacramento de la Confirmación.
- Soy alimentado en el sacramento de la Eucaristía.
- Soy reconciliado con Dios en el sacramento de la Reconciliación.

Vivo lo que aprendo

Vivo como hijo de Dios.

Sigo a Jesús.

Rezo la Señal de la Cruz.

Conozco estas palabras

Encuentro estas palabras en el *Glosario*:

Acto de Contrición, p. 76   **pecado,** p. 77

Bautismo, p. 76   **Reconciliación,** p. 77

Confirmación, p. 77   **sacramento,** p. 77

Eucaristía, p. 77   **sacramentos de la Iniciación,** p. 77

Comparto con mi familia

Ponemos nuestra esperanza y confianza en Dios. Pide a los miembros de tu familia que compartan cómo Dios les ayuda.

Oración final

Dios amoroso, gracias por el don de Jesús. Ayúdame a permanecer cerca de él.

Living My Faith

I Remember What I Learn

- The name *Jesus* means "God saves."
- I received new life in the Sacrament of Baptism.
- I am strengthened in the Sacrament of Confirmation.
- I am nourished in the Sacrament of the Eucharist.
- I am reconciled with God in the Sacrament of Reconciliation.

I Live What I Learn

I live as a child of God.

I follow Jesus.

I pray the Sign of the Cross.

I Know These Words

I find these words in the Glossary.

I Share with My Family

We place our trust and hope in God. Ask your family members to share ways that God helps each of them.

Closing Prayer

Loving God, thank you for the gift of Jesus. Help me to stay close to him.

Jesús nos perdona

Otra oportunidad

¿Te ha pasado esto alguna vez?

_____ Cometiste un error en tus tareas escolares.

_____ Tu dibujo no te salió como esperabas.

_____ Fallaste un gol en un partido de fútbol.

_____ Tocaste la nota equivocada durante tu clase de música.

Los errores ocurren. Quizás a veces no te gusta lo que has hecho. Quieres intentarlo de nuevo. ¿No es maravilloso tener otra oportunidad?

Oración

Jesús, amigo mío, ayúdame a tomar buenas decisiones.

Jesus Forgives Us

Another Chance

Has this ever happened to you?

_____ You make a mistake in your homework.

_____ Your drawing doesn't turn out the way you hoped.

_____ You miss the goal on a free kick.

_____ You play the wrong note during your piano lesson.

Mistakes happen. At times you don't like what you've done. You want to try again. Isn't it great to have another chance?

Prayer

Jesus, my friend, help me to make good choices.

21

La segunda oportunidad de Mateo

Jesús iba por el camino. Entonces vio a Mateo trabajando tras una mesa. Mateo estaba recaudando impuestos en nombre del gobierno romano. Cobraba a la gente más dinero de lo que debía. La gente se empobrecía cada vez más. Se daban cuenta de que Mateo estaba haciendo algo malo.

Matthew's Second Chance

Jesus was walking down the road. He saw Matthew working behind a table. Matthew was collecting taxes for the Roman government. He took more money from the people than he should have. The people became very poor. They saw that Matthew was doing something wrong.

Cuando Jesús vio a Mateo, vio en él algo más. Jesús miró en lo profundo de su corazón. Vio a un hombre bueno. Le dijo que dejara la mesa y lo siguiera. Mateo dejó su trabajo y se convirtió en discípulo, en seguidor de Jesús. Mateo tomó una buena decisión. Más tarde, Jesús se reunió con Mateo en una gran fiesta en casa de Mateo.

Mucha gente estaba furiosa con Jesús por haberse hecho amigo de Mateo. No querían a Mateo. Jesús les dijo que él había venido para ayudar a las personas que habían pecado. Él quería que todos fueran sus amigos.

adaptado de Mateo 9:9–13

When Jesus saw Matthew, he saw something more. Jesus looked deep into Matthew's heart. He saw a good man. He told Matthew to leave the table and follow him. Matthew left his job and became a disciple, a follower of Jesus. Matthew made a good choice. Later, Jesus joined Matthew at a big party in Matthew's home.

Many people were upset with Jesus for making Matthew his friend. They did not like Matthew. Jesus told them that he came to help people who had sinned. He wanted everyone to be his friend.

adapted from Matthew 9:9–13

*Amarás al Señor tu Dios
con todo tu corazón, . . . y al
prójimo como a ti mismo.*

Lucas 10:27

¿BUENO?

GOOD?

Tomar buenas decisiones

Con el Bautismo comenzamos a vivir como seguidores de Jesús. Vivimos como sus discípulos. Dios nos da la **libre voluntad** para tomar decisiones. Como discípulos de Jesús, queremos tomar buenas decisiones. El Espíritu Santo nos guía en nuestras decisiones. Es nuestro ayudante especial.

Algunas decisiones son fáciles de tomar. Podría elegir entre comer una manzana o un plátano en el almuerzo. Otras decisiones no son tan fáciles. A veces tengo que elegir entre lo que está bien y lo que está mal. A esto se le llama tomar una **decisión moral**.

Si no estoy seguro que una decisión es buena, esto es lo que hago:

1. Me detengo antes de actuar.
2. Pienso en los Diez Mandamientos.
3. Pido ayuda a mis padres, a mi catequista, a un diácono o a un sacerdote.
4. Rezo al Espíritu Santo.

Making Good Choices

In Baptism, we begin to live as followers of Jesus. We live as his disciples. God gives us **free will** to make decisions. As Jesus' disciples, we want to make good choices. The Holy Spirit guides us in making choices. He is our special helper.

Some choices are easy. I might choose whether to eat an apple or a banana for lunch. Other choices are not so easy. Sometimes I have to choose between what's right and what's wrong. This is called making a **moral choice**.

If I am not sure a choice is a good one, this is what I do:

1. I stop before I act.
2. I think about the Ten Commandments.
3. I ask for help from my parents, my catechist, a deacon, or a priest.
4. I pray to the Holy Spirit.

I Listen to God's Word

You shall love the Lord, your God, with all your heart . . . and your neighbor as yourself.

Luke 10:27

¿Bien o mal?

En cada círculo, dibuja una carita sonriente si crees que Juan tomó una buena decisión. Dibuja una carita triste si crees que tomó una mala decisión.

○ Martín le pidió a Juan que le dejara copiar la tarea. Juan le dijo que no.

○ Juan estaba viendo la televisión cuando en el programa empezaron a decir malas palabras. Juan cambió de canal.

○ Ana tenía dulces en su escritorio. Juan tomó uno cuando nadie estaba mirando.

○ Juan terminó de limpiar su recámara. Luego ayudó a su hermana pequeña a limpiar la suya.

○ La vendedora de la tienda le dio a Juan cambio de más. Juan se alegró de recibir dinero extra.

¿Qué puede hacer Juan para convertir sus malas decisiones en buenas decisiones?

Right or Wrong?

Draw a smiley face in the circle if John made a good choice. Draw a sad face if you think he made a bad choice.

◯ Matt asked to copy John's homework. John said no.

◯ John was watching TV when the people started using bad language. He changed the channel.

◯ Ana had candy on her desk. John took a piece when no one was looking.

◯ John finished cleaning his bedroom. He helped his little sister clean hers.

◯ The salesperson at the store gave John too much change. John was glad for the extra money.

What can John do to turn his bad choices into good ones?

Pienso en esto

Los errores y los accidentes no son pecados.

¡Anímate! Dios nos ama pase lo que pase.

Somos tentados a pecar

Incluso cuando intentamos tomar buenas decisiones, a veces somos tentados. Somos tentados a actuar de maneras que nos hieren a nosotros mismos o a otras personas. Cuando nos alejamos de la ley de Dios, pecamos. El pecado daña nuestra amistad con Dios.

A veces alejarse de Dios y de los demás puede ser algo muy serio. Es un **pecado mortal**. Un pecado mortal es una decisión seria de alejarse de la ley de Dios. Nos aleja del amor y de la gracia de Dios. Debemos confesar a un sacerdote nuestros pecados mortales y recibir la absolución.

A veces nos podemos alejar de Dios y de los demás de una forma menos seria. Entonces cometemos un **pecado venial**. Cada vez que pecamos, dañamos nuestra amistad con Dios y con los demás.

Jesús siempre nos ama, incluso si pecamos. Jesús mira en nuestro corazón. Ve que somos buenos. Si hacemos algo malo y nos arrepentimos, Jesús nos perdona. Él nos da otra oportunidad.

We Are Tempted to Sin

Even when we try to make good choices, sometimes we are tempted. We are tempted to act in ways that hurt ourselves or other people. When we turn away from God's laws, we sin. Sin hurts our friendship with God.

Sometimes turning away from God and others can be very serious. It is a **mortal sin**. A mortal sin is a serious choice to turn away from God's laws. It cuts us off from God's love and grace. We must confess mortal sins to a priest and receive absolution.

Sometimes we can turn away from God and others in a less serious way. Then we commit a **venial sin**. Every time we sin, we hurt our friendship with God and with others.

Jesus always loves us, even if we sin. Jesus looks into our hearts. He sees that we are good. If we do something wrong and we are sorry, Jesus forgives us. Jesus gives us another chance.

Hmm ...

I Think About This

Mistakes and accidents are not sins.

Cheer up! God loves us no matter what.

Abriendo camino

Abre camino hacia Jesús tachando con una X las cosas que dañan y debilitan nuestra relación con él. Resalta en un círculo las cosas que restauran y fortalecen nuestra amistad con Jesús. Colorea el dibujo.

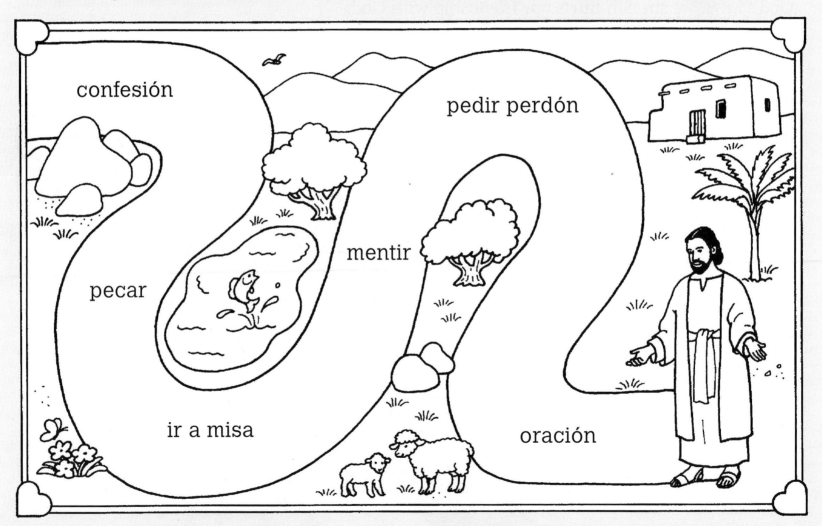

confesión

pedir perdón

mentir

pecar

ir a misa

oración

Clearing the Road

Clear the road to Jesus by drawing an X through the things that damage and weaken our relationship with him. Circle the items that rebuild and strengthen our friendship with Jesus. Then color the picture.

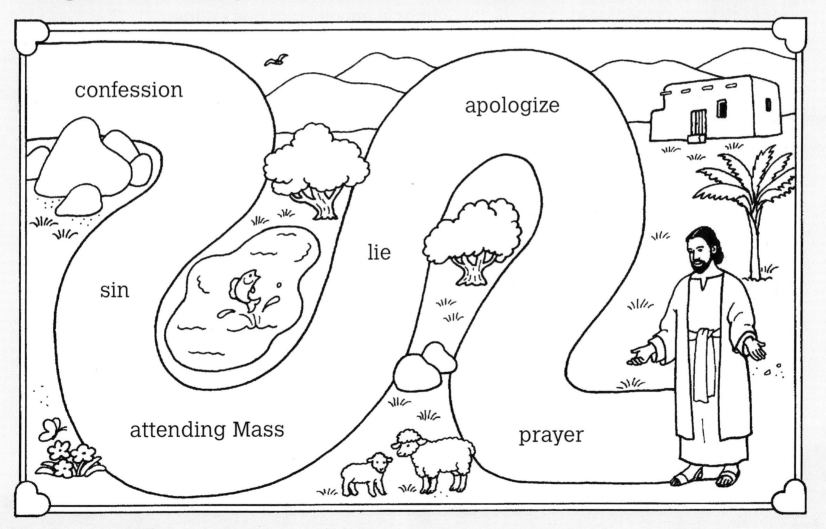

confession

apologize

sin

lie

attending Mass

prayer

Siempre con nosotros

Jesús está siempre con nosotros. Podemos hablar con él cuando queramos. Podemos decirle lo que hay en nuestro corazón. Podemos estar seguros de que nos escuchará. Él nos ama. Quiere estar con nosotros, de corazón a corazón.

Una conversación amorosa

Guía: Jesús está con nosotros.

Todos: Abrámosle nuestro corazón.

Guía: Escuchemos en silencio una lectura de los Salmos, e imaginemos que estamos hablando con Jesús con estas palabras:

Lector: Tú has mirado en lo profundo de mi corazón, sabes todo acerca de mí.
Conoces mis pensamientos.
Te das cuenta de todo lo que hago y adónde voy.

adaptado de Salmo 139:1–3

A Loving Conversation

Prayer Leader: Jesus is with us.

All: Let us open our hearts to him.

Prayer Leader: Let's listen quietly to a reading from the Psalms and imagine we are speaking these words to Jesus.

Reader: You have looked deep into my heart,
and you know all about me.
You know my thoughts.
You notice everything I do
and everywhere I go.

adapted from Psalm 139:1–3

Always with Us

Jesus is always with us. We can talk to him any time we want. We can tell him what's in our heart. We can be sure he will listen. Jesus knows us well. He loves us. He wants to be with us, heart-to-heart.

Cuando rezo

Jesús sabe lo que hay en mi corazón, pero le gusta que se lo cuente yo.

Guía: Ahora que estamos en silencio ante la presencia de Dios, miremos dentro de nuestro propio corazón. ¿Qué hay en tu corazón que te gustaría compartir con Jesús ahora?

Escuchemos en silencio la respuesta de Jesús.

En agradecimiento por la presencia de Jesús en nuestra vida, recemos:

Todos: Gracias, Jesús, por tu amistad y tu amor. Ayúdame a seguirte de todo corazón. Amén.

Prayer Leader: As we sit silently in God's presence, let's take a look into our own hearts. What is one thing in your heart that you would like to tell Jesus about now?

Let's listen quietly for Jesus' response.

In gratitude for Jesus' presence in our lives, we pray:

All: Thank you, Jesus, for your friendship and your love. Help me to follow you with my whole heart. Amen.

When I Pray

Jesus knows what is in my heart, but he likes to hear it from me.

Viviendo mi fe

Recuerdo lo que aprendo

- Jesús ve lo que hay en mi corazón.
- Puedo elegir entre lo bueno y lo malo.
- A veces me alejo de la ley de Dios.
- Jesús me perdona cuando me arrepiento de mis pecados. Dejo que su perdón llene mi corazón.
- Jesús siempre me da una nueva oportunidad.

Vivo lo que aprendo

Antes de tomar una decisión. . .

> me detengo.
>
> pienso.
>
> pido ayuda.
>
> rezo.

Conozco estas palabras

Encuentro estas palabras en el *Glosario:*

decisión moral, p. 78   **pecado mortal,** p. 78

libre voluntad, p. 78   **pecado venial,** p. 78

Comparto con mi familia

¿Cuándo necesitaste tú o un familiar tuyo una segunda oportunidad y la consiguieron? Compartan esas historias en familia.

Oración final

Gracias, Jesús, por llamarme a ser tu discípulo. Ayúdame a seguir la ley de Dios.

Living My Faith

I Remember What I Learn

- Jesus sees into my heart.
- I can choose between what is right and what is wrong.
- Sometimes I turn away from God's law.
- Jesus forgives me when I am sorry for my sin. I let his forgiveness into my heart.
- Jesus always gives me another chance.

I Live What I Learn

Before I choose . . .

I stop.

I think.

I get help.

I pray.

I Know These Words

I find these words in the Glossary.

free will, p. 78   **mortal sin,** p. 78

moral choice, p. 78   **venial sin,** p. 78

I Share with My Family

When did you or a family member need another chance and get it? Share stories with your family.

Closing Prayer

Thank you, Jesus, for calling me to be your disciple. Help me to follow God's law.

Participar

Jesús nos sana

Tratar con amor

Muchas personas nos aman y se preocupan por nosotros. Piensa en algunas de ellas. Escribe sus nombres.

_____

_____

_____

A veces hacemos cosas que hieren a las personas que nos aman. ¿Qué podemos hacer entonces?

Oración

Jesús, Sanador, ayúdame a decir "lo siento" cuando ofendo a los demás.

31

Jesus Heals Us

Handle with Care

Many people love us and care about us. Think of some of them. Write their names.

Dad, Mom, brothers sister, God, Jesus.

Sometimes we do things that hurt the people who love us. What can we do then?

Prayer

Jesus, Healer, help me to say I'm sorry when I hurt others.

31

Sanado mediante el perdón

Un día Jesús estaba enseñando en una casa de un pueblito. Cuatro hombres fueron a la casa cargando a un amigo que no podía caminar. Querían que su amigo viera a Jesús. Pero la casa estaba llena de gente. Ellos no podían entrar.

Entonces los hombres subieron a la azotea. Hicieron un agujero en el techo y bajaron por él a su amigo en una camilla hasta donde estaba Jesús. Jesús lo miró con amor. Vio el interior del corazón del hombre y dijo: "Tus pecados te son perdonados".

Healed Through Forgiveness

One day, Jesus was teaching inside a house in a small town. Four men came to the house carrying their friend who could not walk. The men wanted to help their friend see Jesus. But the house was full. They could not get inside.

So the men climbed to the roof of the house. They broke through the roof and lowered the man on a mat to Jesus. Jesus looked at the man with love. He looked inside the man's heart and said, "Your sins are forgiven."

Lo que Jesús dijo enojó a algunos de los que estaban allí. Ellos decían que solo Dios podía perdonar los pecados. Jesús les preguntó: "¿Qué es más fácil, perdonar los pecados de este hombre o decirle que se levante y camine?". Entonces Jesús le dijo al hombre que se levantara y caminara. El hombre hizo lo que Jesús le indicó. Todos se quedaron sorprendidos.

adaptado de Marcos 2:1–12

What Jesus said upset some of the people there. They said that only God could forgive sins. Jesus asked, "What is easier, forgiving this man's sins or telling him to get up and walk?" Then Jesus told the man to get up and walk. The man did as Jesus said. Everyone was amazed.

adapted from Mark 2:1–12

Pienso en esto

Solo los obispos y sacerdotes pueden perdonar los pecados en nombre de Jesús.

Jesús perdona nuestros pecados

Jesús perdonó los pecados del hombre que no podía caminar. Jesús también quiere perdonar nuestros pecados. Nos acercamos a Jesús en el sacramento de la Reconciliación para recibir el **perdón** de los pecados. En este sacramento **confesamos** nuestros pecados al sacerdote y mostramos **contrición**. Él nos perdona en el nombre del Padre, y del Hijo y del Espíritu Santo, y nos da la absolución. La absolución después de la confesión de pecados graves nos reconcilia con Dios y con la Iglesia. Recibimos de nuevo la gracia que habíamos perdido.

Jesús nos consuela mediante el sacramento de la Reconciliación. Él nos fortalece en nuestro caminar. Nos reconciliamos con Dios, con la Iglesia y tratamos de reconciliarnos con las personas a las que hemos ofendido. Mediante este sacramento, la Iglesia celebra el don del perdón que nos da Jesús.

Jesús te perdona porque te ama.

Jesus Forgives Our Sins

Jesus forgave the sins of the man who could not walk. Jesus wants to forgive our sins too. We come to Jesus for **forgiveness** in the Sacrament of Reconciliation. In this sacrament, we **confess** our sins to a priest and show **contrition**. He forgives us in the name of the Father, and of the Son and of the Holy Spirit, and gives us his absolution. The absolution after the confession of grave sins reconciles us with God and the Church. The grace we have lost is given back to us.

In the Sacrament of Reconciliation, Jesus comforts us. He strengthens us on our journey. We are reconciled with God, with the Church, and we seek to be reconciled with the people we have hurt. Through this sacrament, the Church celebrates Jesus' gift of forgiveness.

Hmm ...

I Think About This

Only bishops and priests can forgive sins in Jesus' name.

Jesus forgives you because he loves you.

Sopa del perdón

En la olla que aparece a continuación, escribe tres ingredientes importantes para el perdón. Después colorea el dibujo.

Forgiveness Soup

In the pot below, write three ingredients that are important for forgiveness. Then color the picture.

Love

Kindness

Apolagising

Celebrar el sacramento

Podemos celebrar el sacramento de la Reconciliación de
diferentes maneras. Nos podemos reunir en privado con
el sacerdote en el confesionario. O nos podemos reunir
con nuestra familia parroquial para una celebración
comunitaria. Durante esta celebración también podemos
confesar nuestros pecados a un sacerdote en privado.
Cualquiera que sea la manera en que lo celebremos, solo
el sacerdote y Dios escuchan nuestros pecados.

Ahora nos estamos preparando para recibir el
sacramento de la Reconciliación. Lo celebraremos antes
de recibir la Sagrada Comunión por primera vez.

Escucho la Palabra de Dios

*Jesús dijo a sus apóstoles:
A quienes les perdonen
los pecados les quedarán
perdonados.*

Juan 20:23

I Listen to God's Word

Jesus told his apostles,
Whose sins you forgive are
forgiven [to] them.

John 20:23

Celebrating the Sacrament

We can celebrate the Sacrament of Reconciliation in different ways. We can meet with the priest privately in the reconciliation room. Or we can gather with our parish family for a community celebration. At this celebration, we can also confess our sins to a priest in private. No matter which way we celebrate, only the priest and God hear our sins.

We are preparing now for the Sacrament of Reconciliation. We will celebrate it before we receive Holy Communion for the first time.

Dos opciones en el confesionario

Nos podemos reunir con el sacerdote en el confesionario.
Luego podemos elegir la manera de confesar nuestros pecados.
Tenemos dos opciones: nos podemos reunir con el sacerdote y
sentarnos frente a frente o nos podemos arrodillar y hablar con
el sacerdote a través de la rejilla del confesionario.

Jesús nos enseñó acerca del perdón.

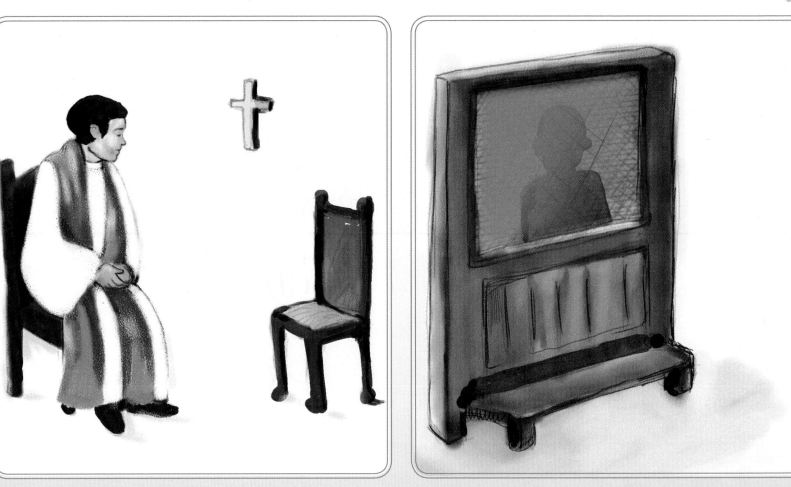

Reconciliation Room Choices

We can meet the priest in the reconciliation room. Then we can choose how we want to confess our sins. We can sit and meet with the priest face-to-face. Or we can kneel and talk with the priest from behind a screen.

Jesus taught us about forgiveness.

Rezar acerca de mi día

Esta es una manera de rezar acerca de tu día. Puedes usar esta oración todos los días para que te ayude a vivir cada vez más como un seguidor de Jesús.

Guía: Al rezar juntos la Señal de la Cruz, recordemos que todos somos miembros de la familia de Dios.

Todos: En el nombre del Padre...

Guía:

Descubre lo que te hizo feliz

Piensa en tu día hasta ahora. ¿Qué sucedió que te hizo feliz? ¿Fue la sonrisa de alguien, la luz del sol o quizás tu desayuno favorito? Cuéntale a Jesús las cosas por las que hoy estás agradecido.

Reza al Espíritu Santo

Pide al Espíritu Santo, con tus propias palabras, que te guíe mientras reflexionas y rezas.

Praying About My Day

Here is a way to pray about your day. You can use this prayer every day to help you live more and more as a follower of Jesus.

Prayer Leader: As we pray the Sign of the Cross together, let's remember that we are all members of God's family.

All: In the name of the Father . . .

Prayer Leader:

Find the Happy Things

Think about your day so far. What happened that made you happy? Was it a smile, the sunshine, or maybe your favorite food for breakfast? Tell Jesus about the things you are grateful for today.

Pray to the Holy Spirit

Use your own words and ask the Holy Spirit to guide you as you think and pray.

Stop and Think

When we make time to stop and think about our day, we start to notice things such as what made us happy or sad, if we have taken time to talk to God, or how we helped or hurt others. When we stop and think about our day, we can share our feelings with Jesus. We can thank him for the good things and ask for his help to do better when things go wrong.

Cuando celebro

Pienso en cómo mis acciones ayudan o hieren a la familia de Dios.

Piensa detenidamente

Al reflexionar acerca de tu día, hazte estas dos preguntas:

¿Cuándo me sentí cerca de Dios?

¿Cuándo me sentí lejos de Dios?

Pide perdón

Dile a Dios que te arrepientes de las veces que te alejaste de él. Pídele que te perdone por las veces que no trataste a los demás con amor.

Da gracias a Dios

Pide a Dios que te ayude a comportarte mejor mañana.

Luego da gracias a Dios por su presencia en tu vida.

Guía: Concluyamos nuestra oración de la misma manera que comenzamos.

Todos: En el nombre del Padre y del Hijo y del Espíritu Santo. Amén.

Think It Over

As you think about your day, ask yourself two questions:

When did I feel close to God today?

When did I feel far away from God today?

Ask for Forgiveness

Tell God that you are sorry for the times you did not stay close to him. Ask him to forgive you for the times you did not act lovingly toward others.

Thank God

Ask God to help you to do better tomorrow.

Then thank God for his presence in your life.

Prayer Leader: Let's close our prayer as we began.

All: In the name of the Father, and of the Son, and of the Holy Spirit. Amen.

When I Celebrate

I think about how my actions helped or hurt the family of God.

39

Viviendo mi fe

Recuerdo lo que aprendo

- Jesús perdonó los pecados del hombre que no podía caminar.
- Confieso mis pecados.
- El sacerdote me perdona en nombre de Jesús.
- Me reconcilio con Dios, la Iglesia y los demás.
- Puedo confesar mis pecados frente a frente o tras la rejilla del confesionario.

Vivo lo que aprendo

Le doy gracias a Dios porque me ama.

Le doy gracias a Dios por la gente que me ama.

Digo "lo siento" cuando hago algo malo.

Le doy gracias a Jesús por su amor y su perdón.

Conozco estas palabras

Encuentro estas palabras en el *Glosario*:

confesar, p. 78   **perdón,** pg. 78

contrición, p. 78

Comparto con mi familia

¿Cuándo celebraron por primera vez el sacramento de la Reconciliación tus familiares y padrinos? Pídeles que compartan sus recuerdos de aquel día.

Oración final

Gracias, Jesús, por el don del perdón. Ayúdame a perdonar a quienes me ofenden.

Living My Faith

I Remember What I Learn

- Jesus forgave the sins of the man who couldn't walk.
- I confess my sins.
- The priest forgives me in Jesus' name.
- I am reconciled with God, with the Church, and with others.
- I can confess my sins face-to-face or from behind a screen.

I Live What I Learn

I thank God for loving me.

I thank God for the people who love me.

I say "I'm sorry" when I do something wrong.

I thank Jesus for his love and forgiveness.

I Know These Words

I find these words in the Glossary.

confess, p. 78   **forgiveness,** p. 78

contrition, p. 78

I Share with My Family

When did your family members and godparents first celebrate the Sacrament of Reconciliation? Ask them to share their memories.

Closing Prayer

Thank you, Jesus, for your gift of forgiveness. Help me forgive those who hurt me.

El Espíritu Santo nos guía

Cálida bienvenida

A veces llegan nuevas personas a nuestra vida. Otras veces, hay familiares o amigos que se marchan durante un tiempo y luego regresan. ¿Te ha ocurrido alguna vez lo siguiente?

_____ Una familia nueva se muda a tu barrio.

_____ Tienes un compañero nuevo.

_____ Tus abuelitos vienen a visitarte.

Comenta lo que hiciste para darles la bienvenida.

Oración

Dios amoroso, ayúdame a recordar que tú siempre me darás la bienvenida.

41

Warm Welcomes

Sometimes new people come into our lives. At other times, family or friends are gone for a while and then return. Has this ever happened to you?

✓ A new family moves into your neighborhood.

✓ A new student joins your class.

✓ Your grandparents come for a visit.

Share what you did to welcome them.

Prayer

Loving God, help me to remember that you will always welcome me home.

41

Regresando a casa

Érase una vez un joven que quería irse de casa y viajar a muchos lugares. Le dijo a su papá: "Quiero que me des ahora el dinero que heredaría cuando te mueras". El papá se puso muy triste. Sin embargo, le dio el dinero a su hijo.

El muchacho se marchó muy lejos. Se gastó el dinero en fiestas y ropa cara. Al poco tiempo, ya no le quedaba nada y necesitaba trabajar.

Coming Home

There once was a young man who wanted to leave home and travel. He told his father, "You know the money that I would get when you die? I want it now!" The father was very sad. Still, he gave his son the money.

The young man went far away. He spent his money on fancy clothes and parties. Soon, he had nothing left and needed a job.

El único trabajo que encontró fue dando de comer a los cerdos. Pasaba hambre y era infeliz. Sabía que había tomado algunas malas decisiones y estaba arrepentido. El joven quería decirle a su papá que no estuvo bien el que se hubiera ido de su casa. Quería que su papá lo perdonara. Quería regresar a casa.

El papá extrañaba a su hijo. Un día, cuando el papá estaba mirando la carretera, lo vio venir. Corrió hacia él y lo abrazó. Le dio una túnica muy fina, un anillo de oro y unas sandalias nuevas. Luego el papá dijo a todos que se prepararan para una fiesta. Estaba muy contento porque su hijo había regresado.

adaptado de Lucas 15:11–24

The only work the young man could get was feeding pigs. He was hungry and unhappy. He knew he had made some bad choices, and he was sorry. The young man wanted to tell his father that he knew he was wrong to leave home. He wanted his father to forgive him. He wanted to go home.

The young man's father missed him. One day, as the father looked down the road, he saw his son coming. He ran to meet his son and hugged him. He gave him a fine robe, a gold ring, and new sandals. Then the father told everyone to get ready for a party. He was happy that his son had returned.

adapted from Luke 15:11–24

El perdón y nuestra voz interior

Dios, nuestro Padre, es como el papá de la historia. Cuando pecamos, nos espera para que regresemos a él. Quiere que sepamos que él nos perdona. Nos quiere dar la bienvenida a casa en el sacramento de la Reconciliación. Este sacramento es una celebración del amor y el perdón de Dios.

La **conciencia** es una voz dentro de nosotros. Nos ayuda a saber lo que Dios quiere que hagamos. Nos ayuda a distinguir entre el bien y el mal. Nos ayuda a darnos cuenta de las maneras en que hemos pecado.

El Espíritu Santo nos ayuda a escuchar y seguir a nuestra conciencia.

¡La conciencia es algo bueno!

Forgiveness and Our Inner Voice

Your conscience is a good thing!

God our Father is like the father in the story. When we sin, he waits for us to come home to him. He wants us to know he forgives us. He wants to welcome us back in the Sacrament of Reconciliation. This sacrament is a celebration of God's love and forgiveness.

Conscience is a voice within each of us. It helps us know what God wants us to do. It helps us know the difference between right and wrong. It helps us know the ways we have sinned.

The Holy Spirit helps us listen to and follow our conscience.

Pienso en esto

*El sacerdote nunca puede decirle a nadie lo que escuchó durante la confesión. Esto se llama el **sigilo sacramental**.*

El examen de conciencia

Necesitamos prepararnos antes de celebrar el sacramento de la Reconciliación. Examinamos nuestra conciencia.

Esta es una forma de examinar tu conciencia antes de ir a confesarte:

- Reza al Espíritu Santo para que te ayude.
- Repasa los Diez Mandamientos y las enseñanzas de la Iglesia.
- Piensa en los momentos en los que no te comportaste como un amoroso hijo o hija de Dios.
- Piensa acerca de los pecados que vas a confesar.

Cuando termines tu **examen de conciencia**, estarás listo para confesarte.

Examination of Conscience

Before we celebrate the Sacrament of Reconciliation, we prepare ourselves. We examine our conscience.

Here is a way to examine your conscience before going to confession.

- Pray to the Holy Spirit for help.
- Review the Ten Commandments and the teachings of the Church.
- Think about the times you did not act as a loving child of God.
- Think about the sins you are going to confess.

After your **examination of conscience**, you are ready to go to confession.

I Think About This

Hmm . . .

The priest can never tell anyone what he has heard in confession. This is called the *Seal of Confession*.

Ir a confesarse

Al empezar la confesión, el sacerdote nos da la bienvenida con la Señal de la Cruz. Nos invita a confiar en Dios, quien nos ama. Quizás leamos juntos un pasaje de la Biblia.

Luego le confesamos nuestros pecados al sacerdote. Debemos confesar todos nuestros pecados mortales. También es bueno que confesemos nuestros pecados veniales.

El sacerdote habla con nosotros y nos da una **penitencia**. La penitencia puede consistir en rezar una oración o realizar una buena obra. Cumplimos con la penitencia para demostrar que queremos enmendar el mal que hemos hecho y que estamos preparados para cambiar nuestra forma de actuar.

El sacerdote nos pide que le digamos a Dios que estamos arrepentidos. Hacemos esto rezando el Acto de Contrición.

Going to Confession

At the beginning of our confession, the priest greets us with the Sign of the Cross. He invites us to trust in God who loves us. We may read a passage from the Bible together.

We then confess our sins to the priest. We must confess all our mortal sins. It is also good to confess our venial sins.

The priest talks with us and gives us our **penance**. This may be a prayer to pray or a good deed to do. We do our penance to show that we want to make up for what we have done wrong and that we are ready to change our way of acting.

The priest asks us to tell God we are sorry. We do this by praying the Act of Contrition.

I Listen to God's Word

Through Jesus Christ, we have been reconciled to God.

adapted from Romans 5:11

Cuando celebro

Sé que el perdón de Dios sana mi relación con él y con los demás. Me trae la paz.

El sacerdote es la única persona que nos puede dar la **absolución**, las palabras de perdón y paz. Nos dice: "Yo te absuelvo de tus pecados, en el nombre del Padre y del Hijo y del Espíritu Santo".

Entonces termina la celebración del sacramento. El sacerdote dice: "Vete en paz" y nosotros respondemos: "Amén".

Nos marchamos y cumplimos la penitencia que nos dio el sacerdote.

La Iglesia festeja con nosotros cuando celebramos el sacramento de la Reconciliación. Es como la fiesta que preparó el papá de la historia cuando dio la bienvenida a su hijo. Me siento consolado como se sintió el hijo. Sé que Dios me ama. La gracia del sacramento nos ayuda a vivir en paz con Dios y con los demás.

Vivir en paz con Dios nos hace sentirnos bien.

The priest is the only one who can give us **absolution**, the words of forgiveness and peace. He says, "I absolve you of your sins in the name of the Father, and of the Son, and of the Holy Spirit."

Our celebration of the sacrament is then finished. The priest says, "Go in peace," and we answer "Amen."

We leave and do the penance the priest gave us.

The Church celebrates with us when we celebrate the Sacrament of Reconciliation. It is like the party the father had when he welcomed his son back home. I feel comforted like the son. I know God's love for me. The grace of the sacrament helps us to live in peace with God and with one another.

When I Celebrate

I know that God's forgiveness heals my relationship with him and with others. It brings me peace.

It feels nice to live in peace with God.

Alegría para compartir

La alegría indica, sin duda, que Dios está con nosotros. Es un don del Espíritu Santo. Nada nos hace más felices que saber lo mucho que Dios nos ama. La alegría es para ser compartida. Cuando estamos llenos de alegría, podemos llevar esa alegría a los demás.

¿Sientes la alegría?

Todos: En el nombre del Padre y del Hijo y del Espíritu Santo. Amén.

Guía: Alabado sea Dios, que llena nuestra vida de alegría.

Todos: Te alabamos cantando con alegría.

Guía: Escuchemos nuevamente la historia del padre que perdona a su hijo.
(De regreso a casa, páginas 42–43).

Adéntrate en la historia. Imagina que estás ayudando al joven a dar de comer a los cerdos. Es un trabajo muy duro. Ambos están muy sucios, cansados y hambrientos. ¿Qué se dicen entre ustedes?

Los dos empiezan a caminar hacia su casa. Es un camino muy largo y hace mucho calor. El joven continúa pensando en qué debería decirle a su papá. Sabe que tomó malas decisiones y quiere ser perdonado.

Can You Feel the Joy?

All: In the name of the Father, and of the Son, and of the Holy Spirit. Amen.

Prayer Leader: Praised be God who fills our lives with joy.

All: We sing to you with joy.

Prayer Leader: Let's listen once again to the story of the forgiving father.
(*Coming Home*, pages 42–43)

Place yourself in this story. Imagine that you are helping the young man feed the pigs. It's hard work. You're both very dirty, tired, and hungry. What do you say to each other?

The two of you begin to walk to his home. It's a long way, and you are hot. The young man keeps thinking about what he should say to his father. He knows he has made wrong choices and wants to be forgiven.

Joy to Share

Joy is a sure sign that God is with us. It is a gift from the Holy Spirit. Nothing brings us more joy than knowing how much God loves us. Joy is meant to be shared. When we are filled with joy, we can bring joy to others.

Cuando rezo

Puedo contar con la ayuda del Espíritu Santo.

Ves que alguien los mira desde lejos. ¿Puedes ver quién es? Es el papá del muchacho. ¿Cómo te sientes al escucharlo gritar con alegría: "¡Mi hijo ha regresado a casa!"?

Con tus propias palabras, da gracias a Dios por su amor y su perdón.

Guía: Dios amoroso, tú nos buscas y esperas nuestro regreso. Tú siempre nos recibes con los brazos abiertos.

Te cantamos con alegría.

Todos: En el nombre del Padre y del Hijo y del Espíritu Santo. Amén.

You can see someone in the distance, watching. Can you tell who it is? It's the young man's father. How do you feel when you hear him shout with joy, "My boy is home"?

Use your own words to thank God for his love and forgiveness.

Prayer Leader: Loving God, you watch for us and wait for our return. You welcome us back with open arms.

We sing to you with joy.

All: In the name of the Father, and of the Son, and of the Holy Spirit. Amen.

When I Pray

I can count on the Holy Spirit to help me.

49

Viviendo mi fe

Recuerdo lo que aprendo

- Dios, nuestro Padre, quiere que le pida perdón.
- Celebro el perdón de Dios mediante el sacramento de la Reconciliación.
- Confieso mis pecados al sacerdote y recibo la absolución.
- Cumplo mi penitencia.
- Me siento en paz.

Comparto con mi familia

¿Cuándo necesitaste la ayuda del Espíritu Santo en tu casa o en la escuela? Comparte con tu familia algunos de esos momentos.

Vivo lo que aprendo

Confío en el amor y el perdón de Dios.

Me arrepiento cuando cometo un pecado.

Confieso mis pecados y sé que soy perdonado.

Conozco estas palabras

Encuentro estas palabras en el *Glosario:*

absolución, p. 79

conciencia, p. 79

examen de conciencia, p. 79

penitencia, p. 79

sigilo sacramental, p. 79

Oración final

Dios amoroso, te doy gracias por el sacramento de la Reconciliación. Ayúdame a vivir en paz contigo y con todas las demás personas.

Living My Faith

I Remember What I Learn

- God our Father wants me to ask for forgiveness.
- I celebrate God's forgiveness in the Sacrament of Reconciliation.
- I confess my sins to the priest and receive absolution.
- I do my penance.
- I am at peace.

I Live What I Learn

I trust in God's love and forgiveness.

I am sorry when I sin.

I confess my sins and know I am forgiven.

I Know These Words

I find these words in the Glossary.

Respond

I Share with My Family

When did you need the Holy Spirit's help at home or at school? Name some times with your family.

Closing Prayer

Loving God, thank you for the Sacrament of Reconciliation. Help me to live in peace with you and with everyone I meet.

Dios está siempre con nosotros

Perdido y encontrado

En el juego de las escondidas, ganamos cuando nadie nos encuentra. En otras ocasiones queremos que nos encuentren.

Si estamos en un lugar donde hay mucha gente y no podemos encontrar a nuestros papás, entonces, queremos que nos busquen. Si nos perdemos, queremos que alguien nos ayude. Estar perdidos puede causar miedo.

¿Te has perdido alguna vez? ¿Qué hiciste?

Oración

Dios, Padre nuestro, ayúdame a recordar que, si me pierdo, tú siempre me buscarás.

Lost and Found

In the game of hide-and-seek, we are winners when no one can find us. At other times, we want to be found.

If we're in a crowd and can't find our parents, we want them to look for us. If we lose our way, we want someone to help us. Being lost can be scary.

Was there ever a time when you were lost? What did you do?

Prayer

God our Father, help me to remember that you will always look for me when I am lost.

El buen pastor

Ser pastor no es un trabajo fácil. El pastor tiene que vigilar a las ovejas para que no se alejen demasiado. Durante el día, el pastor las lleva a las fuentes de agua para que beban y a las praderas para que coman. Por la noche, el pastor permancece despierto para proteger a su rebaño de cualquier animal que pueda hacerle daño.

The Good Shepherd

Being a shepherd is not an easy job. The shepherd watches the sheep so that they don't wander off. During the day, he leads them to water for drinking and to grassy areas for eating. At night, he stays awake to guard his flock of sheep from animals that might harm them.

Jesús contó la historia de un pastor que tenía 100 ovejas. Un día se dio cuenta de que una de ellas se había perdido. El pastor estaba preocupado, así que dejó a las otras 99 en las colinas y fue en busca de la oveja perdida. Buscó por todas partes. Cuando por fin la encontró, la cargó de vuelta adonde lo esperaba el resto de la ovejas. El pastor estaba muy contento. Estaba tan contento que quería cantar y bailar. Y así lo hizo.

adaptado de Mateo 18:12–14

Jesus tells the story of a shepherd who had 100 sheep. One day he saw that one was missing. The worried shepherd left the other 99 sheep in the hills and went in search of the one that was lost. He looked everywhere. When at last he found the lost sheep, he carried it back to where the other sheep waited. The shepherd was very happy. He was so happy that he felt like skipping and dancing. So he did.

adapted from Matthew 18:12–14

El amor eterno de Dios

El pastor cuida de todo su rebaño. También Dios cuida de todas las personas. Quiere que todos sepamos que él nos ama. Hay veces que nos alejamos del amor de Dios. Pecamos. Nos alejamos de Dios, como la oveja que se perdió.

Dios nos ama incluso cuando nos alejamos de él y pecamos. Él sale a buscarnos. Jesús nos dice que Dios, nuestro Padre, nos busca al igual que el pastor busca a la oveja perdida. Dios, como el pastor, se alegra cuando nos encuentra.

God's Everlasting Love

The shepherd cares for his whole flock. God also cares for everyone. He wants all of us to know we are loved. Sometimes we turn away from God's love. We sin. We wander away from God like sheep that get lost.

God loves us even when we wander away and sin. He comes searching for us. Jesus says that God our Father searches for us like the shepherd searches for his lost sheep. Like the shepherd, God is happy when we are found.

I Listen to God's Word

I sin when I do what I know I shouldn't. I sin when I don't do what I know I should.

adapted from Romans 7:19

Rumbo al amor de Dios

Dios nos ama a cada uno de nosotros. Nos alejamos de ese amor cuando pecamos. Cuando nos alejamos, Dios nos ayuda a encontrar el camino de regreso a él otra vez. En el recuadro a continuación, haz una lista de las maneras en las que se nos orienta de regreso a nuestra amorosa amistad con Dios.

Toward God's Love

God loves each of us. We turn away from that love when we sin. When we turn away, God helps us find our way back to him again. In the box below, list ways we are directed back toward our loving friendship with God.

Pienso en esto

Dios siempre está dispuesto a perdonarme, no importa las veces que peque.

Regresar de nuevo

Cuando nos perdemos y terminamos pecando, Dios nos llama a que regresemos a él. Dios nos da otra oportunidad. Podemos hacer **confesión**. Podemos confesarnos en cualquier momento y tan a menudo como sea necesario. El sacerdote puede ayudarnos a aprender formas de cambiar y ser mejores.

El **sacramento de la Penitencia y la Reconciliación** nos ayuda a estar más cerca de Dios, de la Iglesia y de nuestros amigos. Nos ayuda a vivir en paz.

Nuestra vida con Dios es como un viaje muy largo. Dios nos acompaña durante todo el camino. Dios está con nosotros, incluso cuando nos perdemos. Tenemos su ayuda.

Dios está con nosotros, ¡incluso cuando nos perdemos!

Returning Again

When we lose our way and wander into sin, God calls us back. He gives us another chance. We can go to **confession**. We can go any time and as many times as we need to. The priest can help us learn ways to change and do better.

The **Sacrament of Penance and Reconciliation** helps us to be closer to God, to the Church, and to our friends. It helps us to live in peace.

Our life with God is like a long journey. He is with us every step of the way. Even if we get lost, God is with us. We have his help.

Hmm...

I Think About This

No matter how often I sin, God is ready to forgive me.

God is with us even when we get lost!

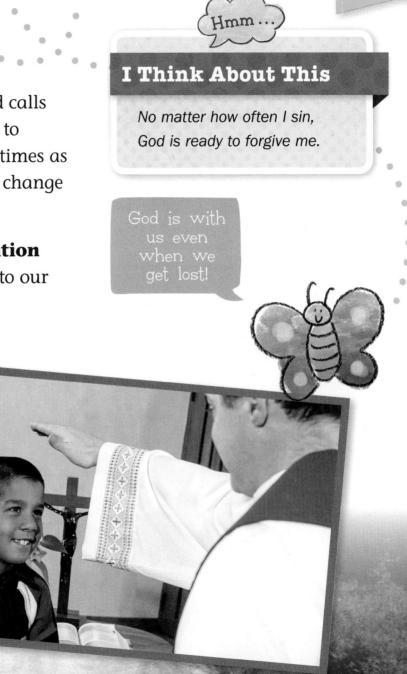

Más ayuda para el camino

Cuando celebro

Se que de verdad el amor de Dios es para siempre.

Sabemos que no caminamos solos durante nuestro viaje de fe. Dios está con nosotros. Nuestra comunidad parroquial también está con nosotros.

Mira el boletín de tu parroquia y escribe en las líneas siguientes la información correspondiente. Fíjate cómo tu parroquia te ayuda a crecer en tu fe y en tu amor a Dios. ¡Disfruta del viaje!

Boletín parroquial

Nombre de la parroquia:

_____

_____
Párroco

_____
Sacerdote

_____
Sacerdote

_____
Diácono

_____
Diácono

Horario de misas

Vigilia del sábado _____

Domingo _____

Días de fiesta _____

_____

Entre semana _____

Horario de confesiones

_____

_____

_____

Horario de la celebración comunitaria de la Reconciliación

_____

_____

_____

More Help for the Journey

We know that we don't travel alone on our faith journey. God is with us. Our parish community is with us too.

Check your church bulletin and fill in the spaces below. See how your parish helps you grow in your faith and love of God. Enjoy the journey!

When I Celebrate

I know for sure that God's love is forever.

Parish Bulletin

Name of Parish: ____________________

	Mass Times	Reconciliation Times
____________ Pastor	Saturday Vigil ________	____________
____________ Priest	Sunday ________	____________
____________ Priest	________	____________
____________ Deacon	________	**Communal Celebration Times**
____________ Deacon	Holy Days ________	____________
	________	____________
	________	____________
	Weekdays ________	
	________	

La gracia que necesitamos

Cuando nos alejamos como la oveja perdida, Dios es el Buen Pastor que sale a buscarnos. Nos espera pacientemente. Se alegra con nosotros cada vez que regresamos a él. El sacramento de la Reconciliación nos da la gracia que necesitamos para regresar a Dios cada vez que nos alejamos de él.

Una y otra vez

Guía: Alabado sea Dios, nuestro Buen Pastor, que nos ama y quiere que permanezcamos junto a él.

Todos: Bendito seas por siempre, Señor.

Guía: Recemos juntos, invocando la ayuda de Dios y dándole gracias por su ternura y su amor.

Todos: Señor, guíame por tus caminos.

Over and Over Again

Prayer Leader: Praise be to God, our Good Shepherd, who loves us and wants us to stay close to him.

All: Blessed be God forever!

Prayer Leader: Let us pray together, asking God's help and thanking him for his kindness and love.

All: Teach me your ways, O Lord.

The Grace We Need

When we wander away like lost sheep, God is the Good Shepherd who comes looking for us. He waits for us with patience. He rejoices with us each time we return to him. The Sacrament of Reconciliation gives us the grace we need to return to God whenever we wander away from him.

Cuando rezo

*Puedo confiar en que Dios
sabe lo que necesito.*

Guía: Muéstrame tus caminos
y ayúdame a seguirlos;
guíame con tu verdad
y enséñame.

Todos: Señor, guíame por tus caminos.

Guía: Tú me proteges,
siempre puedo confiar en ti.
Por favor, Señor, ayúdame a recordar
que tú siempre eres paciente y bueno.

Todos: Señor, guíame por tus caminos.

adaptado de Salmo 25

Guía: Dios de amor, aunque pecamos una y otra vez,
tú siempre nos esperas para darnos la bienvenida.
Danos tu amor y tu gracia. Te lo pedimos en nombre
de Jesús. Amén.

Prayer Leader: Show me your paths
and help me to follow;
guide me by your truth
and teach me.

All: Teach me your ways, O Lord.

Prayer Leader: You keep me safe,
I always trust you.
Please, Lord, help me remember,
you are always patient and kind.

All: Teach me your ways, O Lord.

adapted from Psalm 25

Prayer Leader: God of love, even though we sin over
and over again, you are always waiting to
welcome us home. Give us your love and your
grace. We ask this in Jesus' name. Amen.

When I Pray

I can trust that God knows what I need.

59

Viviendo mi fe

Recuerdo lo que aprendo

- Dios es como el pastor que busca a su oveja perdida.
- Al igual que las ovejas, nos vamos alejando. Pecamos.
- Dios nos ofrece el perdón en el sacramento de la Penitencia y la Reconciliación.
- El sacramento nos ayuda a estar más cerca de Dios.
- Dios está con nosotros a lo largo del camino de nuestra vida.

Comparto con mi familia

Como familia, den gracias a Dios por el don de su amor. ¿Cómo pueden darle gracias por este don?

Vivo lo que aprendo

Voy a confesarme cada vez que lo necesito.

Intento obrar mejor.

Recuerdo que Dios camina a mi lado.

Conozco estas palabras

Encuentro estas palabras en el *Glosario*:

confesión, p. 79

sacramento de la Penitencia y la Reconciliación, p. 79

Oración final

Gracias, Dios amoroso, por darme siempre una nueva oportunidad. Ayúdame a regresar a tu lado cada vez que me aleje de ti.

Living My Faith

I Remember What I Learn

- God is like the shepherd searching for his lost sheep.
- Like sheep, we continue to wander away. We sin.
- God calls us to forgiveness in the Sacrament of Penance and Reconciliation.
- The sacrament helps us to be closer to God.
- God is with us on our journey in life.

I Share with My Family

As a family, thank God for his gift of love. What are some ways you can thank him for this gift?

I Live What I Learn

I go to confession whenever I need to.

I try to do better.

I remember that God walks with me.

I Know These Words

I find these words in the Glossary.

confession, p. 79

Sacrament of Penance and Reconciliation, p. 79

Closing Prayer

Thank you, loving God, for always giving me another chance. Help me to return to you when I wander away.

Vivo mi fe

Me guían en la fe

El Mandamiento Mayor

Los Diez Mandamientos se cumplen en el Mandamiento Mayor de Jesús: "Amarás al Señor tu Dios con todo tu corazón, con toda tu alma, con toda tu mente, con todas tus fuerzas. . . .Amarás al prójimo como a ti mismo. No hay mandamiento mayor que estos".

Marcos 12:30–31

El Mandamiento Nuevo

Antes de su muerte en la cruz, Jesús dijo a sus discípulos: "Les doy un mandamiento nuevo, que se amen unos a otros como yo los he amado: ámense así unos a otros".

Juan 13:34

¡Dios te ha dado un gran corazón!

I Live My Faith

I Am Guided in My Faith

The Great Commandment

The Ten Commandments are fulfilled in Jesus' Great Commandment: "You shall love the Lord your God with all your heart, with all your soul, with all your mind, and with all your strength. . . You shall love your neighbor as yourself. There is no commandment greater than these."

Mark 12:30–31

The New Commandment

Before his death on the cross, Jesus gave his disciples a new commandment: "Love one another. As I have loved you, so you also should love one another."

John 13:34

God gave you a big heart!

Los Diez Mandamientos

Dios nos dio los Diez Mandamientos.
Nos ayudan a hacer el bien y evitar el mal.

Aprendo la Ley de Dios

1. Yo soy el Señor tu Dios. Amarás a Dios sobre todas las cosas.

2. No tomarás el nombre de Dios en vano.

3. Santificarás las fiestas.

4. Honrarás a tu padre y a tu madre.

5. No matarás.

6. No cometerás actos impuros.

7. No robarás.

8. No darás falso testimonio ni mentirás.

9. No consentirás pensamientos ni deseos impuros.

10. No codiciarás los bienes ajenos.

Sigo la Ley de Dios

1. Ama a Dios más que a cualquier otra cosa.

2. Usa el nombre de Dios con respeto.

3. Haz del domingo un día de oración y descanso.

4. Respeta a quienes cuidan de ti.

5. Trata con respeto toda vida humana.

6. Respeta la vida matrimonial.

7. Conserva solo lo que te pertenece a ti.

8. Di la verdad. No hables mal de otras personas.

9. Respeta a tus vecinos y amigos.

10. Sé agradecido cuando tus necesidades sean atendidas.

The Ten Commandments

God gave us the Ten Commandments. They help us do good and avoid evil.

I Learn God's Laws

1. I am the Lord your God; you shall not have strange gods before me.

2. You shall not take the name of the Lord your God in vain.

3. Remember to keep holy the Lord's Day.

4. Honor your father and your mother.

5. You shall not kill.

6. You shall not commit adultery.

7. You shall not steal.

8. You shall not bear false witness against your neighbor.

9. You shall not covet your neighbor's wife.

10. You shall not covet your neighbor's goods.

I Follow God's Laws

1. Love nothing more than God.

2. Use God's name with reverence.

3. Keep Sunday a day of prayer and rest.

4. Respect those who care for you.

5. Treat all human life with respect.

6. Respect married life.

7. Keep only what belongs to you.

8. Tell the truth. Do not spread gossip.

9. Respect your neighbors and friends.

10. Be grateful when your needs are met.

Mandamientos de la Iglesia

Los mandamientos de la Iglesia son unas leyes especiales de la Iglesia. Estos son los mandamientos de la Iglesia:

1. Oír misa entera todos los domingos y fiestas de guardar.

2. Confesar los pecados mortales al menos una vez al año, y en peligro de muerte, y si se ha de comulgar.

3. Comulgar al menos por Pascua de Resurrección.

4. Ayunar y abstenerse de comer carne cuando lo manda la Santa Madre Iglesia.

5. Ayudar a la Iglesia en sus necesidades.

Los días de precepto en los Estados Unidos son

- 1 de enero: Santa María, Madre de Dios

- 40 días después de la Pascua de Resurrección o el séptimo Domingo de Pascua de Resurrección: la Ascensión del Señor

- 15 de agosto: la Asunción de la Santísima Virgen María

- 1 de noviembre: el Día de Todos los Santos

- 8 de diciembre: la Inmaculada Concepción de la Virgen María

- 25 de diciembre: la Natividad del Señor

Holy Days of Obligation in the United States are

- January 1—Mary, the Mother of God

- 40 days after Easter or the Seventh Sunday of Easter— Ascension of the Lord

- August 15—Assumption of the Blessed Virgin Mary

- November 1—All Saints Day

- December 8—Immaculate Conception of the Blessed Virgin Mary

- December 25—Nativity of the Lord

Precepts of the Church

The precepts are special laws of the Church. They include:

1. attendance at Mass on Sundays and Holy Days of Obligation.

2. confession of sin at least once a year.

3. reception of Holy Communion at least once a year during the Easter season.

4. observance of the days of fast and abstinence.

5. providing for the needs of the Church.

Las Bienaventuranzas

Las Bienaventuranzas son las enseñanzas que dio Jesús en el Sermón de la Montaña (Mateo 5:3–10). Jesús nos dice cuáles serán nuestras recompensas por ser fieles seguidores suyos.

Aprendo las Bienaventuranzas

Bienaventurados los pobres de espíritu,
porque de ellos es el Reino de los cielos.

Bienaventurados los que lloran,
porque ellos serán consolados.

Bienaventurados los mansos,
porque ellos poseerán la tierra.

Bienaventurados los que tienen hambre
y sed de justicia,
porque ellos serán saciados.

Bienaventurados los misericordiosos,
porque ellos alcanzarán misericordia.

Bienaventurados los limpios de corazón,
porque ellos verán a Dios.

Bienaventurados los que trabajan por la paz,
porque ellos serán llamados hijos de Dios.

Bienaventurados los perseguidos a causa
de la justicia,
porque de ellos es el Reino de los cielos.

Vivo las Bienaventuranzas

Soy bienaventurado cuando sé que no puedo hacer nada sin la ayuda de Dios.

Soy bienaventurado cuando consuelo a quienes están tristes o a quienes padecen dolor.

Soy bienaventurado cuando trato a los demás con paciencia y bondad.

Soy bienaventurado cuando trato a todas las personas con justicia y cuando comparto lo que tengo con los necesitados.

Soy bienaventurado cuando perdono a los demás y trato a todos con bondad.

Soy bienaventurado cuando Dios y sus leyes son lo más importante de mi vida.

Soy bienaventurado cuando hago todo lo posible para estar en paz conmigo mismo y con los demás.

Soy bienaventurado cuando digo y hago lo que sé que es correcto, aun cuando los demás no lo hagan.

The Beatitudes

The Beatitudes are the teachings of Jesus in the Sermon on the Mount (Matthew 5:3–12). Jesus tells us the rewards that will be ours as his faithful followers.

I Learn the Beatitudes

Blessed are the poor in spirit,
  for theirs is the kingdom of heaven.

Blessed are they who mourn,
  for they will be comforted.

Blessed are the meek,
  for they will inherit the land.

Blessed are they who hunger and thirst
    for righteousness,
  for they will be satisfied.

Blessed are the merciful,
  for they will be shown mercy.

Blessed are the pure of heart,
  for they will see God.

Blessed are the peacemakers,
  for they will be called children of God.

Blessed are they who are persecuted
    for righteousness' sake,
  for theirs is the kingdom of heaven.

I Live the Beatitudes

I am blessed when I know that I can do nothing without God's help.

I am blessed when I comfort those who are sorrowful or in pain.

I am blessed when I treat others with patience and gentleness.

I am blessed when I treat everyone fairly and share what I have with those in need.

I am blessed when I forgive others and treat everyone with kindness.

I am blessed when I put God and his laws first in my life.

I am blessed when I do my best to be at peace within myself and with others.

I am blessed when I speak and do what I know is right even when others do not.

Me preparo para la Reconciliación

Tomar buenas decisiones

El Espíritu Santo nos ayuda a tomar buenas decisiones. También recibimos ayuda de los Diez Mandamientos y de la gracia que recibimos en los sacramentos. Las enseñanzas de la Iglesia y otros cristianos también nos ayudan.

Para asegurarme de que una decisión es buena, hago lo siguiente:

1. Me detengo antes de actuar.
2. Pienso en los Diez Mandamientos.
3. Pido la ayuda de mis padres, mi catequista, un diácono o un sacerdote.
4. Rezo al Espíritu Santo.

I Prepare for Reconciliation

Making Good Choices

The Holy Spirit helps us make good choices. We also get help from the Ten Commandments and the grace of the sacraments. The teachings of the Church and other Christians help us too.

To make sure a choice is a good one, this is what I do:

1. I stop before I act.
2. I think about the Ten Commandments.
3. I ask for help from my parents, my catechist, a deacon, or a priest.
4. I pray to the Holy Spirit.

El examen de conciencia

Un examen de conciencia es una manera de reflexionar acerca de cómo he dañado mi relación con Dios y con las demás personas.

Mi relación con Dios

- ¿Me acuerdo de rezar todos los días?

- ¿Presto atención durante la misa y participo en ella?

- ¿Uso irrespetuosamente el nombre de Dios o de Jesús cuando me enfado?

Examination of Conscience

An examination of conscience is a way of thinking about how I have hurt my relationships with God and with others.

My Relationship with God

- Do I remember to pray each day?

- Do I pay attention and take part at Mass?

- Do I use God's name or Jesus' name without respect or when I am angry?

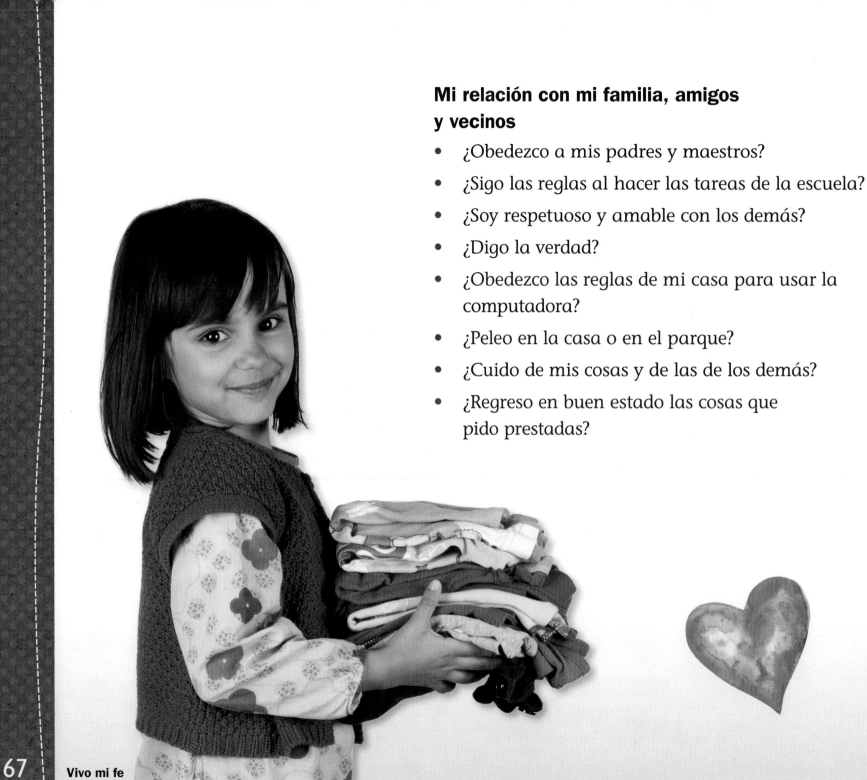

Mi relación con mi familia, amigos y vecinos

- ¿Obedezco a mis padres y maestros?

- ¿Sigo las reglas al hacer las tareas de la escuela?

- ¿Soy respetuoso y amable con los demás?

- ¿Digo la verdad?

- ¿Obedezco las reglas de mi casa para usar la computadora?

- ¿Peleo en la casa o en el parque?

- ¿Cuido de mis cosas y de las de los demás?

- ¿Regreso en buen estado las cosas que pido prestadas?

My Relationships with Family, Friends, and Neighbors

- Do I obey my parents and teachers?

- Do I follow the rules with my schoolwork?

- Am I kind and respectful of others?

- Do I tell the truth?

- Do I follow rules about using the computer at home?

- Do I fight at home or on the playground?

- Do I take care of my belongings and those of others?

- Do I return things that I borrow in good condition?

Celebro la Reconciliación

Rito de la Reconciliación individual

Después del examen de conciencia, estoy listo para confesarme.

1. **El sacerdote me saluda.**

   El sacerdote me da la bienvenida y juntos rezamos la Señal de la Cruz. Me invita a que confíe en Dios, quien me ama.

2. **Leemos la Palabra de Dios.**

   Puede ser que el sacerdote lea en voz alta un pasaje de la Biblia o que me invite a mí a leerlo.

3. **Le digo mis pecados al sacerdote.**

   El sacerdote me ayuda y me aconseja. Luego me asigna una penitencia.

I Celebrate Reconciliation

The Individual Rite of Reconciliation

After my examination of conscience, I am ready to go to confession.

1. **I am greeted by the priest.**

   The priest welcomes me, and we pray the Sign of the Cross. He invites me to trust in God who loves me.

2. **We read the Word of God.**

   The priest may read aloud a passage from the Bible, or he may invite me to read it.

3. **I tell my sins to the priest.**

   The priest helps or counsels me. Then he gives me a penance.

4. Le pido a Dios su perdón.

Expreso mi arrepentimiento por los pecados que he cometido. Rezo el Acto de Contrición u otra oración de arrepentimiento.

5. Recibo la absolución del sacerdote.

El sacerdote me absuelve de mis pecados en nombre de Jesús.

6. Le doy gracias a Dios y me marcho en paz.

El sacerdote y yo damos gracias a Dios por su amor y misericordia. A continuación el sacerdote dice: "Vete en paz". Me marcho y cumplo, lo antes posible, la penitencia que me asignó el sacerdote.

4. I ask for God's pardon.

I express sorrow for my sins. I pray an Act of Contrition or another prayer of sorrow.

5. I receive absolution from the priest.

The priest absolves me from my sins in Jesus' name.

6. I give thanks to God and go in peace.

The priest and I thank God for his love and mercy, and then the priest says, "Go in peace." I leave and do the penance he gave me as soon as possible.

Rito de la celebración comunitaria de la Reconciliación

Cuando celebro el sacramento de la Reconciliación con mi comunidad parroquial, esto es lo que hago:

1. **Me reúno con la comunidad parroquial.**

   Me uno al sacerdote y a todos los que están reunidos para cantar un himno y rezar una oración inicial.

2. **Escucho la Palabra de Dios.**

   Escucho atentamente las lecturas de las Sagradas Escrituras. Puede ser una lectura de uno de los Evangelios o varias lecturas con un salmo entre medio. Luego escucho la homilía para que me ayude a entender la Palabra de Dios.

The Communal Rite of Reconciliation

When I celebrate the Sacrament of Reconciliation with my parish community, this is what I do.

1. **I gather with the parish community.**

   I join with the priest and all those gathered in singing a hymn and praying an opening prayer.

2. **I listen to the Word of God.**

   I listen carefully to the readings from Scripture. There may be a reading from one of the Gospels or several readings with a psalm in between. Then I listen to the Homily to help me understand God's Word.

¡La sensación de paz es algo maravilloso!

3. Examino mi conciencia, reconozco mis pecados y rezo el Padrenuestro.

Me uno a la comunidad en un examen de conciencia. El sacerdote o el diácono nos invita a reconocer nuestros pecados en oración. Luego todos juntos rezamos en voz alta el Padrenuestro.

4. Confieso mis pecados y recibo una penitencia y la absolución.

Espero mi turno para hablar con un sacerdote. Luego confieso mis pecados. El sacerdote me impone una penitencia. Él me absuelve de mis pecados.

5. Doy gracias a Dios y me marcho en paz.

Cuando las confesiones individuales han terminado, me uno a la comunidad en una oración de alabanza y gratitud a Dios. Entonces el sacerdote nos bendice y nos despide en paz.

3. **I examine my conscience, admit my sinfulness, and pray the Lord's Prayer.**

   I join the community in an examination of conscience. The priest or deacon invites us to express our sinfulness in prayer. Then we all pray the Lord's Prayer aloud.

4. **I confess my sins and receive penance and absolution.**

   I wait for my turn to talk with a priest. Then I confess my sins. The priest gives me a penance. He absolves me from my sins.

5. **I give thanks to God and go in peace.**

   When individual confessions are over, I join the community in a prayer of praise and thanks to God. Then the priest blesses us and dismisses us in peace.

Peace feels so wonderful.

Rezo estas oraciones

Señal de la Cruz

En el nombre del Padre
y del Hijo
y del Espíritu Santo.
Amén.

Padrenuestro

Padre nuestro que estás en el cielo,
santificado sea tu Nombre;
venga a nosotros tu Reino;
hágase tu voluntad
en la tierra como en el cielo.
Danos hoy
nuestro pan de cada día;
perdona nuestras ofensas,
como también nosotros perdonamos
a los que nos ofenden;
no nos dejes caer en la tentación,
y líbranos del mal.
Amén.

I Pray These Prayers

Sign of the Cross

In the name of the Father,
and of the Son,
and of the Holy Spirit.
Amen.

Lord's Prayer

Our Father, who art in heaven,
hallowed be thy name;
thy kingdom come,
thy will be done
on earth as it is in heaven.
Give us this day our daily bread,
and forgive us our trespasses,
as we forgive those who trespass against us;
and lead us not into temptation,
but deliver us from evil.
Amen.

Avemaría

Dios te salve, María,
llena eres de gracia;
el Señor es contigo.
Bendita Tú eres
entre todas las mujeres,
y bendito es el fruto de tu vientre, Jesús.
Santa María, Madre de Dios,
ruega por nosotros, pecadores,
ahora y en la hora de nuestra muerte.
Amén.

Gloria al Padre

Gloria al Padre
y al Hijo
y al Espíritu Santo.
Como era en el principio,
ahora y siempre,
por los siglos de los siglos.
Amén.

Hail Mary

Hail Mary, full of grace,
the Lord is with you.
Blessed are you among women,
and blessed is the fruit of your
  womb, Jesus.
Holy Mary, Mother of God,
pray for us sinners,
now and at the hour of our death.
Amen.

Glory Be

Glory be to the Father
and to the Son
and to the Holy Spirit,
as it was in the beginning
is now, and ever shall be
world without end.
Amen.

Puedes rezar para pedir perdón.

Acto de Contrición (u Oración del Penitente)

Dios mío,
me arrepiento de todo corazón
de todo lo malo que he hecho
y de todo lo bueno que he dejado de hacer,
porque pecando te he ofendido a ti,
que eres el sumo bien
y digno de ser amado sobre todas las cosas.
Propongo firmemente, con tu gracia,
cumplir la penitencia,
no volver a pecar y evitar las ocasiones de pecado.
Perdóname, Señor,
por los méritos de la pasión
de nuestro Salvador Jesucristo.

Acto de Contrición

Dios mío, me arrepiento de todo corazón
de todos mis pecados y los aborrezco,
porque al pecar, no sólo merezco las
penas establecidas por ti justamente, sino
principalmente porque te ofendí, a ti sumo
Bien y digno de amor por encima de todas
las cosas. Por eso propongo firmemente, con
ayuda de tu gracia, no pecar más en adelante
y huir de toda ocasión de pecado.
Amén.

Palabras de absolución que pronuncia el sacerdote

Dios, padre misericordioso,
que reconcilió al mundo consigo
por la muerte y la resurrección de su Hijo
y envió al Espíritu Santo para el perdón
   de los pecados,
te conceda, por el ministerio de la Iglesia,
el perdón y la paz.
Y yo te absuelvo de tus pecados,
en el nombre del Padre, y del Hijo,
y del Espíritu Santo.

Act of Contrition

O my God, I am heartily sorry
for having offended Thee, and
I detest all my sins because of
thy just punishments, but most
of all because they offend Thee,
my God, who art all good and
deserving of my love. I firmly
resolve with the help of Thy grace
to sin no more and to avoid the
near occasion of sin.
Amen.

Act of Contrition (or Prayer of the Penitent)

O My God,
I am sorry for my sins with all my heart.
In choosing to do wrong
and failing to do good, I have sinned against you
whom I should love above all things.
I firmly intend, with your help,
to do penance,
to sin no more,
and to avoid whatever leads me to sin.
Our Savior Jesus Christ
suffered and died for us.
In his name, my God, have mercy.

Words of Absolution Spoken by the Priest

God, the Father of mercies,
through the death and resurrection of his Son
has reconciled the world to himself
and sent the Holy Spirit among us
for the forgiveness of sins;
through the ministry of the Church
may God give you pardon and peace,
and I absolve you from your sins
in the name of the Father, and of
the Son, and of the Holy Spirit.
Amen.

You can pray for forgiveness.

Confiteor (Yo confieso)

Yo confieso ante Dios todopoderoso
y ante ustedes, hermanos,
que he pecado mucho
de pensamiento, palabra, obra y omisión.
Por mi culpa, por mi culpa, por mi gran culpa.
Por eso ruego a santa María, siempre Virgen,
a los ángeles, a los santos
y a ustedes hermanos,
que intercedan por mí ante Dios,
nuestro Señor.

Oración al Espíritu Santo

Ven Espíritu Santo, llena los corazones
   de tus fieles.
Y enciende en ellos el fuego de tu amor.
Envía tu Espíritu y serán creadas todas
   las cosas.
Y renovarás la faz de la tierra.

Oremos:
¡Oh Dios, que has instruido los corazones
de tus fieles con luz del Espíritu Santo!,
concédenos que sintamos rectamente con
el mismo Espíritu y gocemos siempre de
su divino consuelo. Por Jesucristo Nuestro
Señor.
Amén.

Prayer to the Holy Spirit

Come, Holy Spirit, fill the hearts of your faithful.
And kindle in them the fire of your love.
Send forth your Spirit and they shall be created.
And you will renew the face of the earth.
Let us pray:

Oh God,
by the light of the Holy Spirit
you have taught the hearts of your faithful.
In the same Spirit
help us to know what is truly right
and always to rejoice in your consolation.
We ask this through Christ, our Lord.
Amen.

Confiteor

I confess to almighty God
and to you, my brothers and sisters,
that I have greatly sinned,
in my thoughts and in my words,
in what I have done
and in what I have failed to do,
   [And, striking their breast, they say:]
through my fault, through my fault,
through my most grievous fault;
therefore I ask blessed Mary ever-virgin,
all the Angels and Saints,
and you, my brothers and sisters,
to pray for me to the Lord our God.

Conozco estas palabras

Capítulo 1

gracia: don que Dios nos ha dado sin que lo hayamos tenido que ganar. La *gracia* nos llena de la vida de Dios y nos hace sus amigos. *[grace]*

pecado original: resultado de la decisión de Adán y Eva de desobedecer a Dios. Necesitamos recibir la gracia santificante en el Bautismo para ser liberados del *pecado original.* *[Original Sin]*

reconciliar: volver a la gracia de Dios al confesar nuestros pecados en el sacramento de la Reconciliación. Jesús vino para *reconciliarnos* con Dios. *[reconcile]*

Salvador: Jesús, el Hijo de Dios, que se hizo hombre para reestablecer nuestra amistad con Dios. El nombre de Jesús significa "Dios salva". Jesús es el *Salvador* que Dios envió para liberar al mundo del pecado original. *[Savior]*

tentación: pensamiento o sentimiento que nos puede llevar a desobedecer a Dios. La *tentación* puede surgir tanto dentro como fuera de nosotros mismos. *[temptation]*

Capítulo 2

Bautismo
Baptism

Acto de Contrición: oración que expresa arrepentimiento por nuestros pecados y el deseo de mejorar. Rezamos el *Acto de Contrición* durante el sacramento de la Reconciliación. *[Act of Contrition]*

Bautismo: sacramento que nos libera del pecado original y que nos da una nueva vida en Jesucristo, por medio del Espíritu Santo. El *Bautismo* es el primero de los tres sacramentos de la Iniciación, por los que nos hacemos miembros plenos de la Iglesia. Los otros dos sacramentos de la Iniciación son la Confirmación y la Eucaristía. *[Baptism]*

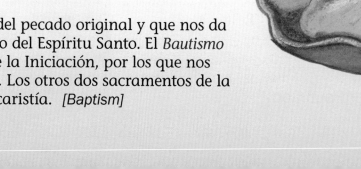

I Know These Words

Chapter 1

grace: the gift of God given to us without our earning it. *Grace* fills us with God's life and makes us his friends. *[gracia]*

Original Sin: the result of the choice that Adam and Eve made to disobey God. We need to receive sanctifying grace in Baptism to free us from *Original Sin.* *[pecado original]*

reconcile: being restored to God's grace by confessing our sins in the Sacrament of Reconciliation. Jesus came to *reconcile* us with God. *[reconciliar]*

Savior: Jesus, the Son of God, who became man to make us friends with God again. The name Jesus means "God saves." Jesus is the *Savior* whom God sent to free the world from original sin. *[Salvador]*

temptation: a thought or feeling that can lead us to disobey God. *Temptation* can come either from outside us or inside us. *[tentación]*

reconcile
reconciliar

Chapter 2

Act of Contrition: a prayer of sorrow for our sins and of our desire to do better. During the Sacrament of Reconciliation, we pray an *Act of Contrition.* *[Acto de Contrición]*

Baptism: the sacrament that frees us from original sin and gives us new life in Jesus Christ through the Holy Spirit. *Baptism* is the first of the three Sacraments of Initiation by which we become full members of the Church. The other two Sacraments of Initiation are Confirmation and the Eucharist. *[Bautismo]*

Confirmación: sacramento que completa la gracia que recibimos en el Bautismo. La *Confirmación* es el sacramento de la Iniciación mediante el cual somos fortalecidos en la fe. Los otros dos sacramentos de la Iniciación son el Bautismo y la Eucaristía. *[Confirmation]*

Eucaristía: sacramento durante el cual el Cuerpo y la Sangre de Cristo se hacen presentes bajo las especies del pan y el vino. La *Eucaristía* es el sacramento de la Iniciación en el que alabamos y damos gracias a Dios por habernos dado a Jesucristo. Los otros dos sacramentos de la Iniciación son el Bautismo y la Confirmación. *[Eucharist]*

pecado: la libre elección de desobedecer a Dios. El *pecado* daña nuestra relación con Dios, con nosotros mismos y con los demás. *[sin]*

sacramento: una de las siete maneras mediante las cuales la vida de Dios entra en la nuestra por obra del Espíritu Santo. Un sacramento es una señal de la gracia que recibimos a través de Jesucristo. Los siete *sacramentos* son el Bautismo, la Confirmación, la Eucaristía, la Reconciliación, la Unción de Enfermos, el sacramento del Orden y el Matrimonio. *[sacrament]*

sacramentos de la Iniciación: los tres sacramentos que nos hacen miembros plenos de la Iglesia. Los *sacramentos de la Iniciación* son el Bautismo, que nos libera del pecado original; la Confirmación, que nos fortalece en la fe; y la Eucaristía, en la que recibimos el Cuerpo y la Sangre de Cristo. *[Sacraments of Initiation]*

Reconciliación: sacramento en el que celebramos el perdón de Dios por los pecados que hemos cometido. En el sacramento de la *Reconciliación* expresamos nuestro arrepentimiento por nuestros pecados y se los confesamos a un sacerdote. *[Reconciliation]*

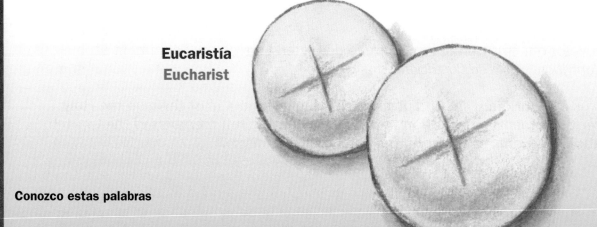

Eucaristía
Eucharist

Confirmation: the sacrament that completes the grace we receive in Baptism. *Confirmation* is the Sacrament of Initiation in which we are made stronger in our faith. The other two Sacraments of Initiation are Baptism and the Eucharist. *[Confirmación]*

Eucharist: the sacrament in which the Body and Blood of Christ is made present under the form of bread and wine. The *Eucharist* is the Sacrament of Initiation in which we give praise and thanks to God for giving us Jesus Christ. The other two Sacraments of Initiation are Baptism and Confirmation. *[Eucaristía]*

sacrament: one of seven ways through which God's life enters our lives through the work of the Holy Spirit. A sacrament is a sign of the grace we receive through Jesus Christ. The seven *sacraments* are Baptism, Confirmation, Eucharist, Reconciliation, Anointing of the Sick, Holy Orders, and Matrimony. *[sacramento]*

Sacraments of Initiation: the three sacraments that make us full members of the Church. The *Sacraments of Initiation* are Baptism, which frees us from original sin; Confirmation, which strengthens our faith; and the Eucharist, in which we receive the Body and Blood of Christ. *[sacramentos de la Iniciación]*

sin: the free choice to disobey God. *Sin* hurts our relationship with God, with ourselves, and with others. *[pecado]*

Reconciliation: the sacrament in which we celebrate God's forgiveness of the sins we have committed. In the Sacrament of *Reconciliation*, we express our sorrow for our sins and confess them to a priest. *[Reconciliación]*

The Holy Spirit is present in the Sacraments of Initiation.
El Espíritu Santo está presente en los sacramentos de la Iniciación.

Capítulo 3

decisión moral: decisión de hacer lo correcto. Tomamos una *decisión moral* porque es lo que creemos que Dios quiere que hagamos. *[moral choice]*

libre voluntad: nuestra capacidad de elegir entre el bien y el mal. La *libre voluntad* es un don de Dios. *[free will]*

pecado mortal: decisión seria de alejarnos de Dios. Un *pecado mortal* nos distancia del amor y la gracia de Dios. *[mortal sin]*

pecado venial: decisión que tomamos que debilita nuestra relación con Dios o con los demás. Un *pecado venial* es menos serio que un pecado mortal. *[venial sin]*

Capítulo 4

confesar: admitir que hemos hecho algo malo. Durante el sacramento de la Reconciliación *confesamos* nuestros pecados a un sacerdote. *[confess]*

contrición: expresión del arrepentimiento que sentimos por haber pecado y de nuestro deseo de mejorar en el futuro. Durante el sacramento de la Reconciliación rezamos un Acto de *Contrición*. *[contrition]*

perdón: don de Dios que repara nuestra relación rota con él por medio de las palabras del sacerdote. Recibimos el *perdón* de Dios mediante el sacramento de la Reconciliación. *[forgiveness]*

Chapter 3

free will: our ability to choose between right and wrong. *Free will* is a gift from God. *[libre voluntad]*

moral choice: a choice to do what is right. We make a *moral choice* because it is what we believe God wants. *[decisión moral]*

mortal sin: a serious decision to turn away from God. *Mortal sin* cuts us off from God's love and grace. *[pecado mortal]*

venial sin: a choice we make that weakens our relationship with God or with others. *Venial sin* is less serious than mortal sin. *[pecado venial]*

Chapter 4

confess: to admit having done something wrong. During the Sacrament of Reconciliation, we *confess* our sins to a priest. *[confesar]*

contrition: an expression of sorrow for our sins and of our desire to do better in the future. During the Sacrament of Reconciliation, we pray an Act of *Contrition*. *[contrición]*

forgiveness: the gift of God that repairs our broken relationship with him through the words of the priest. We receive God's *forgiveness* in the Sacrament of Reconciliation. *[perdón]*

Jesus promised forgiveness of our sins.
Jesús prometió el perdón de nuestros pecados.

absolución: el perdón de los pecados que recibimos de Dios por medio de la Iglesia en el sacramento de la Reconciliación. Después de rezar el Acto de Contrición, el sacerdote nos da la *absolución*. [absolution]

conciencia: la voz interior que nos ayuda a conocer la Ley de Dios y que nos guía para que sepamos lo que está bien y lo que está mal. Nuestra *conciencia* nos ayuda a tomar buenas decisiones. [conscience]

examen de conciencia: acto de reflexionar en oración acerca de lo que hemos hecho o dejado de hacer. El *examen de conciencia* es una parte necesaria de nuestra preparación para celebrar el sacramento de la Reconciliación. [examination of conscience]

penitencia: oración u obra buena que el sacerdote nos pide que hagamos después del sacramento de la Reconciliación. El cumplir la *penitencia* demuestra que estamos arrepentidos y que queremos alejarnos del pecado y vivir como Dios quiere que vivamos. [penance]

sigilo sacramental: deber que tiene el sacerdote de mantener en secreto cualquier cosa que aprende sobre alguien en el sacramento de la Reconciliación. Los sacerdotes están obligados, por el *sigilo sacramental*, a mantener en secreto lo que confesamos en privado. [Seal of Confession]

Capítulo 6

confesión: acto de decir nuestros pecados a un sacerdote en el sacramento de la Reconciliación. Recibimos la gracia de Dios cuando participamos en la *confesión*. [confession]

sacramento de la Penitencia y la Reconciliación: sacramento con el cual celebramos el perdón de Dios por los pecados que hemos cometido. En el *sacramento de la Penitencia y la Reconciliación* expresamos nuestro arrepentimiento por nuestros pecados y se los confesamos a un sacerdote. [Sacrament of Penance and Reconciliation]

absolución
absolution

absolution: God's forgiveness of our sins that we receive through the Church in the Sacrament of Reconciliation. After we pray the Act of Contrition, the priest gives us *absolution*. *[absolución]*

conscience: the inner voice that helps us know God's law and guides us to know what is right and wrong. Our *conscience* helps us make good choices. *[conciencia]*

examination of conscience: the act of prayerfully thinking about what we have done or failed to do. An *examination of conscience* is a necessary part of preparing to celebrate the Sacrament of Reconciliation. *[examen de conciencia]*

penance: the prayer or good deed the priest asks us to do in the Sacrament of Reconciliation. Doing our *penance* shows that we are sorry and want to turn away from sin and live as God wants us to live. *[penitencia]*

Seal of Confession: the duty of a priest to keep secret anything that he learns from someone in the Sacrament of Reconciliation. A priest is required by the *Seal of Confession* to keep secret whatever we confess in private. *[sigilo sacramental]*

Chapter 6

confession: the act of telling our sins to a priest in the Sacrament of Reconciliation. We receive God's grace when we go to *confession*. *[confesión]*

Sacrament of Penance and Reconciliation: the sacrament in which we celebrate God's forgiveness of the sins we have committed. In the *Sacrament of Penance and Reconciliation,* we express our sorrow for our sins and confess them to a priest. *[sacramento de la Penitencia y la Reconciliación]*

Índice temático

Índice bíblico

Index

Scripture Index

Reconocimientos/*Acknowledgments*

Todas las ilustraciones de las mariposas y los lápices son obra de/*All butterfly and pencil art by Carrie Gowran*

Créditos de las fotografías/*Photography Credits:*

En las páginas con varias ilustraciones, los reconocimientos de las ilustraciones están enumerados de izquierda a derecha y de arriba hacia abajo. Las páginas "(a)" indican las páginas de la izquierda y las páginas "(b)" indican las de la derecha.

On pages with multiple images, credits are listed left to right, top to bottom. "(a)" page numbers indicate left pages, "(b)" page numbers indicate right pages.

Introducción/*Front Matter*
i Susan Tolonen. **iii** Ariel Skelley/Media Bakery. **iv** © iStockphoto.com/Kemter. **iv**(b) Fosten/Corbis. **v**(a) KidStock/Media Bakery; © iStockphoto.com/pringletta; Blend Images Photography/Veer. **v**(b) © iStockphoto.com/markmortensen.

Capítulo/*Chapter 1*
1 Laura Doss/Media Bakery. **2** Anna Leplar; © iStockphoto.com/tomograf. **3** Anna Leplar. **4**(a) Frans Lanting/Corbis; Sean Davey/Water Rights/Corbis; Robert Sablan/Design Pics/Corbis. **4**(b) Allan Seiden/Design Pics/Corbis; Garcia/photocuisine/Corbis. **5**(a) Blend Images Photography/Veer. **5**(b) Jamie Grill/Media Bakery. **6** Joy Allen. **8–9** Joy Allen. **10**(a) Allen Donikowski/Moment Select/Getty Images; iStock/Thinkstock. **10**(b) Design Pics CEF/Media Bakery.

Capítulo/*Chapter 2*
11 Ron Nickel/Media Bakery. **12** Anna Leplar. **13** Anna Leplar. **14**(a) Candle, catholicserenity.com. **14**(b) iStock/Thinkstock; Philippe Lissac/Godong/Corbis. **16**(a) Phil Martin Photography; Bill Wittman. **16**(b) Marina Seoane. **18**(a) Warling Studios; © iStockphoto.com/EasyBuy4u. **18**(b) Warling Studios. **19**(a) Pascal Deloche/Godong/Corbis; Kasey Hund Photography; © iStockphoto.com/EasyBuy4u. **19**(b) Alis Photo/Veer; © iStockphoto.com/Mgov. **20**(a) Simon Marcus/Corbis. **20**(b) Ken Seet/Corbis; © iStockphoto.com/Tiax.

Capítulo/*Chapter 3*
21 Fancy/Media Bakery. **22** Anna Leplar. **23** Anna Leplar. **24**(a) © iStockphoto.com/tilo; ©iStockphoto.com/voltan1.**24**(b)©iStockphoto.com/Barabasa; © iStockphoto.com/Muralinath. **26**(a) Kevin Dodge/Corbis. **26**(b) Gelpi JM/Shutterstock. **27** Yoshi Miyake. **28**(a) Prixel Creative/Shutterstock; Jutta Klee/Corbis. **28**(b) Prixel Creative/Shutterstock; © iStockphoto.com/jaminwell. **29**(a) Hemera/Thinkstock; Kim JongBeom/TongRo Images/Corbis; Ciaran Griffin/Media Bakery; Joseph Furtado/age fotostock Spain S.L./Corbis; (merged) © iStockphoto.com/shaun. **30**(a) Edvard March/Corbis; James Daniels/Shutterstock. **30**(b) Tim Pannell/Corbis.

Capítulo/*Chapter 4*
31 Blend Images/Alamy. **32–33** Anna Leplar. **34**(a) Warling Studios. **34**(b) Godong/Media Bakery; Jupiterimages. **35** Yoshi Miyake. **36–37** Joy Allen. **38**(a) © iStockphoto.com/Liliboas; © iStockphoto.com/redmal. **38**(b) iStock/Thinkstock. **39**(a) Hemera/Thinkstock; Corbis Photography/Veer; Potapov Alexander/Shutterstock. **39**(b) Collage Photography/Veer. **40**(a) Westend61/Getty Images. **40**(b) Fancy Photography/Veer.

Capítulo/*Chapter 5*
41 © iStockphoto.com/Lorado. **42–43** Anna Leplar. **44**(a) Digital Vision/Getty Images. **44**(b) Brooke Fasani Auchincloss/Corbis; Philippe Lissac/Godong/Corbis. **45**(a) © iStockphoto.com/CreativeFire. **45**(b) Mytopshelf/Alamy. **46**(a) Lighthouse/Veer; Jupiterimages. **46**(b) Warling Studios. **47**(a) Warling Studios; Bill Wittman. **47**(b) 2/Colorblind/Ocean/Corbis. **48**(a) Zack Seckler/Corbis; © iStockphoto.com/GlobalP; Robert Kyllo/Hemera/Thinkstock. **49**(a) John Fedele/Blend Images/Corbis; (merged) © iStockphoto.com/fotandy; Svitlana Pavzyuk/Media Bakery. **49**(b) Christina Kennedy/Alamy; Fancy Photography/Veer. **50**(a) Jupiterimages/Stockbyte/Thinkstock; Christian Draschl/Hemera/Thinkstock. **50**(b) Monkey Business Images Ltd/Monkey Business/Thinkstock.

Capítulo/*Chapter 6*
51 Fancy Photography/Veer. **52–53** Anna Leplar. **54**(a) Jose Gil/Shutterstock; iStock/Thinkstock. **54**(b) John Lund/Tom Penpark/Media Bakery. **55** Yoshi Miyake. **56**(a) Warling Studios; Dennis MacDonald/Alamy. **56**(b) Bill Wittman. **57**(a) © iStockphoto.com/helgy716. **57**(b) © iStockphoto.com/helgy716. **58** Joy Allen. **59**(a) Godong/UIG/Bridgeman Images; iStock/Thinkstock. **59**(b) LWA-Dann Tardif/Corbis; iStock/Thinkstock. **60**(a) David P. Hall/Corbis. **60**(b) © iStockphoto.com/viafilms.

Sección final/*End Matter*
61(a) Ivan Vdovin/Media Bakery. **61**(b) iStock/Thinkstock; © Adam Hester/Corbis. **62**(a) © iStockphoto.com/jallfree. **62**(b) Steve Skjold/Alamy. **63**(a) Mary Evans Picture Library/Alamy; © iStockphoto.com/small_frog. **63**(b) iStock/Thinkstock; Digital Vision/Alamy. **65**(a) Rafael Lopez; Media Bakery. **65**(b) Markus Moellenberg/Corbis; Dennis MacDonald/Alamy. **66**(a) Image Source Photography/Veer; SW Productions/Photodisc/Getty Images; iStockphoto.com/Crisma. **67**(a) iStock/Thinkstock; iStock/Thinkstock; © iStockphoto.com/Erdosain. **68**(a) Warling Studios; Steve Collender/Shutterstock.com. **68**(b) Warling Studios. **69**(a) Ocean Photography/Veer; Colonial Arts.com. **69**(b) © iStockphoto.com/FrankyDeMeyer; Warling Studios. **70**(a) © iStockphoto.com/pringletta; Jupiterimages/Polka Dot/Thinkstock; AJD images/Alamy. **70**(b) Hemera Technologies/PhotoObjects.net/Thinkstock; Phil Martin Photography. **71**(a) © Sebastien Desarmaux/Godong/Corbis; Edward Lara/Shutterstock.com. **71**(b) © iStockphoto.com/CEFutcher. **72**(a) vadim kozlovsky/Shutterstock.com. **72**(b) © Johan Willner/Etsa Images/Corbis. **73**(a) © iStockphoto.com/Mirrorimage-NL. **73**(b) John Warburton-Lee Photography/Alamy; Ralph Brannan/Hemera/Thinkstock. **74**(a) Cristina Fumi/iStock/Thinkstock. **74**(b) wavebreakmedia/Shutterstock.com. **75**(a) The Crosiers/Gene Plaisted, OSC. **75**(b) Luca Morreale/iStock/Thinkstock; naluwan/Shutterstock.com. **76–79** Susan Tolonen.

Chapter 2 / Capítulo 2

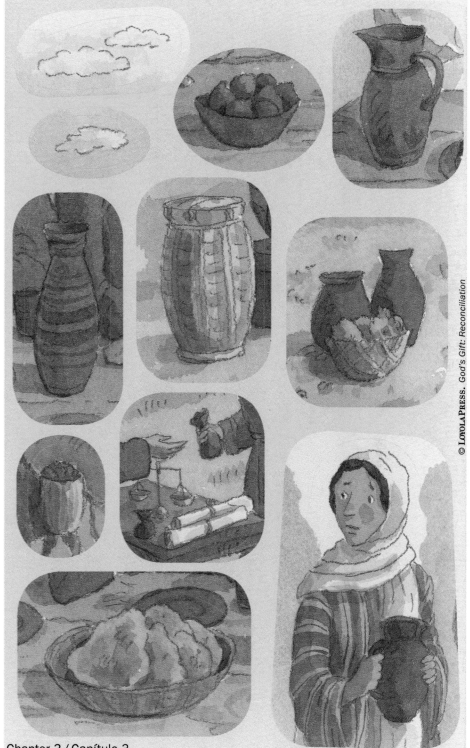

Chapter 3 / Capítulo 3